1985

University of St. Francis
GEN 741 C696
Collier
F

W9-ADS-053

0301 00023498 5

FORM,
SPACE,
AND VISION

FORM,
SPACE,
AND VISION
discovering design through drawing

GRAHAM COLLIER

Foreword by SIR HERBERT READ

PRENTICE-HALL, INC., Englewood Cliffs, N. J.

LIBRARY
College of St. Francis
JOLIET, ILL.

Third printing. . . . . August, 1964

© 1963 by PRENTICE-HALL, INC.,
Englewood Cliffs, N.J.
All rights reserved. No part of
this book may be reproduced
in any form, by mimeograph
or any other means, without
permission in writing from
the publishers. Library of
Congress Catalog Card No.:
63-8513. Printed in the
United States of America.

32947–C

PRENTICE-HALL INTERNATIONAL, INC., LONDON
PRENTICE-HALL OF AUSTRALIA, PTY., LTD., SYDNEY
PRENTICE-HALL OF CANADA, LTD., TORONTO
PRENTICE-HALL OF INDIA (PRIVATE) LTD., NEW DELHI
PRENTICE-HALL OF JAPAN, INC., TOKYO
PRENTICE-HALL DE MEXICO, S.A., MEXICO CITY

741
C696
c. 3

115,124

Dedicated to my children

WENDY,

RUTH,

and ANDREW

foreword

I am often asked if it is possible to teach "modern art"—by which the questioner means whether there is a short cut to skill or efficiency in such contemporary styles as the abstract or non-figurative. My first inclination is to evade the question—I do not like being responsible for other people's destinies. But if I am compelled to answer, I murmur something about "contact with things," "immersion in physical materials," "the discipline of the senses." Go to the potter's wheel, I have sometimes said, and when you can throw a bowl with a perfect outline, you will be ready to indulge in action painting. Spontaneity is not enough—or, to be more exact, spontaneity is not possible until there is an unconscious coordination of form, space, and vision.

These are the three elements which Mr. Collier has chosen as the prime concern of the teacher of art; and, good teacher that he is, he knows that the nature of these elements cannot be realized conceptually, but must be discovered experimentally. This is a book of "exercises," and is not only clear and practical, as every manual must be, but is throughout informed by the author's awareness of the limits of art and of the dangers of dogmatism. He knows also that art involves imagination as well as skill, and that even imagination cannot be left to chance, but has laws of its own origination, as Coleridge called them. It will be said that imagination is a gift and cannot be taught— turn then to Part Two of this book and you will find such a superstition refuted. This is the most original contribution that Mr. Collier has made to the teaching of art, and I know of no previous treatise that has dared to define the laws of visual imagination, and to build an educational method on them.

Mr. Collier is not unknown to me. For a few years we were neighbors in England and I had an opportunity then of observing the inspiring character of his teaching. We have lost his physical presence in our schools, but I am happy to find that he can express himself so clearly that teachers everywhere can now adopt and adapt his methods to the needs of their pupils. This is an illuminating book and will help even the general reader to a better understanding of art.

HERBERT READ

preface

A book owes its origin to many influences experienced from many different sources that have affected its author. The years past are, in many ways perhaps, more important than the present, for the formative influences necessarily lie behind us. I must, consequently, admit my debt to those special among my friends in England who have enlarged my understanding of the phenomena of art, while at the same time acknowledging the encouragement and opportunity to write this book afforded me in the United States.

I remember many searching, stimulating conversations at Lancing with John Dancy, now Master of Marlborough College, pertaining to the nature of the creative impulse and its importance in education. The rare insight and sensitivity to the visual arts of my old friends and colleagues at Lancing, Roger Lockyer and Henry Thorold, helped shape much of my own attitude, while our mutual friend, the late Martin Wigg, conspired also to increase my understanding. Among painters, I must acknowledge the valuable hours spent at Fawley Bottom with John Piper, where an ineffable sensitivity to the urges of the spirit and an awareness of the sacred elements present in even the simplest things pervade the atmosphere. Among writers and philosophers, Herbert Read stands as a constant source of inspiration through both his writings and his friendship.

The drawings illustrating this text are the work of students in basic drawing courses at Western Washington State College. Individually, they are too numerous to list, but I must thank them all for allowing me to reproduce their work. The over-all standard of the drawings is reasonably good for beginning students, who have in many cases no previous experience in art, but I should mention that these illustrations were not selected with any professional standard in mind, rather for their directness and sincerity as beginners' drawings.

Photographs of some aspect of nature are to be found in almost every chapter. Some of these are my own; but many of them, and the best of them, come from the observant eye of John Albaugh.* I am grateful to him for spending so many months searching these things out and identifying himself so much with the spirit of the book. Other photographs of nature

---

* Figs. 4-3, 4-4, 4-5, 4-20, 5-1, 5-2, 5-4, 5-9, 9-1, 9-11, 11-14, 17-2.

have come from Mildred Sutherland (Fig. 8-2), and Leona Sundquist gave me a free hand with many of her fine biological photographs from which I selected two (Figs. 8-3 and 20-1). I wish to thank them both.

I must also express my appreciation to the galleries, collectors, and artists who so willingly supplied the illustrations I desired, especially to Victor Pasmore in London for allowing me to select from very recent drawings, paintings, and constructions, and to Ernest Mundt in San Francisco for affording me a similar wide selection from his sculpture.

I have made considerable use of many of my colleagues at Western Washington State College. I wish to thank particularly Dr. Arnold Lahti, Dr. Edward Neuzil, and Dr. William Bender for their help with those chapters dealing with dynamics in art; also Professor James Hildebrand for his advice on many issues that have arisen concerning the mathematical implications of form structure and dynamics. I am grateful to Dr. William Proweller for allowing me to use Review Fig. 3 and for his constant willingness to argue difficult points; and to Dr. James L. Jarrett for clarifying problems in the presentation of the subject matter. Robert Bragg has given me considerable help in making the right emphases among the many concepts argued in the text.

I am indebted to Dr. Herbert Taylor and the Research Advisory Committee of Western Washington State College for their generous help in the preparation of the manuscript, and to Jane Clark for her patient and skillful typing. I must record my thanks to Robert B. Davis for his enthusiastic support from the beginning, to the early reviewers of the material for their sympathetic reception and wise suggestions, and to that fine editor, James M. Guiher. His skillful pruning of verbosity, clarification of concepts, and empathy for the manuscript generally have played an important part in the writing. Finally, my appreciation to Maurine Lewis for her hard work in the production stages of the book, and to Marvin Warshaw for the many hours spent in designing and laying it out.

I wish to thank my wife, Mary, for her patient understanding and tolerance in leaving me so well alone to work.

GRAHAM COLLIER

contents

introduction

It may sound odd for the author of this book to announce at the outset that he has always been dubious about the effectiveness of a book dealing with the practice of art. Artists are engaged in an extremely complex activity. They try to express their attitudes to life through visual images—better say they experience a compulsion to do this— and it is hopelessly wrong to suggest that skills constitute the most important criterion of quality in the visual arts. Proficiency in handling materials is not proof that one is an artist.

If technical competence is not of prime importance, what should be the subject of a book concerned with the creative acts of art? Our answer in this volume is that skill is less important than awareness, that the appearance of things is less important than their meaning and aesthetic significance, and that imaginative reality is at least as important as sensory reality. The thesis is not easily explained, for words convey but poorly the mysterious power of the visual image. We are affected by shape, color, and texture, by form and space, in a way that is all but impossible to describe verbally. But the attempt must be made if we believe that art greatly enriches human experience and enlarges our world by adding a new dimension to it.

Our aim is to produce a book that is worthy of this higher

1

function of art, the function that Sir Herbert Read describes as "the mental processes which lead to the creation of the most permanent achievements of mankind. . . ." [1] Since it is our theory that the best way to understand art is to "do" it, we shall approach the subject through drawing; and through "doing," we hope to initiate a creative experience. At the same time we shall bring in broader aesthetic ideas and relate them to specific exercises, so that some understanding of the revealing function of art will also be gained. There is an unnatural tendency in higher education to separate the practice of art from the history of art—an unfortunate dichotomy and one that does not exist for any artist worthy of the name. Today, all artists are powerfully influenced by the art of the past: the artist lives with the images of art; there is a sort of mystical "laying on of hands" from the great artists in history to those of today. Providing historical perspective, references will be made throughout the text to art and architecture of the near and distant past. The concepts discussed here are essentially timeless. They are to be found in the art of differing ages, and "modern art" should be seen as evolving logically and naturally from the art of the past.

The urge to draw is instinctive in all children. They use drawing as a very personal and intimate way of making statements about memory, about desire, and about mood. Accurate representation is generally not their concern. But as children grow up in our strongly rational civilization, in our verbal culture, their early affinity for personally created images dies away, and drawing becomes associated with "commercial" art, "industrial" art, or "fine" art. The philosophy of this book is that drawing should be used by beginning students to record their personal and instinctive reactions to all kinds of stimuli, whether initiated by the senses, by the intuition, by the emotions, or by the intellect. We also maintain that drawing is the *first* means of expression; that a piece of sculpture, a work of architecture, a painting, a contemporary table lamp, more often than not, takes shape first as a drawing—hence the subtitle, *Discovering Design through Drawing*. If "design" means *bringing into being*—the visual and technical organization of a work of art—then drawing and design are inextricably linked, though

---

[1] Sir Herbert Read, *The Forms of Things Unknown* (New York: Horizon Press, 1960), p. 28.

we may draw without any intent to design. Rather does design grow inspirationally out of the act of drawing. "Drawing," in this context, signifies the use of any medium to mark on a drawing surface some concrete visual form embodying an idea, a feeling, or a picture in the mind.

The drawing experiments in the book will attempt to *involve* the student in a series of fundamental experiences. He will be asked to look intently at many things and to search and analyze rather than tacitly to accept. He will be confronted with many problems of form and the all-pervading element of space. After sharpening his perception, and thereby his greater understanding, of both form and space (actually we are incapable of perceiving either one separately), the reader is asked to develop an attitude or mood about them—to generate an aesthetic response to form and space, an involvement which we hope is built into every experiment. This aesthetic response can spring from two sources: from the intellect and from feeling. Both are ways of knowing and recognizing those special qualities of form and space which activate our aesthetic sensibilities. Both are required to make an adequate response, and both are called upon in these experiments.

An act of perception alone, even when acute, is insufficient to produce a work of art. There must also be the compulsive force of the imagination, for only the imagination has the power to turn fact into art. We say a person has "vision" when he combines a capacity for heightened perception with a sensitive imagination and is strongly affected by mood. Part Two of the book introduces the student to the imaginative reality of art.

The chapters of the book are conceived as a sequence of experiments, for the later work builds on the experiences of the earlier sections. But there is nothing rigid about this format; the instructor or the student can elect to complete the work dealing with form before he becomes involved with space—or vice versa—should he so desire.

The aim of this beginning work in art is to awaken the reader's visual curiosity; to give him confidence, so that he can readily express himself through drawing; to encourage him to deepen his awareness of the objects and forms around him; to sharpen his ability to respond through drawing to these forms; to induce personal attitudes, of which he becomes aware, to form and space—in summary, to increase his capacity for personal vision. All these are basic factors which are necessary for any future specialized study in art.

Everyone is capable of a creative act in the visual arts. This is manifestly true for children, but it also holds for older youths and adults, providing the unsophisticated attitude of the child can be restored, the curiosity and wonder. All people should not be measured against a Paul Klee or an Henri Matisse, but they can be held to the same standards of imagination, insight, and creativity that we expect of them in papers written in an English or philosophy course. It is our hope that this book may provide the reader with a vocabulary of art and with an insight into its workings that will enable him to place greater reliance on the creative, rather than the imitative, act of drawing. And he should gain some standards of aesthetic judgment that will help him distinguish the genuine from the fake, the natural from the contrived, art from craft.

As Max Scheler says, the purpose of art is "not to reproduce what is already given (which would be superfluous), nor to create something in the pure play of subjective fancy (which can only be transitory and must necessarily be a matter of complete indifference to other people), but to press forward into the whole of the external world *and* the soul, to see and communicate those objective realities within it which rule and convention have hitherto concealed." [2]

---

[2] Max Scheler, *The Nature of Sympathy,* trans. P. Heath (London: Routledge, 1954), p. 253.

PART ONE

form and space

We have no visual knowledge of any kind except that of form and space. The dimensions of space determine the world in which we move and live; and space, in turn, is defined by the objects or forms that occupy space. The artist, concerned with giving visual expression to his perceptions and creative imagination, cannot avoid re-creating form in space, for there can be no visual communication that is formless and spaceless—there is just nothing at all.

This seems very obvious, but it must be impressed on the reader how fundamental in art are the concepts of form and space. The practice and philosophy of art must start with them. The eleven chapters in the first half of this book are designed to involve the reader in certain aspects of form and space, and with the interrelationship between the two. The experiments are not meant to be comprehensive, but merely an introduction to two of the three basic factors underlying the whole structure of the visual arts. The third is the element we call "vision," which is the concern of Part Two.

The five aspects of form with which we shall be concerned are its structural, aesthetic, organic, tactile and dynamic qualities. Each experiment is only a starting point for further discoveries about these qualities. Involving the student in a personal awareness of space is more difficult. As you will see, space must be approached through an awareness of form. Consequently, the experiments dealing with space also involve form. The operation of forces in space, the space appraisal of the intuition, the reasoning of the mind, and the "natural" perception of the third dimension are the prime concerns of the experiments involving spatial awareness.

5

1

structural
families:
the skeletal object

In this first drawing experiment, our principal objectives are:

1. To train your powers of *observation* so that you can better analyze the structure of form.

2. To develop your ability to *make a drawing* on the basis of this observation and analysis.

3. To expand your *knowledge of form* through drawing of this kind.

4. To enhance your ability to see the *creative potential* in a drawing based on analysis of structure.

5. To point out that form is entirely *dependent on structure*.

These are five basic statements about drawing. If the words in italics are extracted from each statement, we can summarize the objectives in this way. Observe and analyze the object to make a drawing based on your knowledge of **form**, keeping an eye on the creative potential of the drawing. The final drawing should reflect the fact that form is dependent on structure. These words sum up the aims which are behind most beginning student work. They do not tell the whole story about the creative, revealing function of art, but they are the bones on which the whole body of art will grow.

Some artists would not agree that observation is crucial in

RITE OF PASSAGE
Theodore Roszak
Sculpture in steel, nickel, and copper. The figure abstracted to a skeletal form which, nevertheless, makes strong suggestions of volume and sharply defines regions of space.
(Pierre Matisse Gallery, New York. Photograph by Flair Studios)

7

the work of a mature painter or sculptor; and in the sense that we are using the word, implying a conscious looking, they would be justified. But for the student, a capacity for observation is vital. However, at any stage of development, the memory of a thing seen is a prototype image on which the artist's imagination will build. Even the nonobjective artist is immersed in the world of things seen, from which he gathers much of his knowledge of form. There are many ways of regarding an object, from a superficial glance to a penetrating scrutiny, casually and disinterestedly or with intent and involvement. When we look with intent we try to see beyond the immediate, apparent shape of the object into its true and essential structure to understand "how" it is. This will also yield understanding of "why" it is, what is its function, and what part it plays in its particular setting. It is this type of looking which enables us to see the design potential of the object and to reveal its form through a drawing. We are led to the essential, permanent nature of the object.

Obviously, external appearances do not tell the whole story about an object. Asked to describe a tomato, the average person would say that it is a small, round, and reddish object. Some might go further and describe its softness to the touch, but relatively few would cut it open and describe its internal cross section. Yet a drawing of the tomato's cross section is just as much the tomato as the round and red object. When purchasing a new automobile, few people decide to buy solely on the basis of the "looks" of the car; they want to know how it performs and perhaps how well it is built. Similarly, to make a significant drawing of any object, one should know about its structure and function as well as its external appearance.

An inquiring person is alive with all his senses, restless with curiosity, eager to know more about himself and the worlds beyond himself. He tends to regard objects much as the prospective automobile purchaser views his gleaming new model, as objects which are *his* to enjoy and to explore visually and intellectually. Then he may, through drawing, express these several attitudes to objects. Such a person tends to identify himself with the natural world and does not restrict his curiosity and interest to the comparatively few objects he calls his own, but develops an awareness of the entire range of natural phenomena. Even in the mid-twentieth century, nature is still the master designer. Poor is the man who feels attachment only to his own possessions, for the world of nature can be more intimately "possessed" than any automobile.

We can all heighten our experiences of form by learning more about the principles of structure, for structure determines the shape of form and also its functional capacity. From a structural analysis of form, we discover that the *spatial element* of an object—the space in and around the object—is very important in our total comprehension of it. There are three important aspects of our perception of form. We search out *form-structure* in order to understand how the shape we see is constructed; we give some meaning to the object when we can ally the structure and shape to *form-function;* and when we are aware of the shape of the *surrounding space*, we have a heightened perception of the significant shape of the object. And following close on our perception of form comes our inevitable aesthetic response to it.

We can learn much from children, whose continual sense of wonder about the world is so evident in their paintings and sculpture. But like many other childhood faculties, with the coming of "mature" years, this imaginative capacity disappears. Although a few of us retain it to some degree, most of us have to redevelop it before we can take a childlike delight (which is a difficult feat for an adult) in our surroundings, and thus create the conditions under which we might enjoy an aesthetic experience. For an aesthetic experience is part wonder, part recognition. We are moved to wonder when our imagination is so strongly affected that we recognize a quality of completeness that approaches perfection. Under ideal conditions this experience can approach the transcendental.

But before we can expect to look successfully "with intent," we must train ourselves in the more elementary aspects of visual analysis, in such things as proportions, directional movements, rhythms, and organic growth—to mention just a few. In so doing, we are led inevitably to the object's structure. The aim of this first experiment is to initiate you into the processes by which simple observation can grow into the greater understanding of perception and perhaps, finally, into the full imaginative significance of "vision."

THE FIRST STRUCTURE DRAWINGS

The student should now collect four or five specimens of objects with a skeletal structure: grasses, twigs, seed-head formations, leaves, the backbones of fishes, and the bony skeletons of small animals are some possibilities (Figs. 1-4, 1-5). Once engaged in the search, you will be amazed at the variety of skeletal forms at hand. In the conclusion to this chapter skeletal structure is defined as structure which "can be represented by a number of lines moving in different directions, but all must be connected to a main stem by a series of joints in what is known as an 'articulated system.'" It is form possessing a discernible skeleton.

That discernible skeleton is what we are looking for now. Our purpose is to make a strong black-line diagram that reveals how the object "holds together" through its skeletal limbs. In the case of a leaf, we are concerned with only the central skeleton, ignoring the flesh of leaf area (Fig. 1-5). A straightforward sketch representation of its appearance is not our purpose.

To make these drawings, it is best to use a black grease pencil or a broad-nibbed drawing pen and black ink. Also, it is a good thing to make some tentative line diagrams on a rough newsprint pad, in order to get to know the object before producing the finished black drawing on a good quality offset paper. To make these drawings effective, ignore secondary detail and the outlines or edges of the form: an X-ray approach is required. A glance at Figs. 1-1 to 1-3, will show how these drawings appear. In the drawing, you could make a distinction between principal and secondary skeleton lines by means of thick and thin lines—that is, make the main growing stems or central limbs with a thicker line. When the skeleton limb makes a change of direction, indicate a joint by means of a dot before moving the drawing line off in the new direction. Watch for proportionate lengths of the lines in relation to other lines of the structure and also for the subtleties of the varying angles in changes of linear direction.

FIGS. 1-1 to 1-3

Three plant structure drawings carried out with a broad nib. The result is a clear and bold linear design. The space divisions, linear proportions, and directional movements differ considerably because the natural objects themselves are so different. These three skeletal forms are reasonably regular, but many will be found to be wildly irregular and dynamic.

Weed

FIG. 1-1

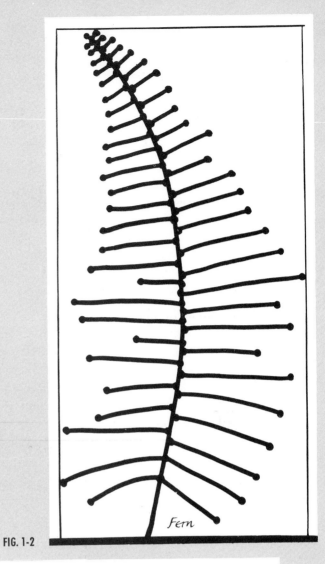

Fern

FIG. 1-2

Weed

FIG. 1-3

When the drawing is complete, enclose it in a black line rectangle and put three or four drawings on one sheet of paper (pad size about 22″ x 18″) in order to make easy comparisons between them.

CONCLUSIONS

Look at the drawings as they now appear side-by-side. You will notice perhaps for the first time the divsions of space between the limbs of each structure drawing and the relationship in both area size and suggested direction of movement each space-division bears to the other. Such relationships can be studied in the space divisions side-by-side in the same drawing, and then they may be compared with the very different divisions of space occurring in the other structure drawings. Having made this observation, we can now begin to appreciate "flat"[1] space-division design and to be critically aware of how such structure drawings divide up space in so many different ways over an apparently flat two-dimensional surface.

Look again at your sheet of drawings. Which of the structures appears to provide the most interesting visual arrangement of jointed lines and areas of space? You will probably find that the structure having the least symmetrical and least regular space divisions and the fewest parallel lines has the most appeal. This is the first crucial point: Sameness or regularity tends to produce an inanimate and mechanical structure. On the other hand, a linear structure composed of diverse and opposing elements is vital and visually stimulating if held together by a structural unity. (A sense of structural unity is imparted when the organic movement from limb to limb is a characteristic of the structure rather than a contrived, artificial arrangement of the parts.)

The second vital point is that the fundamental form of a skeletal object is not realized by merely following the apparent edges of the object, either when regarding it or when drawing it. The important elements are the proportion of its parts, the joints and directional arrangement of the limbs that are its structural parts, and the nature of the space in and around the object.

---

[1] The word "flat" is used here with some reservations. Space 1 indicates the relationship between two- and three-dimensional space.

FIG. 1-4

Byssus threads anchoring young scallops. In this complex linear structure, the space divisions defined by the threads play an important part in our perception of the skeletal form itself. (Shell International Petroleum Company Ltd.)

FIG. 1-5

Decomposed leaf revealing the delicate skeletal structure supporting the "flesh" of the leaf.

FIG. 1-4

FIG. 1-5

We can now summarize the essential characteristics of a skeletal object.

1. Its outward shape is entirely dependent on the articulated structure of its limbs, and the form of the object is *its shape determined by its structure*—hence the importance of understanding structure. For example, we cannot make a valid drawing of the human hand unless we understand the jointed skeleton of the bones that are its underlying structure. The apparent edges of the fingers merely indicate the flesh or clothing of the basic structure.

2. A skeletal object, unlike an object of mass, constitutes a number of parts jointed together as a series of limbs.

3. The linear structure of the object defines the space which the object occupies. A skeletal object breaks up the space around it very considerably through the extension of its limbs. Consequently, we must be aware of the space immediately surrounding and penetrating such an object in order to comprehend its form.

4. An object with a skeletal structure can be represented by a number of lines moving in different directions, but all connected to a main stem by a series of joints in what is known as an "articulated system." Such a drawing will effectively realize the structural form of the object.

Opposed to the skeletal object is a second family of objects composed of mass. A boulder, a pebble, a loaf of bread, and a cloud do not possess limbs. They are objects of volume or mass and will be discussed in Form II (Chapter 4).

Finally, it should be stressed that a close analysis of objects from nature should enable you to solve many different types of design problems calling for either objects having mass or a predominant skeleton. We have been working here with relatively small-scale items, but the structural principles remain the same even with objects of gigantic size.

A famous master at depicting structure was the great French painter, Paul Cézanne, who attempted to render the permanent character of things (see Chapter 12). He spoke of art being "theory developed and applied in contact with nature . . ." of treating nature "by the cylinder, the sphere, the cone, everything in proper perspective so that each side of an object is

FIG. 1-6

ANATOMICAL EXPOSITION
OF A TIGER
George Stubbs
A drawing illustrating the artist's preoccupation with structure. The discernible skeletal form of the rib-cage defines the space-volume of the body, while the bone structure of the limbs, articulating the animal's movements, can also be seen and "felt" just beneath the surface.
(Victoria and Albert Museum, London)

FIG. 1-7

RITE OF PASSAGE

14

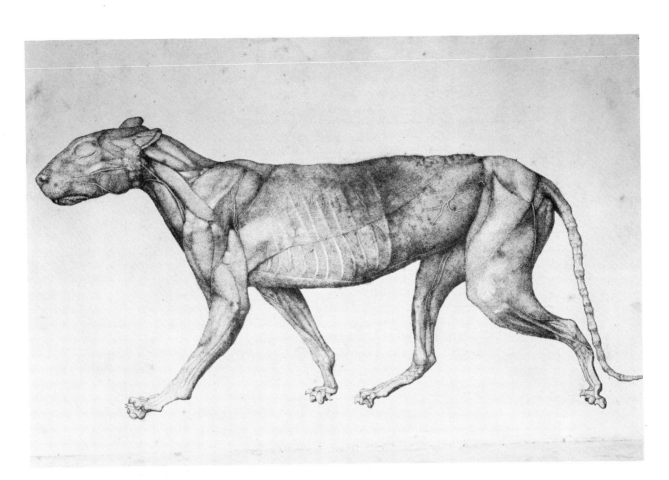

FIG. 1-6

FIG. 1-7

directed towards a central point." [2] But Cézanne did not simply impose an arbitrary geometric formation onto nature; rather, he attempted to reveal structural truths by removing confusion and clutter from visual sensations. He sought to achieve this by deliberately organizing objects within the cone of vision (the natural cone of focus made by the eye when concentrating on any single distant point). Through such an organization Cézanne intended to create an order out of confused visual impressions, for in the natural cone of vision the distant point is in focus, while the rest of the cone produces a periphery of vagueness and confusion. This is what Cézanne meant by "réaliser"; to bring all into ordered focus and thus introduce the artist's structural order into visual sensations.

We repeat one of our initial aims: to heighten the ability to perceive nature through this search for structure (Fig. 1-6). It is important to realize that we have made these skeletal structure drawings from actual objects, that the information has come from outside one's self. Too often the layman imagines that the artist and designer are suddenly struck by a flash of inspiration from nowhere. Usually, however, it is a sharpened faculty of observation and an acute perception that triggers the imaginative vision. A twig structure can suggest a tubular steel chair frame, or the movement of a figure in action (Fig. 1-7). Look at some of the skeletal structure drawings upside down, and see how they change their character completely, suggest new objects and usages. If you will examine the twenty small drawings of tree formations in Fig. 3-4, made by a student walking through the woods, you will notice the many differing space arrangements produced by a relatively few vertical lines, which could be exploited for design purposes. All were derived from observation. A capacity to observe is a necessary part of the beginning student's artistic equipment; and to record what he sees, his sketchbook should always be within handy reach. Finally, note the architectural form of the Brussels Atomium, derived from the skeletal molecular structure of an iron molecule (Fig. 1-8).

[2] Sir Herbert Read, *A Concise History of Modern Painting* (London: Thames & Hudson, 1959), p. 17.

FIG. 1-8

THE ATOMIUM, BRUSSELS INTERNATIONAL EXHIBITION (1958)
A. & J. Polak, architects
An example of skeletal structure in architecture. This structure is a model of an iron molecule enlarged 165 million times. It is 360 ft. high.
(The Architectural Review, London)

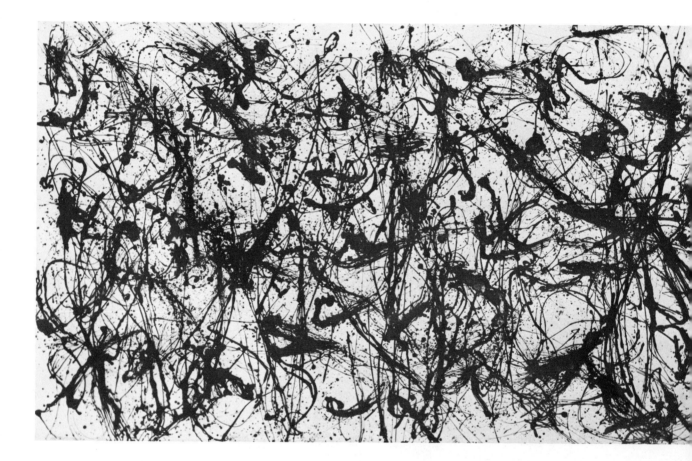

2

lines
and marks
with ink

So much could be written about line quality that it is presumptuous to discuss it in only one chapter of this book. But since this whole book deals with drawing in one form or another, and constant references will be made to "the line," we must at least present a brief introduction to the subject.

When someone draws a line, it is as personal to him as his own fingerprint. Consider the factors involved: a line is a person's direct response, through drawing, to an experience. It may or may not be a sensitive drawing response, for the degree of sensitivity depends on the expressiveness of the person's touch, the quality of his mood, and the type of medium he employs. The use made of lines in Form I was almost mechanical. They were drawn to give certain information in a diagram drawing, and they varied only in weight to distinguish the more important structure lines from the less important. But when a drawing is rendered freely and naturally—more spontaneously—a line governed by "touch," "mood" and "medium" becomes a personal commitment (Figs. 2-1 to 2-4). Your personal response to stimuli will be different from that of your neighbor—therefore your mood, your feeling, will be different, also; and this in turn, will affect your touch sense so that your line or mark will have a unique quality. If you are using charcoal, the results will be quite different from those produced by

NUMBER 32 (1950)
Jackson Pollock
A configuration of marks and lines which is expressive, intense, and urgent. The drawing mark has become the only vehicle for the artist's spontaneous creativity. (Collection, Mrs. Lee Krasner Pollock. Photograph by Hans Namuth, New York)

19

the medium of pen and ink. If you sing to yourself while drawing the line, the line will reflect your mood; if you mutter
angrily beneath your breath, then the line, even though describing the same object, will be a different kind of line. Some
people are almost hypnotically relaxed in drawing; others
feverishly bite their tongue. And as you draw, the paper, depending on the type of surface, will set up a resistance to the
pen or brush or finger or piece of wood. How you overcome
this resistance will obviously also determine the quality of your
line. Just contrast for a moment the sensations you would experience in using soft charcoal over a coarse paper surface or
using a hard, spiky nib over velvet smooth paper. You can *feel*
the kind of line that will result, without having to draw it. The
line of drawing, however it is accomplished, evolves from the
attempt to reconcile the tensions that exist between perceiving
the object and imaginatively re-creating it through drawing—
between the factual, substantial reality of the object and the
artist's imaginative exploration of it. You may create a line
without actually drawing it, where two areas of different tone
or color meet in a design.

Throughout this book you will find that drawing is used as
the catalyst between knowledge and invention. To draw a
thing is to *know* a thing; and from the illustrations, you will see
that more value is placed on the direct, personal mark that
is the spontaneous result of a person's excitability about an
object and the ideas it engenders, or an experience, than on a
"neat," technically good, but dead-as-mutton representational
drawing.

THE EXPERIMENTS

Starting with a blank sheet of white paper (about 15″ x 22″—
rough or smooth, according to preference), try to produce as
many different vertical lines as possible, working over the sheet
from left to right. First, however, assemble as much drawing
"equipment" as possible, from the conventional pen and brush
to more unorthodox materials such as rubberbands, pieces of
twig or wood, edges of paper, the edge of a thumbnail, hair
grips and curlers, and so on—as varied a range of things as can
be dipped in black ink to make a line of drawing.

FIG. 2-1

*Sheet of experimental lines
and marks.*

20

Start at the left with the lightest possible lines (hair lines). Gradually build up as you move across the paper to heavy, thick lines. After this, combine both thick and thin into one line, a swelling line that is alternately thick and thin throughout its whole length. Try doing this first with the pen and the brush and leave a little space between the marks; then, in these spaces, repeat the variations of line, but this time use all the equipment you have gathered together. Experiment with every single piece—metal, wood, bone, paper, or plastic. As the lines go down, be aware of the quality of mark produced—sharp or dull, gray or black, firm or broken—and try to remember the particular "feel" of the instrument that made the mark as it was moving over the paper surface. You will probably remember some that particularly suited you, producing a definite feeling of control and of satisfaction while the line was being made. Finally, draw lines with your left hand, lines starting at the bottom of the paper and finishing at the top, lines where you press hard on your drawing instrument, overcoming strong paper resistance, lines when the instrument is almost dry of ink, and lines when it is flooded with ink. Then, on top of all this, try a few lines which will have a completely different character, lines which you will *print* rather than draw. For example, ink the edge of a ruler, press the ruler onto the paper, and see what you have; repeat this ruler-line, but this time dampen the paper area beneath the ruler and then compare this line with the first. You might even print a line from a piece of string. All these variations—and there are many more you can invent—produce a different line quality.

When this sheet of line marks is complete (Fig. 2-1), it should reveal a wide range of drawing possibilities. To complete these line experiments and to see what kind of free approach to drawing they might have induced, here is a concluding piece of work.

Concluding experiment

Take one of the natural objects used for the structure drawings of Form I (Chapter 1) and redraw it. But this time draw it spontaneously and naturally. Use any drawing instrument and line method (or combinations of them) which you found particularly attractive when making the line sheet. On this occasion, you are not analyzing or probing structure; you have to

FIG. 2-2

Rapidly executed drawings of twigs, using line, blob, and smeared tone.

FIG. 2-2

attack the object and work spontaneously and rapidly to complete it in two or three minutes at the most. The drawing you produce will be an *impression* of the object—yet it will be more than this. Your attack is based on knowledge—the knowledge of the fragmentation of space and the line direction determined by the organic quality of the object, which you have learned from previously drawing its skeletal structure. And because your recently gained knowledge of ink marks and lines will help you to "let go" in your quick, two-minute attack, the resulting drawing will be both a swift statement of appearances and a remembered statement of fact. In Figs. 2-2 and 2-3, notice the vitality and immediacy of impact these quick sketches produce, which tell more about the living aspect of nature than any number of careful and labored detailed drawings could do. Drawing of this free and experimental character is constantly demanded throughout the book, and you will find that the sheet of line experiments can be used for constant reference.

FIG. 2-3

A series of rapid twig notes of expressive line quality. A searching for structure can be seen, but no amount of "finished" drawing would capture the sheer feeling for twig form that these spontaneous drawings evoke.

FIG. 2-4

NUMBER 32

FIG. 2-3

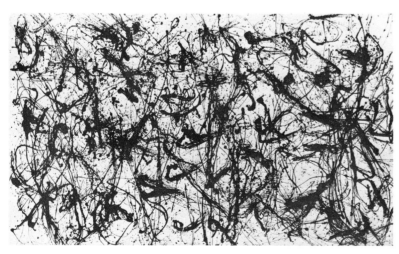

FIG. 2-4

115,126

LIBRARY
College of St. Francis
JOLIET, ILL.

3

the relationship between two and three dimensions

The work described in this chapter provides a logical continuation of Form I (Chapter 1), where we made drawings or diagrams that were meant to provide positive information. By means of lines moving out from joints in lateral (that is, two-dimensional) directions we revealed the structural characteristics of an object; and once a frame was placed around this structure drawing, a flat grid pattern emerged. On looking at these finished drawings, the eye is first aware of the areas of space between the lines of the structure and sees them in terms of length and breadth only, or simply as a flat pattern of divisions. Then, gradually, certain other factors become apparent, and we realize that our eyes are apprehending not only up, down, and across, but also in. We find ourselves visually probing the possibilities of the third dimension, depth.

This ability to comprehend depth is a mental-optical faculty we use constantly. Every time you put out your hand to grasp a door handle you make an automatic appraisal of the distance your hand should travel in order to make contact with the handle. Sometimes when this combined optical, mental, and kinesthetic apprehension of space is upset, you will find yourself misjudging the distance and either hitting the door hard with your hand or stopping short in mid-air before reaching the handle. If you close one eye and then reach out to pick up

PERSIMMONS
Mu-Ch'i
In this thirteenth century painting, the associations in depth between the objects are achieved by the weight and quality of the brush mark. Although the five fruits are disposed along the same horizontal line (which rules out mechanical perspective depth illusion), each fruit possesses a differing degree of frontality.
(Daitoku-ji, Kyoto)

27

a book, you will find it surprisingly difficult to judge the depth of space involved. Some people are afflicted with a more limited depth perception than others, and such misjudgment of depth can be a frequent cause of highway accidents; a driver making a left-hand turn in front of oncoming traffic may have a collision because he considered the approaching cars far enough way to allow plenty of time for the turn.

We obviously live our lives "in depth." That is, we move and we constantly exist in space. As we found in Form I (Chapter 1), when we isolate any skeletal object in order to look at it more closely, we discover that the space immediately around the object is just as important as is the solid fact of the object itself. Faced with many objects in close juxtaposition, we make a subconscious pinpointing of their positions in space. If we were then blindfolded we would attempt to weave a way among them as we plot their positions on our mental object-in-space screen. This natural ability to see and comprehend a three-dimensional world remains with us and operates even when we are confronted by a flat, two-dimensional surface such as a piece of drawing paper. So long as the paper remains unmarked, no suggestion of space penetration occurs; but put on some lines which start a demarcation of flat areas, and the eye begins to search for depth.

It would be a good thing at this stage to turn back to Form I and look again at the structure drawings. Do any of the spaces between the lines of the structure seem to recede more into the distance than other spaces in the same drawing? Or do some spaces appear nearer than others? Does your eye return to one space which suggests a dominant frontal area? Or does it search out a hole, a receding area? Such a dominant place would be a focal point in the drawing, and it is interesting to note that a focal point can be either a hole or a forward-projecting area. If you notice such a dominant frontal or receding area, then without having recourse to perspective you have produced depth on a flat piece of paper.

Since its inception during the early Renaissance, the method of creating the illusion of depth over a flat surface has been performed by establishing vanishing points and disappearing lines. This perspective has been the traditional means of taking the onlooker into the picture. But this mechanical illusion, by becoming merely a formula, can blind the artist to an inten-

FIG. 3-1

RELIEF CONSTRUCTION IN WHITE, BLACK, AND MAROON
Victor Pasmore
Varying degrees of depth are achieved over this flat surface. Assess for yourself the differing degrees of projection and recession achieved by these lines and rectangular panels. Tonal dominance and line weight and quality produce the spatial perceptions experienced.
(Victor Pasmore)

FIG. 3-2

NORHAM CASTLE
J. M. W. Turner
Turner's landscape dissolves into misty regions of space. Depth is achieved through varying intensities and weights of tone and by the strength of dominant marks. Compare this with the painting of the persimmons by Mu-Ch'i.
(Trustees of the Tate Gallery, London)

FIG. 3-1

FIG. 3-2

sive personal experience of space, to the natural experience of depth perception. And as we have tried to show, natural depth perception does occur without perspective (see Fig. 3-1). The purpose of the following experiment is to create an awareness of *natural* depth perception as opposed to mechanical systems of perspective.

But before going on, it would be well to point out that when the illusion of perspective is used creatively rather than automatically, the result can impart a genuine and personal experience of space. A great authority on Italian Renaissance art, the late Bernard Berenson had this to say about the work of Perugino (1445-1523), the Umbrian (central Italian) painter who was a master of perspective.

Space composition can take us away from ourselves and give us, whilst we are under its spell, the feeling of being identified with the Universe, perhaps even of being the soul in the Universe. . . . For those of us who are neither idolators nor suppliants, this sense of identification with the Universe is of the very essence of religious emotion—an emotion by the way, as independent of belief and conduct as love itself. . . . The religious emotion, for some of us entirely, for others at least in part, is produced by a feeling of identification with the Universe; this feeling in its turn can be created by space composition. It follows then that this art can directly communicate religious emotion—or at least the religious emotion that many of us really have, good church members though we may be.[1]

Berenson has put his finger on one of the fundamental purposes of art: to heighten man's instinctive awareness of the cosmos and to enable him to identify himself with the vast range of things within the universe. When this new world is revealed by a design, as in the case of Perugino, our instinctive links with the great systems of space, matter, and energy are more consciously realized, and we are "taken away from ourselves." Look at Turner's space in Fig. 3-2. Painters, sculptors, and architects, even though working in abstract forms, today concern themselves with space and our feeling for it; space is one of the permanent conditions of life—and thus of art, as well. Perhaps when man knows more about the space which surrounds him and its relationship with time, the artist will have to change his approach to space and his sensitivity to it may be modified. But at the moment it still remains a vital constituent of our aesthetic response to human experience.

---

[1] Bernard Berenson, *The Italian Painters of the Renaissance* (London: Phaidon, 1952), p. 122.

FIG. 3-3

PERSIMMONS

FIG. 3-4

Twenty notes, made out-of-doors, indicate the wide range of vertical-line space divisions that can be extracted from tree groupings. There are the curvilinear and the straight, the symmetrical and the asymmetrical, the interesting and the dull. They draw one's attention primarily to two-dimensional space in vertical and lateral directions.

FIG. 3-3

FIG. 3-4

THE EXPERIMENTS

The stimulus for the drawings made in Form I came from observing actual skeletal objects; and for the work at hand, we shall also turn to objects in nature. We are to illustrate *space in depth* without having recourse to the more mechanical disappearing lines of perspective—to see, in fact, how a natural depth perception operates. This can best be done by observing rather than by inventing some gimmicky manipulation of abstract geometry. Fifteen minutes outside with a sketch pad and a soft, black drawing crayon will be sufficient. Since we have had some experience now of linear or skeletal structures, we shall retain this kind of form. Look at a clump of tree trunks and note how they are grouped together in bunches of three, four, or five trunks. As you look around, notice the different grouping arrangements of other clumps of trees. On your pad, draw about a dozen small squares, freehand, about 2″ x 2″. In each square, make a simple and direct line sketch of vertical trunks, a different formation in each square for the different clumps you see. These are not meant to be pictorial views of trees; the lines, heavy or light as appropriate, indicating the position of each tree, will serve as notes or diagrams, as in Fig. 3-4. As you make these drawings, you will notice the distance between trees. You will notice the space *sideways* between each tree and also the fact that some of these vertical trunks are *farther back* than others—that there is space between them in depth as well as horizontally.

As you make your drawings, you will probably automatically attempt to show the space in depth by thickening the lines which represent the trees in front, and by so doing you will push the thinner lines to the rear, *together with the space between these thinner lines* (Fig. 3-5). This will produce some depth in the drawing. The horizontal space organization is extremely simple to depict. So now the eye penetrates the drawing to the thinner lines which appear to be behind, as well as crossing the lateral distances between the trunks. One other thing you may have done automatically to increase the apparent depth between the tree lines: you may have started some of the lines higher in the square than others, from the base

FIG. 3-5

Specific frontal areas have now been created by the thickening of certain lines in these three drawings. The greater depth or recession in the bottom drawing is due to the introduction of more delicate, secondary lines.

FIG. 3-6

Unlike Fig. 3-5, this drawing has no differing weight of line to produce frontal or receding regions. Instead, depth is achieved by contrasting the totally enclosed areas (which appear frontal) with the more open regions (which appear to recede) where space can move in and out.

FIG. 3-7

Two drawings where depth perception operates in several ways. Line weight brings forward both line and immediate space. Although no areas are totally enclosed, more open space around a line tends to produce a greater suggestion of distance within this particular rectangular frame. There is also a suggestion of perspective in the size and position of the lines, introduced quite unconsciously by the student; yet it is a lively perspective, not mechanical or dead.

FIG. 3-5

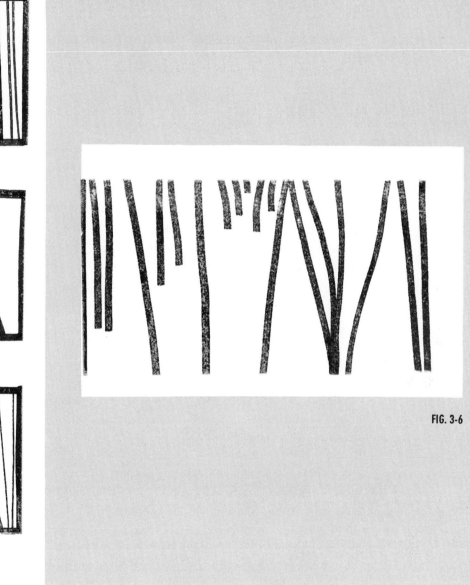

FIG. 3-6

FIG. 3-7

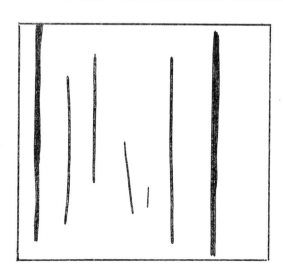

line up to perhaps a third or half the distance up the square (Figs. 3-6 and 3-7).

Conclusions

What significant conclusions are to be drawn from such instinctively produced notations of tree groupings? The three most important ones which are well illustrated in Figs. 3-5 to 3-12 are

> 1. When an area is not completely contained by lines—when space penetrates it from neighboring areas—the area recedes.
>
> 2. The heavier the weight of line, the more frontal dominance it and the surrounding space will have.
>
> 3. The quality of a line may also relate to depth. Examine the sheet of lines previously made in Chapter 2 (Fig. 2-1). Sharp, incisive lines come forward; broken, blurred, or gray lines recede. You will notice that even a heavy line that is grayish and "spongy" will appear to be farther back than a much slighter line possessing sharpness and a biting edge quality.

These three points are borne out when they are applied to industrial design artifacts. Look at the refrigerator illustrated in Fig. 3-8. In any visual context, depth perception tends to operate in similar ways.

These three conclusions help explain how your eye, in the first structure drawings in Form I distinguished between frontal areas and receding areas and eventually seized on one area as the dominant focal area. That the eye, or rather that the total visual organization of eye and brain, naturally seeks to measure in depth has already been demonstrated. This analysis of the simple drawings of trees illustrates how the three-dimensional illusion operates in drawing without recourse to the mechanical help of perspective. Since we possess the capacity to be aware of the depth of space occupied by an object, this awareness is obviously an important factor in any visual design. As we said in Form I, an awareness and an appreciation of the space immediately surrounding the object is very necessary to apprehend completely the object itself. The space in's and out's of a piece of furniture (between the legs, through the chair arms) contribute very substantially to our perception of

FIG. 3-8

REFRIGERATOR BY PRESTCOLD
The dominant black strips at top and bottom of the front panel give a strong emphasis to the white region which we thus perceive as a positive region of defined space, rather than form. The stereoscopic sharpness of the handle projects further forward, strongly indicating its function. Our total perception of the form is cunningly aided by these simple devices. (Photograph by Council of Industrial Design, London)

FIG. 3-9

OFFICES FOR BRITISH OLIVETTI LTD., LONDON
Misha Black and John Diamond, designers
A further example of spatial illusions created through an exploitation of line weight and quality and degrees of tone. Full practical use is made of the wall for the typewriter tables, yet the visual barrier of the wall surface is diminished by exploiting our natural depth perception. The sharp, black frame of the table projects forward from the wall, while the heavy, black "O" on the wall is more frontally dominant than the mosaic trade mark. Thus three regions of depth are suggested, and the wall may be used without being visually or psychologically oppressive. (The Architectural Review, London)

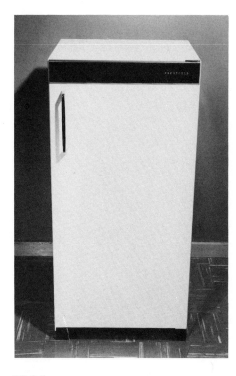

FIG. 3-8

FIG. 3-9

the form of the object, a fact that every designer must take into account. In this chapter we have now developed the space concept somewhat further. Rather than regarding a single form in its individual envelope of space, we have moved into a large space field containing several forms and studied their positions in depth, both in relation to the total space and to each other.

We can now say that form is complementary to space, and space is complementary to form. In painting a landscape or a portrait, in forming a piece of sculpture, or in designing an automobile interior or an office (see Fig. 3-9), this relationship must be taken into consideration.

Concluding experiment

To reinforce this elementary lesson in depth perception, we will present a more developed and more consciously organized problem. Take one of the simple tree trunk studies, and in the studio make a larger and more finished drawing in pen and ink, along the following lines. (About 8″ x 8″ is a good size for this new square, which should be enclosed with a good firm pen line.) Redraw any one of the small sketches in the larger square, with thin, delicate pen lines all of equal weight. This now gives you a design of vertical lines, the special arrangement of which has been taken from an observed source in nature, and in which you have some totally enclosed areas (frontal areas) and some space-penetrated areas (receding areas). But since the lines are all of equal weight, the drawing will not appear very three-dimensional. Now, with a pen or brush, thicken up two lines which almost, or totally, enclose an area, in order to achieve a stronger frontal dominance for that area and for those particular lines. Look over the design again (remember you are no longer thinking about tree trunks) and decide which verticals should be thickened only slightly in order to produce some frontal dominance but not as much as in the first area. In other words, this area will appear behind the first. After these two operations, the design is now composed of three differing weights of line—the forward-thrusting heavy lines, the medium lines in the middle distance, and the thin lines of the original drawing which now appear well recessed. One more thing remains to be done. From the page of line experiments made in Chapter 2, choose one type of line of some definite quality, either very sharp or very diffuse, and

FIG. 3-10

Enlargement from small, outdoor, tree-grouping note. Frontal, middle, and distant regions have been produced with line weight, line quality, and enclosed and open areas. Notice the importance of line quality in such a space context. The thin, yet sharp line in the center of the drawing is almost stereoscopic in its jump forward, despite its lack of weight and its position, surrounded by much empty space.

FIG. 3-11

Subtle depth relationships have been established in this drawing using the four verticals of differing weight and positioning them to allow varying degrees of space penetration within the rectangle. The frontal projecting horizontal bar gives a space-focus to the four verticals and helps the eye to make a more positive assessment of their depth position in space.

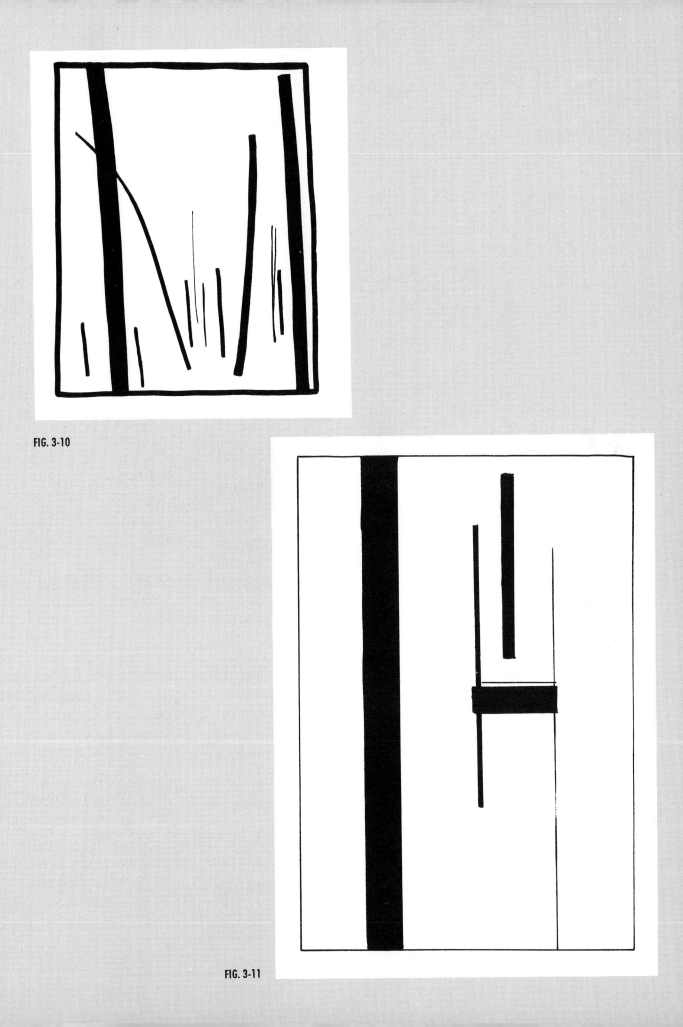

FIG. 3-10

FIG. 3-11

insert a similar line anywhere in this design. Does this line of definite quality appear near or far away in relation to the other black lines? Figures 3-10, 3-11, and 3-12 illustrate similar situations.

The drawing is now complete. Once again, rather like the structure drawings, it has become almost a diagrammatic design, but nevertheless a design giving considerable information. Regions of varying depth have been created, and the vertical lines have a relationship to each other based on their depth positioning rather than on rhythmic, proportional, or tensional considerations.[2] A re-examination of the three "Conclusions" arrived at from our notations on tree groupings should help to clarify why this is so.

SOME FURTHER OBSERVATIONS

While discussing space in depth, it is interesting, and I think necessary, to draw attention to some approaches to art, that achieve a three-dimensional realization of the world through apparently flat, two-dimensional design.

I am referring, of course, to Eastern art and to the art of children the world over. Japanese woodcuts, Chinese scroll paintings, Mogul and Rajput paintings in India, and a six-year-old's drawing from anywhere—all have several factors in common. During the last sixty years, art in the West has finally broken away from the limitations of "realism," from the 600-year-old struggle to portray "appearances" (as depicted by the mechanical rules of perspective) and has utilized some of the flat-pattern techniques of the East and of primitive painters, with no great loss of spatial depth and a definite gain in meaningful expression. Obviously, then, the two-dimensional space of the paper surface can become three-dimensional regions of depth, without the artificial imposition of Western perspective formulas. Our aim in Space I has been to indicate how this can be done consistent with the way we naturally perceive spatial relationships in depth. The "Conclusions" to the first space experiment of this chapter present three specific situations which produce three-dimensional space.

FIG. 3-12

Two drawings which illustrate how varying regions of depth are more obviously perceived when the natural scene is reduced to the linear abstraction. When the natural scene is re-created from the abstraction, as in the drawing on the right, it also gains in depth contrasts over a first, quick sketch.

---

[2] Linear tensions are discussed in Space IV (Chapter 11).

Eastern art (and incidentally some early Western medieval art) uses the size-proportion-color method of achieving emphasis and dominance for the important parts of the design. These are the parts that are ideologically significant, rather than the parts that are visually significant. Most Western artists have found visual significance their greatest concern. In primitive art, for example, the important figure in a composition is drawn as the largest figure, irrespective of his position visually in the design. Conversely, "crowd" figures and unimportant figures are drawn smaller, even if they are in the very front of the picture (Fig. 3-13). Young children do exactly the same thing. They play up the objects and the people in the picture that are important to them, rather than being concerned with visual accuracy. Color is used, too, for producing emphasis and to enrich the decorative effects of the painting rather than to indicate spatial relationships.

The space elements created in this so-called "two-dimensional" art possess depth as a result of frontal dominance achieved by parts of the design, in much the same way as the heavy lines of the tree diagrams were forward-thrusting. This depth is not obvious to Western eyes, so accustomed to the converging lines and diminution of perspective—it is more natural, more subtle (because it has an abstract quality to it), and perhaps more expressive, since the artist is freer to use the space relationships for purely aesthetic ends throughout his work. Perspective can be a very demanding master, and the danger is that the "means" become more important than the ends.

In 1908, the French painter Henri Matisse wrote:

> Expression to my way of thinking does not consist of the passion mirrored upon a human face or betrayed by a violent gesture. The whole arrangement of my picture is expressive. The place occupied by the figures or objects, *the empty spaces around them*, the proportions, everything plays a part.

There is little conscious use of perspective in the paintings of Matisse (Fig. 3-14), but depth is created naturally through the organization of his design in the manner we have discussed. The idea that space, empty space, can be expressive was quite a perceptive statement to make in 1908, even though the Japanese print had then been in vogue for some time.

FIG. 3-13

HUNTERS SHOOTING DEER
Fragment of fresco from Alpera, Spain. The deer are the largest objects, irrespective of their space position in the design, because they are the most important objects. (The American Museum of Natural History)

FIG. 3-14

THE JOY OF LIFE
Henri Matisse
Space and form in a complementary association. An example of the expressiveness of Matisse's "empty" spaces.... (© 1963 by the Barnes Foundation, Merion, Pennsylvania)

FIG. 3-13

FIG. 3-14

4

structural families:
objects of mass
and the structure of volume

The second family of objects which now concerns us differs in every way from the skeletal forms in Form I. Experience there showed us that when we can determine structure, we must do so if we are to draw with complete understanding; and we also learned that since space often intrudes between the parts of the skeleton, we must take account of the space surrounding such an object if we are to draw successfully its significant proportions, movement, and structure.

Drawing is an act of discovery. Either as a conscious reaction to an objective stimulus or as an act of spontaneous creativity, it is concerned with knowing, and awareness of skeletal structure is one aspect of knowing about form. However, objects that are composed of mass—a pebble or a loaf of bread—have no such skeleton (see the definition of skeletal structure under the heading, "Conclusions" in Form I) and thus form a second family of object-types which may be called the "mass" group (Fig. 4-1). Such objects are not made up of a jointed series of skeletal parts, are usually static rather than vibrant, and have a "lumpy" or "massive" quality—characteristics in direct contrast to the linear objects we first examined. And it is not easy to look at a pebble and decide how it can be structurally explained in visual terms. Nevertheless, if one sets out to determine how a sense of structure operates with these solid objects,

FIG. 4-1

MUSE

Constantin Brancusi
Bronze on stone base. An object of mass. The highly polished surface of this heavy swelling mass invites your hand to experience its fullness and appraise its weight. It is the very antithesis of the skeletal object. (Portland Art Museum, Oregon. Photograph by Eliot Elisofen)

43

how their form and weight and space displacement are apprehended through observation, then one does discover a common structure characteristic which is effective in explaining them in drawing. This structural characteristic operates in a way very different from the skeletal limbs of the first group. See Fig. 4-2, which shows the natural contour line in a piece of wood.

Let us call this common structure characteristic for objects of mass the "continuous contour line." It moves without any break over and around the planes and curved surfaces of a solid form object, constantly making a progression in its exploration of surface and surface inclination (Fig. 4-3). This contour line is both imaginary and real. For many people, as their eyes travel over the surface of a form, they trace "lines of information" relevant to the surface under observation rather as if the tips of the fingers were exploring the form. In some cases, the tactile and the visual senses are so intimately attuned that it is possible to "feel" a surface on one's fingertips merely by intensive looking. The contour line, traveling over and around the surface, is apprehended imaginatively even when it disappears from view around the other side of the object. The following illustration is a good example of this inter-operation of the senses. If you were asked to estimate the weight of a watermelon placed before you, your eyes would travel over the surface, appraising the swell and form of the surface, to judge the total mass or weight. They would repeat their assessment on the side that is out of sight; and at the same time, you would be imaginatively "feeling" the heaviness of the melon in your hand. The continuous contour line does all this with an object of mass, *entirely through drawing*. It defines solid form as these different levels of perception, sight and touch, work together.

At this stage, a complication occurs, inasmuch as the title of this section refers to "the Structure of Volume," for volume has a dual role. Volume denotes the space occupied by solid form or mass but it also signifies defined regions of space. Volume may refer to a solid like a pebble (Fig. 4-4), or to emptiness like a hole (Fig. 4-5). There is no real contradiction here: there are two kinds of volume that exist independently of each other or can exist side-by-side as properties of the same object. A

FIG. 4-2

Photographic magnification of a small wood piece. The contour delineation of the mass is well shown. This photograph could illustrate planes and curved surfaces (Form V) and become an aerial view of a rocky canyon. It is only a question of scale. (Photograph by Wayne Bitterman)

FIG. 4-3

A good, natural example of an object of mass whose form is defined by a continuous contour groove. Notice how the light and shade assists the groove in our perception of the mass.

FIG. 4-4

A hole. This simple, round stone is made the more significant because, through the hole, we become aware of the other side.

FIG. 4-5

Compare this shell with the human ear. It is an object which defines space-volume most delicately.

FIG. 4-6

FROG EATING A LIZARD
Eduardo Paolozzi
Bronze sculpture. On skeletal limbs stands this fearsome form of mass and volume. The holes give suggestions of its mysterious space-cavity, while the projections and protrusions of its surface suggest a molten growth. (Martha Jackson Gallery, New York)

FIG. 4-3

FIG. 4-2

FIG. 4-4

FIG. 4-6

FIG. 4-5

stone is mass volume; an egg or a snail shell is space volume. But volume, to have any discernible shape, must be defined; and this is the important function of the continuous contour line; it will define the space volume of a hole or the mass volume of a rock; and where the rock is pierced with holes, the same contour line will define both kinds of volume (see Fig. 4-6). It will be easier to understand this by looking at the illustrations, Figs. 4-7 to 4-9.

It will be apparent that both Figs. 4-7 and 4-9 are contour drawings which express mass volume—the solidity of the form is reasonably apparent, and the structural shape characteristics of the surface of a mass are defined by the contour line. The figures represent two different kinds of pebbles. By contrast, Fig. 4-8 is a drawing of space volume; the contour line encloses a volume of space rather than a solid form, and it appears as a square hole into which you could place a finger (see also Fig. 4-10). These three illustrations show how effective is the continuous contour line in drawing both volume of mass and volume of space. Try to imagine the pebbles in Figs. 4-7 and 4-9 if they were outlined, only. Would this convey any sense of the structural implication of their surface, or their space displacement or heaviness?

One more factor remains to be introduced into contour-line structure drawing, that of the quality and weight of line. We became acquainted with this important factor in both Drawing Marks I and Space I. It is further illustrated in Figs. 4-11 and 4-12, which indicate how the introduction of line quality and line weight modify one's perception of the form.

You will see that in Fig. 4-12 the heavier weight of the line and the more incisive quality of line are at the "front" of the form, and the line becomes more neutral and less positive as it moves away down the form. In Fig. 4-11, however, these linear emphases are reversed, and our perception of this form is different. By its linear emphases Fig. 4-12 suggests the structure of a hollow space and Fig. 4-11 appears to be a more solid object. A further study of the two illustrations reveals that this difference between "hole" and "solid" is achieved by using linear emphasis in a way that can be stated simply as follows: *If the dominant emphases of weight and quality are introduced where the revolving line converges, an object of more solid*

FIG. 4-7

Contour - line diagrammatic drawings of mass form.

FIG. 4-8

Contour - line diagrammatic drawing of space-volume.

FIG. 4-9

FIG. 4-10

STAIRWAY IN BERLIN
*The structure of space-volume revealed in architecture. Here is the continuously revolving contour line defining a hole in a building in the same way that you defined a hole in a piece of wood.
(Ullstein, Berlin. Photograph by Fritz Eschen)*

FIG. 4-11

Contour line expressing a projection of form.

FIG. 4-12

Contour line expressing a recession or hole.

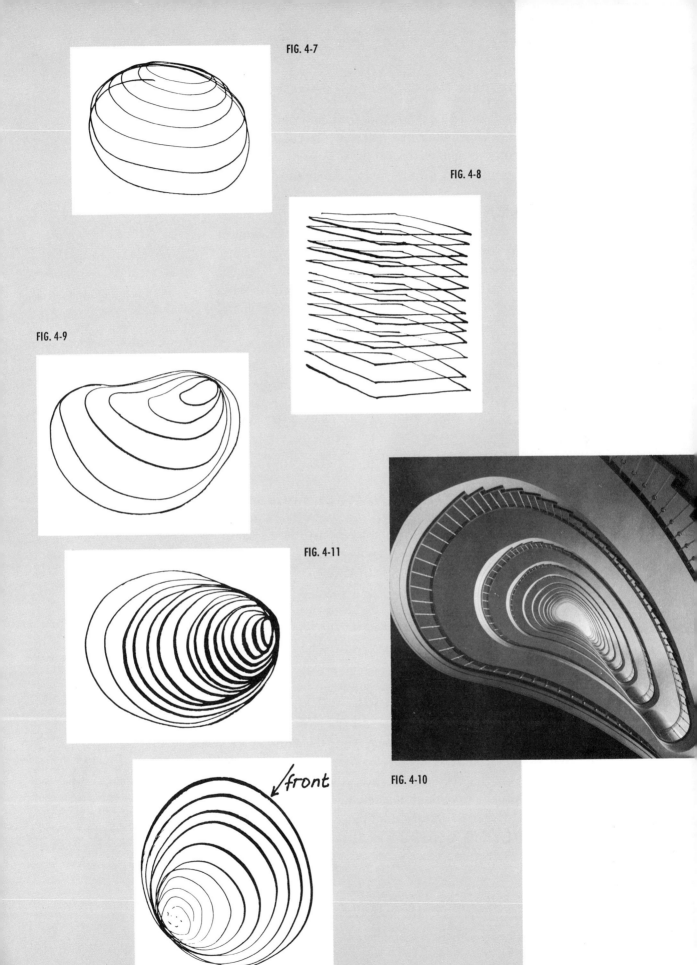

FIG. 4-7

FIG. 4-8

FIG. 4-9

FIG. 4-11

FIG. 4-10

front

FIG. 4-12

form is perceived. When the reverse is true, and *the revolving contour-line quality is lighter and less sharp in the regions of convergence, then a hollow space form is perceived*. This proposition is consistent with the *frontal dominance* or *recession in space* discoveries made in Space I.

But the contour line, like all things perceived by human sight, suggests different things to different people. Although it gives structural suggestion to volume, it is not always immediately apparent *which* volume: that of space or mass. A longer look at Figs. 4-11 and 4-12 will render you undecided as to which is which. Now the reinforcement to the contour line is to be found in the conventional use of light and shade. The drawings in Fig. 4-13 indicate how, by determining the regions of highlight and shadow and "building them into" the contour structure, a more positive perception of hollow form or solid form can be achieved.

THE EXPERIMENT

Contour lines that are continuously exploring surface or space-volume demand exceptionally free and unforced drawing (Fig. 4-14). The whole arm, rather than just the wrist or the fingers must move, and a rhythm must be built up while the drawing is in progress. The first experiment will help to achieve this rhythmic freedom. Draw on your paper a large freehand shape and "pierce" it with holes of differing shapes and sizes.

Attempt to go deep—and in some cases right through—by using a continuously revolving contour line which varies in its quality and in its weight. Within the same freehand shape try to "pull out" a few projections to contrast with the holes and do not be afraid of any experimentation, such as dropping a blot of ink onto the paper and allowing your revolving line to grow out of the blob. A study of Figs. 4-15 and 4-16 will indicate some idea of the possible inventive variations produced by this exploratory structure drawing. Figure 4-16, particularly, reveals how the surface movement of form, its holes and projections, can be expressed with the rhythmic freedom of the contour line.

FIG. 4-13
A sequence of experiments with the contour line in drawing holes and projections, with conventional tone shading used to supplement the contour line and heighten our perception of the mass or space. Black tone (shadow) helps to suggest how deep is the hole, while highlights catching projecting surfaces help to indicate the degree of projection possessed by the mass. Here, black suggests recession rather than frontal projection because we associate darkness with the depth of a hole. In the context of a projecting form, strong white tone comes forward because we associate the projecting high point of a mass with light reflection. This reverses the natural depth perception discussed in Space I and reveals the difficulty of postulating rules of perception, for—depending on the context—there is an ambiguity about our perception of form and space in which "meaning" plays an important role. This might be termed the factor of psychological association in perception.

FIG. 4-13

Now let us be more objective and examine in detail the human ear. You will notice that its form is made up of a series of holes or hollows situated between projecting ridges. Were you to take a photograph and make a tremendously enlarged print, the ear would look just like an aerial view of a mountain range. It is this very quality of hollows and ridges that the contour line is suited to describe and with which the whole of this chapter has been concerned. But first make a conventional drawing of the ear, in any medium you wish, to produce as accurate a representational drawing as you can with line and tone shading. Second, make a continuous contour-line structure drawing of the same ear, showing all the surface movements, all the holes, and all the projecting ridges. Work very objectively. Use the line as boldly as in making the holes in the freehand shape. By the time you have finished this structure drawing it will probably resemble a contour map of a hilly ground area, rather than a drawing of an ear, such is the definition of surface movement. Yet if we are to make a comparison between the two drawings, the representational and the structural (see Fig. 4-17), I think you will agree that it is the contour drawing that tells you more about the structure of the ear and the organic relationship between the parts of the ear. In making such a structure drawing, it becomes necessary to understand "how" the ear is, in order to re-create it as a form with structural and organic reality.

Conclusions

Objects of mass and the dual nature of volume have now been tentatively explored through structural drawing. If we add skeletal objects to objects of mass and volume, we have examples from each of the two principal families of form. It is very difficult to think of any kind of form which does not take its place in either of these families—from the substantial object, or the shell which is merely a defined region of space, to the hairlike thread.

This emphasis on structure is not just a frill. An attempt was made in Form I to relate structure to the process of comprehending form. Drawing is meaningless without it. Leonardo da Vinci and many lesser artists have attempted to establish that art (and drawing is the foundation of art) is a mental

FIG. 4-14

A typical student sheet of practice drawing with the contour line. The line's insistence on expressing volume, both mass and space, is shown here.

FIG. 4-15

A drawing, made without reference to any object, of a wood form having holes and projections.

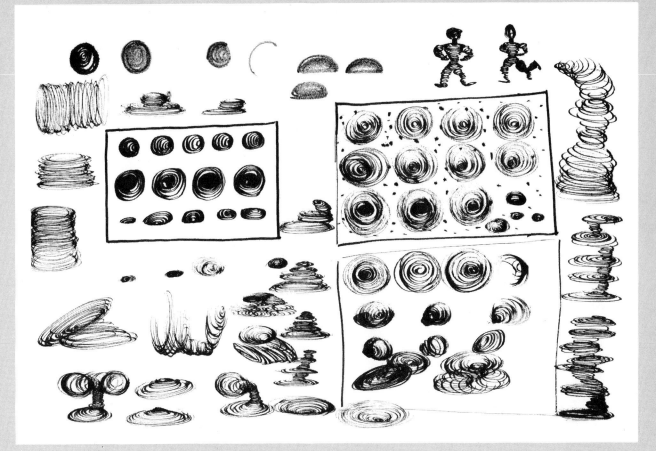

FIG. 4-14

FIG. 4-15

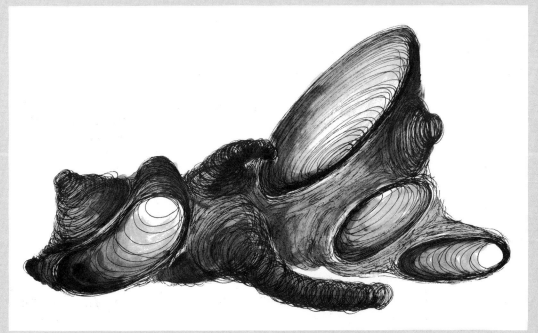

activity and a science searching for objective reality. In the present day, we admit that it is also an intuitive, sometimes clairvoyant means of revelation about life, individual consciousness, and subjective experience. The searching for the structural "how" of an object is a mental part of the process of perception when one is looking with intent. Eventually, this search for the structure becomes an intuitive faculty of the artist or designer, for without it drawing can become second to photography. Both your studies of the ear were from direct observation. The traditional drawing is a portrait of a particular ear with emphasis on its sensory appearance in terms of what the eye sees. The contour drawing, while still faithful to local peculiarities, is nevertheless concerned with an "earness" common to all ears everywhere—an absolute quality of earness —and has resulted from what you *know* about the ear, after analysis of its surface mass, as well as what you see. The knowing is as important as the seeing.

In writing this, I realize how misleading these separations can be. The world's great works of art embody a complete marriage between appearance and structure, knowing and seeing, feeling and understanding, all synthesized by the catalyst of vision. Art is art. When one explains art, there is no art. Here lie the difficulties for the writer and the teacher dealing with the visual creative process.

Knowledge of this family of form—of mass or volume objects with which this section has been concerned—has wide application. The cylindrical stalk of a plant, clouds and holes in clouds, eyes situated in sockets, the mass of a boulder, the volume of the human thigh—these are perceptively realized through the structural implications of the revolving contour line. The drawings in Fig. 4-18 are good illustrations of an exploratory search for mass and volume. Would these forms be as graphic without the drawings' insistence on surface contour?

It becomes apparent from structure drawings that by an objective process of reduction to structural realities, we find one way to arrive at the abstract form in art. It was Paul Cézanne, in fact, whose research in this direction charted the path to cubism.[1] From there it was a short step to the abstract or non-representational form; for in delving this deep into structure,

---

[1] See reference to Cézanne in the Conclusion to Form I.

FIG. 4-16

Drawing of an imaginary wood form. Contour line expresses the various surface movements and rhythms.

FIG. 4-17

A first, observed drawing of the human ear and a contour-line structure drawing which heightens perception of the surface movement of the form, of the "plains" and "ridges" of the ear.

FIG. 4-16

FIG. 4-17

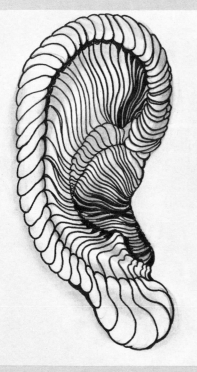 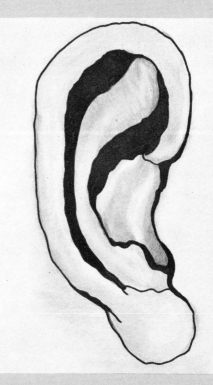

new shapes emerged, derived from the object, yet now existing in their own right. Once the artist realized that such nonrepresentational shapes possessed an aesthetic content and power in their own right, then it was but a short step to produce such abstract forms without recourse to an object at all. And thus nonobjective art was born.

SKELETAL STRUCTURE AND VOLUME

Even the slenderest twig has weight and volume. Although predominantly linear or skeletal in appearance, it is, nevertheless, also an object of mass and volume, as we would see if we were to cut through it and expose a cross section.

The branching marine animal to which the queen scallop is attached (Fig. 4-19) is essentially skeletal, yet its limbs, too, have roundness and volume.

In short, all skeletal objects are also objects of mass and volume. It does not work in reverse, however: objects of mass do not automatically have a skeleton. What, then, is the point of dividing objects into two families if fundamentally they all possess volume? The reason is that we want to bring out the dominant structural characteristic. Everybody would agree that the branching marine animal of Fig. 4-19 is predominantly a linear, multi-directioned, articulated object. This is so obviously its principal structural characteristic that its volume does not intrude greatly on our perception of the object. But look at Fig. 4-20, a brain coral formation from Samoa. Here the situation is the other way around; it is the object's *volume* that we principally perceive, even though it is made up of a series of fine linear branches.

Thus the division of objects into structural families is based on our perception of the dominant structural aspect of the object—whether linear and skeletal or volume and mass. And we are now familiar with the methods of structural drawing which best reveal the skeletal or the voluminous type of form. For example, since we perceive the brain coral predominantly as volume, we should draw it with the continuous contour line, to express its volume, and then put in the skeletal formation to indicate the linear means by which the volume is achieved. In

FIG. 4-18

Contour-line diagrammatic experimental drawings describing volume and mass.

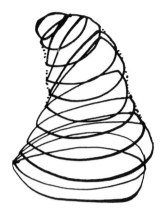
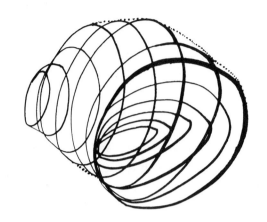

the case of the marine animal, its predominantly linear and branching form is best revealed by drawing it first as a jointed skeletal line. But since a line has no volume, we could add contour lines *around* the skeletal line to give the animal mass.

An imaginative use of both methods of structural drawing can often help reveal the dominant form of an object. A bottle, for example, is pure volume. It is not made up of delicate linear branches like the brain coral, and it has no skeletal form present in its structure. Yet, in drawing the bottle, it helps to draw an imaginary skeletal structure around which the volume can expand. This is suggested in the experiment described in Vision II, where, before drawing the space volume of the bottle, an imaginary skeleton composed of a central vertical line and horizontal "width" lines is drawn. This plots the shape and proportion of the volume which the contour line will then describe. A bottle drawn in this way results from an intelligent application of the principles behind structural drawing, rather than from a mechanical use of a formula.

FIG. 4-19

Branching marine animal with queen scallop. Although our perception of this form is primarily of a skeletal object, the volume or mass aspect of its limbs is also realized in this photograph. (Shell International Petroleum Company Ltd.)

FIG. 4-20

Brain coral from Samoa. Our perception of this form is primarily of an object of mass or volume, yet the coral is made up of many fine skeletal threads.

FIG. 4-19

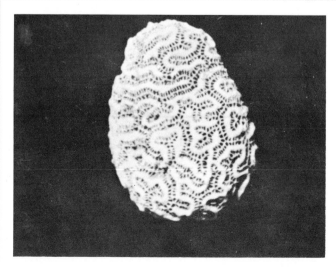

FIG. 4-20

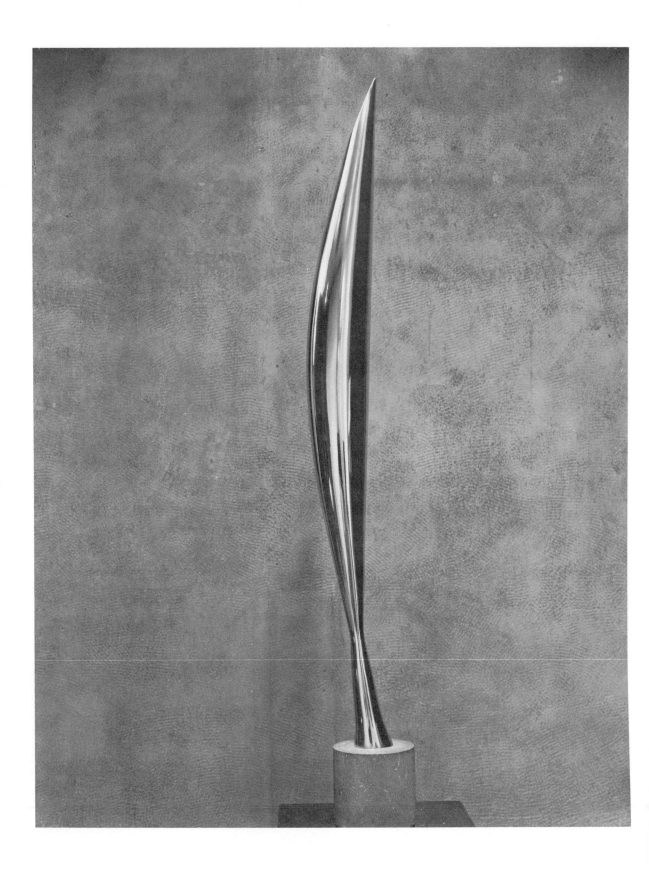

5

the aesthetic implications of form

Examining form in terms of structure, we have come to the conclusion that two basic family types exist: skeletal form and mass form. We discovered structural qualities that are capable of description through drawing and that enlighten our understanding of "how" an object is. They help our eye, mind, and instinct to operate together in appraising the *modus operandi* of the object when it confronts us and demands comprehension rather than mere identification. An awareness of structure directs our attention and interest to search for the inner, more permanent nature of the object. It helps us to recognize associational affinities with other objects and insures that we perceive more about an object than merely the shape of its external appearance. This is the importance of work in structural analysis.

In Form I, we said, "Form or outward shape is dependent entirely on structure. . . ." Although this is true, it would be a mistake at this stage to pursue too far the separation between skeleton and clothing. This section, therefore, will serve as an introduction to the aesthetic implications of form as a complete phenomenon. Webster's definition of form as "the shape and structure of anything" is concise and adequate, but it does not go far enough for the artist who wants to imply that form has an *aesthetic potential*, that the "shape and structure

BIRD IN SPACE (1919)
Constaintin Brancusi
Bronze, 54 inches high.
The soaring of a bird or the
human spirit, symbolized
and suggested through form.
(Collection, The Museum of
Modern Art, New York)

59

of anything" provokes some kind of reaction in the beholder. I would prefer to define form as "a particular organization of shape capable of arousing the emotional and intellectual participation of the individual."

From a potato to an orchid, a jam jar to a Cellini saltcellar, form is inescapable. Even with closed eyes we can appreciate form through our sense of touch. The form of things comprises the total substantial element of our world and is a large part of our conscious orientation. We all have personal reactions of thought and feeling to the ubiquitous presence of form. At the lowest level comes the simple act of accepting or rejecting something when we are shopping. At the highest level comes an experience of recognition, understanding, and sympathy so intense that it approaches ecstasy—a complete self-identification with the object through a heightened total consciousness. It can happen when one is confronted with some extraordinary quality of completeness in the forms of nature, when one is face to face with a work of art, inspiring and transcendental like a Gothic cathedral, a Renaissance bronze figure, a Baroque altarpiece, or even a primitive clay vessel.

There is obviously a distinction to be made between the commonplace and the powerfully moving. When form appears complete and unalterable, when we sense that any addition or subtraction would ruin this completeness, when form is charged with meaning, when it coincides with our desires, invites our physical or imaginative possession and the subsequent loss of our own identity in self-identification with the form—when we are affected in any of these ways, then for a moment we become involved with the mystery of an aesthetic response. For some, this is an intimation of the divine. It is what Bernard Berenson meant in his comments on Perugino's space composition, quoted in Space I—an aesthetic experience of a visual nature. Perugino heightens our awareness of space sufficiently for us to become significantly involved. This kind of experience accounts for an artist's being moved by form and a designer's preoccupation with it. (If we must have a pot to cook in, why not have one to enjoy aesthetically?)

Between the highest and lowest levels of such experience lie many levels of degree. Yet all form contains some interest and audience involvement, for we react to what might be called "pure" form, to squareness or roundness or sharpness (Figs. 5-1, 5-2), irrespective of any meaning the form may have. The sculptor who is actually handling three-dimensional

FIG. 5-1

Two stones from a river bed, shaped by the flow of water. They are magnificent manifestations of "roundness." Herein lies their aesthetic implication.

FIG. 5-2

A river-bed stone that is beautiful in its thin, rounded, flatness. Compare it with the stones of Fig. 5-1. This one arouses different sensations and ideas.

60

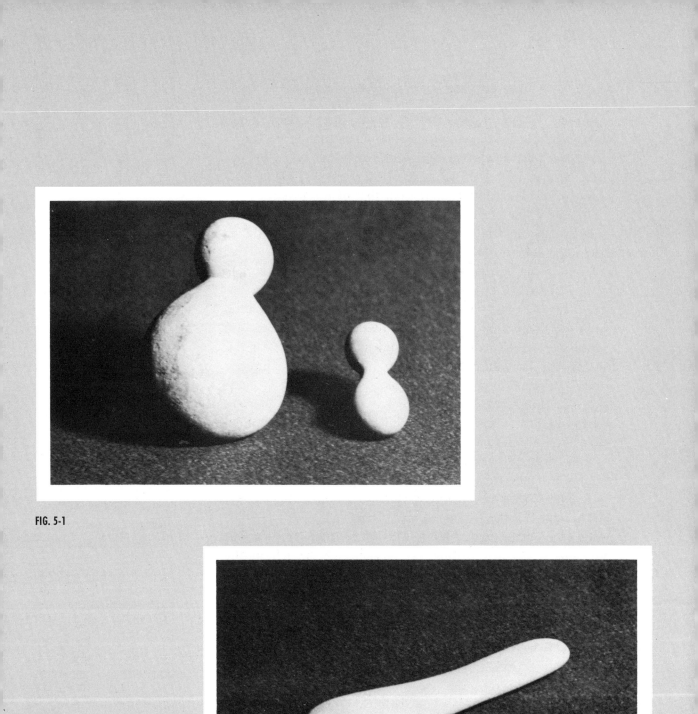

FIG. 5-1

FIG. 5-2

form may be more interested than the painter in these "pure" aspects of form. The sculptor may find motivation in the "pure" form of a potato, whereas the painter would have no interest in it at all. Yet both artists' range of interest in form spreads more widely and more acutely than that of the nonartist.

In nature, "pure" form and meaningful form are to be found side-by-side: the white, smooth bone and the rough, weathered rock; the folds of the hills and the swell of abdomen and breasts in the human torso. It may be the "pure" form that excites the artist, or it may be the significance for him of its meaning—but more than likely both of these aspects of form are inseparably bound up in his aesthetic awareness. For man is still part of the natural world, and forms in nature can stir in him the recognition of common affinities between all forms and their presence in his own physical shape (Fig. 5-3). Such a recognition provides a glimmer of truth—the truth of common qualities of shape among things, and this is a fundamental part of aesthetic awareness (Figs. 5-4 and 5-5).

This chapter touches on only the essential aspects of the aesthetic implications of form. The meaning of beauty and perfection, the psychology of aesthetic sensitivity, the urge for possession, and the faculty to identify with the object—all of which are part of our innate sensitivity to form—must be left to more specialized writing.[1] It is sufficient enough in the early stages of an involvement with art to be aware of the intimate part played by form in stimulating our desires, our moods, our imaginings, our hopes and fears. Knowledge of form is the basis of a whole range of visual imagery which includes both memory of the past and imaginative explorations of the future. What, for example, is "mountain-form"? You have seen mountains, and a generalized image of mountain-shaped characteristics remains with you; you live with the memory-form of the mountain rather than with the mountain. But have you seen an Angel or a Spirit? Probably not. In that case, what form might such an airy creature have? You will be familiar with art's treatment of such things over many hundreds of years—idealized human bodies wearing long flowing garments and often sprouting wings from somewhere around the shoulder blades—a treatment determined by using a form

FIG. 5-3

IDEAS FOR SCULPTURE (1941) Henry Moore sketchbook *Forms of nature, developed into shapes of heightened aesthetic implication by the artist's vision through drawing.* (Henry Moore)

FIG. 5-4

Compare this stone from the river bed with the Cycladic head of Fig. 5-5. This form suggests "head," and it is powerful in the natural state, with just a hint of the features of the face. Its mysterious authority would be lost if the features became intelligible.

FIG. 5-5

CYCLADIC HEAD FROM KEROS *The head simplified to an abstract form by "primitive" artists of the Aegean, about 3000 B.C. The fine simplicity of the form, like the stones taken from the river bed, makes a strong aesthetic appeal per se. Add to this its significance as a symbol of the human head, and we have a powerful object.* (Musée du Louvre, Paris. Photograph by M. Chuzeville)

[1] Cf. Kenneth Clark, *Moments of Vision* (Oxford: The Clarendon Press, 1954); Herbert Read, *The Meaning of Art* (Baltimore: Penguin Books, Inc., 1961); Laszlo Moholy-Nagy, *The New Vision and Abstract of an Artist* (New York: George Wittenborn, Inc., 1947).

FIG. 5-3

FIG. 5-4

FIG. 5-5

(the human figure) already known to the artist and embellishing it with symbols of purity and flight. Modern art has tackled this problem much more imaginatively, particularly in sculpture, where new and powerful forms have denied any representational allegiance to the human body and have evoked powerful and mystical suggestions of pure "Spirit" (see Fig. 5-6). This is the creative function of art: to produce form in a variety of mediums, form which is capable of enlarging our own individual experience and constantly revealing hidden aspects of life and nature.

The mystery of Francis Bacon's intangible materializing shapes (Fig. 5-7) are a painter's forms to which we react with a feeling of foreboding. In contrast, the distillation of maternal tenderness and madonna-like innocence in Fra Filippo Lippi's "Virgin" (Fig. 5-8), expressed through the translucent and evocatively modeled head and column of the neck, attains a quality of remoteness and spirituality that is almost spine-tingling in its unearthiness. It is the quality of Lippi's form that says all these things to us.

We live surrounded by form: landscape, the human figure, the dream, the legend and the myth, the fantastic minutiae of biochemistry or nuclear physics, the products of industry, commercial advertising, architecture, and townscape, the teeming complexities of nature. We retain images of the shape of all these things. If there is no form, then space is all that remains. (But we shall see in Chapter 12, "Form and Space," that we would not be aware of space without the marker buoys of form to chart it.) This is one of the difficulties in trying to imagine an immortal spirit.

Because of ever-present form and our inescapable involvement with it, architects, designers, and town planners must always consider the aesthetic implications of the objects they sponsor. Living in a visual slum is hardly likely to foster human creative aspirations, and such creativity is a part of the scale on which we measure "progress" and civilization. We live surrounded by too much visual squalor that is man-made—hence our frequent refreshment at the springs of nature, our urge to get into the country "away from it all" (Fig. 5-9).

"The shape and structure of anything," this is the dictionary definition of form, to which we have added an aesthetic qualification. Through our mysterious capacity to be affected by form, we find ourselves in love with all kinds of things. At one and the same time we both belong to the world and yet

FIG. 5-6

BIRD IN SPACE

FIG. 5-7

FRAGMENT OF A CRUCIFIXION
Francis Bacon
A spirit of unease and foreboding haunts these macabre, materializing forms. Here are a painter's forms possessing aesthetic implications not of beauty, but of truth, the truth of the horror of crucifying. (Hanover Gallery, London)

FIG. 5-8

LA MADONNA COL BAMBINO
E ANGELO
Fra Filippo Lippi
The form of the neck and head of this madonna evokes an imaginative response to the theme of maternal, yet virginal, womanhood. (Uffizi Gallery, Florence)

FIG. 5-9

Man-made visual squalor.

FIG. 5-6

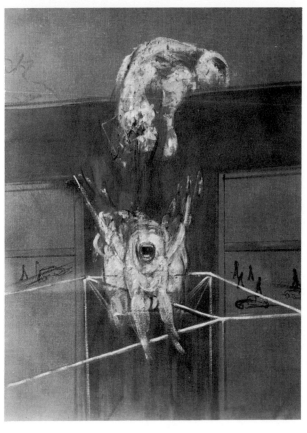

FIG. 5-7

FIG. 5-8

FIG. 5-9

transcend it through this aesthetic sensitivity which allows us to possess it so intimately.

As we have stressed several times now, drawing must constantly be used by a student as a means of realizing aspects not immediately discernible in an object. Presenting things in this way, the drawing offers new suggestions of form to be studied, responded to, and then imaginatively developed into a more significant graphic image. Drawing is the principal way the artist brings form into being. At this point it is now possible to make the equation:

FORM = shape derived from structure + aesthetic aura

These factors have been separately discussed; first, the two main structure families of form and the dependence of shape on structure; second, in the implications of the aesthetic aura of form as it occasions a response in the individual. In Drawing Marks I, the expressive and meaningful nature of lines and marks was introduced, and the student was initiated into the possibilities of a personal quality in drawing, by means of a line that is vital, yet sensitive—spontaneous, yet considered. It has been stressed also that objects exist in space and that an awareness of space displacement or space entry plays an important part in an act of perception. It is with all these things in mind—the structure and aesthetic of form, the means of drawing, and the implications of space—that you should approach the following suggested projects.

One factor involved in this work, however, has not yet been touched upon. This is the factor of the imagination, which usually operates at some level when one makes any kind of personal statement, either verbally or visually in drawing. When one is concerned with design—in this case the making of a new form for a specific result—it is the imagination which suggests the development from one stage to another through a series of drawings. But this aspect of the creative process is the sole concern of the experiments in Part Two, "Vision," and we shall not pause to discuss it here. We shall apply our recently gained structural and spatial knowledge to a personal drawing statement.

THE EXPERIMENTS

Use a rough or smooth-surfaced drawing paper (according to taste), minimum size about 16″ x 16″; a pen, brush, or finger, with ink, or a charcoal stick, or pencil. Make a free, and yet

FIG. 5-10

These weathered wood forms, drawn without reference to any object, are dependent upon the contour line to express their mass and their space-volume or holes.

FIG. 5-11

A piece of driftwood drawn with the contour line where the surface direction of the mass demanded emphasis.

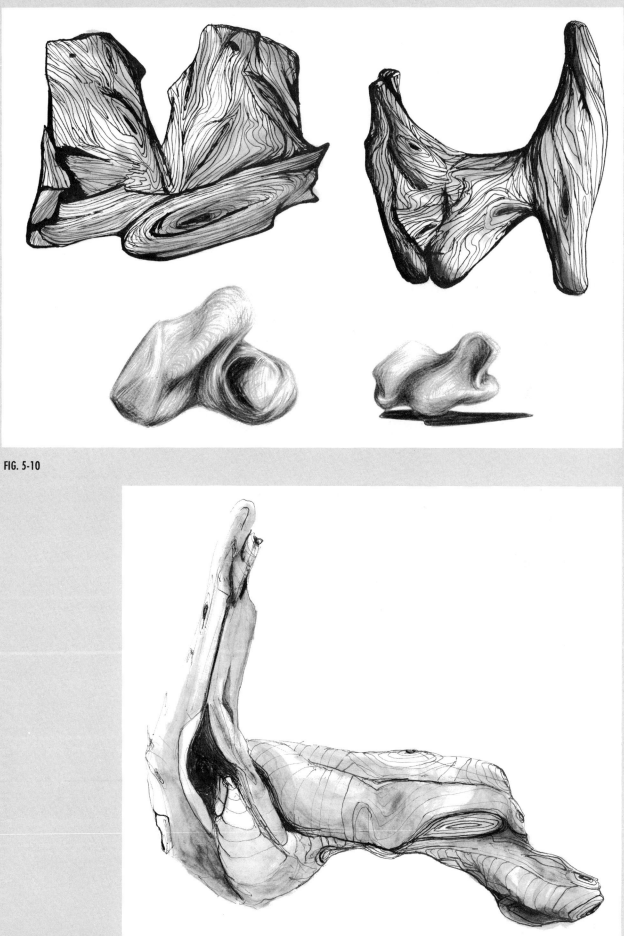

FIG. 5-10

FIG. 5-11

considered, design of the form suggested by each of the following propositions. Start by tentatively exploring the possibilities in drawing loosely, and perhaps vaguely, on a newsprint pad, filling the sheet with suggestions after the manner of doodling. Gradually, your drawing will become more definite as you find one shape suddenly appearing more interesting than the others. Begin to exploit and develop this shape, or a part of it newly discovered, into a fuller indication of the form it suggests. Even when this stage is reached, it is still a good thing to let it continue to evolve through several drawings, before turning to make the finished drawing. Look back for a moment at Henry Moore's drawings for sculpture, to see the progressive shaping of form by drawing (Fig. 5-3).

Use all your resources for this design. Conjure up shapes from memory, build shapes in the mind, "feel" the form as the line explores the paper; allow your knowledge of structure—the jointed limbs of the skeleton or the contour line of the mass— to direct your line. Sense the aesthetic aura emanating from this new thing beginning to grow before you on the paper. Let it grow, rather than try to visualize it before drawing. Start by "scratching about," and fill the wastepaper basket with rejected sheets; but when the drawing is finished, attempt to analyze your aesthetic response to it in terms of the statements made in this text.

Experiment 1

A single and integral free-standing form. Imagine a free-standing rock or wood form which has been weathered by all the elements over a long period of time.

Do you see this as a skeletal object or as a mass/volume object? How does it intrude into space? How does space enter it: through cracks, holes, or tunnels? What is its surface quality as you run your hand over it? Is it the kind of form to be associated with the sound of a high-pitched shriek or with the sound of a dull thud? All these and similar imaginative questions should be running around in your head as the design develops. And do not be afraid to experiment with drawing marks as you feel the need to express special vital elements in the character of your form (see Figs. 5-10 to 5-12).

Experiment 2

A conglomerate form, not free-standing. Consider a bird's-eye view of a section of a dried and rock strewn river bed.

FIG. 5-12

An imaginative metamorphosis of form. The once solid rock has been broken down into what is almost a skeletal object. Compare this imaginative drawing with Fig. 4-20, the brain coral from Samoa.

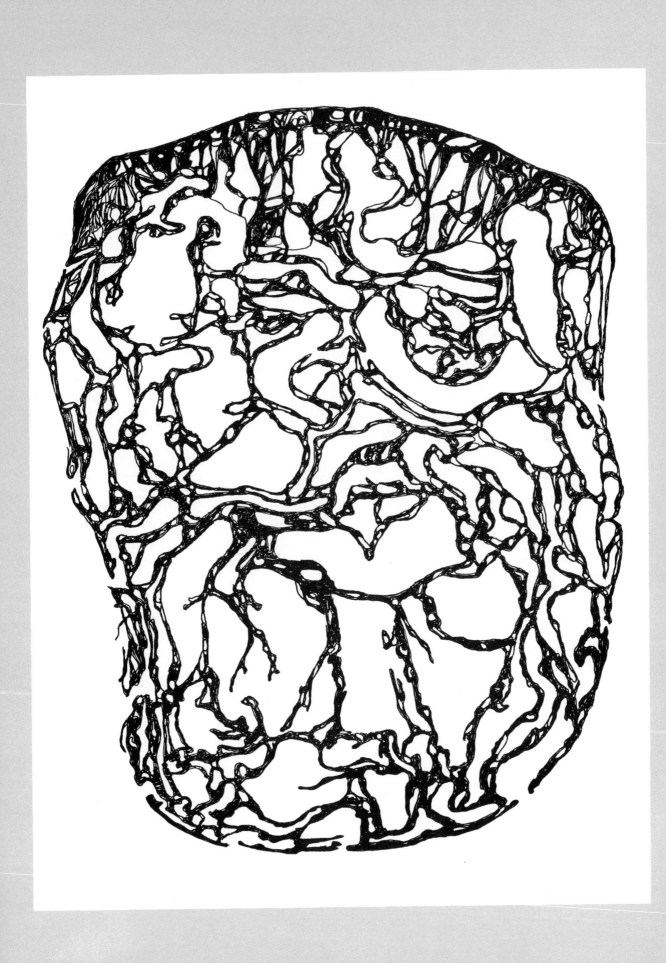

Unlike Experiment 1, which concerns itself with a single monolithic presence, this experiment suggests a more mobile, flowing situation in which many small and independent elements come together to make a compound form. Engagement with this type of form introduces a completely new consideration—the factor of forces, the special study of Space IV, "Dynamic Relationships." Later, when we discuss how forces operate in space to create shifting and fluid organizations of conglomerate form, we shall refer back to this experiment, in which we let our intuition and present knowledge compensate for a lack of knowledge about forces; we depend here on our familiarity with form and space.

Large pebbles, small pebbles, big rocks, all either sharp or smooth, lie on the river bed. But the *way* they lie on the river bed is determined by the water flowing over them, the force involved in this imaginative proposition. The composite form created by the many rocks and pebbles has been created by the force of water. Consequently, the design should show the directional flow of water currents over the stones and account for their clustering and positioning in terms of the water's force. A large stone will act as a barrier to water and to smaller moving pebbles—hence a cluster is formed around a larger or more powerful unit. This is often a characteristic of conglomerate form. Thus two things are happening here: water is flowing smoothly and then a barrier is created which will cause a new direction of water flow. With a new direction of flow, new forces are exerted on the arrangement of other pebbles. These pebbles will, in turn, set up their own opposition and barriers. It is a constantly changing pattern. But, again, such impermanence is a characteristic of conglomerate form.

In the summer when there is no water, the rocks and pebbles exist as a witness to the force that created their formal arrangement. The drawing, when complete, should indicate all these things. The form will have no real beginning and no obvious ending, for it is constantly attracting and expelling the units which shape it. One aesthetic element of this created form will lie in the degree of credibility achieved by the drawing through recognition of how the form was achieved (see Figs. 5-13 and 5-14).

FIG. 5-13

In this river-bed drawing, form is less important than force and movement. The lack of any homogenous quality among the stones, particularly in direction and grouping, produces a dynamic movement of disintegration throughout the design.

FIG. 5-14

This is a fairly static river bed, by comparison with Fig. 5-13. The channels of water force are more regular and not as strong—hence, a more homogenous grouping of the stones as a compound form. Notice the build-up of the stones behind the larger rocks, and the diminution in size of the stones as they disappear in holes in the deeper parts of the channel. This design is descriptive of forces at work and at the same time aesthetically satisfying as an image of organic compound form (growing form made up of many small units).

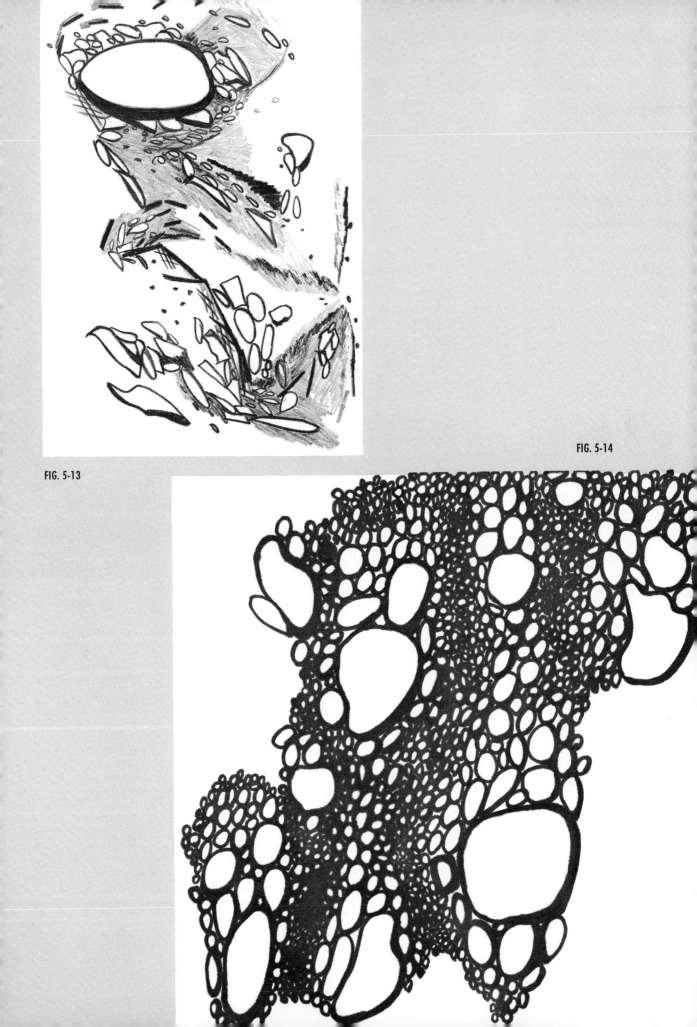

FIG. 5-13

FIG. 5-14

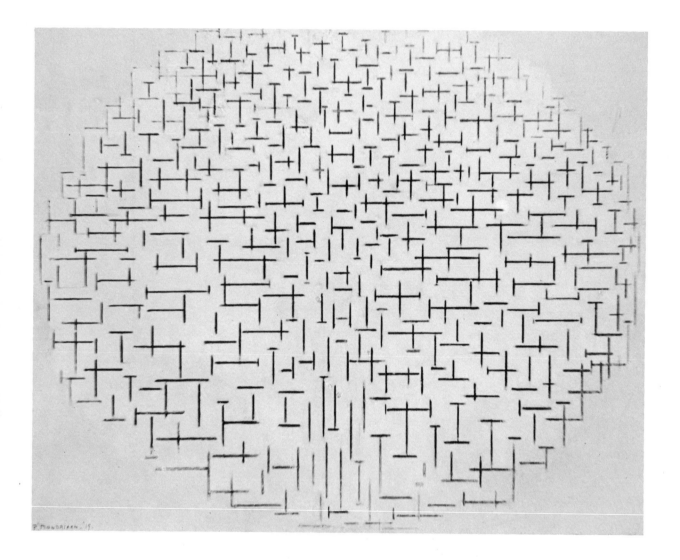

6 the intuitive organization of space

COMPOSITION NO. 10
Piet Mondrian
Here is space disturbed by marks, but unlike your experiment in making free, instinctive, brush marks in an empty space, this is tremendously organized and controlled. Where does your eye finally come to rest in this composition? Notice the subtle changes in space distribution creating a "rushing in" of the marks to one particular region. Space IV discusses how the compression of space suggests force movement.
(Rijksmuseum Kröller-Müller, Holland)

So accustomed are we to our three-dimensional world that our eyes are instinctive depth finders. In Space I (Chapter 3) when we studied the relationship between two and three dimensions, we looked at lines on a flat page and saw them in positions in depth. To further understand this natural tendency, let us consider the three main objectives of this section: (1) to establish that most of us have an instinctive or intuitive tendency to organize the placing of objects or marks in empty space, to create a seemingly "right" and organic grouping within the space available; (2) to show that we tend to see relationships between marks or objects on a piece of paper or in space, even though such marks or objects have no direct connection to each other; (3) to make a two-dimensional drawing into a three-dimensional model by taking it off the paper and giving it a three-dimensional structure in space. Three related space experiments, each one of which depends initially on an intuitive feeling for spatial relationships; will serve as a proving ground.

The first experiment is short and is intended to illustrate the instinctive tendency to distribute focal points of major and minor interest in space. Although it is extremely difficult to free the mind of all association and ideas, instinct operates so strongly in our awareness of form and space that it is

73

possible to approach the experiment with an open mind and to allow our subconsciousness a freedom of expression. There is no doubt in my mind that knowing (by which I mean a realization in whole or in part of both the visible and the invisible) does not work only at the conscious level, but also through the mysterious channels of the subconscious mind. The artist more than anyone (except perhaps the mystic) realizes the importance of this kind of knowing.

Many people distrust the intuitive approach of some artists; others distrust an intellectual attitude. But there is really no need for suspicion on either side. Both are valid ways of knowing. Our knowledge of life is built up through both our intuition and our intellect. We should realize that they make it possible for us to make different statements about the same thing. We are always affected by the dimensions of space in which we live and in Space I we attempted to give a logical explanation of space perception. Now, let us turn to our intuitive faculties.

THE EXPERIMENTS

Experiment 1

This work has to be carried out on a sheet of white paper, not less than 20″ x 15″ in dimension, pinned to a drawing board and then erected on a semi-vertical easel at about shoulder height. You will need a regular sable water-color brush of medium size, the handle of which should be lengthened by tying it to a piece of dowel stick about 12 inches long. The lengthening of the brush handle by this means insures a lack of deliberation in handling the brush and maintains a distance between you and the paper which helps to preserve the detachment necessary for inducing an intuitive response. Now, standing at least three feet from the easel and holding the brush right at the end of the dowel stick, dip the brush into a saucer of black ink and proceed to dab the paper with the brush point. It must be stressed that there should be no attempt to *draw* with the brush: the movement should be just a touch with the point before moving back. It should be done

FIG. 6-1

An example of intuitive mark making and space filling. Focal points are made by concentrations of dabs, and depth is created by the frontal projection of dominant marks over the recession of minor ones.

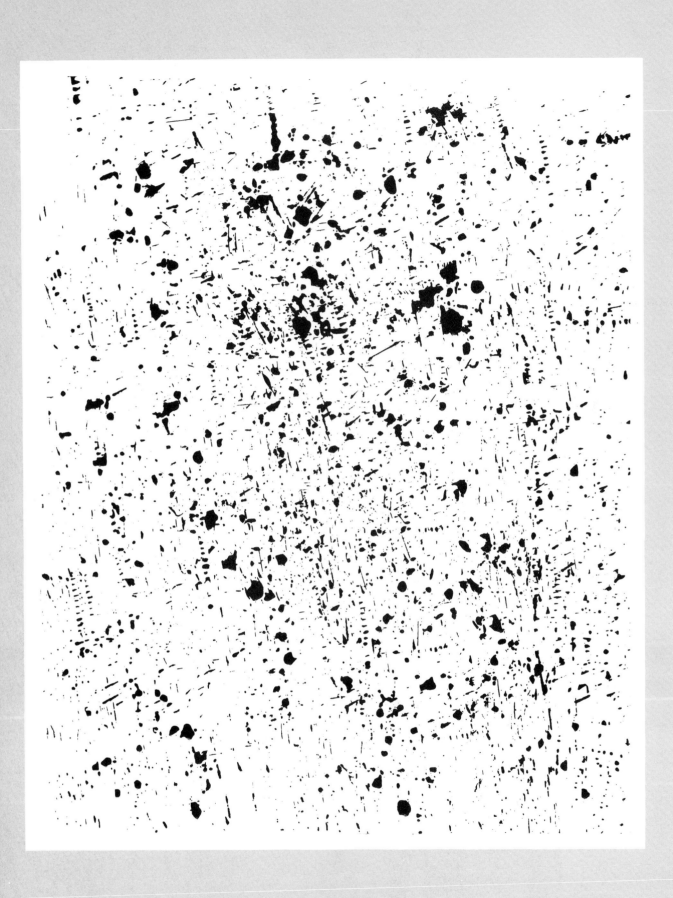

with complete relaxation, both physical and mental, the mind as complete a blank as you can make it, and the whole body loose as you move rhythmically backwards and forwards making the dabs. When there is an automatic reaction against continuing to dab, then stop. Don't think about when to stop; just stop on some such automatic impulse. Figure 6-1 is such a sheet of dab marks.

The whole thing will occupy only about three or four minutes, so when you are finished, put another piece of paper up and do another; and possibly another one after that, in order to make comparisons between the three pieces of paper which have been so marked. The first thing you will notice is that some of the dabs were made with a stronger impact than others and have produced dominant and minor marks. The differences suggest a change in strength of mechanical movements involved in making the marks, some variation in depth perception [1] as the backwards and forwards movement was repeated, and an emotional urge (present in all activity) that varied between positive and neutral degrees of stimulus as the paper space became more crowded with each new brush mark.

The second thing to be noticed if you allow your eye to wander freely over the papers is that in one or other of them your eye will probably come to rest at one particular region where there is a confluence of dabs, a concentration of dabs around one or two strong dominant marks. This represents the major focal point. (Where is the focal point in Fig. 6-2?) There may be other minor areas of concentration, or there may be no such point of concentration at all. If the marks are distributed uniformly over the total area, then the space relationships are equidistant and similar, and the eye rests nowhere. Such a regular, and therefore dull, arrangement of marks indicates a minimum intuitive ability to organize space interestingly; it also suggests that you were activated by a relatively low emotional charge.

The third and final lesson to be taken from this experiment provides a direct connection with Space I. It is that the strong black dabs project forward over the weaker gray dabs, thus making areas of depth where the eye penetrates. Now this might be accidental or still part of the whole intuitive process.

---

[1] See Space I (Chapter 3).

The dabs would be blacker and more powerful when the brush was newly charged with ink. The forcefulness could be related simply to the act of dipping into the ink when a purely mechanical need arose. Or one may dip in the ink to recharge the brush when he instinctively wishes for a stronger mark. But a mechanical explanation would not satisfy the question as to why certain marks should be made by flattening the brush onto the paper with some force, whereas others are the result of a delicate touch with the tip. There is a connection here with the drumbeat. A mechanical succession of beats with none louder than any other and with a regular period interval between each beat is meaningless. Only when the interval between beats is irregular and some beats are louder than others are we affected by the sound.

A number of dab experiments carried out with groups of people have indicated one thing: that in about 70 per cent of the cases, an intuitive marking of white space with black marks produced a more interesting visual result than a deliberate and conscious attempt to organize the space as a design.

Experiment 2

This work takes the previous intuitive mark-making experiment a stage further. It should produce two results: reinforcement of what has already been stated about our instinct for space organization, and an indication of how we make visual jumps of perception when faced with a scattered and random arrangement of marks in space—how we imaginatively project lines between the marks that appear significant. These lines seem to connect the marks in such a way that they form shapes on the page.

First, take a handful of variously sized pebbles and lay them out ready for easy selection. You will need another sheet of large white drawing paper, brush, and black ink. Once again attempt to relax completely; and selecting random pebbles from your collection, place them quite unself-consciously anywhere on the white paper. There is no conscious aim behind this, no particular end in view—just an instinctive putting down of the stones in the area at your disposal. As with the first experiment, don't think about when to stop; just stop when it seems right to stop. With a pencil now, draw a line around each pebble on the paper and remove the pebbles. Finally, take the brush and fill in the rings with ink.

What you now have is a collection of much larger marks, more positively shaped than the dab markings of the first experiment. Figure 6-3 is a typical example of such an instinctive pebble-placing arrangement.

This illustration reveals how well-balanced is the organization of large pebbles with smaller ones and how natural and "right" the groupings seem to be. As you continue to look, you will find that your eye tends to start at the bottom right-hand corner of the paper and move up through each pebble mark, creating an imaginary line as it does so. Your comprehension of this sheet is first a collection of black marks agreeably dispersed, but then a line is suggested moving through the marks and pulling them, rather like the beads on a string, into a linear organization. This effect is similar to the fascination of joining dots with lines that one experienced at a younger age with children's puzzles. The eye is always ready to be led onwards, particularly when new and interesting changes of direction are suggested by the next jump. A distribution of marks thus leads the eye and the imagination a merry dance—perhaps from a starting point to a finishing point, or perhaps to no definite end at all but just in a perpetual movement. The fact remains, however, that our eye is led over surfaces through points of emphasis and points of directional change. This is true as well for the surface of a canvas or the wall of a building (see Fig. 6-4). The eye also sees the marks in depth by assessing their relative degrees of darkness and size. Obviously, then, the placing of accents (dominant marks) by the artist or designer, the child drawing, or the housewife placing furniture over a floor area greatly affects our perception of the total space involved (Fig. 6-1).[2] Dominant marks also guide our perception of the linear relationships between units that occupy the space (Fig. 6-3).

For evidence that an instinctive attitude in placing the marks in space produces results aesthetically[3] superior to those placed through a conscious attitude, see Fig. 6-5.

FIG. 6-2

COMPOSITION NO. 10

FIG. 6-3

Sheet recording the non-deliberate placing of pebbles.

FIG. 6-4

FAÇADE, PALAZZO FARNESE, ROME (1530-1548) Sangallo and Michelangelo, architects. *Horizontal divisions created over a wall surface. One's eye jumps along the top of the window pediments, bridging the gaps between and thus creating horizontal lines which make proportionate divisions of the total wall surface. (Photograph by Alinari)*

FIG. 6-5

Sheet recording the deliberate, "design-conscious" placing of pebbles and the commonplace result.

---

[2] Chapter 12, "Form and Space," points out that we are not aware of space until it is identified by form acting as a marker buoy.

[3] See Form III (Chapter 5) for an understanding of the word "aesthetic."

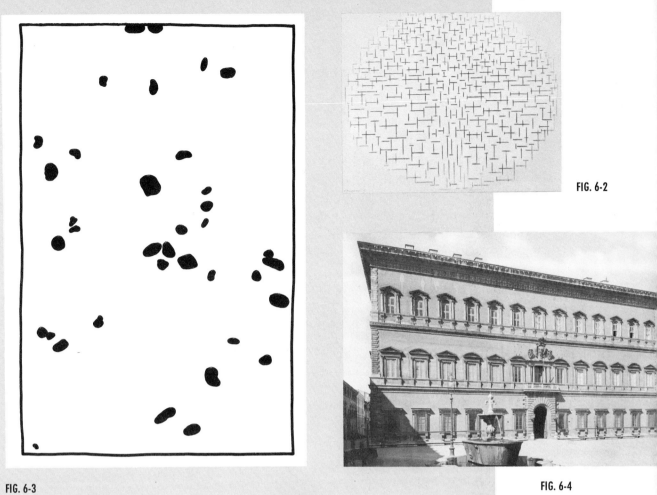

FIG. 6-2

FIG. 6-3

FIG. 6-4

FIG. 6-5

This illustration shows what often happens when the student is told to arrange the pebbles in as pleasing and rhythmical a way as he can, utilizing the space at his disposal to the best possible advantage. This illustration shows an obviously contrived attempt to be decorative and to suggest movement. It is highly derivative from plant form, and there is no mystery about the form the pebble marks suggest as the eye connects them into a line of drawing. In contrast, the intuitive organization of Fig. 6-3 allows the eye to wander in and out of possible combinations of linear connection, always changing and at differing depth levels of three-dimensional suggestion. These two illustrations provide a good example of how the instinctive judgment is often better than the calculated decision.

Experiment 3

To round out this section dealing with the intuitive appreciation of three-dimensional space, we shall go back to the pebble drawing of the last experiment. The problem is to translate this drawing into three-dimensional wire sculpture. It has already been pointed out that a line of drawing exists imaginatively as the eye moves from blob to blob; so draw in this line now in pencil and see what movement and form it suggests. Yet because this is a drawing on paper, this line moves in only two dimensions. (Whatever suggestions of depth or three-dimensional movement are made come through the factors discussed in Space I, Chapter 3.) But if you take a length of heavy-gauge pliable wire and attempt to reproduce in space the imaginative line passing through the pebble marks, you are actively engaged in translating this line into a true, three-dimensional environment.

This, then, is the experiment: Examine the marks of your pebbles and produce a wire sculpture in which the movement and shaping of the wire are directly inspired by the linear form which the pebble drawing suggests. Look again at Fig. 6-3, where the drawing gives the suggested line of wire sculpture only in the form of a flat silhouette. The special difficulty of this project, therefore, requires the translation of this line actually into another dimension without losing the character of the original pebble arrangement. To do this effectively demands an imaginative handling of the wire. But

FIG. 6-6

Wire models made from the pebble-placing record sheets. (Upper model by courtesy of the instructor, Walter Wegner)

FIG. 6-7

Shell with markings from Samoa. Observe the differing size and weight of the marks, the irregular clustering of marks, and the emergence of focal points. These natural markings give considerable visual interest to the surface of the shell.

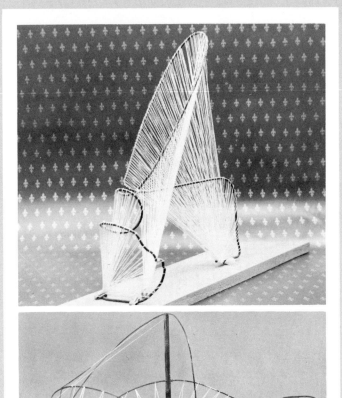

FIG. 6-6

FIG. 6-7

since all the work in this chapter has been produced so far by an immediate and therefore part-intuitive response to a situation, do not at this stage become too deliberate with the wire. Start it moving, attempt to interpret the rhythm of the pebble drawing, and be as relaxed and casual when you bend the wire into shape as you were when idly placing the pebbles on the paper. When you have finished, make some kind of heavy base to support the sculpture and then take a good look at it.

The flat line on the paper has become a line describing volume in the air. It is quite a transition from a few black marks made without thinking. But it should serve to indicate what common factors are present in all visual problems. One last thing remains to be done to complete the wire model. Pick out the planes or curved surfaces that might exist between the lines of the wire as they move in and out through space. Take some black or white cotton and by stringing up a cotton "wall" between the wires, delineate such surfaces in one or more parts of the sculpture. The finished result will resemble the models in Fig. 6-6, both of which originated from pebbles placed freely on a piece of paper. Also look at Pevsner's "Developable Column," Fig. 6-8.

This ability to translate images from one medium to another, from one dimension to another, both in imagination and in practice, is a rewarding accomplishment. It instills a knowledge of how the process of point-to-line perception works, of how important a part is played in this perception by the element of space, and of how our intuitive powers can produce space-form relationships that are aesthetically significant.

FIG. 6-8

DEVELOPABLE COLUMN (1942)
Antoine Pevsner
Brass and oxidized bronze, 20¾ inches high. Compare this sculpture with the wire forms illustrated in Fig. 6-6. Pevsner's form is doing the same thing, only in a more highly sophisticated and controlled manner. It heightens our awareness of three-dimensional regions of space and movement in these regions by its own movement out from the center and its arcing, curved surfaces. (Collection, The Museum of Modern Art, New York)

7 the
conscious
organization of space

The intuitive is constantly at war with the rational in the visual arts. In the previous section, the intuitive side of this struggle was discussed. Now we shall take up a "drawing" that results from logical and calculated decisions. It is true that when working freely and experimentally with no specific end in mind, one's hand is guided by intuition; but as soon as an objective problem is posed, a strong calculating attitude often takes over, and the intuition is frequently swamped. This explains why Fig. 6-5 is so commonplace. It was the response to a definite proposition put by the instructor, to which the student reacted calculatingly, and unless one has the mental powers of a Raphael, calculation can fail.

Does this mean that only the intuitive response produces art? No, it does not. But it does mean that a completely logical approach to art tends to inhibit feeling or attitude and spontaneity, which are vital to the creative process. An intellectual perfectionism devoid of these things is pretty sterile. We should strive, then, to keep our instincts alive, even when the objective is clearly stated and demands a conscious and logical application by the artist.

Here lies the reason for this experiment. It is to present a problem that will require you to think in terms of a deliberate use of space, and yet rely on the lessons of intuitive awareness

FIG. 7-1

DANCE 1
Ernest Mundt
A line in the air defining certain regions of space.
(Ernest Mundt. Associated Press News Photograph)

85

which were demonstarted in Space II (Chapter 6). The answer to the question "does only the intuitive response produce good art?" is thus that it must always be present in some degree. As you begin to explore space in this experiment, you will be required to make mental decisions, yet at the same time preserve an attitude of feeling for the spatial values your aerial construction will be creating. The necessity for the preservation of the intuitive in art is stated by Sir Herbert Read in his essay, "The Realist Heresy."

The virtue of a symbol lies, and always did lie, in a relative degree of unintelligibility. A symbol loses its grip once its significance has been rationalized and it has become generally understood. But so long as it remains unintelligible, it can if it is a good symbol, exercise astonishing powers.

When you draw on a flat surface, your arm is restricted to making only lateral and vertical movements, and as we have seen in previous work (Space I), the third dimension of depth is introduced by the eye's innate ability to search it out—to make depth distinctions between marks and areas bounded by marks, and so on. But now we must come to grips physically with the third dimension and translate from line which bounds *area* into line which contains *volume*. See Figs. 7-1 and 7-2 for the transition from line-bounded space to volume, per se.

One way of handling space is to take a line into the air and "draw" with it. This is how the wire models of the previous section were produced. Yet wire, easily bent to produce a rhythmical cutting through space, did not demand of you any calculated decision concerning changes of direction; neither did you physically have to construct the line piece by piece when a change in direction was made. Since a strip of wood used as a line of drawing in the air does demand this greater degree of control, we will employ it in this experiment, which is to make a construction from one continuously moving line. Instead of drawing a line two-dimensionally on a flat surface, we are now going to take a line of wood strip into the air and "draw" with it three-dimensionally in space. However, before taking this line off the ground, one important stipulation has to be made: the line must move only at

FIG. 7-2

DANCE 2
Ernest Mundt
*When the linear form of Fig. 7-1 revolves, the space regions become defined volumes, and the previously linear object becomes an object of volume or suggested mass. The artist's eye regarding "Dance 1" may well see the movement form of "Dance 2" without the help of motorization.
(Ernest Mundt)*

right angles to itself; every time it changes direction, the angle must be 90 degrees. There are two principal reasons for this stipulation. First, it simplifies the actual making of the construction, since the wood strip, being square in section, glues together easily at a right-angle joint. Second, it will make you concentrate on proportionate lengths and three-dimensional direction. This experiment will help you see that a line moving in space creates volumes or compartments of space and that these volumes also have proportional relationships to each other and to the total construction. In addition, you should get a peculiar fascination in "drawing in depth" in the three-dimensional freedom of the air (see Fig. 7-3).

THE EXPERIMENT

The most suitable wood strip to use for this work is a balsa strip of the sort normally used in making model aircraft. About four to five feet in length is required and this should be ⅜₆″ or ¼″ in section. Any of the appropriate cement fixatives will be satisfactory.

Before the line of strip wood can ascend into the air and start its wanderings, there should first be a base to support the construction, although the very ingenious construction illustrated in Fig. 7-4 balances perfectly on the single point of the first vertical length of strip. In making the base, leave it open (unconnected to its other members) at the point from which the vertical line takes off into the air. This will help the viewer establish the starting point. On leaving the base at the appropriate point, the strip should now ascend vertically into the air at right angles to the base. After this stage, you are very much on your own. It is your job now to move the strip constantly in changing directions, once it is safely airborne. Obviously, the strip will require constant support while the cement of the angle joints is hardening. But while this is happening at one part of the construction, the next few moves of the line may be seen in advance and can be prefabricated, ready to attach to the part that is drying. With every length of strip attached to the growing object, you will

FIG. 7-3

THE PALACE AT 4 A.M.
Alberto Giacometti
Construction in wood, glass, wire, and string. An objective organization of architectural space made by drawing with wood strip in the air. The symbolic forms are cunningly placed in their respective compartments for both meaningful and visual considerations. (Collection, The Museum of Modern Art, New York)

be forced ino making decisions which involve both physical and visual balance, the compartmentalization of space, and the working out of directional and angular forces. (Forces are the subjects of Form V and Space IV. In this experiment these forces may briefly be described as the tensions created in the structure by a sudden change of direction. See Fig. 7-5.) That you can now actually *see* these aspects of drawing, in handling them to put up the construction, should not blind you to the fact that the same decisions and elements exist in drawing on a flat surface.

At some point you should both think and feel that any further change of direction or further prolongation of the strip would merely confuse rather than clarify the form of the construction. Stop at this point. When completing the construction, make sure the strip line emerges into the open, so it can be seen clearly in relation to the starting point on the ground.

Conclusions

What can we learn from this experiment? Figure 7-4 provides an excellent example of a conscious working out of the problem where a feeling for space volumes and linear progression has worked hand in hand with reason. The starting point of the line can clearly be seen, and the continuation of the line through its many right-angled phases can be followed out to both finishing points. The construction has a nice asymmetrical balance, both in terms of line and volume. At the same time, as we pointed out earlier, it is also perfectly balanced physically. The thrust of line against line creates tensions in the structure of which the viewer is aware; he is also aware of the resolution of these tensions through the equilibrium achieved by the construction. Space is obviously a crucial element here. The space compartments contained within this strip drawing are organically part of the design, and they grow out of the construction; the outside space becomes a part of the drawing by entering into the construction. This interchangeability of space *contained* with space *surrounding* is an important factor, not only in the act of perceiving an object, but also in our aesthetic response to an object.

FIG. 7-4

Student wood strip construction.

Figure 7-6 is rather different. Here there is no immediately obvious following through of the strip from its beginning to its end. Neither is there the same concern with volume or the cubic disposition of air. The student, in this case, became so interested in the visual effect created by lone, soaring lengths of line and monumental proportions, by the contrast of large rectangles with smaller ones, and by the interplay of the square and thin rectangular areas, that he took the experiment beyond the immediate class problem and produced a work of creative architectural suggestion. The fact that he ignored the rules and developed more than just one line is not really important. True, he has not created the three-dimensional drawing of Fig. 7-4, but he has done automatically what I hope many people will do *after* working through these experiments; that is, go ahead on their own and produce work which is very personal, yet based on an awareness of the structural and spatial elements involved.

FIG. 7-5

MODEL OF YORK MINSTER CHAPTER HOUSE ROOF
On one side, the common rafters are omitted for clarity. This is a complex example of a linear construction defining space. Although the skeleton of this late thirteenth century timber roof was purely functional, the model may be enjoyed aesthetically. (Yorkshire Archaeological Society)

FIG. 7-6

Student wood strip construction.

FIG. 7-5

FIG. 7-6

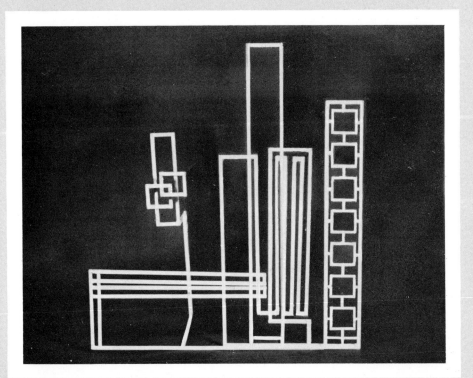

8

form
in the plant:
the structural unit

FIG. 8-1

A sea of thistle seeds more than one foot deep. The form of the single seed, made up of delicate spiky units, can be seen in the top left-hand corner, as the seeds fall to the ground. The complexity of the ground mass, comprising several thousand identical seed-head units, cannot be described.

We now come to a piece of work which could fit quite happily into either Part One or Part Two of this book. It is concerned with form and structure, yet also with vision and imagination. But since the basic aims underlying the experiment concern form, we rightfully should take it up here. Already we have examined the two structural families of form and the aesthetic implications of our response to form. Now we come to the stage of analyzing a particular kind of form, where search and discovery should be second nature to the inquiring eye confronted by a structure of some complexity.

It is all too often obvious, however, that not every person possesses an inquiring eye. In too many of us, curiosity, the capacity for wonder, and any sense of a personal response to the complex forms of other life in the world (Fig. 8-1), have given way to the perceptive lethargy of an automatic and mechanized civilization. Even the machines, things often of rare beauty and structure, are taken for granted by a great many people, for whom the analytical and inquiring faculty of eye fused with the imagination has become stunted.

The practice of drawing (and all the design activities that spring from drawing), makes first this demand of the eye: that it should search out objects of interest, and, concentrating, fix them in the mind that they may be more completely under-

95

stood; thus will the imagination become active and the emotions quickened. Some of the most complex forms readily available to us, on which we can sharpen the failing powers of an inquiring eye, lie all around us in nature. Everyday things such as the dandelion seed-head, the thistle seed-head, the various types of fir cones, and the wide range of weed flowers turned to seed—these are the plant specimens to choose in order to study how the form is made up. Nature is a most efficient designer, in whose complex world of form the superfluous and the wasteful have little place. Nature is very much concerned with the *unit* of structure—with the basic part which, constantly repeated, makes up the total form. It is with this unit of structure, with the small elemental part cunningly used in a built-up system to create the whole, that this section on form is concerned (see Figs. 8-2, 8-3). The student is required to look hard at the seed form he has chosen, to select the smallest basic unit from which the complete object is built and then to use this unit in a new *structural system* to produce a new seed form. For the artist, this looking for a unit of structure becomes a habit, whether he is regarding a dandelion seed, a contemporary architectural structure (Fig. 8-4), or the honeycomb of the bee. His eye searches to discover the structural unit.

It is in the making of the final drawing demanded by this section, the drawing of the new seed form, that one very important factor about the multi-unit characteristic of form becomes apparent. For the mutation or new seed to be convincing, it must appear to be the result of organic-structural growth, rather than an apparent attempt to create an artificial novelty. It is, of course, necessary for the imagination to project from what is to what might be, but equally important is a realization of what is meant by an "organic structure," [1] by the growing, living, purposive organization of parts of a form.

THE EXPERIMENTS

Seed-head formations of plants probably provide the most complex natural objects for study, and it is possible you will

---

[1] A full explanation of organic structure is provided in the Conclusion to this section.

FIG. 8-2

The unripe pine cone showing the closed units that make up its form.

FIG. 8-3

The clematis seed structure, showing the unit organization.

FIG. 8-4

CENTRAL WASHINGTON STATE COLLEGE LIBRARY
Bassetti and Morse, Seattle, architects
*Sun screen of clay tiles. Each screen is a complex honeycomb made from a small, standard unit of structure. The smaller picture shows the honeycomb units in process of construction, set up without mortar. In the background, the screens wait to receive them.
(Bassetti and Morse, Seattle. Photograph by Hugh N. Stratford)*

FIG. 8-2

FIG. 8-3

FIG. 8-4

find some so complex that a magnifying glass will help in finding the unit of structure. Depending on the season, some flower formations, as well as all kinds of pond weeds and seaweeds composed of repeated units, can be found. When the chosen plant is before you, examine it closely to determine the smallest unit of structure to which it can be reduced and then extract this part and study it individually. Now on a clean sheet of drawing paper, make lots of little drawings of this unit part, with pen or pencil or wood in ink (Fig. 8-5). Make drawings from many angles until you know this part pretty thoroughly, for this is the structural unit of the plant. Drawing an object is one of the best ways to know an object. By the time you have sorted out proportions and parts from many different viewing positions, in order to describe them by drawing, you will know a great deal more than you did when you were just observing the objects.

At this stage, return to the principal object itself and examine it again. Notice particularly how the small unit attaches to the head or stem or core of the object, or even to itself. Notice the regularity of the pattern of attachment, the point of attachment, the angle of attachment, and so on. When you are fairly confident that you understand how the complete object works, both structurally and organically, make a drawing of the complete seed-head or plant. This drawing will be the more convincing because of your analytical observation. Such a drawing need not be fine enough to illustrate a nature book, but just an honest and direct result of observation and an awareness of how the thing is made. The illustrations indicate the variety of approaches students will make to this procedure of analysis through drawing. If you look at Figs. 8-6 to 8-10 you will see the stages through which such analytical probing moves. Figure 8-6 shows the bald core of the salsify seed head; in 8-7, the student is assembling the parts onto the core, and in 8-8 the unit-complex structure is complete. Then under further observation, this large complex is broken down into a dispersal of points in Fig. 8-9, eventually to become a disintegrating series of point forces in Fig. 8-10. Yet in this last drawing, notice how even the furthermost points are still dynamically retained by the center nucleus; they are still part

FIG. 8-5

Drawing notes made at random as a student begins to dissect several natural objects.

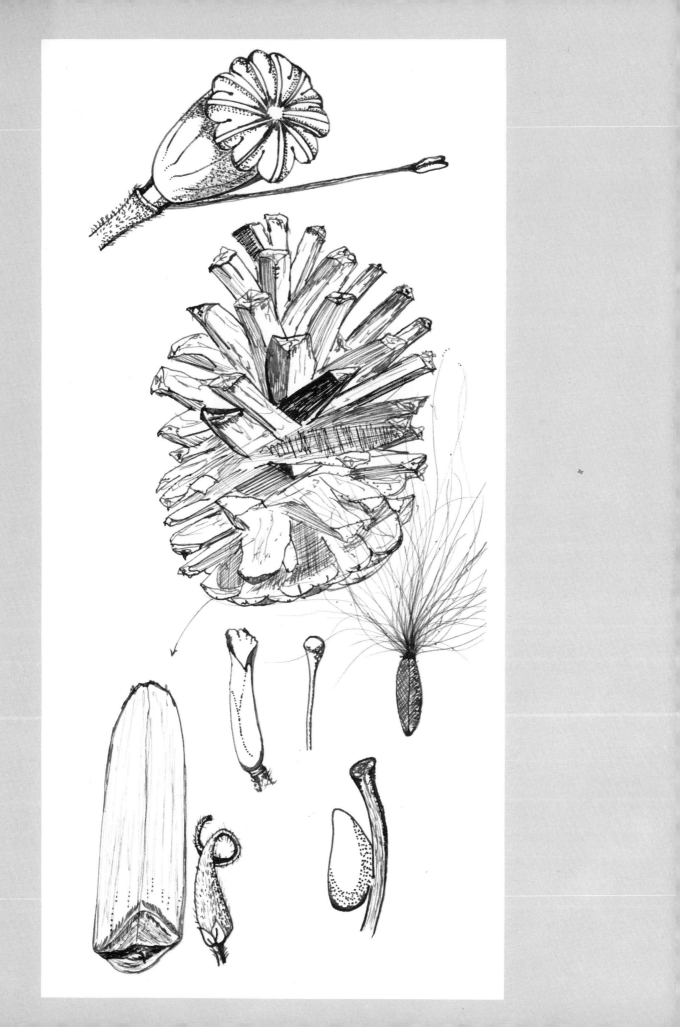

of the system, and one senses that no further disintegration will occur. This final drawing has become an abstract dispersal of points, yet it must be understood that such an accurate simplification can be achieved only when the artist knows the "how" of the seed, after analytical surgery through drawing. You now have made drawings of the unit of structure and of the major object itself. To produce them, you had, in fact, to be a surgeon—to take to pieces and then build up again. Now with this knowledge of the *parts* and of the *whole,* you are asked to use your imaginative ability to design a new plant form. You must take the small unit of structure and by inventing a *new grouping system* of the parts, a *new organization of structural pattern* having its own principles of attachment and directional movement, produce a new total object. This new object will be a variant from the original, the kind of object not yet seen in nature, but which could be produced by some interference with the biological laws governing heredity and growth—in other words, a mutation or new development (see Figs. 8-11 to 8-16).

Conclusions

Many of the obvious conclusions to be drawn from this work have already been stated in advance, both in the introduction to this section and in the description of the project itself. But always when a task of this kind is completed, one or two factors loom up large and clear as the most important aspects of it to remember. In this case a clue is provided by the three words used earlier in the final paragraph of the Introduction, the phrase "organic structural growth." The implication of the word "organic" is one of a living condition or a systematic, nonaccidental organization of parts. The dandelion and the fir cone are living objects, and their parts consequently are structured in an organic way. Our perception of these objects as "living" and "growing" is assisted by this organic structural organization. Take an object like a steel desk, which has not arrived at its final shape through the living, growing process of the repetition of a structural unit or cell, and we perceive it as an inanimate object, artificially made.

By far the greatest problem you had in creating your

FIG. 8-6

The bald core of the salsify seed-head.

FIG. 8-7

Assembling the structural units onto the bald core.

FIG. 8-8

The complex unit structure of the salsify seed-head, complete.

FIG. 8-9

The abstract dispersal of points of the seed-head.

FIG. 8-10

The seed-head reduced to a disintegrated series of point forces.

FIG. 8-7

FIG. 8-8

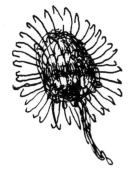

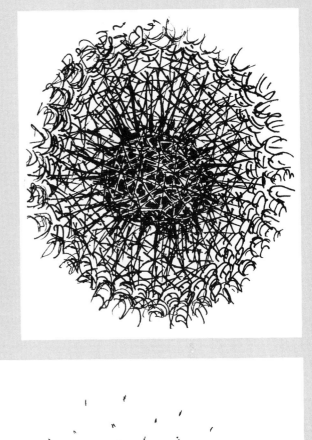

FIG. 8-6

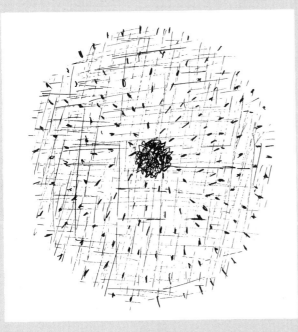

FIG. 8-9

FIG. 8-10

mutation lay in the organization of the new structural pattern, using the old structural unit, because—at the end of it all— your new plant form would either appear artificial and incapable of life or it would be as believable an organic structure as the original object.

The deduction to be made from this is that your early analysis of the plant should contain an appreciation of its organic element, for such an appreciation is part of one's aesthetic response to this kind of object. Such an appreciation would be sensitive to the rhythmic structural relationship of part to part and of all the parts to the complete form. Such a relationship of parts does not necessarily imply a mathematical or geometric regularity of structural organization although this is how the Greeks understood it (see Fig. 8-17, Greek vase about 650 B.C.). The structure can be completely irregular and curvilinear to a degree or angular to a degree, yet still possess an organic structural growth.

If you were concerned with designing a chair to be made completely from wood, you probably would try, consciously or otherwise, to make the legs belong structurally to the seat, to make the back grow from the seat—and to give both back and legs some relationship, some kinship which is imparted to them through an organic rhythm or sense of living structure.

A chair design which is just "thrown together," the parts at sixes and sevens with each other, will appear ludicrous by comparison and quite unconvincing. The dissection of the original plant form to its basic unit of structure helped to reveal its organic growth pattern. This was the purpose of suggesting such an analysis.

There are, of course, relationships between the parts of an object or the parts of a design which are not organic in the living, growing sense, but depend upon other associational elements such as a common scale, a suggested equal weight, a common color, or something of this kind. In painting, for example, such relationships may be more important than any sense of organic structure. But I think it is true to say that as soon as one becomes concerned with the object existing in space as a three-dimensional form, then the organic sense of its parts is one of the fundamental appraisals we give it—one might almost say "that we demand of it."

FIG. 8-11

The natural pine cone in its ripe, open state.

FIG. 8-12

The extracted unit of structure.

FIG. 8-13

The cone mutation. The tight clustering of the units around a central nucleus or core is in direct contrast to the horizontal stratification of the ripe and open cone. By comparison, one feels the tightness of the units in the mutation. It would not be easy to pry one away, as in the natural object.

FIG. 8-14

The complex of nuclei and trailing threads of the wild cottonseed formations.

FIG. 8-15

The extracted unit of nucleus and threads.

FIG. 8-16

The mutation or new plant form. This has been accomplished by grouping several nuclei together into a centrally organized motif, thus producing this comparatively regular, radial structure.

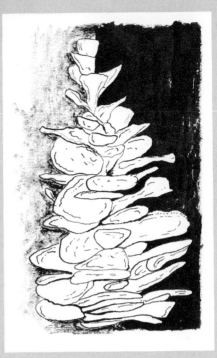

FIG. 8-11

FIG. 8-12

FIG. 8-13

FIG. 8-14

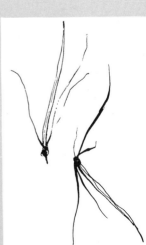

FIG. 8-15

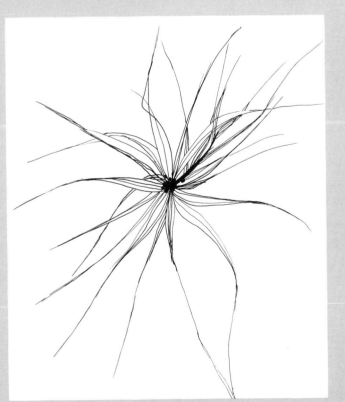

FIG. 8-16

The study, through drawing, of the unit-structure type of natural object, focuses our attention on its smallest unit, providing we are prepared to probe and analyze it sufficiently. When we know about the small unit, we know about the whole. It is important that we are able to understand and recognize that kind of form which is made up of a multiplicity of small repeating parts and see the significance of this kind of structure for the architect, the industrial designer, and anyone concerned with building a structure in space.

FIG. 8-17

GREEK AMPHORA
(675-650 B.C.)
The complete symmetry and logical regularity of this ceramic form makes a calculated appeal to the intellect. This is how the Greeks understood structure and form, through a system of harmonious linear and area relationships—a refined and perfect structural geometry.
(The Metropolitan Museum of Art, New York)

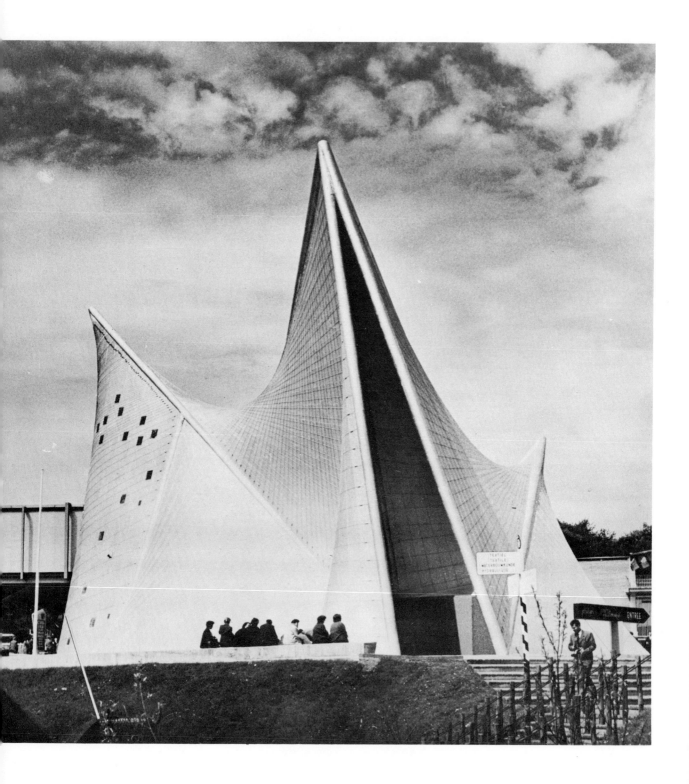

9

planes
and curved surfaces:
forces and surface tension

PHILLIPS PAVILION, BRUSSELS
INTERNATIONAL EXHIBITION
(1958)
Le Corbusier, architect
*Like a huge piece of tent
cloth, the folds of this structure are organized around the
points of force, the gigantic
"tent poles" from which the
walls are suspended.*
(The Architectural Review,
London)

Before proceeding through this chapter we should briefly re-capitulate the aspects of form previously touched upon. We started by defining two structural families of form, then dis-covered something about a person's reactions to form in terms of what was called an "aesthetic response." After this, plant life came in for examination, so that we might see how the repeti-tion of a unit makes up a complete form of organic significance. Now we shall move into the wide-spreading regions of space, into landscape and architecture, where our attention is not focused on the single, free-standing object, but explores ex-pansive areas of surface. Nevertheless, the principles discussed, which are of forces and pressures affecting the surface organ-ization of form, apply equally to the smaller, individual object, but they can best be studied in landscape, in the spreading surface of the earth in its movements from mountain to valley. Similarly, when standing within the gracious space-sculpture of much contemporary architecture, we are led visually through organizations of undulating wall movement and sweeps of ceiling, with surface movement on a grand scale taking us through large areas of space. The surface aspect of form is not perceived at any one single point of focus, but the eye skates over varying directional surfaces, to be bounded in landscape only by a horizon. And in architecture which some-

107

times appears to have no bounds at all, wall and ceiling surfaces move out and then return to their source in an apparently self-perpetuating system (see Fig. 11-3).

So now we move from the object in isolation to the motion of the continuous surface of the sea, of the land, and of architecture—we move, in fact, to the surface of form.

This aspect of form is concerned with planes and curved surfaces, with the external aspects of form, with the constant movement of surface as the shape is revealed. Altogether in this book there are six chapters on form dealing with fundamental issues of which every student of art should be aware. In addition, of course, there are other important aspects of form not dealt with here, and a book about them all would be a very thick volume.

If you put your mind to imagining "landscape" for a moment, you will realize that the surface movement just described can be of two kinds. It can be gentle and curvaceous or sharp and angular—gentle *folds* or crevicelike *angles*—the rolling countryside or the precipitous mountain. And in architecture, too, these same kinds of surface movement occur. It is therefore possible to make two general statements about surface movement: that it is (1) a series of multi-directional planes producing through their juxtaposition an *angular* surface quality where plane meets plane; and (2) an undulation of curved surfaces producing a *folded* surface quality. It is, of course, possible to find both types of surface side-by-side in the same form, the sharp angle and its plane giving way to the fold with its curve. Architects, particularly, make use of this sudden transition of surface movement.

The work which this section is now going to propose makes a definite statement. It suggests that the folds and angles of a crumpled piece of paper have a direct relationship to the planes and curves of the earth in landscape and to the planes and curves of surfaces in architecture. The fact that the scale of a crumpled piece of paper is so much smaller than that of a mountainside or the dome of a cathedral is no objection to this proposition. Scale is not relevant because the degree of commonality in other ways is so pronounced—the common characteristics of surface plane and surface curvature shared by forms, irrespective of their relative sizes. For example, if a photograph of the crumpled paper were to have a part of it

FIG. 9-1

Grooves formed in the soft sand by the action of the incoming tide. An interesting illustration of surface formation resulting from the operation of forces.

greatly magnified, it would appear perfectly credible as an aerial view of a mountain range. The planes, angles, and valleys of the paper are only a smaller version of the surface characteristics of mountain terrain. This is rather an important point: the realization that all surface formations are made up of planes in juxtaposition or curved surfaces in series, either separately or together, and that it is only in scale that differences occur. No other formations of surface exist. So once again for the artist, the minutiae of form are as important as the monumental, and a study of the surface of the one yields information about the surface organization of the other. Hence, the crumpled piece of paper can become Mount Everest or the folds in the lay of the land. *The surface of the form*—this is our concern in the drawing experiment of this section. But before moving on to a description of the work, another important aspect of surface organization must be described. The surface of form is merely an indication of operating forces (see Fig. 9-1).

If one allows one's eye merely to play over the planes and curves, without at the same time sensing the forces that have worked within the form or pressed upon it, then he loses the complete significance of plane and curve as the surface manifestation of force or tension to which the mass is subject (see Fig. 9-2).

This then is the implication of the words "structural organization" as applied to surface. The word "organization" is used to imply that the surface of form takes the shape it does because of the forces exerted on it, either from within or without. For example, if one attempts to straighten out a piece of curved bark, the surface detail of the bark will change its formation. Or think of it another way: if one drapes a piece of material over the top of a vertical pole, the resulting folds are organized by virtue of the vertical point-thrust beneath; but if one drapes the same material over the seat of a chair, then there will result quite a different organization of surface fold because the resistant pressure force beneath is a different kind of pressure. As another example, take a flat sheet of aluminum which, lying on the table, constitutes a plane surface and which, held vertically, is still a plane surface. But if mechanical force is exerted to pull the two sides round together, then the aluminum sheet is no longer a plane surface, but a curved surface.

FIG. 9-2

WOMAN COMBING HER HAIR
Alexander Archipenko
A sculpture of planes and angles, curved surfaces, depressions and protrusions. As the surface of the crumpled paper represents the pressure exerted, so does the surface organization of this sculpture represent the artist's forceful shaping of his medium into the pressure forms of the human figure. The point thrust and pressure thrust which are described in Space IV (Chapter 11) play an important part in Archipenko's dynamic abstraction of the figure.
(Collection, The Museum of Modern Art, New York)

110

The stronger the force applied, *the more apparent is the tension over the surface of the curve.*[1] Surface tension is thus greater over any curved surface than over any plane surface, and the more pronounced the curve, the more surface tension is induced. From this it will be seen that when eventually a curve becomes an angle (as it does with the aluminum sheet if great force continues to be exerted at the sides), then the surface tension over the *angle* is very considerable. Hence, skin stretched tight over projecting bones has considerable surface tension as it changes direction. This is why skeletal-form surfaces are more dramatic than gently curving bulbous-form surfaces. The surface tension is both seen and felt by the viewer (see Fig. 9-3).

In landscape, the earth has been worked on by forces—internal and external—and the surface form we see is the present *status quo* achieved by these forces. The architect achieves equilibrium in a building through the interaction of forces, through the pressure force of roof against wall, wall against foundations, and so on. Sometimes the tension of his surfaces is indicative of the operation of these forces (see Fig. 9-4). When a mountain is drawn by a man who both sees and feels the surface to be a manifestation of the forces that shaped the earth, then he produces a dramatically revealing statement about "mountain." To see this, look at John Piper's "Slope of Tryfan" (Fig. 9-5). Yet when another man merely draws the surface appearance of the mountain without equating this with the forces that shaped it, then all we have is a piece of stage scenery.

THE EXPERIMENT

First, select two pieces of paper, each one about 2′ square, one a crisp, strong paper and the other a soft, absorbent paper. Using both hands, deliberately crumple up each piece separately, not so strongly that you reduce it to a small and formless ball, but with just enough strength to produce a complex of planes, angles, and folds. With this accomplished, you now have some personal experience of force being responsible for surface organization. At the same time, you will notice a difference between the crumpled papers. The strong paper will have

---

[1] Surface tension is the result of forces in opposition, the molecular forces of the substance versus the mechanical forces exerted on it.

FIG. 9-3

WOMAN'S HEAD (1909)
Pablo Picasso
*Bronze, 16¼ inches high.
The cubist tendencies of this sculpture give a pronounced emphasis to the planes and curved surfaces of the head. Structure is dominant, and the sharply formed angles produce a surface tension which heightens the dramatic quality of the form.
(Collection, The Museum of Modern Art, New York. Purchase)*

FIG. 9-4

PHILLIPS PAVILION

FIG. 9-5

SLOPE OF TRYFAN (1950)
John Piper
*A mountain drawn by a man who sees the planes and curves of the form's surface as a manifestation of the forces that shaped the earth.
(John Piper)*

FIG. 9-3

FIG. 9-4

FIG. 9-5

formed sharply defined planes and clean angles; the soft paper will be altogether more "blurred," less angular, and with a suggestion of curved surfaces rather than planes. This difference is due to the varying resistance that the paper offers the pressure. After seeing this, we are now in a position to make a further generalization about the formation of surface planes and curves: *the stronger and more rigid the material, the sharper will be its angles and the more distinct its planes when forces operate to shape the form.* For the softer, less rigid materials, the converse is true. Hence, soft fabric under such conditions develops a surface that is curved and folded rather than planed and angular.

Two drawings of each crumpled paper form have now to be made. Choose your own drawing medium for this. The first drawing of each piece of paper is to be entirely a line drawing (Fig. 9-6). This will be an attempt to describe the surface formation of the angles and planes of the crisp, strong paper form, followed by the folds and curved surfaces of the soft paper form. The second drawing of each piece of paper is to dispense with line altogether. Half-close your eyes and see the form as an organization of surface areas (planes or curves) *but do not look for their edges.* Now, using shading or tone, build up the form, bit by bit, by "blocking in" with tone each plane area or curved area over the whole shape—rather like building up piece by piece with bricks (Fig. 9-7). Any lines or edges that are formed will occur automatically where the tone shading stops or changes intensity (Fig. 9-8). The dark or light quality of the tone should be taken directly from the objects. Where the planes or curves appear lighter or darker, adjust your tone shading to a similar intensity. If a pen is being used, then tone is best indicated by lines, heavy or light, closely concentrated or widely spread across the face of the plane or curve (Fig. 9-9). With these four drawings complete, some conclusions should now be made, conclusions which add more to our knowledge of the surface organization of form and which suggest the importance for the artist of an awareness of forces and tensions when he is faced by surface movement of plane and curve.

Conclusions

The carefully crumpled piece of paper is no simple form; and when one has the task of drawing it, deciding where to start is

FIG. 9-6

Line drawings with pen and pencil of a crumpled piece of hard paper. Both drawings are well-observed expressions of the form with its complicated surface of planes and curves produced by the crumpling force. Points 1 and 2 made in the Conclusion to Form V are borne out in these drawings.

FIG. 9-7

The crumpled paper is built up through areas of tone, with each plane acting rather like a chunk of masonry. Any linear quality is merely the result of changes in tonal intensity. This form is credible as a piece of paper, a large piece of rock, or an aerial view of a range of hills.

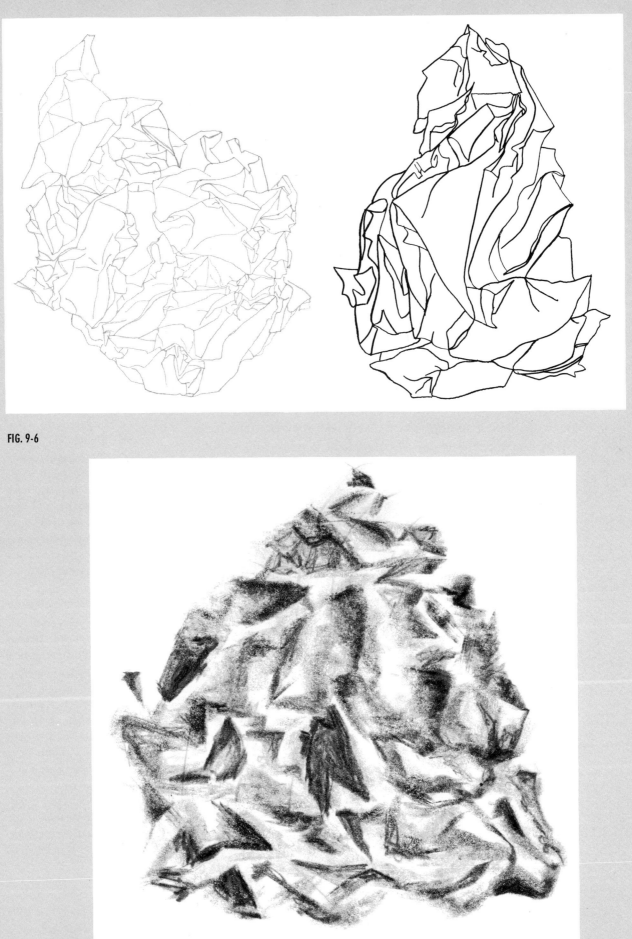

FIG. 9-6

FIG. 9-7

a difficult decision. As the eye searches the surface, moving from plane to plane and angle to angle, the mind is also working along with the eye, trying to relate the surface to forces in the form pushing out and forces from outside the form pushing in; for in crumpling the paper, a thumb might have pushed in, while a finger pushed out.

The statement has been made elsewhere in this book that drawing is a way to knowledge, that looking with intent increases our understanding of form, and the quality of our attitude to it. This applies perfectly to these pieces of crumpled paper. After drawing them, the following facts about the structural organization of their planes, angles, curves, and folds are apparent.

1. Surface planes and curves tend to be organized two, three, or more to a group, and planes or curves in the same group all tend to emanate from a single point. The arrangement can be seen by following the angle lines through to a group source. It is fairly obvious what this point is: it is the point of force operating internally or externally on the form. Think again of the cloth over the vertical pole: all the folds will originate from the point of suspension or pushing-up force. So a plane with its angles does not exist alone on a multidirectional surface. It is organized with other planes, angles, and curved surfaces about a point of force. If this is not understood in a drawing, then this special relationship between the surface of the form and the forces that have operated to shape it will not be conveyed, and the drawing will not convince.[2]

2. The material of the form will tend to move either vertically or laterally until it meets an opposing directional movement occasioned by a second and different force. To take the example of the cloth over the vertical pole once more, the folds of this material hang vertically throughout the whole length of the material, and no horizontal folds run contrary to them. But as soon as the cloth is supported at a second point—say halfway down, by placing an arm beneath it—then a horizontal movement develops which interrupts the sweep of the vertical. Thus a connection between points of force is to be found in the opposing horizontal and vertical movements of the planes

---

[2] Students' still-life drawings and paintings, in which plane and curved surfaces abound, often fail to show an awareness of surface relationships that result from the forces at work. This is particularly true of draped fabrics, folded papers, etc.

FIG. 9-8

Two carefully analyzed paper forms. Elimination of some detail reveals the organization of the folds around points of force. The dotted-line technique permits a conscious visual probing of the form while drawing and also prevents too strong a concentration on the edge of the form.

FIG. 9-9

In this drawing of a crumpled piece of soft paper, the tone is produced by lines rather than by "shading." The contour line lends itself to the drawing of varied surface movement and, for this student, is a legacy from Form II (Chapter 4). It could easily become a mechanical cliché if used indiscriminately. Each drawing problem should suggest its own method of expression and technical solution.

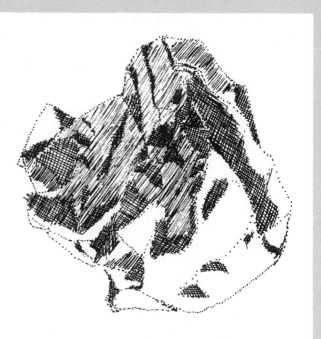

FIG. 9-8

FIG. 9-9

or curves. The vertical movement has the upper hand, since the force of gravity constantly pulls the material in a downward direction.

This scheme of vertical plane, opposed and met by horizontal plane, can be seen in the crumpled paper or on the mountainside. In architecture, the same principle is observed where the horizontal ceiling meets the vertical wall. As long as the forces are roughly equal in strength and capable of being contained by the material (the paper did not disintegrate under the forces exerted upon it), then equilibrium results. The crumpled paper represents an organization of planes and curved surfaces in vertical and lateral opposition, yet in a state of stability rather than disintegration.

The final experiment

To see how you retain all this theory and use it in a project which deals with the organization of surface, let us tackle an imaginative problem of surface design. Using pen or pencil, line or tone, make a drawing of a strange and fantastic rock surface. It can be cliff or free-standing rock; it can be composed of planes or curved surfaces; it can be stratified horizontally, vertically, or in both directions. To do this you may wish to work from the crumpled paper, using it as a stimulus for an imaginative projection involving expression or distortion; or you may just sit down and let the surfaces and their shaping forces take over and grow on the paper imaginatively. Either way, you should now have enough background knowledge to work confidently. The proof will be in the drawings, which will indicate how strongly you have felt and expressed "force" as the cause of surface structure. See Fig. 9-10 as an illustration of this imaginative surface design.

FIG. 9-10

The crumpled paper becomes the imagined mountain range. All the knowledge gained from the study of planes, curved surfaces, and forces has gone into this drawing.

FIG. 9-11

Surface organization of the underside of the mushroom. The vertical planes with their sharp edges could be simulated with sharply folded paper.

FIG. 9-10

FIG. 9-11

surface

texture

FIG. 10-1

CORNER REPEAT PATTERN
Anthony Hollaway and
William Mitchell, designers
*From concrete cladding
panels designed for the
London County Council.
The rich texture of this surface brings to mind the sculptured stonework of twelfth
century Norman stonemasons.
The drab, sterile emptiness
of the concrete cube has been
associated too long with the
contemporary use of the
material. Here is richness
and strength imparted to the
material through an imaginative texture of surface.
(The Architectural Review,
London)*

There is a tremendous interrelationship between the visual sense and the tactile sense, between *looking* and *touching*. More than once we have drawn attention to one's ability to "feel" an object imaginatively with one's fingertips, merely by looking hard at it. This interrelationship probably exists among all the five senses; for example, a particular smell will create in the mind's eye an image of the object associated with it. But sight and touch, especially, have this power to stimulate each other.

Any study of form would be incomplete without some discussion of "touch" quality—of its hardness or softness, dryness or dampness, smoothness or roughness, and so on. This aspect of form is most often revealed by its surface texture. In the work just completed, dealing with surface structure, little reference was made to texture, although it vitally affects our reaction to form. Strongly contrasting textures have considerable power to arouse a strong aesthetic response—attraction or repulsion. Think of a smooth stone half-covered by a soft growth of moss; or an apple smooth and shiny on top but soft, rotten, and fungus-covered on the bottom; or the skin of a woman's face against the texture of a fur collar; or silk stockings in contrast to woolen ones; or, finally, imagine drinking cold milk from a fur-lined bottle. The list could be continued

121

indefinitely. Contrasting textures act as contrasting colors: they complement each other or heighten our awareness of their differing quality.

The architect, the sculptor, the designer in industry, and the painter—all use surface textures to capitalize on the sensitive relationship between sight and touch. An immediate question arises: how effective is an artificially contrived texture when compared with the natural texture of a material? Although we ask the question here specifically about surface texture, this issue of the contrived versus the natural has wide ramifications in the field of art. We would suggest this answer to the specific question: when the surface treatment of a material disguises the true nature of the material, then the aesthetic possibilities of the surface are reduced rather than enhanced.

Examples of such falsification abound in the history of art and design. When the baroque style of architecture was at its summit in eighteenth-century Europe, wood and plaster were skillfully treated to resemble marble, bronze, gold, or silver (see Fig. 11-3, the church of "Die Wies" in Bavaria). The immediate effect on entering the church is wonderful. But as one moves in and touches a "marble" column, it is not cold, crystalline, and smooth; it feels of wood, and immediately something is wrong. The total effect of the building still remains a delight, but it cannot be enjoyed intimately and lovingly through knowledge of its detail. An aesthetic flaw remains.[1]

Some materials possess an unattractive surface quality. Plaster is one. There are things one can do to plaster to enhance its textural quality, but it should never be falsified to resemble some other material. Most artists try to choose a material for its natural surface texture, and they interfere with it little. The art lies in the selection rather than in excessive interference. When the painter uses water color, he wants its transparent, limpid softness; when the architect stipulates concrete, he wants its surface quality in his design [2] (see Fig. 10-1).

The following experiments are intended to bring the student into firsthand contact with surfaces—to involve him in looking and selection, then in the actual touching of the surface, and finally in representing surface textures through drawing.

---

[1] For a fuller understanding of why this should be so, read again the description of aesthetic implication in Form III (Chapter 5) with its suggestion of "completeness" or realization of "truth."

[2] Obviously, structural reasons for choosing concrete may be more important than surface requirements.

FIG. 10-2

Sheet of collected surface rubbings, mounted to show a range of varied textures.

THE EXPERIMENTS

For the first part of this work you will need a large, soft draw-ing pencil or a large, black grease crayon, together with some small sheets of tracing paper. (Any reasonably strong semi-transparent paper will do.) For the next hour or so, attune your eye toward a sensitivity for surfaces, both indoors and out: wood, metal, plastic, concrete, textiles, bricks, rocks, leaves, skins—any surface that excites the eye and imaginatively acti-vates the touch sense. From each surface take a rubbing of a small area (about 3″ x 3″); use the tracing paper and the soft lead or grease pencil, so that you produce a graphic simulation of the surface quality of the material. When you have some thirty of these, gather them all together, trim down the edges of each piece, and mount them all together on a large sheet of paper. The result will be something like Fig. 10-2, which in-corporates rubbings ranging from an auto tire to an iron-stranded cable, to a loaf of bread.

The second part of the experiment is to select three of these mounted rubbings in order of visual dominance—that is, select the texture which stands out from the rest by virtue of its in-tensity of black and vitality of surface. Then choose a texture that is neither very dominant nor very weak—a middle distance texture. Finally, pick out the most unobtrusive texture, the sur-face that recedes more than any other in the collection.

Having made these selections, reproduce the three textures in a drawing, remembering the means by which a variety of drawing marks was produced in Chapter 2 (Fig. 2-1). In order to put the textures "in their place," make a rectangle approxi-mately 9″ x 6″ and divide it by means of three lines into four areas. Let this division be freely executed, the lines forming a natural, twiglike skeletal structure. This will give you space division of an irregular, curvilinear quality like the rectangle-enclosed skeletal drawings of Form I (Chapter 1) especially if the dividing lines are not of equal weight. In that division of the rectangle which appears most frontal,[3] reproduce the domi-nant texture just selected, using any drawing or mark-making means. The texture should fill the area completely. Follow this

---

[3] See Space I (Chapter 3), areas enclosed or bounded by lines of differing weight and quality.

FIG. 10-3

Textures produced by draw-ing. The three textures were selected in each case from the sheet of mounted rubbings and were to suggest three depth levels when placed together in a diagram.

FIG. 10-4

Strange textures given to familiar objects. Are they any longer objects to eat or to touch?

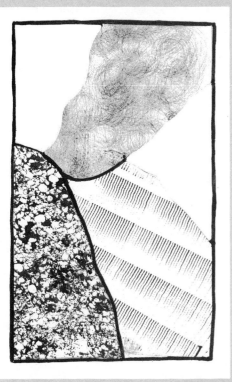
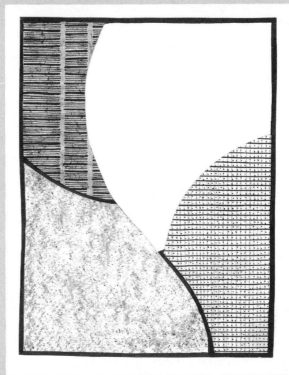

FIG. 10-3

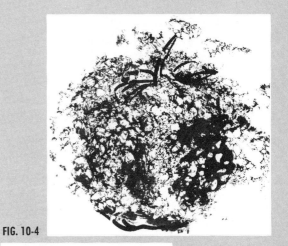

FIG. 10-4

by reproducing the moderately strong texture in the middle distance division of the rectangle, and then draw the meekest texture in any other division of the rectangle. For purposes of contrast, one area in the rectangle will be empty, both texturally and spatially. Black drawing ink is the best medium to use, with pen, wood, dry brush, piece of sponge or any other effective instrument. Figure 10-3 shows two illustrations of textures that have been skillfully simulated through such drawing. They also indicate the degree of immediacy or partial recession which textures in this kind of spatial context possess.

Finally, as an imaginative exercise, let us see what strange and mysterious effects are produced when a familiar form is given an unfamiliar texture. Make a series of small drawings of objects with which you are reasonably well acquainted— things like apples, faces, fish, or eggs—and invest them with a new and alien surface quality. The results appear incongruous and, on the whole, repulsive because now they possess a surrealist quality. It is the violation of the familiar that causes our repulsion, or possible attraction. But it should be sufficient indication of the importance of surface texture in determining our attitude to an object (see Figs. 10-4 and 10-5).

The cold clammy feel of a toad . . . the slimy scales of a fish . . . the silken pattern of a butterfly's wing . . . the smooth fine surface of a new potato . . . the glossy shine of white-painted walls . . . sleeping between sheets or blankets . . . the sackcloth of the penitent . . . ceramic pieces and glazes. . . . Eye, touch, and mood respond immediately to the texture of the form presented to us.

FIG. 10-5

The human eye is given an unfamiliar surface texture of scales, while the lids become speckled and strongly pored. Apart from its surrealistic suggestions, this is technically an interesting textural drawing.

FIG. 10-6

The increased visual interest created by extremes of light and shade over surfaces of uniform texture is demonstrated in this photograph. The strongly lit white stone in the middle foreground makes a dominating focal point.

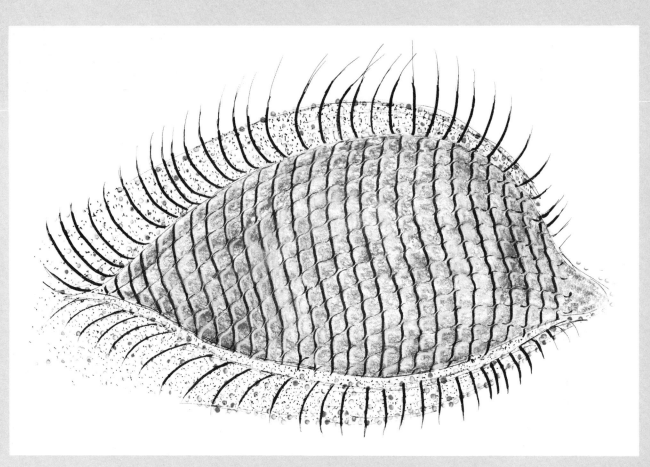

FIG. 10-5

FIG. 10-6

11

dynamic relationships:
forces,
tensions, and equilibrium

We have already had one or two previous introductions to this question of dynamic relationships between objects. For example, in the Imaginative Projects described in Form III (Chapter 5), the second of these projects asked you to consider making a drawing of a dried out, rock-strewn river bed, where large rocks and smaller pebbles lie in some kind of purposive order. The text then asked you to imagine *how* this purposive positioning was achieved—what force pushed or pulled these stones to the position they occupy—it asked you to think of the cause behind the effect, of the force of water to which the new dry stones bear silent testimony.

Before reading on, go back and have a look at Figs. 5-13 and 5-14, for these drawings provide good visual descriptions of dynamic relationships between objects—between stones, in this particular case—relationships that result from some force which has brought the objects to their present position.

Now refer back to Fig. 6-3, the drawing which was the outcome of a chance placing of pebbles on paper, where the eye jumps from one black mark to another, threading them along an imaginary line as beads on a string. Here again it is the dynamic relationship between the marks which binds them together, the directional *movement* that is suggested between mark and mark. But you will notice in this drawing that any

CHOIR VAULT, AMIENS
CATHEDRAL, FRANCE (1247)
*(Photograph by
Clarence Ward)*

129

suggestion of the force involved is weak by comparison with the river bed drawings, because space is fairly evenly distributed between the marks. As soon as space becomes compressed and the objects begin to "cluster," then an operating force becomes apparent. Hence, in the river bed drawings, the smaller stones tend to be forced in, close to the larger stones. When no space remains between them, their grouping indicates that the force was a strong one. A good illustration of such clustering is provided by the salsify seed (Fig. 8-10). Does this suggest a force of attraction to the center or a force of repulsion from the center? It could be either, but it is quite obvious from this drawing that the more *diffuse* the space becomes between the seed marks, the weaker grows the force. So a concentration of objects and a compression of space is evidence that a powerful operating force was involved (see Fig. 11-1).

We had better define some of these terms before going on to the next experiment. The word *dynamic* implies activity and movement; it is the opposite of "static." *Force* is that entity which determines the movement of mass, as the water moving the stones of the river bed, the wind blowing a tree, growth opening the leaves of a bud, or gravity attracting an object to the earth. (In the previous chapter, the word "force" was also used to describe pressures operating *in* form and *on* form, thus affecting the shape of the form.) This chapter is concerned with the dynamic aspect of things in space—with the movement or suggested movement of mass, and with pressure tensions. When several opposing forces are operating in the same region, tensions are created. Tension is simply a force opposing a force. When forces oppose each other in the parts of a building, for example, or in a rocky landscape in nature, and when they are in balance, a state of equilibric tension is achieved, or, simply equilibrium. Tensions in a state of equilibrium represent permanence and stability. When forces, because of their strengths or directions, remain unresolved and in restless opposition, the tensions created within the region, or over the form of the mass, or between the parts of the object, are not in balance and a state of nonequilibric tension or disintegration is apparent. Unstable tensions represent impermanence and instability—a fluid rather than a static situation. (Consider the tension operating over the curved surface of a bent piece of aluminum as described in the previous experiment. The tension is caused by

FIG. 11-1

Visual suggestions of movement associations (dynamic relationships) between objects in space.
(1) A regular grouping of marks and an even distribution of space, where movement suggestions between the marks are weak.
(2) An irregular grouping with an uneven distribution of space, where movement suggestion is strong, suggests a force in operation and puts each mark in a dynamic association with its neighbor.
(3) Marks affected by a centrifugal force, producing the strongest dynamic (as opposed to static) relationships.

FIG. 11-2

CHOIR VAULT, AMIENS CATHEDRAL

FIG. 11-3

PILGRIMAGE CHURCH "DIE WIES," UPPER BAVARIA (1745-1754) Dominicus Zimmermann, architect
(Photograph by Hirmer)

FIG. 11-4

The three basic forces that are used in this experiment.

FIG. 11-5

The point thrust forces of the salsify seed-head.

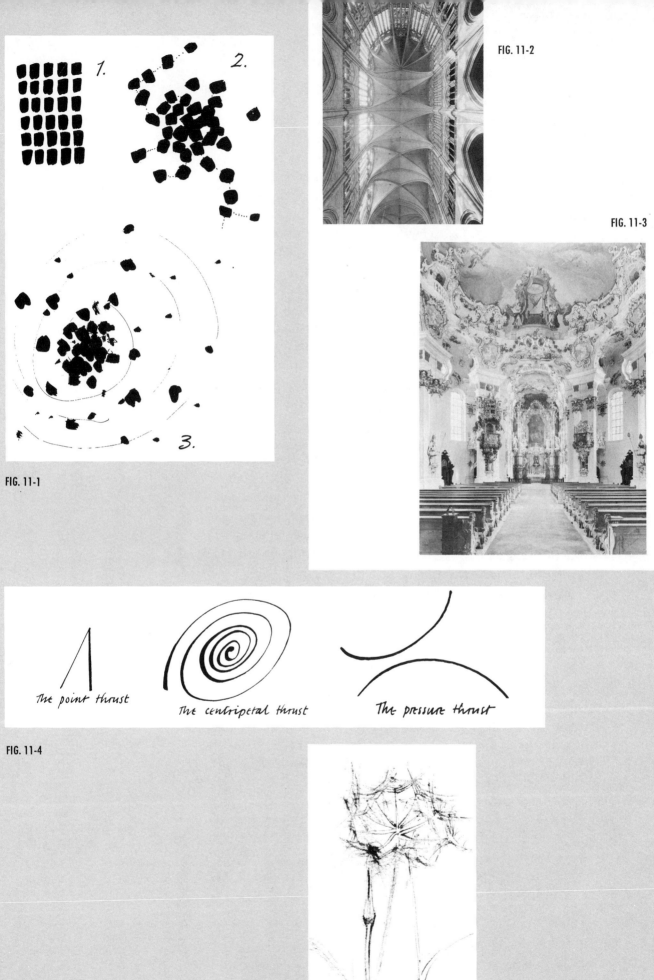

FIG. 11-1

FIG. 11-2

FIG. 11-3

The point thrust

The centripetal thrust

The pressure thrust

FIG. 11-4

FIG. 11-5

strong mechanical forces pulling against the molecular forces of the aluminum itself—by forces in opposition. In this case, equilibrium is maintained until, in bending, the balance point between the two forces is passed, when disintegration of the aluminum sheet becomes a possibility.) A building stands because forces are in balance, creating equilibrium. A stone falls because no counterbalancing force opposes gravity.

For an example of equilibrium, look at Fig. 11-2, the choir vault of Amiens Cathedral, where the mass of the roof vault is concentrated and directed through stone ribs making a downward thrust to fixed points. These fixed points are met by the counterthrust of the vertical, up-pushing piers; and to complete the stability (although it cannot be seen in this photograph), a flying arch is thrusting in to the same point from an outside free-standing buttress. This concentration, up, down, and across to one point in the structure creates a dynamic equilibrium which is the essence of Gothic architecture. What we see are the actual structural tensions by which equilibrium is achieved undisguised by any superimposed design. For an example of a fluid, seemingly impermanent situation in architecture, see Fig. 11-3, the interior of the eighteenth-century church, "Die Wies," in Bavaria. In this baroque style of architecture the rational, precise use of forces we see at Amiens in the thirteenth century, gives way to a deliberate suggestion of a profusion of forces of varied strengths and directions, which fling the eye into a bewildering dance and give no suggestion as to how the stability of the building is achieved. The tensions suggested through the design are nonequilibric tensions, disguising the true structure. When the word "pressure" is used, it signifies forces operating in a particular way. The action of one force against an opposing force, such as a horizontal beam supported by two vertical beams, produces pressure. Pressure forces of this kind are operating in any object which is made up of a series of parts; the pressure occurs between the parts, whether the object be natural or man-made. We shall examine this aspect of form later in the chapter.

Through a system of lines, we tend to perceive the type of force that is involved in moving objects in space and the types of pressure produced in objects. We will use this system of lines to tell us what forces and pressures are at work, whether in a drawing, a piece of furniture, a plant, or a landscape. Our

FIG. 11-6

Sheet of nine free drawings exploring the possible interactions of the three given forces.

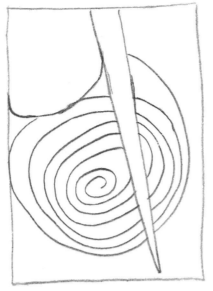

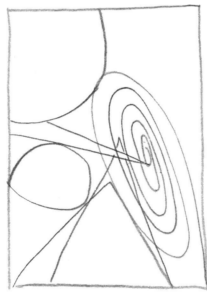

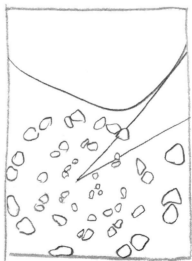

practical problem will be to make drawings in which space is disturbed by forces.

The three basic force movements that we shall use are: (1) the point thrust, (2) the centripetal thrust, and (3) the swelling pressure thrust. These three movements are illustrated in Fig. 11-4. A *point thrust* is force concentrated to one point, like a punch straight from the shoulder. A *centripetal thrust* is delivered outward from a center. For instance, a centripetal thrust produces the ripples on the surface of water when a stone is dropped, as well as the slow, uncoiling movement from the wound-up mainspring of a watch. Or imagine whirling a stone tied to a piece of string around your head. A *swelling pressure thrust* is a movement distributed over a surface, like that produced when you bend a flat piece of paper into a cylinder or expand a surface by blowing up a balloon. It is a swelling, expanding surface.

In the Gothic Cathedral of Amiens you can see an example of the point thrust, of point thrust opposing a point thrust and achieving equilibrium. The baroque church of "Die Wies," on the other hand, contains a restless suggestion of centripetal and swelling pressure thrusts, producing a feeling of tension, not equilibrium.

All three force movements are to be found in nature, sometimes operating in space—as the concentrated thrust of water over the river bed—sometimes existing singly in one object, as in Fig. 11-5, where the drawing of the salsify seed displays a concentrated point-thrust series of pressure forces comparable to those involved in the Gothic Cathedral of Amiens.

THE EXPERIMENT

One of the difficulties to be avoided in a text such as this is the danger of giving the student too rigid and dogmatic a briefing for an experiment. It is, of course, perfectly possible to make some kind of drawing or design by following a set of numbered instructions, but it is unlikely that the result will bear any of that stamp of personal awareness which is part and parcel of art. I hope that all the illustrations in this book indicate individual approaches by students who have taken the text briefing merely as a starting point. The practical work of this section is particularly difficult to describe without making too

FIG. 11-7

The selected drawing from the sheet of force explorations treated first as a line drawing and second as a black and white design. An expanding centripetal force and two point thrusts are displacing forms in the region. In five minutes, the situation could be quite different as the forces continue to operate; therefore, this could not be described as a drawing of stability.

FIG. 11-8

Two drawings where concentrated point thrusts expre operating forces. In the le hand drawing, the irresisti force meets the immova object. The drawing on right expresses stabilit equilibrium as equal fo hold each other in bala

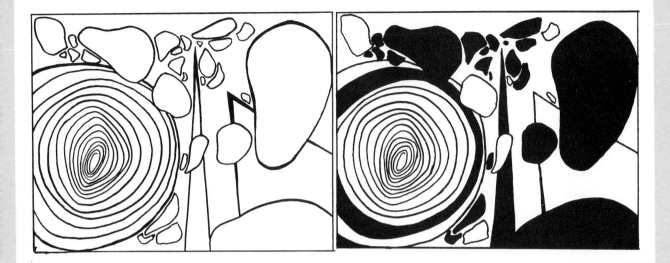

FIG. 11-7

FIG. 11-8

rigid a framework, so I shall mention here only the essentials and suggest that a study of the illustrations will yield more information than a long verbal description.

There are three parts to the work, each one dealing with different aspects of forces at work. First, using all three force movements (point, centripetal, and pressure), make a series of free drawings on one sheet of paper as in Fig. 11-6. These may be left as line drawings or may be "filled in" drawings in black and white. The problem is to contain the three different forces within the limiting size of the rectangle. Study how the space is disturbed, what direction the forces take, what the relationship is among the forces operating in the confined space, and which force dominates. Or perhaps the forces will all be equal in importance. In Fig. 11-6, the point thrust dominates in at least three of the drawings.

It is important to be very free in the manner of drawing and in the expression of the forces. Try to let yourself actually feel the type of energy they represent.

Now select from this sheet of drawings the one which conveys the most dynamic suggestion of forces and, on a larger scale, redraw this as a finished drawing, making whatever refinements you feel are necessary to intensify this feeling of energy. Make this drawing in line only, but then repeat it, blocking in areas of solid black so that you have two drawings, as in Fig. 11-7. Compare the two drawings. Which treatment helps to suggest the greatest dynamic activity, the more restless disturbance of space, and so on?

The drawings you have made so far may be drawings of equilibric tension or disintegrating tension; it depends on how you instinctively dispose the three forces. In the last stage of this work, however, produce as many drawings as you like, but with two definite aims in view: to depict forces that are in balance, creating stability, as in the Gothic Cathedral of Amiens, and forces that are in opposition, producing restless tension, as in the baroque church of "Die Wies." In making these drawings, use one type of force movement—the point thrust, for example—or use two together, or again all three. In Figs. 11-8 to 11-12, the force movements have been employed singly and together in what are essentially exploratory drawings where lines symbolizing forces in operation are used to introduce the dynamic element into drawing and design.

FIG. 11-9

A design of point thrusts aligned to fixed points in space. Movement, time, and intense concentrations of force are suggested by this drawing.

FIG. 11-10

Two drawings of forces. Notice in the drawing at the left how the three point thrusts are balanced. Only the centripetal force (caused by the intruding point force) is menacing and will eventually break through the stabilizing point force on the right. How long will this situation last? It is important to appreciate the time factor suggested in these drawings.

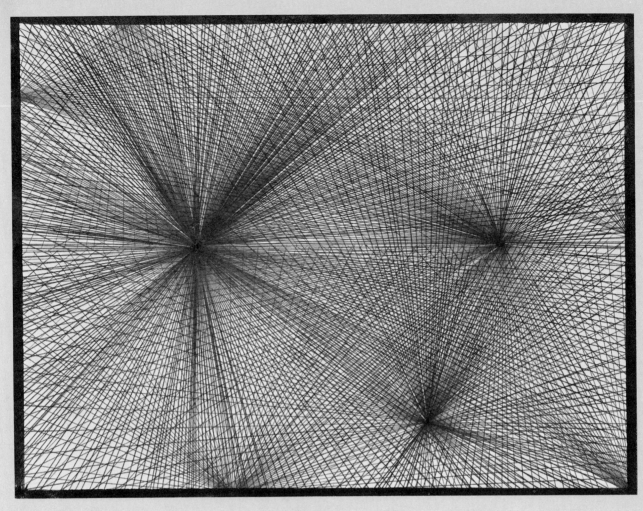

FIG. 11-9

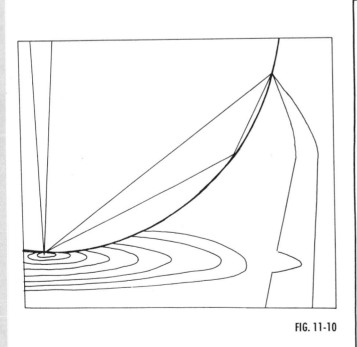

FIG. 11-10

Conclusions

First, how important are dynamic pressure relationships in the single object? Can you think of any complex object that lacks such relationships? Look at the table lamp in Fig. 11-13, for example. It is not difficult to pick out the dynamic operation of the pressure forces of its several parts. The base provides a solid and reassuring pressure thrust, giving stability. The stem with its white, inner shade produces a point thrust down to and against, the base, which is counteracted by the outer shade with its suggestion of an upward thrust away from the base. In our visual appraisal of the lamp, these dynamic suggestions profoundly influence our perception and reaction. An earlier section of the book talked about the aesthetic implications of form; now, having worked with forces, you should realize how strongly the dynamic element influences our aesthetic response. Their power was hinted at in Form V when our response to surface organization was examined, and surface was related to forces at work. Fig. 11-13 convincingly illustrates how important this dynamic connection between the parts of an object is to the industrial designer.

When we move from a single object to a group arrangement of many objects in space, the same factors hold—the suggested dynamic connection between the objects. Remember the pebble marks on the paper, and the imaginary line stringing them together? Can you imagine a living room with the furniture placed at regular, equidistant intervals, a room with no focal points? It rarely happens. Or a landscape where tree, rock, river and mountain are all disposed in a perfect geometric order repeated ad infinitum as far as the eye can see. Impossible. But if it were so, we would work to push some boulders into a group, fell a few trees to break the pattern—anything to introduce dynamic tension, the result of operating forces, into the situation. In nature, rock thrusts against rock; the river scours its resistant banks; trees and plants thrust up into the sky; air currents whirl around; all is in a state of tension, a state of dynamic expansion (growth) and contraction (decay). This is not the unchanging equilibrium of forces, the perfect balance of forces of the Cathedral of Amiens—nature knows no such stability (Fig. 11-14). As in nature, so in art. No work of art can be completely devoid of some dynamic quality; although,

FIG. 11-11

Two drawings of forces of intrusion where a foreign body is exerting pressure on, or in, a substance. The result is tension, due to the lack of balance between the forces, and ultimately, perhaps, disintegration of the substance.

FIG. 11-12

Three drawings of forces expressing movement and pressure. Only the lower right drawing suggests a fairly permanent situation.

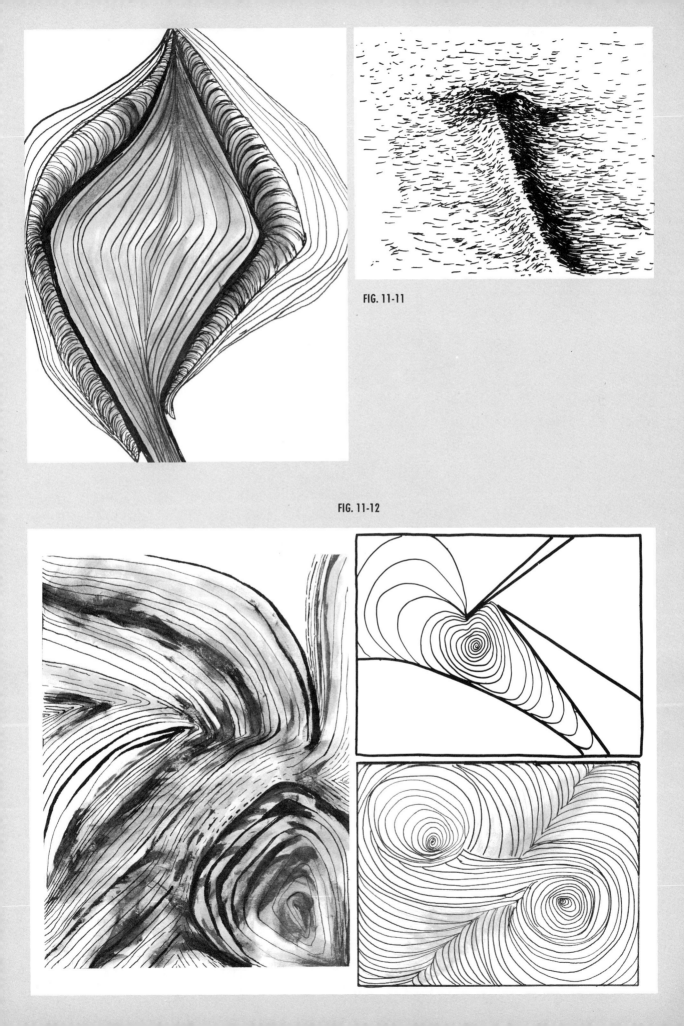

FIG. 11-11

FIG. 11-12

FIG. 11-13

FIG. 11-14

FIG. 11-15

FIG. 11-16

FIG. 11-17

FIG. 11-18

141

as we now know, spatial regularity and directional uniformity can reduce it to a minimum (Figs. 11-15 to 11-17). Possibly the greatest painting in which tremendous forces are held for a moment in a state of equilibrium is Michelangelo's "Creation of Adam," on the ceiling of the Sistine Chapel in Rome (Fig. 11-18).

In this great design, the forces producing the parallel movements of God and Adam are, for a fraction of time, held suspended, as the point thrusts of their outstretched arms and extended forefingers create an intense, yet delicate, stability— a stability charged with electrical energy. The visual dynamics in this painting are strongly buttressed by its deeply significant religious content.

We should now be able to recognize the dynamic elements in architecture (Fig. 11-19), in painting and sculpture (Fig. 11-20), in industrial design, and in nature (Fig. 11-21). Your drawings of forces in this series of experiments are actually symbols of force. Such symbols derived from personal experience and knowledge of the forces affecting form and disturbing space, can be one approach to abstract art. And the designer of artifacts should be aware of the pressures and forces symbolized by the line systems we have described and used.

The essence of composition in art is the disposition of forms in space, and that is what we have been dealing with in this section. We have been concerned with the movement tendencies between forms produced by the play of forces responsible for their present position in space. We have also studied the pressure forces operating between the parts of a single object. Attempting to understand composition without an awareness of the dynamic relationships that exist between forms in space, or between the several parts of one form, is like trying to speak French without knowing a word of the language.

In the plates accompanying this section, the three designs by Victor Pasmore, a contemporary English artist, illustrate particularly well what we have said here. Although they are abstract art, they reveal the forces that govern the disposition of things in the world of space.

FIG. 11-19

STAIRWAY, OFFICES IN LONDON
(1958)
Erno Goldfinger, architect
An example of the centripetal force in architecture. The spiral movement through space is initiated and sustained by forces originating at the center.
(The Architectural Review, London)

FIG. 11-20

ESCAPE AND OPPRESSION
Ernest Mundt
The massive concentration of power in the downward moving point thrust effectively contains the more dispersed thrust force that is attempting to move up and out.
(Ernest Mundt. Associated Press News Photograph)

FIG. 11-21

Pressures in nature: rocks in a state of equilibrium. But move one of the rocks and gravitational force would cause the structure to collapse, as each rock would move to a new position until it met an opposing pressure force. The pressures which are producing the stability of this structure can be visually experienced; there is no need to place a finger between the stones.
(Photograph by Wayne Bitterman)

FIG. 11-20

FIG. 11-19

FIG. 11-21

12

the
equilibrium
of forces in landscape

In this final chapter of Part One, form and space must be brought together and must be seen in a closer association. The two preceding chapters have already started us in this direction. An introduction was made in Form V to the structural organization of surface and the dynamic aspect of form. This was followed in Space IV by an examination of how the dynamic factor operates in space between objects and between the parts of a single object. We must now take the dynamic aspects of both form and space out of the studio and into the spacious world of landscape. By so doing, we shall see how integral are the relationships between them.

Like a leitmotiv, running through this whole book is one constant message—that art is concerned with clarifying particular aspects of our world, aspects perceived through those intellectual and intuitive processes that trigger the act of drawing. Artists such as Perugino, Leonardo, Cézanne, and Matisse have been mentioned in earlier chapters, always to reinforce this message. Now, in this the most difficult section of the book, the inspiration will come almost entirely from Paul Cézanne, the French painter who was born in 1839 and died in 1906. We shall analyze the dynamics of landscape; and in concentrating on this, we shall complete our discussion of forces, begun in the two previous chapters. Form and space

FIG. 12-1

THE THEBAID
Gherardo Starnina (?)
(*Uffizi Gallery, Florence*)

145

will now be brought together, and we shall become aware of the pressure each bears on the other. These patterns of reciprocal pressures between form and space, as seen in Cézanne's landscape paintings, reveal a universe of energy and matter held in a state of dynamic stability.

First, *how* do we perceive space? If you think about this, you will realize that an awareness of space occurs only because we are aware of form. If there were no form to touch or to see as substantial shape, then how would we be aware of nothingness, or nonshape . . . or space? So we really start off by thinking of form as *nonspace* and of space as *nonform*. Make sure you understand this concept before reading on. Figure 11-1 provides a helpful illustration. In the three drawings, groupings of black marks are separated by varying regions of space. The more these marks converge, the more the space is compressed. If the marks come completely together, they lose their individual identity and merge into a conglomerate form. Where there was space, there is now form. In such a merging of these marks—a movement of the marks—a force must act on the marks and *against* space. And when this new conglomerate form is complete, it continues to exist because it continues to exert a force or pressure against space. Were it not to do so, the form would disintegrate, because space, pushing back against it, would meet no resistance. This system of reciprocal pressures between form and space is explained by Newton's Third Law which states, "That for every action there is an equal and opposite reaction." Thus we have a pattern of pressure systems, of forces compressing space to produce form, of form continuing to exert pressure on space to counteract the equal and opposite reacting pressure space exerts on it—in short, an interplay of pressures between space and form. It is by such an interplay of pressures that the jet aircraft gains its momentum. The burning gases forced out at the rear of the jet exert tremendous pressure on space; it is the reacting thrust of space to this pressure which rams the aircraft forward. This reacting pressure is the *force* which moves the aircraft in space.

Space can now be visualized as a region identified as space by virtue of the "marker buoys" of form present in it. We know form as an occupant of space, exerting pressure against space and, in its turn, invoking a reacting pressure of space against it. Thus, these reciprocal pressure patterns are in operation *once form is introduced into a region.* Through these pressures, form exists and is allowed to continue its existence; for were this pressure system to cease operating, then there would presumably be a disintegration of form, and also of space, since without form we do not know space.

Now we can get a better idea of why form and space are so closely related. No doubt you have heard of the word "claustrophobia," a morbid fear of being in closed rooms or narrow spaces. One often gets this feeling in a room overfull of furniture and drapery. Claustrophobia is a human reaction to strong pressure patterns operating in a restricted region; one longs to flee to a larger space. As forms continue to be introduced into a region, the pressures that build up between form and space become more and more complex. We ordinarily call this "overcrowding." But in a spatial context, it is a concentration of pressure that produces the tensions.

In a landscape, in the countryside, the pressure relationships between form and space are quite complicated. The space we call "the sky" envelops the moving growing forms of nature (and where there is a growing movement, there is an intensification of pressure) and hovers over the pressure swell of the earth, the skyward thrust of mountains and the gravity pulled rocks. The artist has long been sensitive to these complex pressure patterns; even in the fourteenth century they were expressed in art.

In the painting, "The Thebaid" (Fig. 12-1) by the fourteenth-century Florentine painter, Starnina, the thrusts of the earth against space are powerfully felt. The small trees standing against the sky seem subject to the most intolerable pressures from space (gravity is not very strong); they almost collapse as one looks at the picture. Newton's Third Law is in some danger here!

The importance of Paul Cézanne as a landscape artist lies in his introduction of space-form pressure patterns in art. For Cézanne, space was nonform and form was nonspace. Before Cézanne, artists had sensed these pressure forces; since Cézanne, they have been consciously aware of them. Look for a moment at this drawing "Valley with a Bright Cloud" (Fig. 12-2) by the English artist, Samuel Palmer (1805-1881).

This is a drawing weighty with pressures. Every leaf, every

blade of grass is growing against the opposition of space. Every form reveals the hidden pressure of its own swell or point thrust. The drawing is alive with point thrusts, centripetal thrusts, and pressure thrusts, although Samuel Palmer was undoubtedly not thinking in such terms when he made the drawing. But notice how the forms are in opposition: the log is pushing against the ground, and the ground against the log; the trees and bushes push against the sky, and the sky pushes back against them. The drawing is so "pressurized" that you feel the intrusion of one more form would cause an explosion. If one more toadstool were to break through the ground, the scene would blow up.

Now we must turn to Cézanne to see Newton's Third Law in operation, to see the pressures between form and space brought together into what could be a contradiction of terms —dynamic stability. Although this reproduction of "Mont St. Victoire" (Fig. 12-3) is in black and white, it will serve our purpose in discussing Cézanne's pressure patterns.

Compare this painting with the Palmer drawing. In the Cézanne, one is not aware of the opposition between form and space, as one is when regarding the Palmer. There is no opposition between form and space in Cézanne; in almost all of his painting he manages to achieve a stability, a harmony of pressures which convey a feeling of permanence. It is, in fact, difficult to distinguish between form and space in a Cézanne landscape, so closely are they integrated. How does he do it? It is achieved by his developing a structural design for his picture which both reveals and stabilizes the hidden pressures of form and space. In this pictorial design, Cézanne simplifies the natural form to a shape which suggests the pressure force of the form. Similarly, space is not treated as mere emptiness, but it becomes a shape suggesting the pressure force of that particular region as it opposes forms in the vicinity (Fig. 12-4). The painting that results is a visual statement of Newton's Third Law. It is Cézanne's way of creating a visible order in landscape; he reveals the invisible reality of pressure forces which lie behind the phenomena of form and space, the reality of *how* the world is, as explained by physical science.

As we study the "Mont St. Victoire," it is the stillness, the sense of permanence that strikes us. With all the pressure tensions that are revealed, it is Cézanne's genius to hold them

FIG. 12-2

VALLEY WITH A BRIGHT CLOUD
Samuel Palmer
*(By courtesy of the
Ashmolean Museum, Oxford)*

FIG. 12-3

MONT SAINTE-VICTOIRE SEEN
FROM BIBEMUS QUARRY
(c. 1898-1900)
Paul Cézanne
*(The Cone Collection, The
Baltimore Museum of Art)*

FIG. 12-2

FIG. 12-3

in a state of equilibrium. By permanence, then, we mean nondisintegration. Equilibrium or permanence represent pressures under control, and Cézanne was a master at exercising this control in his landscapes. The exercises in this chapter are concerned with the rather difficult concepts that have been presented here.

THE EXPERIMENTS

We are to make three drawings of landscape. Select some small and intimate corner of a landscape which has positive character and distinct features with which one can come to grips, rather than a widespreading vista.

The first drawing is straightforward. Using pen, pencil, charcoal, or brush—any drawing medium—draw just what you see with as much expression as you can. The sketch should be about 12″ x 9″ in size (Fig. 12-5). When it is finished, keep it easily accessible, for you will be working from it for the other two drawings.

The second drawing is to be of the same landscape; but this time, rather than concentrating on the immediate appearance of the view, try to reduce the forms in the landscape to a shape which suggests their pressure against space. The drawing will be one of suggested pressure forces of forms. It is better to start by working outdoors, to see, feel and intuitively grasp for yourself the pressure of the landscape forms against space. Do this by making many small drawings of forms or parts of forms. In these drawings, try to reduce the form to a shape which suggests how and where it exerts its dominant thrust against space. This will vary between the extremes of a point thrust, and a swelling pressure thrust spread over an area. Centripetal thrusts will not be so common, as this force operates more usually in space (air currents) than in form. But we will not attempt a similar reduction of *space* to pressure-shaped regions in this experiment, although this could be a further development of a fourth and more complex drawing.

To be sure we understand what is meant by the "pressure-force" shape of form, let us examine it in more detail.

FIG. 12-4

Sketch extracts from the paintings of Paul Cézanne indicate the pressure shapes given to form and space in landscape.

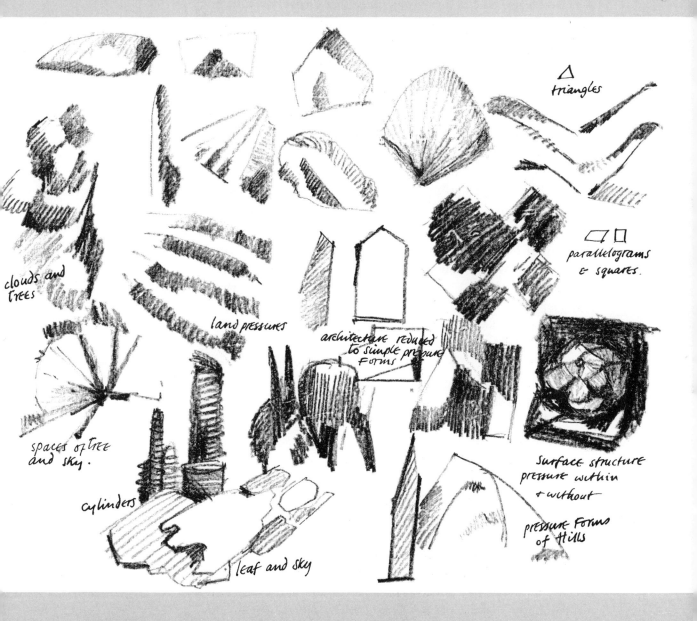

△ triangles

▱ ▢ parallelograms & squares.

clouds and trees

land pressures

architecture reduced to simple pressure forms

spaces of tree and sky.

cylinders

leaf and sky

surface structure pressure within + without

pressure forms of Hills

Pressure-force shape

You will remember that in the preceding chapter, Space IV, lines of force were used to represent the forces operating between objects. These lines suggested the directions of the forces that had brought the objects to their present position or the pressure forces between the parts of a single object. In this experiment, we are not concerned with *movement*, but with the thrust against space exerted by an object from one position, the position in which we perceive the object. Consequently, we need not a line of force, but an area of force, or what we might call a "pressure-force shape." It must have area, mass or volume, and reveal whether the surface is plane or curved, regular or irregular. Obviously, there will be suggestions in such a figure of point thrusts or swelling pressure thrusts, but they must be a part of, and subordinate to, the whole figure. The pressure-force shape is an abstraction from the natural form, to symbolize how, and in which direction, the form exerts its dominant thrusts into and against space. The sketches in Fig. 12-4 show how Cézanne simplified form, and gave shape to space, to reveal their pressure relationships, in a structural design that looks like interlocking pieces of a jig-saw puzzle.

Figure 12-6 shows some examples of forms reduced to simple pressure-force shapes, although these are crude and obviously contrived by comparison with Cézanne's forms.

You should now be reasonably familiar with your landscape subject, having made one complete drawing and several small ones of it. With these drawings before you, redraw the landscape, again about 12" x 9", and simplify all the forms to pressure-force shapes. If you bear in mind what has been said about pressure shape, you can probably assess the pressure aspect of an object instinctively. Also, sensitivity to the tactile qualities of the forms can prompt the hand to "feel" the pressures, and be aware of them in this way. And finally, you may become aware of the pressure implications of forms through a mental appreciation of the laws of physical science. In all three ways, some imagination is required.

Figure 12-7 provides a good illustration of the simplification of landscape forms to pressure-force shapes, producing what might be called a "pressure abstract" drawing. Figure 12-7

FIG. 12-5

Direct landscape drawing.

is not a complete drawing. It is but a step on the way to a more integrated abstract design where the space regions surrounding the forms would also be given a pressure-force shape, in order to reveal the reciprocal pressures exerted on form by space. But significantly, in this drawing form has been reduced to abstract shapes, symbolic and expressive of pressures felt, rather than seen.

We come now to the third and final drawing. If the previous drawing can be called a "pressure abstract" drawing, then this one can be described as a "force movement" abstraction. Our concern will be with the dynamic relationships existing in space between all the forms in the region. In a study of the first drawing, Fig. 12-8, we shall examine the inclining relationship of objects, either toward each other, away from each other, grounded by gravitational pull, or moving up into the sky, and try to discover what type of force brought the objects to their present position. The three types of force we have previously described in Space IV are:

1. The point thrust moving in a straight line; think of the vertical growth of a tree or plant, or the downward pull of gravity.

2. The centripetal thrust uncoiling itself from a central impetus like a spring; think of currents in air or water.

3. The pressure thrust of force distributed over a large surface area; think of the wind, of tide water, of the scooping force of glacier movement, or the swelling growth of a watermelon.

We have demonstrated how forces operate in the preceding chapter; the water pushing the stones of the river bed, gravity forces rolling rocks down hillsides, the growth forces of nature pushing up trees, and the equilibrium gained in architecture when forces are deliberately countered and the fall of a roof or a wall is thus prevented. We should associate force with the idea of movement. But although a pressure is a force, it suggests a more static state of affairs. It suggests an opposition to movement. When you blow up a balloon, you oppose the air pressure; when you place a book on a table, you oppose the pull of gravity; in both cases, you have the action of a force against an opposing force. Consequently, the movement is comparatively limited, or you have a stationary situation. Here lies

FIG. 12-6

Form reduced to simple figures representing pressure force against space.

FIG. 12-7

Forms from the direct landscape simplified to pressure-force shapes. A pressure-abstract drawing.

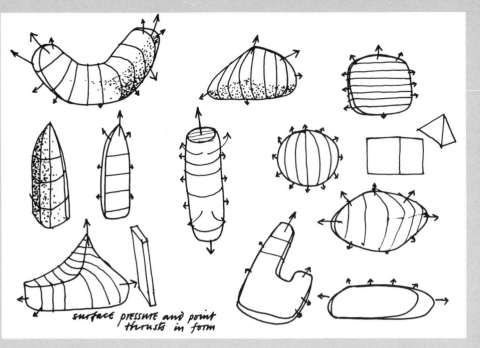

surface pressure and point thrusts in form

FIG. 12-6

FIG. 12-7

the difference between the "pressure abstract" drawing and the "force movement" one to be produced in the third drawing. Look at your first landscape drawing again. What are the dynamic factors involved? What forces have disposed these forms? You will be able to distinguish between *growth* forces, *gravity* forces, or *elemental* forces (wind, water). Each of these may operate via the point thrust, the centripetal thrust, or the pressure thrust.

Using the linear symbols for these forces, make a "force movement" drawing expressing the dynamic factors responsible for the disposition of forms of your first landscape drawing. This will mean creating a spatial design representing the forces that have acted, and are still acting, on the forms in the landscape. The point thrust symbol could represent the growth force of a tree or a blade of grass. The forms themselves need not appear in such a drawing.

Figure 12-9 is a "force movement" abstraction that has been made from the parent drawing, where signs and symbols have replaced objects.

Conclusions

In this section we have attempted to combine two concepts: that of strong forces that produce *movement* and of forces in opposition that produce *pressure*. Both play an important part in the dynamics of art and design. Since this is a long and involved section of complex propositions, we will try to sum up the most important ideas behind these drawing experiments.

1. *The derivation of the abstract form*

As the artist probes beyond the appearance of things, other aspects of reality impinge on his awareness. In this study of space and form, we have been concerned with the invisible rather than the visible. In so doing, we have used signs and symbols which attempt to describe the forces that lie behind the world of appearances. Form is thus reduced to a symbol, and space is rendered meaningful by signs. The result is an abstract or nonrepresentational design. It is important to realize that these new abstract forms now constitute powerful visual images in their own right; they can even be used and developed without further recourse to the object. The artist

FIG. 12-8

Direct landscape drawing.

156

today realizes that he is free to invent, from his own imaginative resources, new shapes of symbolic and emotive power, and the object is no longer the first stimulus. Unfortunately, too many people consider themselves to be working in "the abstract" when all they are doing is producing jazzy patterns or derivative clichés. That is why these experiments are important. They provide a clue to how art works, how it is rooted in a tradition of inquiry, and they show that "modern art" has not just dropped from the sky. Cézanne blazed a trail to a new visual revelation and illustrated once again how necessary it is for the artist to have an inquiring eye and the capacity for imagination. It is the eye that triggers the intuition, the intellect, or the feeling, whichever happens to be the dominant muse for the artist.

2. *Forces of pressure*

The relationship of form to space, and space to form, can be perceived as a system of reciprocal pressure patterns. These patterns provide one ingredient of the dynamic in art and are the basis of the work for the second landscape drawing. Once again, this is an aspect of the invisible reality behind the scenes. Note the closely integrated structure of form with space—a synthesis of form and space—in this "Still Life" by the English painter, Ben Nicholson (Fig. 12-10). The forms are simplified to shapes that suggest their pressure potential, while the immediate space is organized into defined regions which exert pressure against the forms. At the same time, giving space a positive shape in this way helps us to appraise the aesthetic quality of the forms themselves. In still life as in landscape, space and form are complementary to each other.

3. *Forces of movement*

Forces of movement provide a second ingredient of the dynamic in art and govern the compositional elements in design. Such forces have been described at length in Space IV and in the discussion of the third landscape drawing in this chapter. As we perceive the positions of the forms in the landscape before us, we realize that their arrangement is due to the action of forces. Look at the elegant drawing by Victor Pasmore reproduced in Fig. 12-11. In it, the forces moving through space—point thrust, pressure thrust or centripetal—have created

FIG. 12-9

The direct landscape reduced to signs and symbols representing the force movements involved in the landscape. A force-movement abstraction.

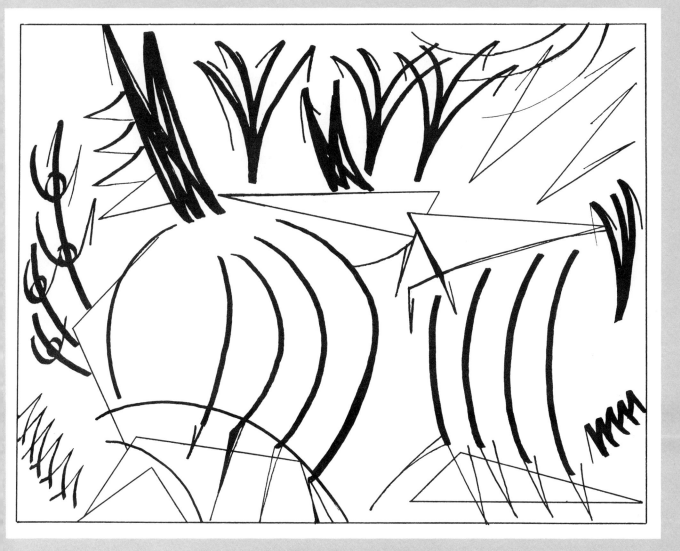

compartments, or defined regions of space. Notice the movement *between* these compartments. The space immediately inside the frame becomes part of the space of the inner rectangle, via the thrust of the heavy black line. No region can escape the forces at work. Even space outside the frame is part of the picture. One can imagine how objects within these regions would be affected by these forces, although the objects themselves do not appear in the drawing. The artist, in this drawing, sharpens our awareness of space by revealing to us the forces, rather than the forms.

4. *Possibilities of development*

The drawings you made should open the door to an invisible world of forces, forces of movement and of pressure. They are really shorthand notes that may be developed into paintings or used for ideas in design and research problems. They are also one introduction to abstract art. These drawings could become as meaningful as those of Pasmore and Nicholson, but only if you develop a spirit of inquiry, a heightened awareness of the possible causes of physical phenomena, and an imaginative ability to express your attitude and your understanding through drawing.

FIG. 12-10

STILL LIFE (1931-1936)
Ben Nicholson
*(Collection the British
Council)*

FIG. 12-11

LINEAR MOTIF (1961)
Victor Pasmore
(Victor Pasmore)

FIG. 12-10

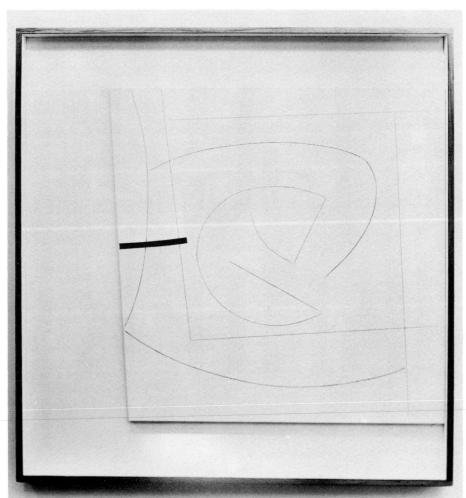

FIG. 12-11

REVIEW

Form I

An awareness of skeletal form, an ability to express it in drawing, a realization of how summarily its limbs divide space, and a knowledge of when to use linear structure in drawing and design problems—all should be developed through further work. The drawing experiments suggested below provide opportunities for development.

1. Consciously apply the skeletal structure of natural objects to the designing of screens, street lamps, wood and metal chair frames, or similar artifacts (see Review Figures 1 and 2).

2. By means of articulated skeletal structures, experiment with the figure in action and repose, with or without the model.

3. From observation of forms that are strongly skeletal and demand an appreciation and expression of linear structure, make still-life and plant drawings.

4. Draw imaginatively from the stimulation of trees, plants, biological magnifications of organisms, and other natural objects whose skeletal form encourages linear abstraction and personal expression.

5. Draw to give ideas for pictorial development; take your first inspiration from a linear organization of surface derived from some visual skeletal stimulus such as the tracery of floating pond weed, veins on the back of the hand, a bare vine in winter.

REVIEW FIG. 1

Drawings for a laminated wood chair frame, a concrete street lamp, and a metal screen. These drawings represent a development of the skeletal structure drawings made from natural objects. They reveal the student's increased awareness of space-to-form relationships in this type of object and his attempts to produce a linear form which possesses a strongly organic structure.

Drawing Marks I

A sensitivity to the quality of lines and marks, to degrees of tone, and to surface can be developed only by constant exposure to these aspects of drawing. Consequently, from time to time, further experiments must be suggested to call on the student's initiative in the selection of material and in the personal use he can make of them in both objective and nonobjective experimental drawing.

Space I

Further work to continue the development of natural depth perception and spatial relationships can be accomplished in many different ways, but here are a few suggestions.

1. Reproduce a complex grid taken from one of the linear structure drawings of Form I (Chapter 1) and fill in a minimum of six spatial regions with freehand vertical lines. Create six positions in depth by varying the concentration of lines in each space and by changing line weight and quality. The same exercise can be repeated by filling in the grid spaces with paint, moving from black to gray to lighter gray, etc., according to the depth position desired.

2. Make a free charcoal drawing in a nonobjective composition that, once again, achieves spatial relationships through degrees of drawing weight and intensity of tone.

3. Achieve variations on the "space-grid" idea (see Fig. 10-3), in which surface textures create degrees of frontality or recession, through the use of collage materials, as in Review Figure 3.

4. Take a newspaper sheet containing type and photographs and allow your natural depth perception to operate over the areas of blackness, grayness, or comparative whiteness. Build up a grid with brush and line around these perceived areas of varying depth, allowing the grid line, by means of weight and quality, to emphasize and accentuate the depth positions of the perceived regions.

Form II

The many uses of the contour line as a means of expressing both space and mass volume are fairly obvious but further

REVIEW FIG. 2

A sheet of quick notes experimenting with a chair's skeletal structure and frontal and receding stripes, preparatory to producing finished drawings.

projects requiring the contour line are suggested as follows:

1. Draw the figure, from the model if possible, in many positions, as a series of contour volumes, perhaps *over* an articulated skeleton, as suggested in the review to Form I.

2. Try an expressive drawing of objects possessing strong mass form and/or holes, where both contour line and contour tone can realize the form. Experimenting with the dry brush and the finger as drawing instruments for both contour line and tone gives surprising results.

3. Draw free, imagined forms expressed through contour line and tone—forms in significant juxtaposition possessing pictorial suggestions.

4. Make free and imaginative drawings of space—of air formations, of smoke, vapor, steam, etc.—where form is moving and constantly changing.

5. Make large charcoal drawings (5′ x 3′) of imagined wood forms, using the contour line to produce a sweeping rhythm of arm movement (Fig. 4-16).

Form III

Perhaps it is not a good thing to develop too strong a conscious attitude to the aesthetic implications of form, as so much of this is intuitively present in a personal drawing. In any case, that which constitutes the aesthetic cannot be rigidly or even simply defined; but some awareness of it is helpful, and so the following suggestions for further development of this chapter are made.

1. Select a flower or a leaf which has a strong aesthetic appeal as form. Draw it freely, deliberately exaggerating the particular aspect that appeals. Observe the drawing and decide if it appeals as much as the original object. Analyze why the answer is "yes" or "no." Determine why, and when, over-idealization defeats its own ends.

2. To induce a mental and deliberate appreciation of form, take a simple cube, like the building brick, and draw it very lightly and quite large. Now work over this drawing by cutting into the cubic form and adding facets and more cubic volumes to produce a drawing of a sculptured brick form. Organize the design consciously and appraise

REVIEW FIG. 3

Black and white collage using type and newsprint. Notice the disposition of the heavier type to produce rhythms of dominance and to give focal emphasis to regions of space.

This is a development experiment to follow the intuitive brush-dabbing exercise.

it at each stage. Justify the design on intellectual grounds of proportion, symmetry, balance, etc.

3. Repeat the second exercise, this time freely and as the spirit moves you, with very little deliberation about the way you modify the brick cube. Compare the result with the first drawing and determine whether the deliberate or the free attitude has produced the more satisfactory design.

Space II

The instinctive tendency to organize space into "regions of space" by the introduction of form has been shown in this chapter. Further work in space perception and in the "designing" of space is best carried out as suggested for Space I.

Space III

Many experiments can be devised to attack the problem of consciously having to express space perception through drawing. Here are three suggestions.

1. Observe the operation of a water sprinkler on the grass in summer as it moves through a complete circle. Make a series of freehand sketches which indicate the height and curvature of the water jet's arc in perhaps fifteen or twenty positions throughout the complete circle of movement. In the studio, translate these sketches into one diagrammatic drawing which attempts to show the full circle of movement followed by the sprinkler, the constant or varying arcs of the jet in different positions on this circle, and the regions of space in depth created by the moving arc.

2. Using a series of lines of differing weight and quality, design a space-grid in which some areas are almost entirely enclosed by lines and therefore project forward, while others, more open, recede at various depths. Separately, design a simple form which suggests a fast-revolving, metallic body, and then draw this in four or five of the space regions. In the space which is most frontal, this body should be large and strong in line and weight; in the chosen space most receding, the revolving body should be small and light in drawing. In between

these two extremes, the size and weight of the body should depend upon the relative space position of the region it is to occupy. The drawing, when complete, should suggest a space region of infinite depth with materializing bodies flying in from outer space.

3. "Draw" with different types of wire, using a line in the air to work out various problems three-dimensionally; for example, "The Disappearing Square," "The Square and the Round," "Space Compressed," "Diminution of a Theme," and so on.

Form IV

The understanding and use of the structural unit is important principally to the designer. Some further experiments are as follows:

1. Build a free-standing model, using one repeating unit of structure; for example, matchsticks, plastic hair curlers, nails, paper clips, etc.

2. Make further imaginative drawings of "freaks" in nature, using an actual unit of structure taken from a natural object.

3. Design an architectural unit from which to construct a screen wall.

4. Examine some models of molecular structure—zinc or hemoglobin, for example. Select one that is not too complex and draw it simply as a system of lines and black blobs. Taking this drawing as the unit, create a complex pattern in a 9-inch square. At the same time, vary the line weight as the unit is repeated over the whole area to produce regions of depth in the spaces thus formed.

Form V

All drawings of complex surfaces demand visual analysis of the organization of planes, curves, and angles, automatically making the artist aware of the pressure forces operating in and on the object. The following exercises are suggested to continue this pressure force aspect of form.

1. Draw the forms made on material other than paper after it is crumpled, bent, squeezed, or subjected to any

169

other mechanical action. Use silk, aluminum foil, plastic sheeting, clay, etc., and notice the diverse surface formations created, owing to the different resistances of the various materials.

2. Draw still life made up entirely of complex, folded materials, from pleated paper to folded textiles.

3. Using a magnifying glass, make an enlarged drawing of wrinkled skin. There are several regions on the back of the hand and fingers that serve for this. Notice what happens to the surface when the skin is tensed by clenching the hand and when it is relaxed.

4. Make five drawings which illustrate the development of a form to complexity. First make a simple, solid triangle from a sheet of aluminum foil, and then push into it once, with a finger. Draw the result. Push in the triangle again at another point and draw the result. Proceed in this manner until five drawings have been produced.

5. Fill a drawing notebook with sketches of quarry walls, rock formations, rock surfaces, the wrinkles of cabbages and bark—anything, in fact, of interesting surface structure.

Form V: Surface texture

Some suggestions for further work to develop sensitivity to surface texture.

1. Ink over surfaces possessing interesting qualities and take a print on sensitive paper; for example, take a print from the end of a cut log. Build up a collection of such prints for reference purposes.

2. Experiment with the monoprint to produce textures. Select several differing surfaces from the prints and put them together in the form of a collage.

3. Select a poem that evokes mood, one that suggests laughter, sorrow, tranquillity, anger, and so on. Attempt to make a translation of the poem in terms of textures, either by collage, or drawing, or both.

Space IV

Many possible developments for this chapter are available in the drawings already made. These abstract sketches can be developed into full-scale abstract designs, incorporating tone, line, texture, and spatial depth, all of which have been previously discussed. Other suggestions would be

1. Set up still-life groups which have a strong dynamic factor operating (a bottle right on the corner of the table, almost falling off, or objects supporting other objects rather tenuously). Translate such a group into a drawing of forces, both movement and pressure.

2. Attempt to work out some design problems, such as possibilities for a six-light chandelier or a large water fountain. For a beginning express only the forces involved, both movement and pressure. See what *shapes* that might develop into the actual object are suggested by these force drawings.

Form and space

Again, developments here can be made from the abstract and semi-abstract drawings already made, as suggested for Space IV, above. Here are some other possibilities.

1. Draw additional landscapes that reduce space as well as form to pressure shape, to produce an integrated space-form pictorial structure.

2. Thinking of the same space-form integration, and either the pressure-abstract drawing or the force-movement drawing, work with still life, the figure, or the portrait, treating the space around the object or head, between the legs and arms, as shape positively related to the object, head or figure. Or draw from architecture and townscape with the same intention. (Study the paintings of Lyonel Feininger, for example.)

3. Trees, particularly, make fine subjects for translation to force-movement patterns, with integrated spatial pressure regions. (Piet Mondrian's tree abstractions would repay study in this regard.)

PART TWO

vision

One major theme runs through Part Two. It is that the creative imagination feeds on images, that image begets image for the artist, as idea begets idea for the writer.

The word "image" as we use it has two meanings. It may signify the mental image, *the picture formed in the mind's eye as the result of ideas produced by some stimulus to the imagination. Or it may signify the* concrete image, *the drawing, painting, or object which possesses the power to stimulate the imagination. The concrete image may also be the practical result of an act of the creative imagination. Both types of image owe their significance to the human capacity for imaginative experience. All kinds of things can stimulate the imagination to produce mental images; but in the eight experiments in the second half of this book, we shall assume that the stimulus that most affects the imagination of the artist is the visual stimulus, the stimulus of the thing seen and the thing experienced. Any visible thing may be such a stimulus; and when it is, it may accordingly be termed a "concrete image." The degree of imaginative significance we are capable of giving to things depends on how well-developed our vision is. We use "vision" here to mean the ability to recognize the potential aesthetic significance of the thing seen, its secretive meaning and associations, its power to heighten mood, or its possible emergence as a symbol.*

Not everybody possesses a capacity for the type of vision we are talking about here; yet many people, when faced with unusual objects or interesting drawings, will make some kind of imaginative jump to a new and more significant mental image. This is the process we called the "developing idea" in art. Each experiment in Part Two is concerned with these principles. They provide a concrete image of some kind to set off the reflex-like workings of the imagination. The mental image thus engendered is then produced in graphic form by drawing. This drawing is a new concrete image and inspires the imagination to a further picture in the mind, which is realized, in its turn, through drawing. And so the process goes on until the imagination has exhausted itself. The creative imagination in the visual arts works by these means. It is a truism to state that without vision there is no art.

173

the

monoprint

A monoprint is a print made from a design that is engraved in ink lying on a flat surface. Only one, or at the most two prints can be taken from such an inked surface. In Drawing Marks I (Chapter 2), a series of lines and marks was made by direct application of ink to paper, and each line or mark had its own quality, its own expressive character in terms of tranquillity or agitation, frontality or recession. If you draw lines on the inked surface of a piece of glass, as you did previously on a sheet of paper, these lines or marks can be translated to paper by taking a print from the glass plate. But these lines and printed marks will bear a different quality from those drawn on paper, for they make a stronger and more immediate visual impact; they possess a special dramatic quality. Assuming that the ink used is black ink, the dramatic quality is present because white lines on a black background are visually more forceful than black lines on white. It is this forceful quality of the monoprint drawing that we are to pursue.

We should explain what is meant by the "forceful quality" of a drawing. It appears when we recognize marks of drawing that are charged with a possibility for development, as opposed to drawings that kindle no such imaginative sparks. Such forceful drawings catch our attention immediately and continue to involve us imaginatively. The significant thing about the

Figure study by the author. This is a monoprint from the glass slab. It indicates the rapidity of drawing that this medium demands and the possible subtlety of line and tone obtainable from the inked glass plate.

175

monoprint method is that it heightens the visual impact of the drawing, and therefore allows us greater opportunity to recognize its imaginative significance and its potential development. To draw successfully on glass, over the slippery surface of ink, now with line, now wiping out areas of tone, demands spontaneity and intuition rather than deliberation and reason. The freedom this medium gives the artist enables him to produce a greater range of marks that are vital and instinctive and which also have a forceful quality. Artists and designers require a capacity for vision; one element of this, as we have seen, is an ability to recognize the potential aesthetic significance of the thing seen. Consequently, any medium which aids the recognition of this factor in the images created through drawing should be explored.

In the work described in Drawing Marks I, you discovered that all kinds of "instruments" can be used to make drawing marks. On the inked glass plate, an even greater variety can be used. The range in the kind of marks that can be made on the glass is almost unlimited; no other medium allows such rapid expression of a mood, an idea, or an attitude. Consequently, you should approach the monoprint freely and with a certain spirit of adventure. At the same time, you should remember the statements made about "line quality" in Drawing Marks I. But the monoprint introduces another factor, that of tone (the degrees of transition from light to dark), an important aspect of monoprint technique that will be described in company with line.

THE EXPERIMENTS

The equipment required is as follows: a sheet of glass about 18" x 15", some tubes of black water-color printing ink, a roller for inking the glass, an absorbent printing paper or newsprint paper.

Experiment 1

This is a line experiment. First squeeze out an inch or so of ink onto the center of the glass plate, and then roll it out evenly over the whole glass area. Roll it well in several counterdirections, so that the ink layer is evenly distributed and

FIG. 13-1

The monoprint: lines drawn in the ink with wood.

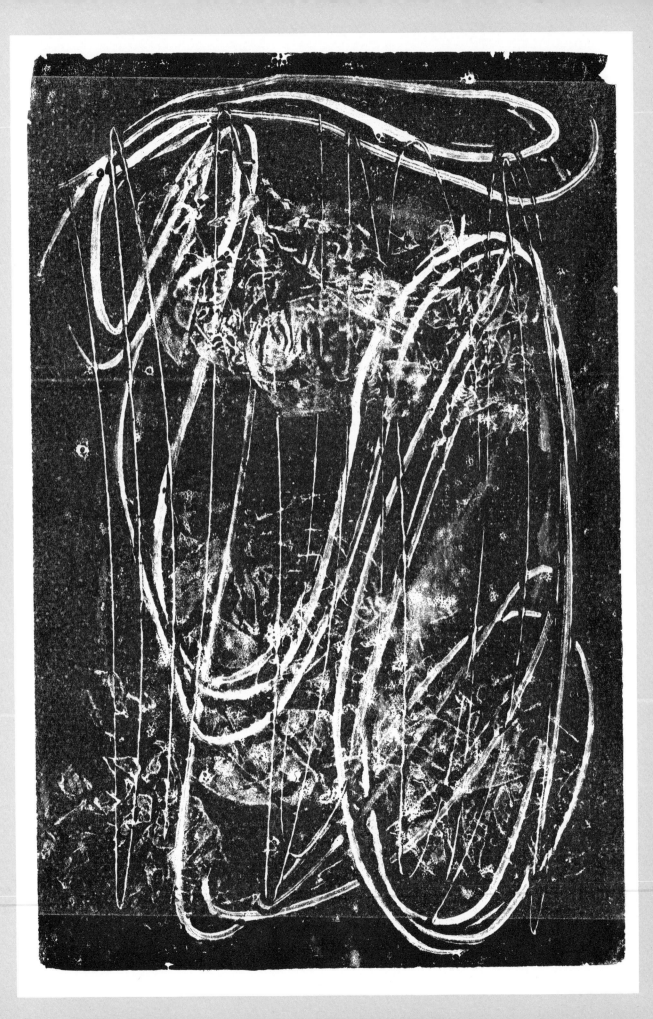

"tacky" to the roller. Now, take a piece of wood (a matchstick or small twig will do) and shape it to a flat, chisel end. This is the first instrument to use in drawing in the ink, and it should be used to produce a line of varying widths as the sharpened end is turned from the flat to the sharp edge as it moves over the glass. There is no conscious aim to this first line. Just work freely, moving the whole arm rather than only the wrist, and produce a rhythmic movement over the whole of the glass area. Stop whenever you feel you have disturbed the ink enough. If a sheet of printing paper is now placed over the plate, then rolled over with a clean roller (or firmly impressed by hand) and peeled off, you will see an interesting reproduction of the line drawn in the ink (Fig. 13-1). Close examination of this printed line will reveal that every subtle nuance of thick and thin, every break, and every variance in the pressure used to make it is faithfully reproduced. A dramatic element of intensity is added because the line is white surrounded by an area of black. But you will notice, too, that this background area is not uniformly black; some parts are grayer than others, or more grained and textured, while other areas are smooth and deep in their blackness. This variation in background is caused by the differing pressures of the roller and the directional changes made by the roller as the printing paper was impressed on the glass. This textural interest of the monoprint background helps give the drawing its forceful intensity.

Now try a drawing instrument of a quality quite different from that of a piece of wood. Roll out the ink smoothly over the glass once more and draw in it with your finger and fingernail, then try a piece of wire (Fig. 13-2), the edge of a folded piece of stiff paper, a piece of rubber, and, finally, press a length of string down into the ink. When you take the impressions from these various line markings, you will get a print of differing types of white line, forcefully presented. It is important to notice how these lines of the monoprint differ from black lines produced on paper by pen, pencil, or charcoal. Which do you think is the more dramatic and forceful?

Experiment 2

This second experiment is concerned with areas of tone rather than line, and with qualities of tone in gray areas between the extremes of black and white. For this work you will need

FIG. 13-2
The monoprint: lines drawn in the ink with wire.

FIG. 13-3

FIG. 13-3

Areas of tone (with some line) produced by drawing with a hairbrush in the ink. The print has strong pictorial suggestions of animal forms.

FIG. 13-4

A result obtained by scraping the ink in a free and rhythmic manner with various folded, stiff pieces of card.

FIG. 13-4

two brushes (a hair and a bristle brush), some pieces of strongly textured rag or canvas, a sponge, wire wool—anything, in fact, possessing a textural surface that will disturb the surface of the ink; you can even use your fingers or the palm of your hand to impress the ink. Once again, prints should be taken at any interesting stage of development, or printing can be delayed until a complex superimposition of marks has been made on the glass. A good starting method is to use one or other of the brushes (you will notice later the different tonal regions produced by hair or bristle) to stroke the ink without consciously thinking in terms of a design.

Don't overcrowd the glass area with these brush markings, and take a print of them first before going on to use the other equipment you've assembled. This print will have black areas of background and gray areas of texture where the brush marked the ink. The surface will appear more subtly variegated than the prints obtained of lines made with the wooden stick, since it is composed of the more delicate markings of the brushes. There may be strong pictorial suggestions produced by the textured shapes these brushed areas of tone have unintentionally created (see Fig. 13-3).

Now let's take this work a little further and see what happens when we scrape off some of the ink. With the glass freshly inked and using either a corner of a rag or the edge of a folded piece of paper, or even parts of your hand, remove large areas of ink from the glass and then work over the whole plate once more with the brush, wood, or finger, dragging the remaining inked areas into the wiped places. The result is a combination of blacks, whites, and grays, multi-textured and charged with a possibility for development (see Figs. 13-4 to 13-6).

Experiment 3

This final piece of work is even more experimental. Select one or two objects such as bottle tops, hair curlers, interesting pieces of wood, bamboo, rush matting, or a simple paper clip and impress them one at a time into the freshly inked plate. Figures 13-7 to 13-10 will help explain how these "instruments" have been used. Place the object in the ink and pull it slightly to one side, or roll it around in the ink producing a range of

FIG. 13-5

A self-sufficient visual statement made by drawing lines in the ink and scraping off the ink with folded card.

FIG. 13-6

The forms in this monoprint were made solely by scraping the plate with a piece of rough card.

FIG. 13-5

FIG. 13-6

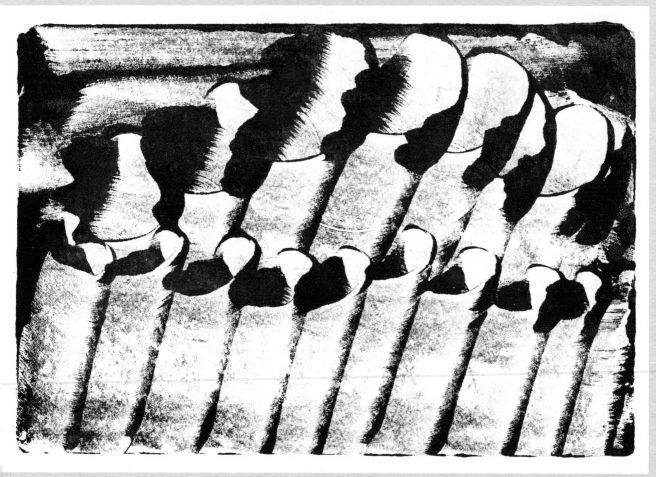

FIG. 13-7

FIG. 13-7

In this example a crumpled handkerchief was pressed into the ink. Notice the good positioning of the impression in the rectangle of black.

FIG. 13-8

Bottle tops were used here to produce these elliptical markings. The slight twist given to the instrument while in the ink gives the mark a three-dimensional quality and creates a sense of depth in the black space.

FIG. 13-9

A plastic hair curler and a short length of bamboo were used to make these distinctive marks in the ink.

FIG. 13-8

FIG. 13-9

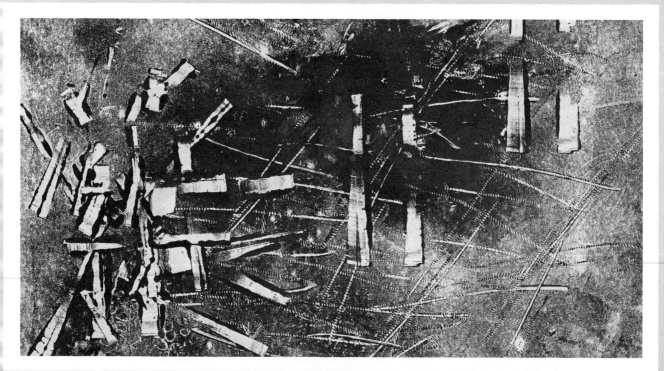

superimposed images. Disturb the ink as many times as seem necessary to produce an interesting image. The print, like its predecessors, is forceful and dramatic, and obviously the strange white forms could not occur on a normal drawing. They have come from a deliberate exploitation of monoprint characteristics. But they involve our imagination and stimulate our capacity for vision; we can see all kinds of pictorial and design possibilities in them—all kinds of shape—many regions of space. This is not to deny the prints significance as "drawings" in their own right; this significance will be touched on in the conclusion.

Conclusions

At the end of this series of experiments, you should have many prints from the glass plate, some interesting and some not so interesting, but all strong in terms of black and white. The images produced on each print owe their expressive quality to the character of the medium—to the sensitive printing surface of glass, to the fluid way water-color printing ink spreads on the glass, to the great variety of means that can be used to disturb the ink, and, finally, to the process of printing itself. But the medium, itself, cannot produce a work of art. To develop the artistic possibilities of the monoprint, to make prints that lead to new ideas about form and pictorial design, the artist must develop his ability to recognize the possible development of a drawing and extend his capacity for expression in the medium. The monoprint can help increase the artist's sensitivity to tone, line, and graphic image, but it is also a powerful medium in its own right. The sensitive artist who knowns the monoprint process well can produce fascinating prints by using the glass plate as a painter would use a canvas (Fig. 13-11). We have employed the medium here to extract images from the ink; later, in Vision VI (Chapter 19), we will use it as the painter might use it, and you will see there further evidence of its power and versatility as a serious drawing medium.

FIG. 13-10

These delicate markings in the ink were made by rolling a fir cone over the inked plate. The vertical lines were then drawn in with a wooden point.

FIG. 13-11

Figure study by the author.

FIG. 13-10

FIG. 13-11

14
addition
and
subtraction

Now that we have had an introduction to form, to space, and to drawing through line and tone, we should introduce the other basic element in art, the element of vision. Vision is the ability to respond imaginatively to the latent aesthetic power of an object or of a visual statement such as a sketch, a roughed-out design, or the first few brush strokes of a painting. Vision may be experienced at varying levels of intensity. At the highest level, the artist may be greatly moved as well as imaginatively transported. In this experiment, vision at a considerably lower level is called for—a capacity for personal involvement and decision in a design situation which is possessed by even the nonartist.

The creative process in the visual arts is usually triggered by some visual stimulus—something seen, however simple and tentative. From my own experience, and after talking to painters, architects, sculptors, and designers for many years, it becomes obvious that only rarely is a person able to visualize the whole or completed project in one flash of insight or inspiration. If most of us sit around waiting for such "inspiration" to strike, it is doubtful if we would ever produce anything. No, there is more to it than this. The theme for a work of art often grows out of a new and sudden awareness of some ordinary, perhaps familiar object, or of a few lines of an incom-

FIG. 14-1

THORN TREES (1946)
Graham Sutherland
A painting made after thorn bushes loomed terrible and significant to the eye and mind of the artist.
(Collection, British Council, London)

189

plete drawing. This new awareness of a thing seen we call "heightened perception," and heightened perception is the herald of vision. It was vision which resulted in the great series of thorn paintings produced a few years ago by the British painter Graham Sutherland (see Fig. 14-1).

A common thorn bush that the artist had passed by without notice on numerous walks, one day detached itself from its surroundings and loomed sharp and terrible to the eye and mind of the painter. For Sutherland, this was a moment of vision, and the spike of thorn later became the motif in paintings symbolizing the suffering and pain to which man is heir. It would be useless for any other artist to try to do the same thing without the vision of the inner meaning and significance residing in the thorns, for his painting would be merely a picture of a thorn bush. Even if we assume that this capacity for vision exists at an intense level for only a few great artists, we all have potentials for imaginative perception that we have not realized. To stretch our imaginations, it helps to build gradually, moving step by step from the first visual stimulus, each stage of development suggesting the next, until we can carry the theme no farther. The work described in this chapter is designed to encourage such chain-reaction growth of the imagination.

"I usually start by scratching about," a well-known industrial designer remarked in conversation one day. This is not a facetious statement. When he says "scratching about," he means that by making a series of scribbles, he will eventually see one that will suddenly leap out as the one with potential for development. But until he has something he can actually see, he has no base around which to build a theme.

There are, of course, endless ways to "scratch about." The least you need is a bit of paper—the back of an old envelope will do—and something to make a mark. The importance of this doodling process is that it produces images which in turn stimulate imaginative perception and, thus, new images in the mind. After many sheets are covered with what is apparently nothing of significance, they can be put aside, apparently wasted. If one returns to study them some minutes later, however, it is surprising how one shape, one partial form, one twist, one angle, one proportion, or one surface texture will suddenly stand out and suggest further development (Fig.

FIG. 14-2

DRAWING (1935)
Henry Moore
A drawing almost of the nature of a doodle, yet notice how the artist suddenly develops the forms suggested by the wandering line, as a twist or an angle helps an image to materialize.
(Collection, Edward Carter)

14-2). From this basic motif or design idea, a theme may be developed until it reaches a point of complete exploitation, when all further additions merely confuse the design. Then it is time to stop, before the intrinsic character of the theme is lost. But the ability to know when a drawing or a design is complete and total is one of the hardest for an artist to acquire.

The experiment described in this chapter attempts to follow the evolution of a design idea from its beginnings as a concrete image (the thing seen) to its proper conclusion. From a simple first mark, a cut on a linoleum block, we will move through a complex process of addition, until addition becomes subtraction (because eventually the block surface is reduced to an area beyond which additional cuts subtract from the printing surface). In the end, we return to a simple statement similar to our first mark, or rather to a negative of this first mark.

THE EXPERIMENT

The necessary equipment includes a block of linoleum about 5" x 3", one or two linoleum cutting tools, a glass slab, a roller, and a tube or so of black, water-color printing ink. The linoleum block can be used either horizontally or vertically, and the work may involve 15 to 25 operations. An operation consists of one or two cuts and the making of a print of the result.

To begin, make a cut anywhere on the virgin block of linoleum. It may be a simple, engraved line or the removal of a small area of the block; do not think long about it, just do it. Figure 14-3 illustrates the first stage.

When the first cut has been made, ink the block with the roller that has been moistened in the ink spread thinly over the glass, and take a print from the block on a sheet of newsprint. The result is not particularly significant. You will see a large rectangle of black broken only by a small white mark. It did not take a great deal of thought or cause you much worry to make the first cut because there was no "subject matter" to create a mental barrier. Now look again at this first print, for your next step is to make a second cut or series of cuts (two or three can be done together) which enlarge on, or develop, the first mark. If two or three cuts are made, make sure that you limit yourself to a comparatively simple extension of the first cut. At this point, you will find yourself weighing the possibilities quite logically. You will be aware of the dominance of the large area of black; you will notice the direction in which the first mark seems to move; you will assess the mark's angular or curvilinear character. You will probably instinctively feel where and how you should make the second cut or cuts.

After this second cutting operation, take another print from the block. Do this on the newsprint beneath the first, in order to make some visual comparisons. You will notice that this print is not so all-over black as the first. The white lines or areas have moved further into the black, breaking it down, and a white pattern is emerging. This method of working should now be repeated, stage by stage. After each additional cut or small group of cuts, a print should be taken. On the block itself, with each cutting stage, when more and more of the surface printing area is disappearing, a white pattern will gradually emerge. After a number of these cuttings and printing stages (which will differ according to each person's method of working), half-way stage will be reached when the area of black remaining approximately balances the area of white. From this point on, as you extend the white marks into the now rapidly diminishing black, you will be achieving a complete reversal of your first prints. Then you had a few white lines in a black area; now you are left with a few black marks in a white area. By the time you take your final print, this reversal is complete. One black mark will stand in a large area of white.

To study all the prints together, mount them individually, in the order of their printing, on a large sheet of paper. (Each print should be numbered as you make it.) Mount the prints in columns with number 1 in the top left-hand corner and then continue the sequence as indicated in Fig. 14-4.

Conclusions

With all the prints mounted, you will now see more easily how the developing process has occurred. From the first, perhaps tentative mark, the block develops an increasing complexity, progressing through the stage of balanced black with white, until it succumbs to the disintegrating cuts of the final stages. The *high point of development* exists when the pattern of lines and shapes and the black and white distribution are just right. Disintegration starts when this balance is disturbed by the addition of just *one more mark*. And yet it is important to remember that you were never consciously subtracting anything, but actually always adding marks.

Eight chapters of this book are devoted to what is called vision or "the developing idea," which is nowhere better illustrated than by this sheet of prints. Look at Figs. 14-5 and 14-6 for a moment and pick out the most complex print of each series. Would it be possible, do you think, to arrive at this particular print *immediately* through a flash of inspiration? It is conceivable, of course—some artists do see the whole thing in their head before starting to work—but it is rare. We know as we look at these two illustrations that the most interesting black-white arrangement on both sheets grew out of a logical and intuitive appraisal of a visual fact—the fact of the first freely cut mark. From making that first step it has been a challenge to break down the solid weight of the block's dominant empty black area. Out of this challenge the design has grown.

Note that in both Fig. 14-5 and Fig. 14-6, the character of the design was determined at a very early stage in the cutting process. It was determined by the third print in both cases. It is difficult to imagine either of these designs having developed other than in the form we see them here. There are no inconsistencies at any stage, yet both these students at the outset declared how hopeless they were "at art." Once past the halfway stage, they gained in confidence and interest, for now the problem was one of organic growth; the white had to grow and eliminate the black. During this exercise, one of the students referred back to one of his earlier drawings of twig structure, to see again how space penetrates linear form.

This, then, is how most designing starts. It grows out of a basic theme which is imaginatively exploited until it reaches a stage of total completeness. In the words of one student busily engaged in scratching about on this particular experiment, "You begin to plan ahead. . . ."

FIG. 14-3

The first cut in the block.

FIG. 14-4

Method of mounting prints.

FIG. 14-5

Mounted series of prints.

FIG. 14-6

Mounted series of prints.

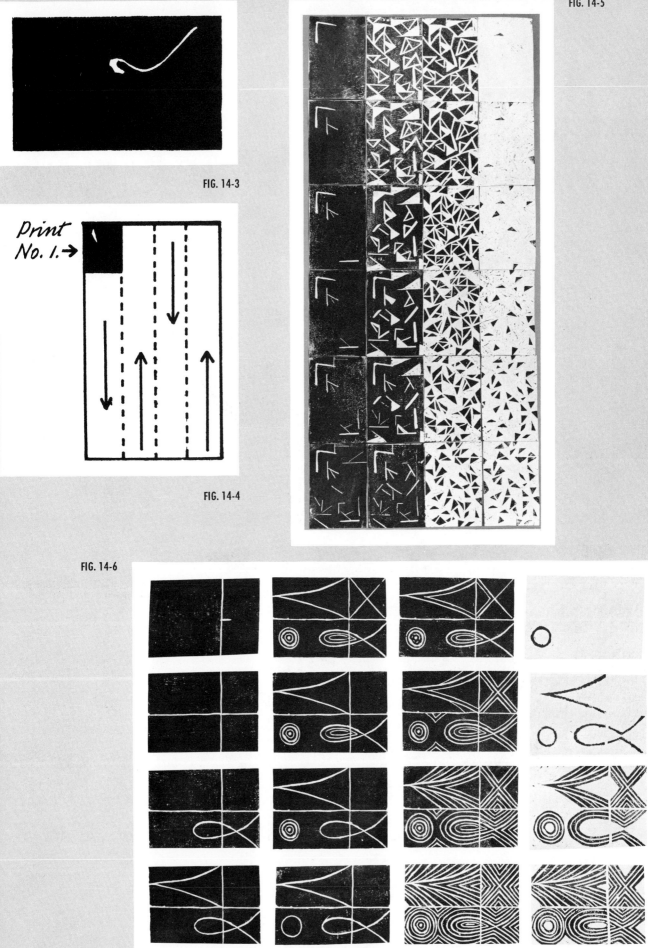

FIG. 14-3

FIG. 14-5

Print No. 1. →

FIG. 14-4

FIG. 14-6

new shapes

from

old

The preceding work with the linoleum block demonstrated how we can build a simple theme into a full symphony of patterns. It enabled us to see when a process of development was complete. And we could also see when the development of the theme had not gone far enough, and when it had gone too far altogether.

Knowing when a work is complete, when any addition or subtraction can be only detrimental, is a major constituent of artistic ability. If you will look again at the drawing by Samuel Palmer (Fig. 12-2), you will perhaps feel that nothing more can be added without causing the taut pressure-patterns to break up. This drawing is thus complete.

Our next experiment is concerned with completeness. Like the exercise in Vision I (Chapter 14), it sets out to develop a theme, but this time in rather a different way, demanding a more conscious imaginative jump from the basic theme to the new shape. It also involves three-dimensional form rather than pattern.

The basic theme is bottle shape. The experiment is short and relatively simple, but it does reveal again that the ability to design results from a capacity to see beyond what *is*, to what *might be*. In the process of visualizing a new form for a familiar object, the artist will imaginatively assess both its structural

GLASSES
S. Fogelberg, designer
It is difficult to visualize any possible change in shape that would improve the form of these glasses. They have an ease of proportion and a purity of form that suggest completeness.
(Thomas Webb and Sons. Photograph by Council of Industrial Design, London)

197

and aesthetic refinement before embodying it through draw-ing as a concrete image.

THE EXPERIMENT

Ordinary glass bottles come in many varied shapes and pro-portions, some pleasing, some disturbingly ugly. The bottle, like the snail's shell, is essentially an object of space volume, a container whose space is enclosed, and consequently defined, by a material substance. We have already discovered that the continuously revolving contour line which moves in a con-tinuous exploration of surface is an effective means of realizing the structure of such objects of volume. But another quality characterizes bottle shape: it is symmetrical or near-symmetri-cal. Unlike the hole in the snail shell, a piece of wood, or a cloud, the volume is symmetrical around an imaginary axis pass-ing through the center of the bottle. When one draws a bottle, then, it is helpful to draw this imaginary axis. As the bottle swells and narrows around its axis, indicate on the axis, by means of horizontal lines, the widest and the narrowest por-tions. This produces an imaginary skeletal structure like the drawing note *a* in Fig. 15-1.

Here is an instance of skeletal form assisting in the drawing of an object of volume, although it plays no real part in the actual structure of the bottle.

Make a random selection of empty bottles, choosing four or five different shapes. Set them up one at a time and make a drawing of each, a drawing which attempts to explain the structure of the bottle. Do several drawings on one sheet of paper as in Fig. 15-1. Any haphazard grouping will do, for this is not intended as a bottle composition. Use both the imaginary skeletal axis and a combination of apparent outline and re-volving contour lines to express the volume of each bottle. Once you have "put the bottle together" in this way, it becomes more significant as a structural form—you have looked inside as well as out.

From this sheet of structural drawings, select two or three which appeal to you most, and on a separate sheet of paper redraw each bottle individually on a large scale, about 12 inches tall. Make these drawings in outline only. The very fact that the bottles have been drawn and understood structurally, as volume, through the continuous contour line, will help to insure that your outline is subtly expressive of volume rather than mere delineation of a flat area. You will recall that in Form II (Chapter 4) we discussed the apparent edge or outline of objects of mass or space volume, and we insisted on drawing over the *surface* of the object rather than around the edge. The revolving contour line, of course, expresses the surface of the object. But for the purposes of this experiment, for which we want to visualize a changed form, an outline drawing will leave us freer to do this.

When these larger drawings have been made, study each of them and try to see a new and improved shape emerging from the basic form. The new shape should keep essentially, the over-all proportions of the first bottle, but should attempt to improve on it through changes in the swelling or narrowing of the volume, changes in the slopes of the surfaces, and so on.

Draw the new shape, which is suggested and inspired by the first, ordinary bottle, *inside* the existing bottle drawing (although in places the new design may protrude beyond these limits). Complete the experiment by filling in with black ink those parts of the old bottle not occupied by the new shape, as in Fig. 15-2.

Conclusions

After the experiment, you will realize how slight a change in shape will produce a radically different form, how easy it is to go too far and produce only a vulgar and ridiculous form. The refinement of form is a subtle process of addition or subtraction suggested by the visual imagination and one's aesthetic sensibility, as we discovered to be the case for pattern in Vision I (Chapter 14). In designing the new shape, you will have made both rational and instinctive decisions—decisions concerning the rhythm of part to part, the proportions of part to part, the structural authority of the new form, and so on. These judgments are part of your aesthetic response to form, and with them must come an awareness of how narrow are the limits of change that affect the aesthetic significance of form. The new shape that is "right" will be the shape that appears to have grown there on the paper; the glasses in Fig. 15-3 meet this criterion. The shape that appears most awkward and ill at ease is the one that has been the most forced or contrived.

The motive for this experiment has been the development of a theme, to help train your imagination to move from what *is* to what *might be*. This experiment assumes that a new bottle shape may be most successfully inspired by an examination of many existing bottles, both to provide a stimulus to the imagination and to set the train of images in motion. The ability to determine the "rightness" of shape is difficult to learn.[1] Natural aptitude for this helps, of course, but this method of starting with existing shapes should help to develop your imaginative and aesthetic awareness.

FIG. 15-1

Skeletal and contour-line structure of bottles.

FIG. 15-2

New shapes from old. The form of the new bottle can be seen clearly for comparative purposes against the black silhouette of the old. The new shapes may or may not be an improvement, but this ready comparison reveals how small are the limits by which the whole character of the original form may be changed.

---

[1] "Rightness" of shape is invariably found in nature, and the artist is tuned to her rhythms. The student who wishes to learn about completeness of form must also look outward to the whole complex field of nature.

FIG. 15-3

GLASSES

FIG. 15-1

FIG. 15-2

FIG. 15-3

FIG. 16-1

pictorial

quality

What is it that moves a person to paint pictures? And what is it that imbues a good painting with a peculiar, magical life of its own which defies logical, cold-blooded analysis? These are big questions, and men have been asking them for a long time; they are worthy of more than the hints that are given in answer here. Yet an introductory hint must be given if this experiment in creating pictorial quality is to mean anything to the reader.

By "pictorial quality" we mean "an expressive and significant combination of shapes and colors." A painting springs from an urge to give expression to some aspect of experience which is affecting us powerfully, and the painter, through an expressive and significant use of shapes and colors, thus reveals his attitude to experience.

The second question is more difficult to answer—perhaps even defies answer—as the whole human capacity for imagination defies analysis, and paintings are the imagination given tangible form. Let us just say that any expressive and significant combination of shapes and colors has a strange power to affect us.

Shape and color in painting are significant in two ways. They affect our mood and suggest ideas. They strike at both the head and the heart. The painter, perhaps, has an advantage

FIG. 16-1

A significant and expressive arrangement of shapes and colors.

203

over the poet and the composer, at least initially, for human beings seem to respond more immediately to a thing seen than to words or sound, which take more time to absorb. The painter also has the advantage of color, which can so strongly affect the viewer, imparting joy or gloom, tranquillity or restlessness, excitement or passivity. Pictorial quality—color and shapes—exists, irrespective of the subject matter of the painting. An abstract or nonrepresentational painting may be totally without pictorial quality; so may a representational painting. On the other hand, both types of painting may possess it. Pictorial quality exists quite independently of the style of the painting, because people can respond to shape and color qua shape and color. We can react to these elements in themselves without having to consider what it is that has a particular shape or color: we can react to them in the abstract. And this response is largely intuitive; we do not have to stop to reason about how we feel about combinations of shapes and colors.

The aim of the following experiment will be to produce a nonobjective painting by free-drawing means. The painting will evolve through a series of mental and concrete images, each stimulating the production of a new image which can then be incorporated in the growing pictorial design. The finished painting may have pictorial quality; it may be "an expressive and significant arrangement of shapes and colors" —or it may not. That will depend on how effectively you are able to capture in concrete form the new images that suggest themselves in the exercise, using the unfamiliar mediums of wax and ink. Obviously, your instinctive response to shape and color will determine how significant and expressive are your images.

THE EXPERIMENT

This experiment will introduce the three basic colors—red, yellow, and blue—and the range of complementary colors that can be derived from them. To exploit this exercise fully, you should be prepared to learn by experience as you go along. The experiment is deliberately designed to keep you one step ahead in your response to the developing situation and to encourage you to make mental notes as results occur. As in much of the work of the previous sections, the value here lies not so much in the particular piece of work as in expanding the range of your aesthetic awareness and expression.

To supply the color for this painting, waterproof inks will be used because they are both intense in color and transparent; they are also quick-drying and extremely permanent. When a red waterproof ink is placed over a yellow one, the resulting color is a pure orange. Since the inks dry very fast and do not mix together, their transparency allows them to show through each other and thus produce an orange which is purer than that gained through normal mixing of pigments. For gaining a firsthand, practical knowledge about the basic colors and their derivatives, waterproof inks offer a much more efficient and exciting method than mixing pigments on a palette and then applying the new color to paper. In addition to the colored inks, we will introduce a resistant medium in this experiment—in this case, wax. The wax will resist the ink and thus render areas of the painting impervious to color. It will enable us to build up both shape and color in a way that could not be achieved by direct painting methods.

Two sheets of paper are required, each about 14″ x 16″ in size, one a sheet of newsprint and the other a good quality, smooth-surfaced white drawing paper. For the wax-resist, you can use an ordinary white wax candle. The best inks for this experiment are red (vermilion or crimson), blue (a light blue rather than a deep purple-blue), and yellow—the three basic colors from which, theoretically, all the others can be made. It is important to use the clearer reds and blues mentioned, because brown-reds and purple-blues do not work well when overlaying the other inks; they produce secondary hues that are muddy rather than clear and distinct.

To begin, cut or tear from an old newspaper a wide range of assorted shapes—just cut or tear quite freely as the inclination takes you, from long and thin shapes to fat and squat ones. When you have a good collection on hand, take the sheet of newsprint and glue a number of these cut and torn shapes onto it. Do this without too much conscious deliberation or selection, but keep an eye on the contrasting qualities of each shape selected, and place each where it would seem best to complement those around it. Some will overlap each other; some will be partially or completely isolated. When you feel that the sheet of newsprint is reasonably well covered, neither too crowded nor too empty, then stop. Each person will group his pieces differently, depending on his individual sense of the arrangement of the forms.

Although you will end up with an apparently meaningless jumble of newspaper shapes, they will finally embody a combination of shapes and colors which will grow through processes of addition and subtraction to an inevitable point of completeness.

For the second stage, you will need the sheet of good quality drawing paper. Make a pencil drawing of the design of the glued newspaper shapes. Do not draw merely the outline of the large figure, but include the overlapping lines of each individual paper piece. Once this is done, the first sheet is no longer required and can be thrown away. It has served its purpose by providing the free and nonobjective arrangement of shapes which you now have as a drawing. Now take the white wax candle and sharpen it down to a good drawing point (you will have to sharpen it quite frequently) so that it can do some intricate work. Approximately one-third of the total paper area has to be waxed over with the candle in this first step; and when you are considering where to wax, the spaces as well as the shapes should be considered. Distribute the wax regions fairly evenly over the whole paper area, applying the wax quite firmly, to close the grain of the paper. It is not necessary to follow closely the pencil outlines of the shapes or spaces; and if you want to, wax only a part of a shape or space. Since it is easier to develop secondary and tertiary colors by this overlay method, if we work from light hues to more intense hues, we will start with the yellow ink.

Using a large water-color brush loaded with ink, lay a rapid wash of yellow over the whole of the paper. Do this in a few quick actions and avoid the temptation to go back with the brush to touch up areas. Notice what happens with this first lay-in of color. The waxed portions, being resistant to the color, remain white, although parts take on a certain speckled quality where the wax did not completely close up the grain of the paper. The result is a yellow sheet of paper, with some white or speckled shapes, and it already suggests some emerging concrete images. It is at this stage that the basic character of the painting can be discerned. You are now in a position to sense the pictorial quality of the painting, as well as to deliberate on what should happen in the next stage of development.

The following steps become more complicated. New areas have to be protected by the wax-resist, and some of the areas first protected have to be scraped clear of wax. The reasons for these steps are fairly obvious. The wax that must be now applied over parts of the yellow area will protect the yellow shapes from the second color to be applied, namely, red. Areas of yellow that are not waxed will become orange; areas that are protected will remain yellow or yellow speckled with red. Scraping off some of the wax from the white or speckled parts will allow certain areas to become pure red. If all these whitish areas which were first protected were to remain waxed, then the red ink could not show up as its own pure color. Which parts of the yellow areas you protect and which areas you scrape off must be your decision. Only when the yellow ink is thoroughly dry and these second two operations are complete should the red ink be flooded over the whole of the paper. (On no account should any attempt be made to "paint in" specific areas or shapes; each color as it is applied must cover *all* the paper.)

After the application of the red ink, examine the design again to see what has happened. Where the red has gone over the yellow, there will be rich and luminous orange shapes. Where the yellow was waxed, pure yellow or yellow-speckled red will remain. The areas of white that were de-waxed will be pure red or red speckled with white. Where the white was left waxed from the beginning, white will remain, although by now it may be speckled with color. A great change has come over the painting with this application of the second color. The process of waxing and de-waxing has created secondary shapes that emerge only as the new inks, brushed over the surface, produce color changes. In fact, it is becoming obvious that you are really drawing with wax, although the results of the drawing appear only as the ink is brushed on. A coherent design is beginning to emerge, a design that has little in common with our first page of newspaper shapes.

Before applying the blue, study the painting closely, for the third color has the power to eliminate all the subtle colors and textures which are now present in the work. Since this color, too, is to be applied over the whole paper, you should try to imagine what effect it will produce. The orange will become brown, the red will become a rich violet, the yellow will be green, and the white will be blue. Blue is a potent colorizer; and of the three basic colors, it should be handled with the greatest care. If applied hastily, the blue can destroy much of the quality that has already been achieved. Therefore, the final layers of wax which are to repel the blue must be carefully applied; and any wax that is to be removed should be thoughtfully considered, so that when the blue is finally brushed over the whole painting, the colors change only where change is desired. Try to work in all the possible color changes somewhere on the painting, but remember that too many white areas are not desirable because they tend to break up the design.

After the blue ink is applied, a complete series of colors should appear: yellow, orange, red, brown, violet, green, and blue. Some of the areas will be speckled, and a few hybrid hues will probably show up. Note that only brown is a tertiary color, that is, a color produced from three sources.

But we are not quite at the end of the experiment. To see the true value of the colors (particularly any white regions), the subtlety of their gradations, and the more distinct outlines of the shapes, scrape the picture clean of wax with a razor blade. With the removal of the opaque film of wax, the whole painting should begin to glow. If you want to continue working on it, you can repeat the procedure with each color, or use other colored inks which are obtainable, to produce a considerable range of new hues. Or you might want to repeat only one color, to enrich the picture here and there.

Conclusions

Figure 16-1 provides a good illustration of pictorial quality. Only the combination of wax and transparent inks produces these special textures and distinctive color harmonies. In other words, some of the pictorial quality results from the natural properties of the materials used; a fact that is always true in painting, and one that makes it important to know your medium thoroughly. The painting produced in Fig. 16-1 is a remarkably homogenous composition. Both shapes and colors combine to form an expressive and rhythmic scheme. It is possible to see where and how the wax has acted as a "drawing" medium to determine a shape or a color area, and the disposition of the semi-white parts shows the artist's sensitivity to the problem of relieving the general redness of the picture. Notice that the yellow ink has all but disappeared (evidently it was not waxed to preserve it from subsequent inkings), and you might think this a deficiency in the work. On the other hand, more pure yellow might destroy the color and shape balance. In making this picture, the student had little conception of the finished result. There was no predetermined and final image toward which she was working. Instead, each stage of the process conditioned the next step and required a response from both the intuition and the intellect.

Figure 16-1 can be considered an effective painting (1) because all the colors in the painting were derived from the three primary colors and therefore possess a natural yet intriguing relationship to each other and (2) because the shapes originated freely and sequentially without being forced or contrived as a self-conscious "design"; they resulted from the gradual, deliberate build-up of color and the intuitive response of the artist to the emerging images. And they have power even though they do not "represent" any object or person.

Not all of your results will be this satisfactory, but in a second and a third painting, when you know more about the medium, you should be able to get an instinctive feeling for the process and have more control over the final outcome. In this exercise you do not have to worry about subject matter. You are free to experiment with pictorial quality in its purest sense. Many variations on this wax and ink method are possible: other colors in addition to the three primaries may be used, and more stages of waxing and de-waxing can be employed, all of which increase the possible number of shape and color combinations. The method can even be adapted to serve a strictly objective painting.

This experiment involving the three basic colors is a good introduction to secondary and tertiary hues, which emerge in the paintings. It should also surpass traditional study of the color wheel in giving you a better idea of how color works, of the nature of related families of color, and of opposite or complementary colors.

209

17

the
pictorial
imagination

We have seen that pictorial quality is an element that grows into the design of a drawing or painting that is intrinsically an organic part of its life, and that appears complete only in the finished work.

A painter usually pursues a direction that evolves from the first shape and the first color that appear on the canvas. He moves intuitively, identifying himself with the painting as it takes on a life of its own and carries him through a complex progression of stages to completion. The previous experiment attempted to reveal the authority of significant arrangements of form and color and the almost magical way they can take over the artist—dictate to him what he should do next. "Pictorial quality" suggests the independent authority of form and color over the artist, irrespective of subject matter or absence of it; pictorial quality affects the painter while he is actually working on the painting.

But what is it that impels him to work in the first place? We use the term "pictorial imagination" to mean the artist's capacity to recognize and to be stimulated by the aesthetic potential of something he sees or otherwise experiences (see Figs. 17-1 and 17-2) and his ability to create an image of greater power and significance in a pictorial context of shapes and colors. "Aesthetic recognition" as a part of pictorial imagi-

THE SLEEPING GYPSY (1897)
Henri Rousseau
Oil on canvas, 51 x 79 inches.
Here is a most mysterious
painting. It is the peculiar
quality of Rousseau's pictorial
imagination which renders
this strange vision.
(Collection, The Museum of
Modern Art, New York.
Gift of Mrs. Simon
Guggenheim)

211

nation, then, might be described as a capacity for heightened perception, which is one aspect of what we have called "vision." Not all artists possess a pictorial imagination. Many are illustrators or recorders of events, the counterparts of journalists in the literary arts.

We have seen how the English painter Graham Sutherland experienced a moment of heightened perception and subsequent vision when a bush of familiar thorns suddenly became terribly significant for him. The thorn painting (Fig. 14-2) is the result of a pictorial imagination, generous in its amount and brilliant in its ability to project new images into a pictorial context. There may sometimes be a long delay between the experience of heightened perception, the subsequent vision which projects images in the mind, and the physical act of creation. The nineteenth-century French painter Eugène Delacroix commented in his *Journal* that sometimes the memory of an object is sharper than the thing seen originally, for the image in the memory is the essential image, freed from irrelevant detail and distracting associations. Consequently, years later, the memory of a thing or an event may still motivate a work of art.

The question arises of whether a "pure" art exists, an art generated entirely from the subconscious resources of the artist, and of whether he need ever refer to visual objects for his inspiration; in other words, is the artist dependent on perception for the creative act? The answer must be left open. It is likely that even when an artist is working in a state of complete detachment and lucidity, divorced entirely from a sensory awareness of the world, the memory of some earlier perception is still the basic influence behind his design. But certainly in any introductory work in drawing and design, one must first attempt to increase one's powers of perception; at this stage, it is the best spur to pictorial imagination, and it is the surest way to accumulate bright, enduring images in the visual memory.

The following experiment attempts to stimulate your pictorial imagination by testing your ability to see things in strange graphic images and to transform these strange shapes into a drawing of imaginative expression.

FIG. 17-1

Large magnification of a tree root mass. What do the strange forms of this surface suggest to the pictorial imagination? Here is an image which must intrigue—but would you ever stop to look at an old root? (Photograph by Wayne Bitterman)

FIG. 17-2

Large magnification of a small patch of light made by hot sun on water. This detail is normally not visible to the naked eye. What forms do you see emerging here? The suggestions to the pictorial imagination may be principally of figures in fluid juxtaposition.

FIG. 17-1

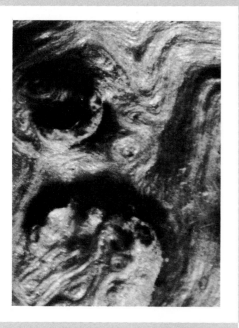

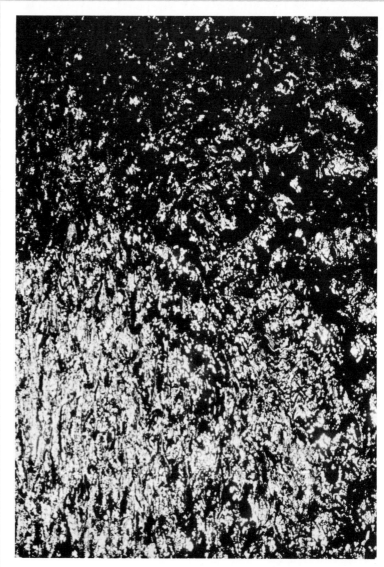

FIG. 17-2

THE EXPERIMENT

You will need a piece of string about 18 inches long, which will be used to make the first strange images. A sheet of white drawing paper not smaller than 22″ x 15″ is also needed. Now make a solution of black drawing ink or black water-color paint in a fairly shallow bowl; but do not dilute the strength of the black too much, or it will produce too pale and watery a mark. Spread some newspapers on the floor for protection and place the white drawing paper in the center. Immerse the string thoroughly in the black solution. On removing it from the bowl, squeeze it lightly to remove surplus liquid and then throw it down on the sheet of drawing paper.

When the string strikes the paper, it will recoil and twist and make a distinctive line or mark. Different types of string will make different kinds of lines and the manner in which the string is used will affect the mark produced. If the string is dropped rather than thrown, or if it is held at one end rather than rolled up in the palm, a different marking of the paper will result.

Once the first marks are on the paper, you may feel that the second throwing should be made with some deliberation, in such a way that it will create a certain relationship with the first mark. If so, this is all to the good. But for the purposes of this experiment, a series of random throwings of the string can be just as effective. When it is apparent that there are sufficient black lines and marks on the paper, that to add any more would confuse the "string drawing" already made, it is time to stop.

Now devote some time to scrutiny and contemplation of this complex pattern. Leave the "drawing" and then return to it, for too intense a scrutiny at one time will deaden rather than enliven your perception. The word "contemplation" suggests a relaxed and passive communion with the object or image, an attitude that is necessary here. After a while, definite shapes will emerge from the jumble of lines, shapes which start off ideas in the mind, stir the feelings, and suggest a new and

214

more eloquent mental image. As you turn the paper around and upside down, you will see a variety of emerging forms, already partially set in a design or composition. The pictorial imagination must now take over. The goal is to realize these new images. Using a drawing pen and black ink, draw over and into the significant shapes that emerged from their background as you contemplated the string markings. Consciously exploit and pull out, through drawing, the new image your imagination has projected into them. But take pains to give some interrelationship to the forms in the drawing and to give the design an over-all spatial organization. The drawing, when complete, should be a homogeneous figure, since all the forms are developed from a common ancestor—the tracery of string marks.

It is interesting to note that when this experiment is performed by a group of students, roughly two-thirds will generally find objective representations in the patterns, such as figures in a landscape, fish beneath the sea, houses, trees, and so on. But here they will be drawn with far more vitality of line, far more expressive distortion, and with a stronger rhythmic movement than would be found in any normal drawing of the same subject matter. A higher degree of perception and imagination allows the other third of the group to find very personal forms in the string drawing (Fig. 17-3). These students will produce forms suggestive of the physical or emotional, or of such abstract concepts as "dignity" and "infinity."

Conclusions

Manipulating a string in this way is, of course, no serious substitute for the personal act of drawing. But it is a way of producing images for a direct stimulus to the pictorial imagination; and once experienced, stimulation will more readily occur in future situations. The capacity for vision, even of this elementary order, is a *sine qua non* for the artist. Without it he is merely a human camera. This experiment should have taxed your imagination and introduced you to the idea of metamorphosis in art. As Picasso has said, "A palm tree can become a horse. . . ."

215

Art operates on two levels: the genuinely creative and the merely derivative. The first tends to be a product of vision, and the second is a matter of reproducing an object or scene. The miracle of art lies in the artist's capacity for imaginative reaches of vision (see Fig. 17-4) and the hope is that the rest of us can keep up with him. William Blake, the nineteenth-century English visionary, once wrote: "He who does not imagine in stronger and better lineaments and in stronger and better light, than his perishing mortal eye can see, does not imagine at all."

Imagination is our most creative faculty. We all possess it to some degree, and we use it all the time. But we can all work to increase its effectiveness. Without it, we would have no sense of curiosity about the wonder of life, no speculative daydreams, and no creation in any of the arts.

FIG. 17-3

The development of a string drawing. The marks made by the string have almost disappeared in the over-drawing with the pen. Nevertheless, they were sufficient to engage the student's pictorial imagination for conscious development into this design. This is the sole purpose of initiating a configuration of lines and marks by means of string: to involve the student in further and more deliberate drawing.

FIG. 17-4

THE SLEEPING GYPSY

FIG. 17-3

FIG. 17-4

18

imaginative drawing
from
the model

Throughout this book we have stressed the importance of observation. Indeed, all of Part One was concerned with an objective and analytical inquiry into the nature of form and space. And drawing was the means by which we revealed the result of our inquiry.

As we have seen thus far in Part Two, the creative process is composed of three stages: perception, vision, and imaginative expression through some medium for giving form to vision. The experiment in this chapter unites these three factors in a drawing exercise. It requires acute observation of an object, going beyond an awareness of its external appearance; this demands perception. At the same time, it suggests certain ideas about the object which will provoke an imaginative attitude toward it; this involves vision. And then, through drawing, the object is transformed into a significant and expressive graphic image; here form is given to vision.

Since the model will be an object of volume and mass, the contour line could be used to reveal the underlying structure of the form. Also, since the object has a complex surface organization composed of planes and curved surfaces, points of thrust, and surface tensions, you might want to refer, for guidance, to the work carried out in Form V (Chapter 9). It is this dramatic quality of its surface which gives the object

LA SAINTE FACE
Georges Rouault
An arresting and compulsive image by one of France's greatest modern masters. The spontaneity of its execution suggests an almost simultaneous realization through drawing of the mental image. Here lies its graphic power. (Musée National d'Art Moderne, Paris)

219

some of the power that is its vitality and its fascination.

In this experiment, the object is the human head. To help stimulate your imagination, we will briefly discuss the type of personal character to be expressed in the new drawing. Late medieval writers often referred to the seven deadly sins of mankind: pride, avarice, lust, anger, gluttony, envy, and sloth. In the religious mystery plays of the Middle Ages, the actor portraying a particular sin would wear a mask that was shaped and painted to represent the sin. The mask was ordinarily semi-flat, to fit across the front of the face. However, the point of this exercise is not to design a mask, but to draw the head, to show the volume of the skull with its holes and bony projections. Nor should you concentrate on a likeness of the sitter. Rather, try to capture the structure of the head as an object of mass.

Select one of the seven deadly sins and let your imagination build up a facial image of it. What kind of a head conveys the idea of pride? Or of envy, or gluttony? As you draw from the model, try to adapt the natural form of the head to express your feelings toward the particular sin you have chosen, and portray your mental image of it. Your drawing should be meaningful as form (this is where the observation is necessary), and expressive of the sin (this is the imaginative element).

THE EXPERIMENT

A formally posed model is not necessary. Ask someone near you to hold his head in profile for a minute or so while you observe him. The profile is deliberately chosen because it aids perception of the structural elements of the head. Look intently at the profile and explore with your eye the movement of the planes and curved surfaces as they move over high points into valleys and along the ridges. More than likely you will find your eyes returning to one point, through which all the rhythms of movement seem to pass: the cheekbone, the high point where the bone of the skull pushes hard against the skin of the face. It reflects light and is a point of strong thrust that creates a surface tension on the skin stretched tightly over it.

There are two other main thrust points on the profile: the chin and the out-jutting frontal bone of the forehead above the eyebrow. The structure of the profile is organized around these three points of the skull. If you will recall the analogy we used in Form V (Chapter 9) to illustrate the proposition that surface planes and curves tend to be organized around a thrust force—the analogy of the cloth over the vertical pole—you will realize that the same thing is happening here over the surface of the face. If we carry this analogy further, we can compare the profile to a tent where the canvas is pulled tight around poles stuck in the ground. Where the canvas pulls against a pole, it changes its plane or direction. The form of the tent is determined by the positions of the poles; although they are not visible, you perceive they are there because of the surface tension of the canvas at the places where its surface changes direction. Our perception of the face and head works in very much the same way. From the surface tension of the skin and the change in surface direction, we learn something about the bony skull we cannot see. The eyes are in sockets or holes (we have done some drawing of holes earlier), while the rest of the profile is high ground or valley.

We are now beginning to go beyond appearances to a perception of the true structure of the head. One significant aspect of this experiment is the use of the contour line. If you will study Fig. 18-1, you will see that a strongly defined "flat" outline of the head does not appear. There is no dominant edge to the head; instead, the plane and curve just disappear beyond the line of sight, because no outline of the profile was drawn in the first place. The drawing was not started at the "edge," but was commenced within the form, at its most projecting point, the high point of the cheekbone.

Using the revolving contour line, draw the projection of the cheekbone, with the same technique you used to make the holes and projections of the wood form in Form II (Chapter 4). Now work *out* from this high point, allowing the pen or pencil to move rhythmically and to describe the planes and curved surfaces surrounding the cheekbone. Suggest the angle and direction of each plane—imaginatively feel it with your fingertips—and notice the rhythmic link these surfaces have with the chin and with the forehead. Each plane and curve can be seen, felt, and drawn as a separate contour region, yet all seem to revolve through and around the thrust points of the cheek, chin, and forehead. Like the canvas of a tent, the movements of the skin indicate the structure beneath. It is possible to draw this head without drawing an outline of any kind. As the line moves out from the cheekbone, exploring the various planes and curves, it stops automatically at the limits of the profile. In this way the mass of the head is realized through the drawing.

A glance at Figs. 18-1 and 18-2 will suffice to indicate how the characteristics of the sin have been expressed. The contour line has expressed the structure of the form, but the sin has been realized through imaginatively exploiting individual features: eyes, nose, and mouth, are specifically designed to reveal the feelings and mental images stimulated by envy and sloth. The features have then been arranged for the maximum of effect: eyes close together or far apart, deeply sunk or protruding, the mouth turning up or down, and the nose shown as beaklike or retroussé. Also, certain parts of the head have been distorted for expressive effect; bulging forehead and disappearing chin, for example. But all these imaginative treatments of the form have been heightened by the use of the contour line which has been adapted to express them.

Your drawing may well take two or three hours to make. The first drawings were made in pencil, with frequent reference to the model for information. These preliminary drawings were based principally on observation, although the contour line was used and the structural basis was derived from the three thrust points. The second drawings, which are those reproduced here, were made by reference to both the first drawings and the model. By then the artists were more confident and better able to give form to mental images without worrying too much about technique or form structure. Thus the head could take on its own imaginative existence as the epitome of the chosen sin.

Conclusions

All the important deductions from this experiment are really self-evident. A study of the drawings reproduced will yield some of them, even without reference to the text. But we should repeat the fundamental reason for making this drawing. It is to indicate that the creative process in the visual arts must integrate several seemingly independent factors. The first of these is sight itself, the process of observation. Second comes

FIG. 18-1

HEAD OF SLOTH
Imaginative drawing from the model.

perception, by which observation produces meaningful knowledge of the thing seen. Third is vision, through which this meaningful knowledge releases a whole range of imaginative ideas and mental imagery accompanied by intensified feeling. And finally we come to the means of expression—line, form, and color, disposed in space—without which, of course, the preceding stages can be nought.

This experiment has used all four of these stages. It has cheated a little because the imaginative idea about the head was injected verbally in the text and did not spring from perception of the object itself. One final point concerns the question of technique. Only when technique is not a conscious problem can the artist really work creatively. One of the values of using the contour line to express structure is that it enables the artist to depict volume and form by second nature, without thinking much about it. He is free to express his attitude, to know himself through drawing.

FIG. 18-2

HEAD OF ENVY
Imaginative drawing from the model.

FIG. 18-3

LA SAINTE FACE

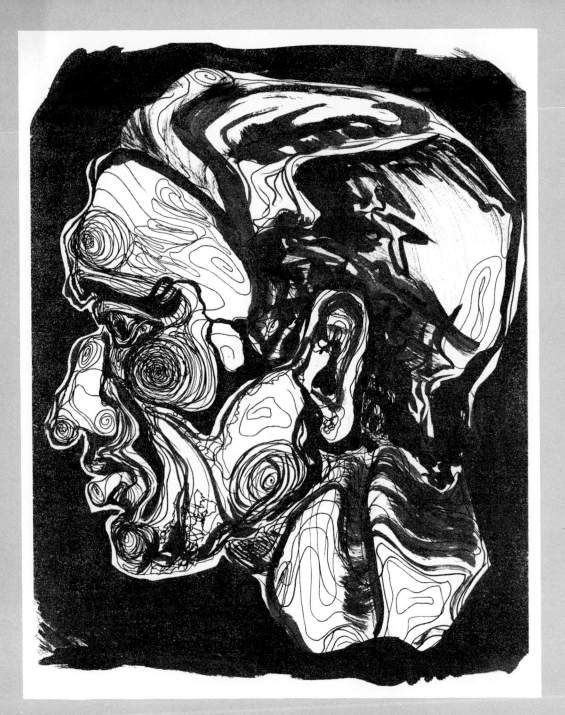

FIG. 18-2

FIG. 18-3

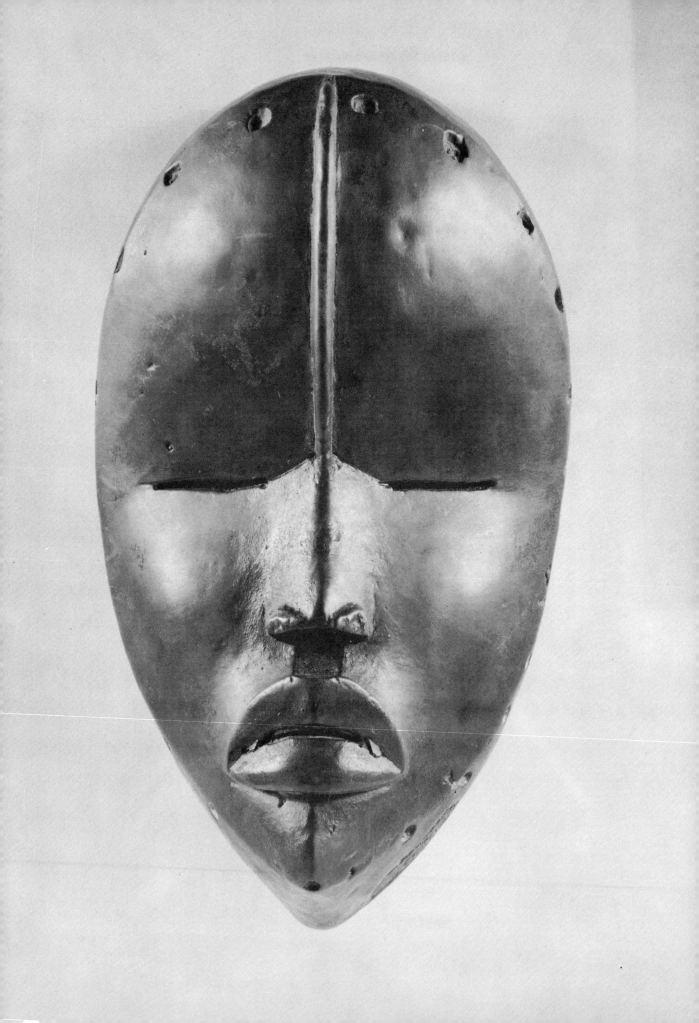

simultaneous observation and imagination

AFRICAN DANCE MASK,
IVORY COAST
*The simplified form given to
the head in this mask is
based on an awareness of the
skull structure beneath the
surface. The forehead, cheek-
bones, and chin become high
points through which all the
facial rhythms move.
(The American Museum of
Natural History)*

In this section, we will follow up the experiment in Vision V (Chapter 18) using the human head again as the subject, but this time with no verbal suggestion in the text to stimulate the imagination. The drawing medium also will be changed.

One of the principal conclusions reached after the last experiment was that a preoccupation with the technical difficulties of drawing or painting stifles the creative spontaneity that we associate with vision in art. Creative spontaneity is closely related to the developing process in art. Both are aspects of the visual imagination. The difference between them is simply one of time. Creative spontaneity refers to the immediate impulse to draw, to the first drawing, which sets the artist working and the sequence of images in motion: something he sees involves his imagination sufficiently for him to draw it and thus invest it with significance. The developing process, on the other hand, signifies the further development of this first drawing, step by step. As a sequence of events, creative spontaneity comes first, followed by the developing process, which is a building on to the graphic *image*, rather than the result of an immediate perception of the *object*.[1] This

---

[1] In the work of the great artists, no such separation can be made. Creative spontaneity and the development of the image are fused, independent of time, in one inspirational act of expression.

experiment is concerned with creative spontaneity, with the quality of the immediate expression in a first drawing. Ask yourself why the drawings of young children about the age of five or six are so appealing. If you watch them drawing, you will see that they are not concerned with technical problems of representation and they have no self-conscious worries about whether others will understand or approve their drawing. The result has an urgent and vital quality because it is an immediate expression, stemming directly from the child's feelings and ideas about the object or the experience.

The purpose of the exercise proposed in this chapter is to help increase your capacity for creative spontaneity. Or to put it another way, it is to produce the conditions under which an immediate and unself-conscious response to an object or an experience can be made, a response or expression through drawing uninhibited by the technical problems of an academic approach.

But first we should explain what is meant by the title of this chapter, "Simultaneous Observation and Imagination." When we look at an object, we see not only its outward appearance but also its personal significance, and in that, we are using imagination. If you see a truck speeding toward you when you are crossing the street, you realize its potential danger and you move quickly out of its path. You have observed the appearance of the truck, but you have also had a significant realization of what would happen if you did not get out of the way. Or if you are thinking of buying some drinking glasses you may observe their shape, size, and color, but you also imagine yourself holding the glass and drinking from it. But the imagining need not be so utilitarian. The object can also take on symbolic significance. A piece of wood in the grass, for instance, could imaginatively become a snake. A drawing which is the immediate response to an object usually manages to combine the observed and the imaginative aspects of the object in a single, urgent expression; such a drawing possesses creative spontaneity.

The artist, by definition, has a highly developed imagination that enables him to visualize in an object many things that do not relate to its utilitarian possibilities. Such imaginative understanding, accompanied by strong feeling, is, as we have seen, of the nature of vision for the artist. He would tend to

FIG. 19-1

Monoprint of the observed head.

see the stick in the grass, for example, as a snake rather than as a club. For the layman, who is less sensitive visually than the artist, this simultaneous operation of seeing and imagining is at a less developed state. But if the layman, when making a drawing, could be as natural as a child—who more often than not has an artist's imagination—he, too, will unconsciously exploit a high degree of creative spontaneity and produce a drawing filled with the magic of art. As John Piper, the contemporary British painter (see Fig. 9-5), once remarked, "Child artists are the natural enemies of adult ones."

The head is a very significant object, expressive of all the qualities we associate with humankind—dignity, nobility, beauty, and on down the list. But it is also difficult to draw—another reason for choosing it as a model. Drawing the head is often given as an exercise in drawing skill, and the result is frequently academic, lifeless, and the very opposite of what we have called "creative spontaneity." In this experiment we will attempt to show how drawing the head can be transformed into a spontaneous and creative experience, for the layman as well as for the artist.

Earlier, we saw the inked surface of a glass plate as a sensitive medium for both tone and line drawing, from which a print can be pulled. Since this medium allows marks of drawing to be achieved rapidly and with ease, we will use it to overcome the technical difficulties that act as a barrier to creative spontaneity. The previous experiment focused our attention on the structure of the head and face and thus provided information about the object which will help you (the self-conscious adult) tackle this new drawing with freedom and surety.

THE EXPERIMENT

The head is a subtle structure of bony protuberances, planes, curves, and holes. This much we have already discovered. To sit down and make the customary pencil sketch of it may be a difficult and laborious task with a number of snares. If one does not observe the head as a whole, he may spend hours on one eye, trying to "get it right," without realizing that it needs the other eye to pull it into its context. The novice draws every-

FIG. 19-2

Monoprint of the observed head.

thing he sees quite separately, and the head becomes a life-less mask, a collection of parts.

In the last exercise (see Figs. 18-1 and 18-2), we found that the three high points of the head—through which all the sur-faces, planes, and curves move and which are the structural bases for the form—are the chin, cheekbone, and forehead. Using the contour line, it was impossible to be sidetracked by all the details of the face: the eye sat simply in its hollow socket, the nose was a projecting plane, and the mouth fitted into the contour line's organization of the surface of the face.

Similarly, the inked surface of the glass plate does not allow preoccupation with individual features. The ink dries fairly rapidly, and one cannot see very much of what is happening on the plate, so there is no stopping to make constant compari-sons with the model and no worrying because the drawing does not "look right."

Drawing the head on the glass plate demands an immediate reaction to the object. What goes down there is a "first seen" quality—the result of the immediate impulse to draw—without fussy drawing of representational details. It is useful to work in pairs for this experiment, with one person modeling and one drawing. Ink the glass plate and assemble all the tools pre-viously found useful for drawing in the ink. (A piece of rag for wiping off ink, to make strong white parts in the drawing, is a necessity for this experiment.)

The plate is ready, and the head is before you. You have about half an hour to work on the glass before the ink becomes too dry. Start by wiping off the ink to give the high point of the cheekbone, and then do the same for the chin and the fore-head, allowing the highly fluid quality of the medium its own freedom of movement. Work rapidly, taking a look at the head and then moving directly into the ink: scrape, brush, scratch, and wipe.

In conclusion, we will let the illustrations speak for them-selves. Four heads drawn in the manner described above are reproduced in Figs. 19-1 to 19-4. Each of these drawings is a simple statement of essentials. There is a minimum of detail and an emphasis on the broad masses of light and dark or, rather, the high points and the depressions (see Fig. 19-5). The forehead, cheekbone, and chin dominate the drawings. The eyes sit in their inky sockets: and where the artist has felt

FIG. 19-3

Monoprint of the observed head.

the need for some linear definition, as in the eyelids of Fig. 19-4, a sharp tool has drawn for a moment in the ink.

After this direct approach for so short a time, the glass gives little indication of the drawing made in the ink. The print, when taken, is quite a shock. The head that emerges is bold in form and vital and convincing as drawing. It is full of life and drama. In it, in fact, observation and imagination have simultaneously produced a drawing of creative spontaneity. When you study your print, think of the pencil drawing you might have made of this head.

FIG. 19-4

Monoprint of the observed head.

FIG. 19-5

AFRICAN DANCE MASK

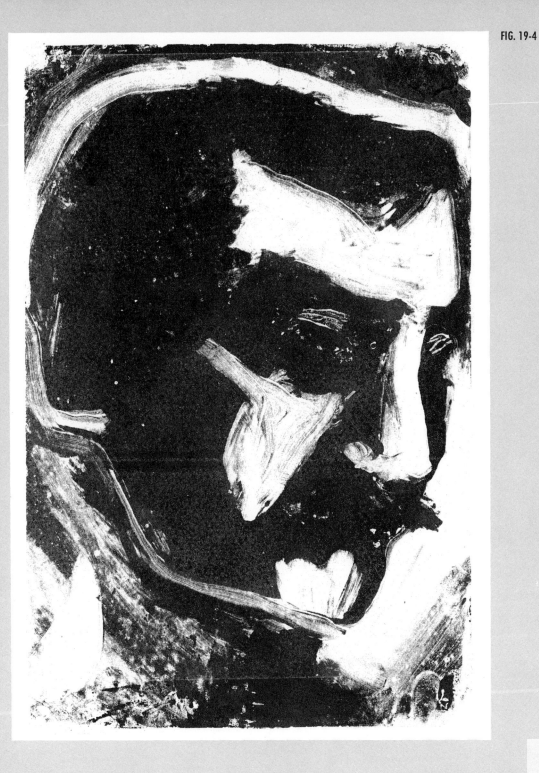

FIG. 19-4

FIG. 19-5

20
looking with intent: simultaneous aspects of objects

The phrase "looking with intent" was used in Part One to suggest that there are degrees of looking, the most common of which is to look at a thing vaguely, merely for purposes of identification, or even just to avoid falling over it. But when we are looking intently, identification is a secondary goal, for we are interested; we are curious to discover all we can, visually, about the object. We also experience what was described in the previous chapter as the simultaneous operation of the imagination. The eye, physically, takes in all it can see, while the imagination speculates on unseen aspects of the object.

What are these "other aspects" of an object? They fall into two categories. There are those that cannot be seen from one particular viewing position, but which we know about through having seen them on other occasions from a different position (the other side of the object, for example). Secondly, there are those that cannot be seen from an external viewing position: the hidden, internal aspects of the object. We must dissect the object in order to project images of these aspects. In the case of some objects, we can actually physically dissect them and reveal their internal prospect (see Fig. 20-1), and this view can later, when we look at the exterior of the object, be conjured up by the mind's eye. Take a tomato, for instance. Externally, it is round and red. But if you slice up enough

VIOLIN AND GRAPES (1912)
Pablo Picasso
An illustration in the late Cubist style of fragmentation of the object, which inevitably occurs when the artist is concerned with revealing several aspects of the form or revealing structural essentials. (Collection, The Museum of Modern Art, New York. Mrs. David M. Levy Bequest)

237

tomatoes, you will become so familiar with their inside sectional appearance that you will never see a tomato without also visualizing its cross section. Many forms and objects, however, cannot be easily dissected. Our imagination has to act like a surgeon's knife and cut through the object to reveal those hidden places of which we have no sensory knowledge.

This kind of X-ray approach, which leads inevitably to the fragmentation of the object, has been one of the major interests of modern painting during this century. The early cubist style of Pablo Picasso and Georges Braque in 1908-1909 imposed the artist's structural geometry on the natural form of the object. When this structural fragmentation was allied to a paint surface of arbitrary tonal planes, the breakdown of the natural form was complete. Eventually, paintings were built up by such "fragmented masonry" without the painter having recourse to any visual subject matter. The form was developed imaginatively, to take on its own life (see Chapter 16, Vision III, "Pictorial quality").

Later phases of cubism introduced the practice of depicting not only what can be *seen* of an object, but also what is *known* about the object, all in one painting. This, of course, produced many difficulties for the viewer, who had been conditioned for so many centuries to an art concerned only with the appearance of things seen from one viewpoint. "Simultaneous projection" in art, the cubist invention of combining differing aspects of the figure or object in the same composition, thus projecting them simultaneously, produced paintings of the head, for example, with a profile superimposed over a full face. Picasso's "Violin and Grapes" (Fig. 20-2) treats the subject matter in the same way. The painter shows us the full face and the profile of the instrument, together with several other aspects of the object. Such an imaginative break-up of the forms will obviously reveal more about the subject than the traditional single-viewpoint representation. It is like getting several paintings for the price of one!

The following experiment will introduce you to the many differing aspects of apparently simple objects. Its primary purpose is to initiate the habit of looking with intent, to instill an awareness of the unseen, to take you once more to the brink of nonobjective art by yet another path. The work will be carried out in three parts. First, through a series of experi-

FIG. 20-1

Cross section of the lily seed pod revealing aspects of the form difficult to imagine from merely external appearances.

FIG. 20-2

VIOLIN AND GRAPES

FIG. 20-1

FIG. 20-2

mental drawings you will imaginatively reveal different exposures of three simple geometric figures. At some stage, a symbol of the object should emerge. Then will follow a series of internal "aspect drawings" made after physically cutting into a fruit. Finally, you will be asked to translate one series of drawings into a composite pictorial design, by projecting simultaneously all the discovered exposures of the object.

THE EXPERIMENTS

Make a cone, a cylinder, and a solid triangle of stiff paper. They do not need to be very accurate or very large—about 6 inches high is large enough to serve as models which can be imaginatively broken down through drawing. Made from paper, they are, of course, hollow; the model is a defined region of space rather than a solid form. As we pointed out in Form II (Chapter 4), volume has this dual role.

In this experiment, the two roles of volume are interchangeable. There is no need to make a base for these figures, since you will need to pick them up and look inside. The first step is to make a series of small drawings of each figure. First, make a straightforward drawing of the model as it appears at the normal eye level. Place this in the top left corner of the sheet of paper, then produce a series of 2-inch squares to the right side of it and beneath in orderly rows. You may need between ten to twenty squares.

The goal is to draw as many different aspects of the paper model as you possibly can. Figures 20-3 and 20-4 are the drawing responses made to this exercise by several students. How are such responses achieved? First, by viewing the object from many different positions and drawing each new observation. This is easy to do, for the model can be picked up and held at many angles and in many positions. Three or four drawings made in this way are sufficient. The drawings which follow are more difficult. For now you are asked to draw not just what you *see* but what your eye and imagination together can reveal. Try to visualize the object cut through and opened out. Imaginative fragmentation of the model is not easy, particularly if the fragment when drawn is to retain its identity as part of a cone, or a cylinder, or a solid triangle. A study of Figs. 20-3 and 20-4 will indicate the many forms that visual-

FIG. 20-3

Drawings exploring the aspects of a cone.

FIG. 20-4

Drawings exploring the aspects of a cylinder.

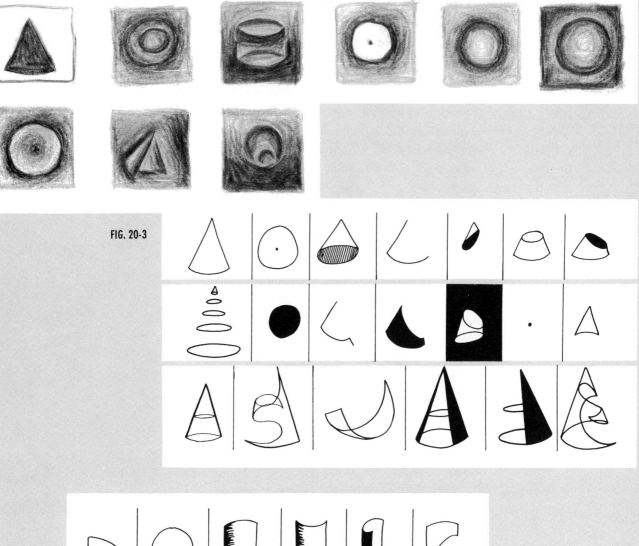

FIG. 20-3

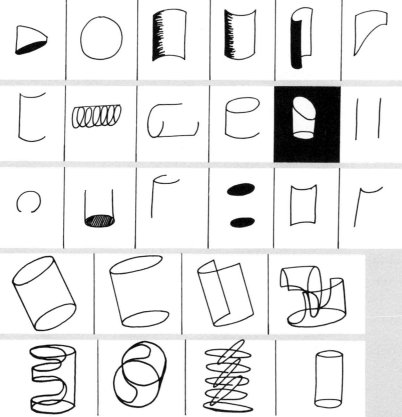

FIG. 20-4

imaginative fragmentation can take. Some of the drawings can be taken as aspects of a solid figure; others are regions of space, partly defined by a shell—such is the imaginative interchangeability between solid form and defined space, to which we previously referred in Form II (Chapter 4). Again, some of these drawings become so simple as linear symbols of the object that they are almost a form of "writing."

Eventually, you will have exhausted the aspect possibilities of this particular object. Some people may have only seven or eight drawings, others as many as twenty. When you have completed the drawings of all three objects, select one drawing from each series which in your opinion is the simplest in terms of drawing, yet which also has the strongest power to suggest the likeness or the idea of the original model. If you have made such a drawing, it could be termed a symbol of the object. A visual symbol must possess strong communicative power; therefore it must be simple, and it must be abstracted from the original object. All the aspects you have made of the three objects are also abstractions of the objects. It follows from this that such an abstraction can possess symbolic power.

The second part of this experiment consists of making drawings similar to those just completed. But, now, instead of *imaginatively* cutting through the object, we shall actually cut it with a knife. Use some kind of fruit, such as a lemon or a tomato. This series of drawings should be set out on a single sheet of paper exactly like the others, with a simple drawing of the whole fruit made in the top lefthand corner. Now, proceed to cut up the model, making a drawing of each new aspect as it is revealed through the surgical operation. You will no doubt find this series of drawings easier to make, for now your imagination is reinforced by a physical reality which can be seen and handled. Figure 20-5 is an illustration based on cutting a lemon. These aspects of lemon are also abstractions of lemon, and at least one drawing could be used as a symbol of lemon.

The final work of this section touches once more on pictorial quality, at least on the part of pictorial quality which has been defined as an "expressive and significant use of shapes." Select one of the sheets of drawings which you have just made, either the aspects of the cone, cylinder, solid triangle, or fruit. You will no doubt select the drawings most successful in revealing interesting and different presentations of the model. The proposition

FIG. 20-5
Drawings revealing the discovered aspects of a lemon.

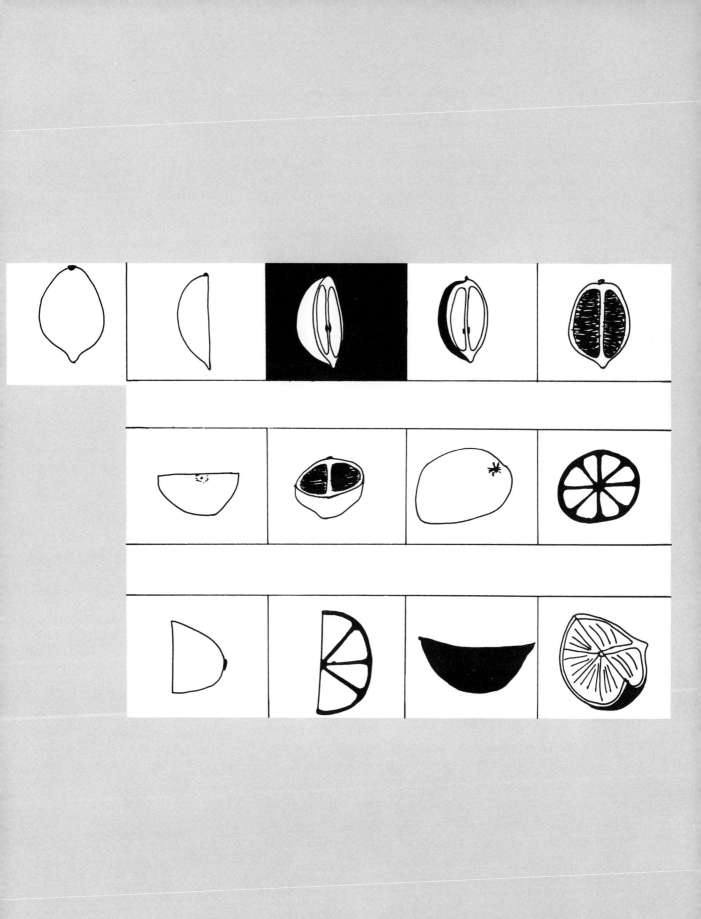

now is to take all aspect drawings of this one particular model and organize them into one pictorial design. You may fit as many as twelve or fifteen aspects into some kind of pictorial organization within a square or rectangular area. A convenient size for the area would be approximately 8″ x 8″. Make the drawing entirely in black and white. Figures 20-6 and 20-7 show two such drawings. Figure 20-7 makes use of solid black against textured white and gray, achieved with a wax-resist. Figure 20-6, however, makes use of tones or washed-in dilutions of ink to achieve the grays. In both of these illustrations, the differing aspects of the one object are projected simultaneously into the picture area to make an expressive and significant organization of shapes. Figure 20-7 is formed from the aspects of the solid triangle; Fig. 20-6 from aspects of the cone.

Conclusions

Now we can see that if new and unfamiliar exposures of an object are revealed when we look with intent, the act of drawing aids such visual, imaginative exploration and, at the same time, fixes and makes permanent the image of the new aspect. Without the drawing, no permanent visual sign or symbol of the discovery remains, either to provide a graphic image for any imaginative development or to elicit a direct response per se.

As you regard Figs. 20-6 and 20-7, one important question should be asked. Could these pictorial designs have been achieved as effectively by a deliberate drawing of a "set" subject, say a pictorial presentation of lemons, or triangles? From the author's experience with his own students, his answer would be "No." Left to your own devices with such a subject, it is more than likely that you would have concentrated in building up a formal composition, say of lemons, as they would appear from one viewpoint, rather than considering their hidden aspects as potential shapes for pictorial design. There is no doubt that the three drawings illustrated have benefited compositionally from all our previous work on structure and on the organization of space. In fact, because of our earlier study, we do not need a set experiment dealing with "composition." Composition involves simply the manipulation of space and a structural significance given to form, and these are things we have been dealing with right from the beginning. The importance of these final drawings, within the context of this chapter,

FIG. 20-6

Aspects of the cone simultaneously projected in a drawing achieving pictorial quality.

FIG. 20-7

Aspects of the solid triangle simultaneously projected in a drawing achieving pictorial quality.

FIG. 20-6

FIG. 20-7

lies in their authentic exposition of a single object. They are both convincing and revealing as studies of "cone-ness" or "triangle-ness." They go beyond a representation of external appearances to show the greater reality of the object's total nature. And although they are nearly abstract, the link connecting them to an act of perception—to looking with intent—may still be recognized.

For the beginning student, the perceptive act is an important factor. He should be able to take the thing seen and consider its total nature, its many aspects rather than recognize merely its external characteristics. Art is not imitative reproduction, or a kind of pretty picture-making, or a purely mechanical exercise of pattern-making. Art is an attitude to life and the things of life; it is an awareness of the structural and organic rhythms of the universe, visually expressed. This is the kind of commitment an artist, and a student of art, must have. It is a commitment to reveal (from a position of inquiry and personal attitude) rather than to imitate. The final works of this chapter should be the result of such an attitude, which is initiated by looking with intent, sustained by inquiry and an increased power of perception, developed by reason, and accompanied by a heightened emotional urge. These elements are synthesized in the two drawings previously mentioned.

Free drawing to find a symbol

By now, you should realize that the ways of drawing can be as varied as the ways of writing a letter, and just as personal. We have seen that the quality of a drawing is not based primarily on the amount of time or sweat put into it—or even on the skill applied. Instead, it depends on how intently the artist has looked at things, and how rich his imagination has been in creating images that carry him beyond mere visual reality or appearances. Any markings made in any medium to record the image, we have called "drawing." How much of this concept will have been assimilated by a person reading and drawing his way through this book cannot be easily assessed. It is probably better if comprehension exists at a subconscious level, for too conscious a striving to attain it destroys spontaneity of vision, so necessary to art.

With all this in mind, a group of students were given a deliberately vague briefing and then left entirely alone. The

FIG. 20-8

Quick studies from observation of the eye.

intention was to follow up the work in Chapter 20 but without any rigid terms of reference. They were asked to pick an object and then reduce it to a symbol through drawing. The symbol was then to be used freely and imaginatively as the motif for the cutting of a linoleum block. Two or three students chose the human eye as their object, and it is their work which illustrates this concluding experiment. First they made some drawings directly from the eye, but with a boldness and vigor that indicates their freedom from worry about technical means (they all used a different medium). It was as if the previous work had released inhibitions about "drawing," enabling them to concentrate on more expressive aspects of the eye.

Figure 20-8 is typical of the first drawings executed with pen, brush, and finger—in ink, pencil, and even monoprint. The treatment of one of these drawings is derived from those rapid sketches of twigs made in Drawing Marks I (Chapter 2). But none of them are characterized by that hesitant groping after irrelevant linear detail which enfeebles beginning drawing.

To simplify the first drawing was the next task. Without prompting, the students executed many small, rapid sketches of various aspects of the eyes, breaking down the first drawing. Each sketch was a graphic image in its own right, and each suggested the degree of simplification required to produce the next drawing. The final drawing produced a concrete image of "eye-ness," to which, in the student's opinion, nothing could be added or subtracted without detriment to the symbol that had emerged. Figure 20-9 shows seven such sketches culminating in a subtle and refined symbol abstraction in the shape of a scroll. This final drawing is a monoprint taken from the glass plate. These seven drawings make use of a cunning interchange of black and white. In drawing number 3, the white space in the center of the eye becomes the black eyeball in drawing number 4, thus clarifying the earlier confusion in this part of the drawing.

These drawings represent the "developing idea" in action once more. When we look at Fig. 20-9, we wonder if drawing number 7 could have been achieved directly from the first eye drawing without the six stages of transition. Probably not. Nor is there much doubt that the enthusiasm and comparative ease with which these drawings were produced came partly from the student's ability to "look with intent," to

FIG. 20-9

Seven drawings illustrating the step-by-step reduction of the eye drawing to its final abstract symbol.

1

2

3

4

5

6

7

discover aspects of objects that otherwise would have been passed over.

When the eye was finally reduced by drawing to a symbol, a symbol that lacked none of the essential qualities of eye but that had added a certain mysterious unintelligibility [1] to the idea of "eye-ness," the final project could be started. The only instruction given to the group at this point referred them back to the linoleum block prints made in Vision I (Chapter 14) and suggested that study of these would indicate good balances of black and white, of line to area, and so on. The problem then was to transfer the eye symbol to the surface of a large block of linoleum. Figure 20-10 illustrates one of the results. In this design, the eye motif is still visible, although in translating the drawing to the block the eye could easily enough have been lost through the expansion of the motif the problem demands. This is an intelligent and pleasing use of the motif. Vital in movement and rhythm, with space and form convincingly integrated through the organic sweep of linear patterns, the design is complete as it stands.

One of the most difficult things to develop is the ability to see a shape or an image in more than one context. For example, a twig with its bud might well become the model for a concrete street lamp, or as we have already seen in Form V (Chapter 9), a crumpled piece of paper can become a mountainside. The students performing the concluding exercise experienced less difficulty in this regard than do most beginners. They moved from the observed object to imaginative abstractions in drawing, and on to the changes in the motif necessitated by engraving a block, without the usual awkward and tentative transitions. They readily jumped from medium to medium to give expression to their ideas and were not overly worried about "how to draw." Their understanding that there are many aspects of reality, their willingness to probe beyond mere appearances, their realization that they, themselves, possess attitudes about things, and that these are spontaneously expressible—all this contributed to their freedom.

No doubt artists are still born and not made. But even the nonprofessional artist may aspire to creative rather than imitative levels of performance.

_____

[1] See Space III (Chapter 7) for Sir Herbert Read's statement concerning the symbol and "unintelligibility."

FIG. 20-10

Linoleum block design based on the abstract eye motif.

REVIEW

Vision I

Building up a nonobjective design through addition and sub-traction can be carried out without using the linoleum block.

1. Scratchboard can be used by scraping out a white shape first, putting part of it back with brush and ink, scraping out again and then inking back, until, by this give-and-take method, the area is eventually occupied by some arrangement of black and white forms.

2. On a white sheet of paper, using two brushes—one for white paint and one for black—build up forms. First add free black forms, then modify them by breaking into them with white paint. Continue this process of alternate addition and subtraction until the design is complete.

3. Work as in 2 above, with charcoal and kneaded eraser. Use the charcoal to lay in areas of black quite freely on the paper and use the eraser actually as a drawing tool, to take off in the black regions. Build up until the design is complete.

Vision II

The following experiments are suggested to develop a stronger realization of common qualities of "shapeness" between forms and of how small a change in form is required to produce a new aesthetic implication.

1. Draw freely with a brush and ink on a large sheet of paper to discover the transitions by which a square becomes a circle. Brush in a solid square at the top left, and working to the right, repeat this square, but make one change in its shape on each occasion. For example, the second square might lose a corner, the third another corner, and so on, until a complete circle results. Repeat this by going from cylinder to cone, square to triangle, etc. Notice the intermediate stages and realize how basically "near" each other are these forms. Try this shape metamorphosis by brush drawing transitions from free forms, and see what shapes result.

2. Using two illustrations from this book for references, the Greek amphora (Fig. 8-17), and the wine glasses (Fig. 15-3), make a series of drawings of each object, each drawing attempting to exploit further the most personally attractive aspect of the original. The aspect might be the object's curvature, or its slim proportion, or its angularity. How far can this expressive change go before it degenerates into caricature or vulgar exaggeration and novelty? Is the original object already at a point of maximum aesthetic expression?

3. Change unitary form into compound form. In a rectangle about 9″ x 7″, brush in a solid black circle occupying approximately one-fifth of the total area. Using the brush, extend this figure into the remaining area of the rectangle by pulling out limbs, protrusions, etc. Stop when the new form is sufficiently complex and when the empty area is satisfactorily occupied. This extension process can be done with many different types of unitary form.

Vision III

Sensitivity to pictorial quality is most effectively induced by a personal involvement with shape and with color, an involvement demanding value judgments of a personal nature. Here are two suggestions for work in this chapter.

1. Try abstracting from great paintings. Select some prints of paintings by El Greco, Rubens, Titian, Raphael, or other great artists (magazine reproductions are quite suitable for this). Pick out the main forms of the design and the main rhythms which hold the design together.

Attempt to express these forms and these rhythms in a black water-color drawing with a full range of tones, one which will be an expressive abstract of the original.

2. Collect a whole range of possible collage material centered around a specific color range—reds to browns or blues to greens—and consider textures and forms as well as color. Select from a wide range of sources. Assemble a design using this material, bearing in mind the phrase, "a significant and expressive combination of shapes and colors." Remember the complementary function of black and white to color. When the assemblage is complete, varnish it. This will give a homogenous quality to the color and the forms of the design.

Vision IV

A constant exercise of the imagination must always be sought in art. The following work is suggested as an appendage to the chapter on the pictorial imagination.

1. Select some large, full-page black-and-white photographs from books or magazines and using four pieces of paper, mask out areas of the picture, thus allowing concentration on one small region. After some experimentation, select one such region and enlarge it into a black-and-white drawing which will almost certainly be abstract, and which may possess its own strong pictorial quality.

2. Spatter some blots, large and small, onto a sheet of drawing paper. What do they suggest? How would you draw into them? Will the finished drawing suggest a landscape or a figure? Find some reproductions of "blot drawings" made by Alexander Cozens, the English eighteenth-century landscape painter.

3. Observe surfaces in nature, stained and molded surfaces of rocks, leaves, tree bark, and similar things. What suggestions of forms are to be found in these variegated surfaces; what do they suggest to the pictorial imagination? Draw!

4. Observe some highly magnified illustrations of biological cross sections. Here is a complete new world of form. Once again, what will the pictorial imagination find here? Make more drawings.

Vision V

For further imaginative drawing from the observed object:

1. From the figure, make a dozen quick drawings of diverse, five-minute poses by the model. Place the figures thus drawn in a new imaginative context in one design. It will be a help to study some of the figure compositions of Nicolas Poussin, the seventeenth-century French artist.

2. From nature, draw a cabbage. Transform this into a face of old, old age.

3. Set up some drapery, three or four separate lengths, having varied organizations of folds, in vertical formation against a wall. Keep about three feet of space between each length. Draw these vertical lengths of cloth using wide paper, and fill in the gaps by introducing an imaginary *draped* figure. This figure should not intrude, but should belong naturally among the folded material and result in an extravaganza of figure and fold.

Vision VI

Many variations can be made in monoprint technique, and they are worth developing; for as a drawing medium allowing the immediate expression of an image or an idea, the monoprint cannot be surpassed. If a drop or two of glycerine is added to the ink, this will retard drying and thus allow more time for drawing and modeling in the ink. Celluloid and plastic may be used instead of glass as the printing surface, and some strange results will occur by printing on experimental papers or materials. The medium is as valuable for free imaginative drawing as for drawing a variety of observed objects.

Vision VII

Further experiments in the breakdown of the object and the revelation of its several aspects in one composite design should be carried out in several different drawing mediums. The subject matter can extend from the natural object to the mechanical one. (Think of the aspects of an engine cylinder block, for example, as a subject for a composite design involving simultaneous projection.) It is also possible to move from the single object to the group, which presents imaginative and organizational problems of some magnitude. Development of the chapter in this way challenges one's creative and technical resources.

index

Authors

Susan Leach Snyder
Earth Science Teacher, Consultant
Jones Middle School
Upper Arlington, Ohio

Dinah Zike
Educational Consultant
Dinah-Might Activities, Inc.
San Antonio, Texas

Consultants

Content

William C. Keel, PhD
Department of Physics and
Astronomy
University of Alabama
Tuscaloosa, Alabama

Stephen M. Letro
National Weather Service
Meteorologist In Charge
Jacksonville, Florida

Safety

Aileen Duc, PhD
Science II Teacher
Hendrick Middle School
Plano, Texas

Reading

Carol A. Senf, PhD
Associate Professor of English
Georgia Institute of
Technology
Atlanta, Georgia

Math

Teri Willard, EdD
Department of Mathematics
Montana State University
Belgrade, Montana

Reviewers

Lois Burdette
Green Bank School
Green Bank, West Virginia

Marcia Chackan
Pine Crest School
Boca Raton, Florida

Annette Garcia
Kearney Middle School
Commerce City, Colorado

Nerma Coats Henderson
Pickerington Jr. High School
Pickerington, Ohio

Michael Mansour
John Page Middle School
Madison Heights, Michigan

Sharon Mitchell
William D. Slider Middle
School
El Paso, Texas

Series Activity Testers

José Luis Alvarez, PhD
Math/Science Mentor Teacher
Yseleta ISD
El Paso, Texas

Nerma Coats Henderson
Teacher
Pickerington Jr. High School
Pickerington, Ohio

Mary Helen Mariscal-Cholka
Science Teacher
William D. Slider Middle School
El Paso, Texas

José Alberto Marquez
TEKS for Leaders Trainer
Yseleta ISD
El Paso, Texas

Science Kit and Boreal Laboratories
Tonawanda, New York

SAFETY SYMBOLS

	HAZARD	EXAMPLES	PRECAUTION	REMEDY
DISPOSAL	Special disposal procedures need to be followed.	certain chemicals, living organisms	Do not dispose of these materials in the sink or trash can.	Dispose of wastes as directed by your teacher.
BIOLOGICAL	Organisms or other biological materials that might be harmful to humans	bacteria, fungi, blood, unpreserved tissues, plant materials	Avoid skin contact with these materials. Wear mask or gloves.	Notify your teacher if you suspect contact with material. Wash hands thoroughly.
EXTREME TEMPERATURE	Objects that can burn skin by being too cold or too hot	boiling liquids, hot plates, dry ice, liquid nitrogen	Use proper protection when handling.	Go to your teacher for first aid.
SHARP OBJECT	Use of tools or glassware that can easily puncture or slice skin	razor blades, pins, scalpels, pointed tools, dissecting probes, broken glass	Practice common-sense behavior and follow guidelines for use of the tool.	Go to your teacher for first aid.
FUME	Possible danger to respiratory tract from fumes	ammonia, acetone, nail polish remover, heated sulfur, moth balls	Make sure there is good ventilation. Never smell fumes directly. Wear a mask.	Leave foul area and notify your teacher immediately.
ELECTRICAL	Possible danger from electrical shock or burn	improper grounding, liquid spills, short circuits, exposed wires	Double-check setup with teacher. Check condition of wires and apparatus.	Do not attempt to fix electrical problems. Notify your teacher immediately.
IRRITANT	Substances that can irritate the skin or mucous membranes of the respiratory tract	pollen, moth balls, steel wool, fiberglass, potassium permanganate	Wear dust mask and gloves. Practice extra care when handling these materials.	Go to your teacher for first aid.
CHEMICAL	Chemicals that can react with and destroy tissue and other materials	bleaches such as hydrogen peroxide; acids such as sulfuric acid, hydrochloric acid; bases such as ammonia, sodium hydroxide	Wear goggles, gloves, and an apron.	Immediately flush the affected area with water and notify your teacher.
TOXIC	Substance may be poisonous if touched, inhaled, or swallowed	mercury, many metal compounds, iodine, poinsettia plant parts	Follow your teacher's instructions.	Always wash hands thoroughly after use. Go to your teacher for first aid.
OPEN FLAME	Open flame may ignite flammable chemicals, loose clothing, or hair	alcohol, kerosene, potassium permanganate, hair, clothing	Tie back hair. Avoid wearing loose clothing. Avoid open flames when using flammable chemicals. Be aware of locations of fire safety equipment.	Notify your teacher immediately. Use fire safety equipment if applicable.

Eye Safety
Proper eye protection should be worn at all times by anyone performing or observing science activities.

Clothing Protection
This symbol appears when substances could stain or burn clothing.

Animal Safety
This symbol appears when safety of animals and students must be ensured.

Radioactivity
This symbol appears when radioactive materials are used.

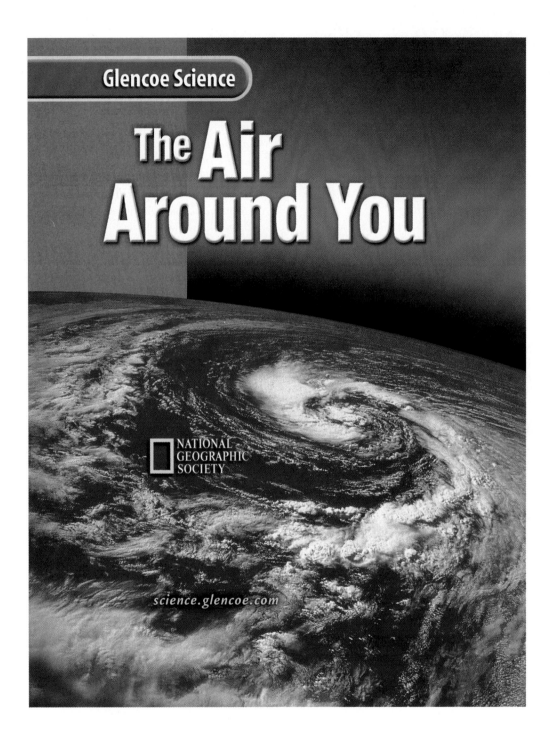

Glencoe Science

The Air Around You

NATIONAL GEOGRAPHIC SOCIETY

science.glencoe.com

Glencoe
McGraw-Hill

New York, New York   Columbus, Ohio   Woodland Hills, California   Peoria, Illinois

Glencoe Science

The Air Around You

Student Edition
Teacher Wraparound Edition
Interactive Teacher Edition CD-ROM
Interactive Lesson Planner CD-ROM
Lesson Plans
Content Outline for Teaching
Dinah Zike's Teaching Science with Foldables
Directed Reading for Content Mastery
Foldables: Reading and Study Skills
Assessment
    Chapter Review
    Chapter Tests
    ExamView Pro Test Bank Software
    Assessment Transparencies
    Performance Assessment in the Science Classroom
    The Princeton Review Standardized Test Practice Booklet
Directed Reading for Content Mastery in Spanish
Spanish Resources
English/Spanish Guided Reading Audio Program
Reinforcement

Enrichment
Activity Worksheets
Section Focus Transparencies
Teaching Transparencies
Laboratory Activities
Science Inquiry Labs
Critical Thinking/Problem Solving
Reading and Writing Skill Activities
Mathematics Skill Activities
Cultural Diversity
Laboratory Management and Safety in the Science Classroom
Mindjogger Videoquizzes and Teacher Guide
Interactive Explorations and Quizzes CD-ROM with
    Presentation Builder
Vocabulary Puzzlemaker Software
Cooperative Learning in the Science Classroom
Environmental Issues in the Science Classroom
Home and Community Involvement
Using the Internet in the Science Classroom

THE PRINCETON REVIEW

"Study Tip," "Test-Taking Tip," and the "Test Practice" features in this book were written by The Princeton Review, the nation's leader in test preparation. Through its association with McGraw-Hill, The Princeton Review offers the best way to help students excel on standardized assessments.

The Princeton Review is not affiliated with Princeton University or Educational Testing Service.

Glencoe/McGraw-Hill

A Division of The McGraw-Hill Companies

Copyright ©2002 by the McGraw-Hill Companies, Inc. All rights reserved. Except as permission under the United States Copyright Act, no part of this publication may be reproduced or distributed in any form or by any means, or stored in a database or retrieval system, without the prior written permission of the publisher.

The "Visualizing" features found in each chapter of this textbook were designed and developed by the National Geographic Society's Education Division, copyright ©2002 National Geographic Society. The name "National Geographic Society" and the yellow border rectangle are trademarks of the Society, and their use, without prior written permission, is strictly prohibited. All rights reserved.

The "Science and Society" and the "Science and History" features that appear in this book were designed and developed by TIME for Kids, a division of TIME Magazine.

Cover Images: Satellite image of Hurricane Bonnie, which struck North Carolina in 1998

Send all inquiries to:
Glencoe/McGraw-Hill
8787 Orion Place
Columbus, OH 43240

ISBN 0-07-825545-7
Printed in the United States of America.
  2 3 4 5 6 7 8 9 10 027/043 06 05 04 03 02 01

Interdisciplinary Connections/Activities

Feature Contents

Science
INTEGRATION

SCIENCE *Online*

THE PRINCETON REVIEW

Storm Scientists

Hurricanes are among nature's most destructive forces. These storms, which have lasting wind speeds of at least 120 km/h, can flatten trees, destroy houses, and kill people. Satellite images of hurricanes help scientists estimate when, where, and with how much force a storm will strike. However, researchers sometimes need detailed information about the internal structure of a hurricane that satellites can't provide. To collect such information, daring scientists fly airplanes where no other travelers dare—directly into the strongest winds of a hurricane.

To measure the fury of a hurricane, researchers must punch through the eye wall—a swirling wall of clouds with high winds surrounding the eye. Sometimes the clouds are so thick in the eye wall that the crew can't see the airplane's wings.

Figure 1
The roof was ripped off this home in Hawaii by the powerful winds of a hurricane.

Figure 2
Scientists use aircraft fitted with high-tech measuring devices to fly into hurricanes and collect data.

Gathering Information

Researchers who fly into hurricanes are blinded by rain. Powerful winds can send the aircraft plummeting to Earth. Despite these dangers, scientists continue to make measurements that require flying into hurricanes.

The NOAA (National Oceanic and Atmospheric Administration) maintains special planes fitted with wind probes and other devices to collect data from hurricanes. These planes fly at maximum and minimum elevations of 6,000 m and 450 m. The low-altitude flying is particularly dangerous because there is little room for recovery if a plane loses control. While flying through hurricanes, scientists sometimes release *dropsondes,* which are small devices that parachute down through a storm taking measurements such as temperature, pressure, wind direction, and humidity.

These data are used in computer models that predict how intense a hurricane is and where it might reach land. The models, in turn, are used to issue watches, warnings, and forecasts to minimize destruction of property and loss of life.

Figure 3
Dropsondes released from aircraft collect information as they fall through a hurricane.

Figure 4
Hurricane Georges wreaked havoc in Key West, Florida, in 1998.

The Study of Weather

Meteorologists are scientists who study weather and make predictions. Meteorologists make weather forecasts using data collected from measurements and observations. Forecasting the strength and movement of hurricanes becomes more accurate if data are collected from many regions.

Even when flying into the eye of a hurricane, researchers must use scientific methods and make accurate observations to make predictions about a storm's strength and direction. Many of these data are gathered by performing a variety of sophisticated investigations, or experiments.

Experimentation

Scientists try to answer questions by performing tests, called experiments, and recording the results. Experiments must be carefully planned in order to ensure the accuracy of the results. Scientists begin by making educated guesses, called hypotheses, about what the results of an experiment might be. Hurricane researchers, for example, hypothesized about what specific data would be most useful for predicting the path of a hurricane.

Variables, Constants, and Controls

When scientists conduct experiments, they try to make sure that only one factor affects the results of the experiment. The factor that is changed in the experiment is called the independent variable. The dependent variable is what is measured or observed in an experiment. Many experiments use a control—a sample that is treated like all the others except that the independent variable isn't applied. Conditions that stay the same in an experiment are called constants.

Constants in the hurricane research included using the same methods and devices to measure the air pressure and the wind strength. However, it's impossible to isolate one independent variable or to use a control. In the case of hurricane research, many observations are obtained and analyzed to compensate for this before conclusions are drawn. In addition, scientists who study hurricanes use computer models to create virtual storms in which they are able to manipulate one independent variable at a time.

Figure 5
Meteorologists study Earth's atmosphere in order to predict hurricanes and other, less extreme weather changes.

Interpreting Data

The observations and measurements that a scientist makes in an experiment are called data. In addition to obtaining images of hurricanes using satellites, scientists who fly aircraft through hurricanes collect many types of data, such as temperature, humidity, wind speed, and wind direction. Data must be carefully organized and studied before questions can be answered or problems can be solved.

Figure 6
Scientists such as Max Mayfield of the National Hurricane Center in Miami, Florida, are responsible for issuing hurricane watches and warnings.

Drawing Conclusions

An important step in any scientific method is to draw a conclusion based on results and observations. A conclusion summarizes what researchers have learned from an experiment.

Timely and accurate conclusions are important in hurricane research. Those conclusions lead to predictions of when and where a hurricane might strike and with what intensity. The predictions then must be communicated to the public. The people who make predictions about where hurricanes might reach land must consider many factors. Safety is the most important concern. However, forecasters also must be careful not to make premature predictions. Hurricane forecasts cause people to prepare their property for the storm, and evacuate the region. These things cost money and can impact local economies. These issues can weigh heavily on the minds of those who issue hurricane watches and warnings.

You Do It

Meteorologists use sophisticated equipment to predict the paths of hurricanes, but the paths of smaller storms often can be predicted reliably with weather maps, barometers, and other common equipment. Design a weather station that could be built at your school to predict when storms might reach your area. Describe how you would use data collected from the station.

Atmosphere

Why is it difficult to breathe at high elevations? Why are some mountain peaks permanently covered with snow? These mountain climbers aren't supplementing oxygen just because the activity is physically demanding. At elevations like this, the amount of oxygen available in the air is so small that the climbers' bodily functions might not be supported. In this chapter, you'll learn about the composition and structure of the atmosphere. You also will learn how energy is transferred in the atmosphere. In addition, you'll examine the water cycle and major wind systems.

What do you think?

Science Journal Look at the picture below with a classmate. Discuss what this might be. Here's a hint: *It "pops" in thin air.* Write your answer or best guess in your Science Journal.

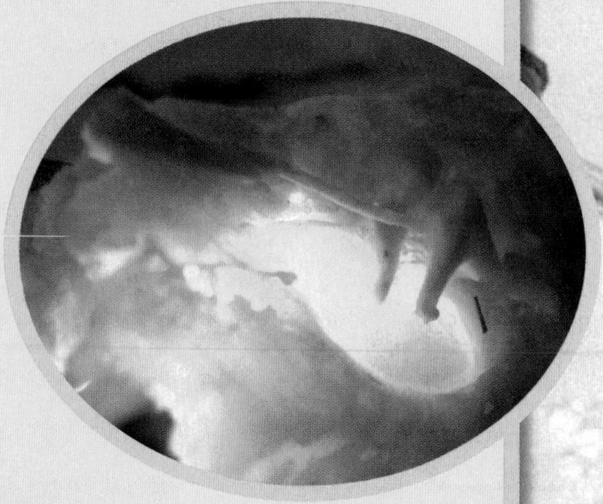

The air around you is made of billions of molecules. These molecules are constantly moving in all directions and bouncing into every object in the room, including you. Air pressure is the result of the billions of collisions of molecules into these objects. Because you usually do not feel molecules in air hitting you, do the activity below to see the effect of air pressure.

Observe air pressure

1. Cut out a square of cardboard about 10 cm on a side from a cereal box.
2. Fill a glass to the brim with water.
3. Hold the cardboard firmly over the top of the glass covering the water and invert the glass.
4. Slowly remove your hand holding the cardboard in place and observe.

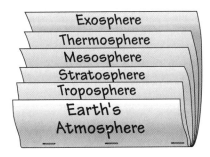

Observe

Write a paragraph in your Science Journal describing what happened to the cardboard when you inverted the glass and removed your hand. How does air pressure explain what happened?

Before You Read

FOLDABLES
Reading & Study Skills

Making a Sequence Study Fold Make the following Foldable to help you visualize the layers of Earth's atmosphere.

1. Stack three sheets of paper in front of you so the short sides are at the top.
2. Slide the top sheet up so that about four centimeters of the middle sheet show. Slide the middle sheet up so that about four centimeters of the bottom sheet show.
3. Fold the sheets top to bottom to form six tabs and staple along the topfold. Turn the Foldable so the staples are at the bottom.
4. Label each flap *Earth's Atmosphere, Troposphere, Stratosphere, Mesosphere, Thermosphere,* and *Exosphere,* as shown.
5. As you read the chapter, write information about each layer of Earth's atmosphere under the tabs.

> Exosphere
> Thermosphere
> Mesosphere
> Stratosphere
> Troposphere
> Earth's Atmosphere

Earth's Atmosphere

As You Read

What You'll Learn

- **Identify** the gases in Earth's atmosphere.
- **Describe** the structure of Earth's atmosphere.
- **Explain** what causes air pressure.

Vocabulary

atmosphere
troposphere
ionosphere

ozone layer
ultraviolet radiation
chlorofluorocarbon

Why It's Important

The atmosphere makes life on Earth possible.

Figure 1
Earth's atmosphere, as viewed from space, is a thin layer of gases. The atmosphere keeps Earth's temperature in a range that can support life.

Importance of the Atmosphere

Earth's **atmosphere,** shown in **Figure 1,** is a thin layer of air that forms a protective covering around the planet. If Earth had no atmosphere, days would be extremely hot and nights would be extremely cold. Earth's atmosphere maintains a balance between the amount of heat absorbed from the Sun and the amount of heat that escapes back into space. It also protects life-forms from some of the Sun's harmful rays.

Makeup of the Atmosphere

Earth's atmosphere is a mixture of gases, solids, and liquids that surround the planet. It extends from Earth's surface to outer space. The atmosphere is much different today from what it was when Earth was young.

Earth's early atmosphere, produced by erupting volcanoes, contained nitrogen and carbon dioxide, but little oxygen. Then, more than 2 billion years ago, Earth's early organisms released oxygen into the atmosphere as they made food with the aid of sunlight. These early organisms, however, were limited to layers of ocean water deep enough to be shielded from the Sun's harmful rays, yet close enough to the surface to receive sunlight. Eventually, a layer rich in ozone (O_3) that protects Earth from the Sun's harmful rays formed in the upper atmosphere. This protective layer allowed green plants eventually to flourish all over Earth, releasing even more oxygen. Today, a variety of life forms, including yours, depends on a certain amount of oxygen in Earth's atmosphere.

Gases in the Atmosphere Today's atmosphere is a mixture of the gases shown in **Figure 2.** Nitrogen is the most abundant gas, making up 78 percent of the atmosphere. Oxygen actually makes up only 21 percent of Earth's atmosphere. As much as four percent of the atmosphere is water vapor. Other gases that make up Earth's atmosphere include argon and carbon dioxide.

The composition of the atmosphere is changing in small but important ways. For example, car exhaust emits gases into the air. These pollutants mix with oxygen and other chemicals in the presence of sunlight and form a brown haze called smog. Humans burn fuel for energy. As fuel is burned, carbon dioxide is released as a by-product into Earth's atmosphere. Increasing energy use may increase the amount of carbon dioxide in the atmosphere.

Solids and Liquids in Earth's Atmosphere In addition to gases, Earth's atmosphere contains small, solid particles such as dust, salt, and pollen. Dust particles get into the atmosphere when wind picks it up off the ground and carries it along. Salt is picked up from ocean spray. Plants give off pollen that becomes mixed throughout part of the atmosphere.

The atmosphere also contains small liquid droplets, other than water droplets in clouds. The atmosphere constantly moves these liquid droplets and solids from one region to another. For example, the atmosphere above you may contain liquid droplets and solids from an erupting volcano thousands of kilometers from your home, as illustrated in **Figure 3.**

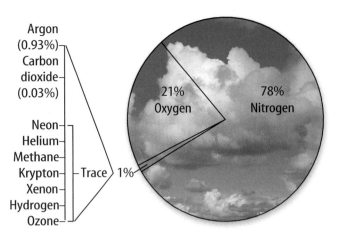

Argon (0.93%)
Carbon dioxide (0.03%)

Neon
Helium
Methane
Krypton — Trace ⟩ 1%
Xenon
Hydrogen
Ozone

21% Oxygen
78% Nitrogen

Figure 2
This graph shows the percentages of the gases, excluding water vapor, that make up Earth's atmosphere.

Figure 3
Solids and liquids can travel large distances in Earth's atmosphere, affecting regons far from their source.

A On June 12, 1991, Mount Pinatubo in the Philippines erupted, causing liquid droplets to form in Earth's atmosphere.

B Droplets of sulfuric acid from volcanoes can produce spectacular sunrises.

Layers of the Atmosphere

What would happen if you left a glass of chocolate milk on the kitchen counter for a while? Eventually, you would see a lower layer with more chocolate separating from upper layers with less chocolate. Like a glass of chocolate milk, Earth's atmosphere has layers. There are five layers in Earth's atmosphere, each with its own properties, shown in **Figure 4.** The lower layers include the troposphere and stratosphere. The upper atmospheric layers are the mesosphere, thermosphere, and exosphere. The troposphere and stratosphere contain most of the air.

Lower Layers of the Atmosphere You study, eat, sleep, and play in the **troposphere,** which is the lowest of Earth's atmospheric layers. It contains 99 percent of the water vapor and 75 percent of the atmospheric gases. Rain, snow, and clouds occur in the troposphere, which extends up to about 10 km.

The stratosphere, the layer directly above the troposphere, extends from 10 km above Earth's surface to about 50 km. As **Figure 4** shows, a portion of the stratosphere contains higher levels of a gas called ozone. Each molecule of ozone is made up of three oxygen atoms bonded together. Later in this section you will learn how ozone protects Earth from the Sun's harmful rays.

SCIENCE
Online

Research Visit the Glencoe Science Web site at **science.glencoe.com** for more information about layers of Earth's atmosphere. Communicate to your class what you learn.

Figure 4
Earth's atmosphere is divided into five layers. *Which layer of the atmosphere do you live in?*

500 km ———

Satellite   Exosphere

Space shuttle

Meteortrails

Thermosphere

85 km ———

Mesosphere

50 km ———

Ozone layer   Stratosphere

Jet   10 km ———

Troposphere

Earth

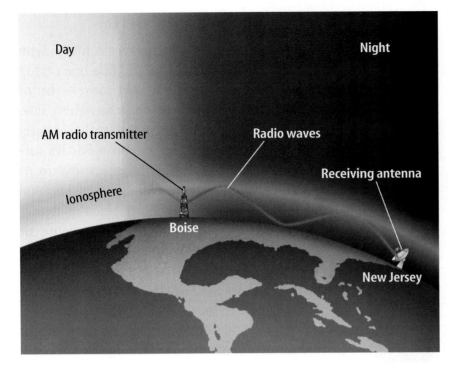

Upper Layers of the Atmosphere Beyond the stratosphere are the mesosphere, thermosphere, and exosphere. The mesosphere extends from the top of the stratosphere to about 85 km above Earth. If you've ever seen a shooting star, you have witnessed a meteor in the mesosphere.

The thermosphere is named for its high temperatures. This is the thickest atmospheric layer and is found between 85 km and 500 km above Earth's surface.

Within the thermosphere is a layer of electrically charged particles called the **ionosphere** (i AHN uh sfir). If you live in New Jersey and listen to the radio at night, you might pick up a station from Boise, Idaho. The ionosphere allows radio waves to travel across the country to another city, as shown in **Figure 5.** During the day, energy from the Sun interacts with the particles in the ionosphere, causing them to absorb AM radio frequencies. At night, without solar energy, AM radio transmissions reflect off the ionosphere, allowing radio transmissions to be received at greater distances.

The space shuttle in **Figure 6** orbits Earth in the exosphere. In contrast to the troposphere, the layer you live in, the exosphere has so few molecules that the wings of the shuttle are useless. In the exosphere, the spacecraft relies on bursts from small rocket thrusters to move around. Beyond the exosphere is outer space.

Figure 6
Wings help move aircraft in lower layers of the atmosphere. The space shuttle can't use its wings to maneuver in the exosphere because so few molecules are present.

✔ **Reading Check** *How does the space shuttle maneuver in the exosphere?*

Atmospheric Pressure

Imagine you're a football player running with the ball. Six players tackle you and pile one on top of the other. Who feels the weight more—you or the player on top? Like molecules anywhere else, atmospheric gases have mass. Atmospheric gases extend hundreds of kilometers above Earth's surface. As Earth's gravity pulls the gases toward its surface, the weight of these gases presses down on the air below. As a result, the molecules nearer Earth's surface are closer together. This dense air exerts more force than the less dense air near the top of the atmosphere. Force exerted on an area is known as pressure.

Like the pile of football players, air pressure is greater near Earth's surface and decreases higher in the atmosphere, as shown in **Figure 7.** People find it difficult to breathe in high mountains because fewer molecules of air exist there. Jets that fly in the stratosphere must maintain pressurized cabins so that people can breathe.

Figure 7
Air pressure decreases as you go higher in Earth's atmosphere.

✔ Reading Check *Where is air pressure greater—in the exosphere or in the troposphere?*

Problem-Solving Activity

How does altitude affect air pressure?

Atmospheric gases extend hundreds of kilometers above Earth's surface, but the molecules that make up these gases are fewer and fewer in number as you go higher. This means that air pressure decreases with altitude.

Identifying the Problem

The graph on the right shows these changes in air pressure. Note that altitude on the graph goes up only to 50 km. The troposphere and the stratosphere are represented on the graph, but other layers of the atmosphere are not. By examining the graph, can you understand the relationship between altitude and pressure?

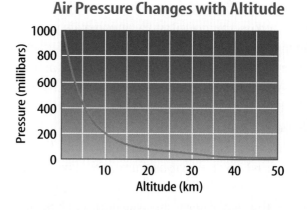

Air Pressure Changes with Altitude

Solving the Problem

1. Estimate the air pressure at an altitude of 5 km.
2. Does air pressure change more quickly at higher altitudes or at lower altitudes?

Temperature in Atmospheric Layers

The Sun is the source of most of the energy on Earth. Before it reaches Earth's surface, energy from the Sun must pass through the atmosphere. Because some layers contain gases that easily absorb the Sun's energy while other layers do not, the various layers have different temperatures, illustrated by the red line in **Figure 8.**

Molecules that make up air in the troposphere are warmed mostly by heat from Earth's surface. The Sun warms Earth's surface, which then warms the air above it. When you climb a mountain, the air at the top is usually cooler than the air at the bottom. Every kilometer you climb, the air temperature decreases about 6.5°C.

Molecules of ozone in the stratosphere absorb some of the Sun's energy. Energy absorbed by ozone molecules raises the temperature. Because more ozone molecules are in the upper portion of the stratosphere, the temperature in this layer rises with increasing altitude.

Like the troposphere, the temperature in the mesosphere decreases with altitude. The thermosphere and exosphere are the first layers to receive the Sun's rays. Few molecules are in these layers, but each molecule has a great deal of energy. Temperatures here are high.

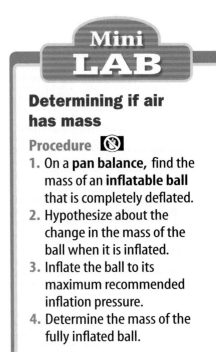

Mini LAB

Determining if air has mass

Procedure
1. On a **pan balance,** find the mass of an **inflatable ball** that is completely deflated.
2. Hypothesize about the change in the mass of the ball when it is inflated.
3. Inflate the ball to its maximum recommended inflation pressure.
4. Determine the mass of the fully inflated ball.

Analysis
1. What change occurs in the mass of the ball when it is inflated?
2. Infer from your data whether air has mass.

Temperature of the Atmosphere at Various Altitudes

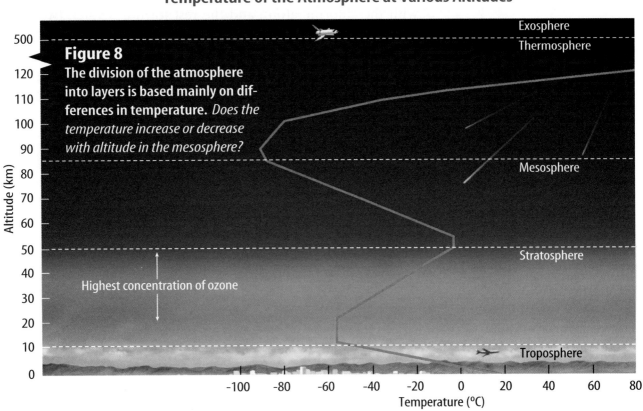

Figure 8
The division of the atmosphere into layers is based mainly on differences in temperature. *Does the temperature increase or decrease with altitude in the mesosphere?*

Highest concentration of ozone

Exosphere
Thermosphere
Mesosphere
Stratosphere
Troposphere

Altitude (km)
Temperature (°C)

Algae are organisms that use sunlight to make their own food. This process releases oxygen to Earth's atmosphere. Some scientists suggest that growth is reduced when algae are exposed to ultraviolet radiation. Infer what might happen to the oxygen level of the atmosphere if increased ultraviolet radiation damages some algae.

The Ozone Layer

Within the stratosphere, about 19 km to 48 km above your head, lies an atmospheric layer called the **ozone layer.** Ozone is made of oxygen. Although you cannot see the ozone layer, your life depends on it.

The oxygen you breathe has two atoms per molecule, but an ozone molecule is made up of three oxygen atoms bound together. The ozone layer contains a high concentration of ozone and shields you from the Sun's harmful energy. Ozone absorbs most of the ultraviolet radiation that enters the atmosphere. **Ultraviolet radiation** is one of the many types of energy that come to Earth from the Sun. Too much exposure to ultraviolet radiation can damage your skin and cause cancer.

CFCs Strong evidence exists that pollutants in the environment are destroying the ozone layer. Blame has fallen on **chlorofluorocarbons** (CFCs), a group of chemical compounds used in refrigerators, air conditioners, aerosol sprays, and foam packaging. If these products develop leaks or are manufactured improperly, chlorofluorocarbons can enter the atmosphere.

Recall that an ozone molecule is made of three oxygen atoms bonded together. Chlorofluorocarbon molecules, shown in **Figure 9,** destroy ozone. When a chlorine atom from a chlorofluorocarbon molecule comes near a molecule of ozone, the ozone molecule breaks apart. One of the oxygen atoms combines with the chlorine atom, and the rest form a regular, two-atom molecule. These compounds don't absorb ultraviolet radiation the way ozone can. In addition, the original chlorine atom can continue to break apart thousands of ozone molecules. The result is that more ultraviolet radiation reaches Earth's surface.

Figure 9
Chlorofluorocarbon (CFC) molecules were used in refrigerators and air conditioners. Each CFC molecule has three chlorine atoms. One atom of chlorine can destroy approximately 100,000 ozone molecules.

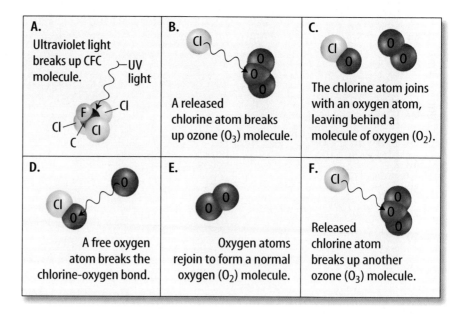

A.
Ultraviolet light breaks up CFC molecule.

B.
A released chlorine atom breaks up ozone (O_3) molecule.

C.
The chlorine atom joins with an oxygen atom, leaving behind a molecule of oxygen (O_2).

D.
A free oxygen atom breaks the chlorine-oxygen bond.

E.
Oxygen atoms rejoin to form a normal oxygen (O_2) molecule.

F.
Released chlorine atom breaks up another ozone (O_3) molecule.

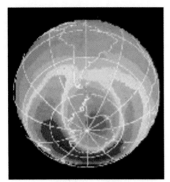
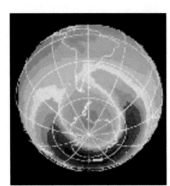
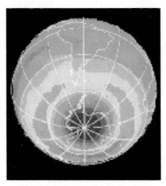
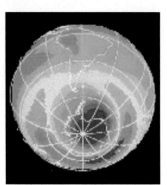

October 1980   **October 1988**   **October 1990**   **September 1999**

Health
INTEGRATION

Ozone Holes Each year, more than 1.3 million Americans develop skin cancer, and more than 9,500 die from it. Exposure to ultraviolet radiation can cause skin cancer. If the ozone layer disappeared, skin cancer rates might increase. In 1986, scientists found areas in the stratosphere with extremely low amounts of ozone. One large hole was found over Antarctica. A smaller hole was discovered over the north pole. **Figure 10** shows how the ozone layer has thinned and developed holes.

In the mid 1990s, many governments banned the production and use of CFCs. Perhaps over time, the areas where the ozone layer is thinning will recover.

Figure 10
These images of Antarctica were produced using data from a NASA satellite. The purple color shows how the ozone hole has grown bigger over time.

Section  Assessment

1. Earth's early atmosphere had little oxygen. How did oxygen come to make up 21 percent of Earth's present atmosphere?

2. List the layers of the atmosphere in order, beginning at Earth's surface.

3. While hiking in the mountains, you notice that it is harder to breathe as you climb higher. Explain why this is so.

4. What are some effects from a thinning ozone layer?

5. **Think Critically** During the day, the radio only receives AM stations from a city near you. At night, you are able to listen to an AM radio station from a distant city. Explain why this is possible.

Skill Builder Activities

6. **Interpreting Scientific Illustrations** Using **Figure 2,** determine the total percentage of nitrogen and oxygen in the atmosphere. What is the total percentage of argon and carbon dioxide? **For more help, refer to the** Science Skill Handbook.

7. **Communicating** The names of the atmospheric layers end with the suffix *-sphere,* a word that means "layer." Use a dictionary to find out what *tropo-, meso-, thermo-,* and *exo-* mean. In your Science Journal, write the meaning of these prefixes and explain if the layers are appropriately named. **For more help, refer to the** Science Skill Handbook.

Activity

Evaluating Sunscreens

Without protection, sun exposure can damage your health. Sunscreens protect your skin from ultraviolet radiation. In this activity, you will draw inferences using the labels of different sunscreens.

What You'll Investigate
How effective are various brands of sunscreens?

Materials
variety of sunscreens of different brand names

Goals
- **Draw inferences** based on labels on sunscreen brands.
- **Compare** the effectiveness of different sunscreen brands for protection against the Sun.
- **Compare** the cost of several sunscreen brands.

Safety Precautions

Sunsreen Assessment			
Brand Name			
SPF			
Misleading Terms			
Cost per Fluid Ounce			

Procedure

1. Make a data table in your Science Journal using the following terms: *brand name, SPF, misleading terms,* and *cost per fluid ounce.*

2. The Sun Protection Factor (SPF), tells you how long the sunscreen will protect you. For example, an SPF of 4 allows you to stay in the Sun four times longer than if you did not use sunscreen. Record the SPF of each sunscreen on your data table.

3. **Calculate** the cost per fluid ounce of each sunscreen brand.

4. Government guidelines say that terms like *sunblock* and *waterproof* are misleading because sunscreens cannot block the Sun, and they wash off in water. List the misleading terms in your data table for each brand.

Conclude and Apply

1. **Explain** why you need to use sunscreen.

2. A minimum of SPF 15 is considered adequate protection for a sunscreen. Sunscreens with an SPF greater than 30 are considered by government guidelines to be misleading because sunscreens will wash or wear off. Evaluate the SPF of each brand of sunscreen.

3. Considering the cost and effectiveness of all the sunscreen brands, discuss which brand you consider to be the best buy.

*C*ommunicating
Your Data

Create a poster on the proper use of sunscreens, and provide guidelines for selecting the safest product. **For more help, refer to the** Science Skill Handbook.

Energy Transfer in the Atmosphere

Energy from the Sun

The Sun provides most of the energy on Earth. This energy drives winds and ocean currents and allows plants to grow and produce food, providing nutrition for many animals. When Earth receives energy from the Sun, three different things can happen to that energy, as shown in **Figure 11.** Some energy is reflected back into space by clouds, atmospheric particles, and Earth's surface. Some is absorbed by the atmosphere. The rest is absorbed by land and water on Earth's surface.

Heat

Heat is energy that flows from an object with a higher temperature to an object with a lower temperature. Energy from the Sun reaches Earth's surface and heats objects such as roads, rocks, and water. Heat then is transferred through the atmosphere in three ways—radiation, conduction, and convection, as shown in **Figure 12.**

As You Read

***What* You'll Learn**
- **Describe** what happens to the energy Earth receives from the Sun.
- **Compare and contrast** radiation, conduction, and convection.
- **Explain** the water cycle.

Vocabulary

radiation	hydrosphere
conduction	condensation
convection	

***Why* It's Important**
The Sun provides energy to Earth's atmosphere, allowing life to exist.

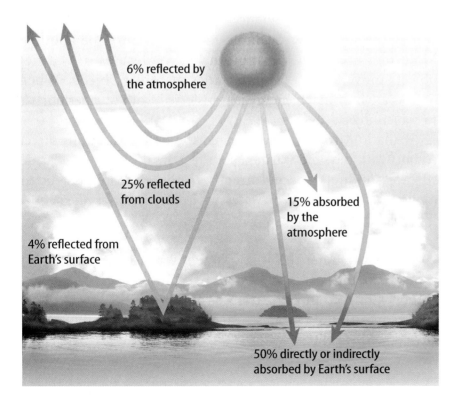

6% reflected by the atmosphere

25% reflected from clouds

15% absorbed by the atmosphere

4% reflected from Earth's surface

50% directly or indirectly absorbed by Earth's surface

Figure 11
The Sun is the source of energy for Earth's atmosphere. Thirty-five percent of incoming solar radiation is reflected back into space. *How much is absorbed by Earth's surface and atmosphere?*

I ◆ 17

Radiation warms the surface.

The air near Earth's surface is heated by conduction.

Cooler air pushes warm air upward, creating a convection current.

Figure 12
Heat is transferred within Earth's atmosphere by radiation, conduction, and convection.

Physics
INTEGRATION

Specific heat is the amount of heat required to change the temperature of a substance one degree. Substances with high specific heat absorb a lot of heat for a small increase in temperature. Land heats up faster than water does. Infer whether soil or water has a higher specific heat value.

Radiation Sitting on the beach, you feel the Sun's warmth on your face. How can you feel the Sun's heat even though you aren't in direct contact with it? Energy from the Sun reaches Earth in the form of radiant energy, or radiation. **Radiation** is energy that is transferred in the form of rays or waves. Earth radiates some of the energy it absorbs from the Sun back toward space. Radiant energy from the Sun warms your face.

✔ **Reading Check**   *How does the Sun warm your skin?*

Conduction If you walk barefoot on a hot beach, your feet heat up because of conduction. **Conduction** is the transfer of energy that occurs when molecules bump into one another. Molecules are always in motion, but molecules in warmer objects move faster than molecules in cooler objects. When objects are in contact, energy is transferred from warmer objects to cooler objects.

Radiation from the Sun heated the beach sand, but direct contact with the sand warmed your feet. In a similar way, Earth's surface conducts energy directly to the atmosphere. As air moves over warm land or water, molecules in air are heated by direct contact.

Convection After the atmosphere is warmed by radiation or conduction, the heat is transferred by a third process called convection. **Convection** is the transfer of heat by the flow of material. Convection circulates heat throughout the atmosphere. How does this happen?

When air is warmed, the molecules in it move apart and the air becomes less dense. Air pressure decreases because fewer molecules are in the same space. In cold air, molecules move closer together. The air becomes more dense and air pressure increases. Cooler, denser air sinks while warmer, less dense air rises, forming a convection current. As **Figure 12** shows, radiation, conduction and convection together distribute the Sun's heat throughout Earth's atmosphere.

The Water Cycle

Hydrosphere is a term that describes all the water on Earth's surface. Water moves constantly between the atmosphere and the hydrosphere in the water cycle, shown in **Figure 13.**

If you watch a puddle in the Sun, you'll notice that over time the puddle gets smaller and smaller. Energy from the Sun causes the water in the puddle to change from a liquid to a gas by a process called evaporation. Water that evaporates from lakes, streams, and oceans enters Earth's atmosphere.

If water vapor in the atmosphere cools enough, it changes back into a liquid. This process of water vapor changing to a liquid is called **condensation.**

Clouds form when condensation occurs high in the atmosphere. Clouds are made up of tiny water droplets that can collide to form larger drops. As the drops grow, they fall to Earth as precipitation, which completes the cycle by returning water to the hydrosphere.

TRY AT HOME
Mini LAB

Modeling Heat Transfer

Procedure
1. Cover the outside of an empty **soup can** with **black construction paper.**
2. Fill the can with **cold water** and feel it with your fingers.
3. Cover the top of the can with black paper.
4. Place the can in the Sun for 1 h. Then pour the water over your fingers.

Analysis
1. Does the water in the can feel warmer or cooler after placing the can in the Sun?
2. What types of heat transfer did you model?

Figure 13
In the water cycle, water moves from Earth to the atmosphere and back to Earth again.

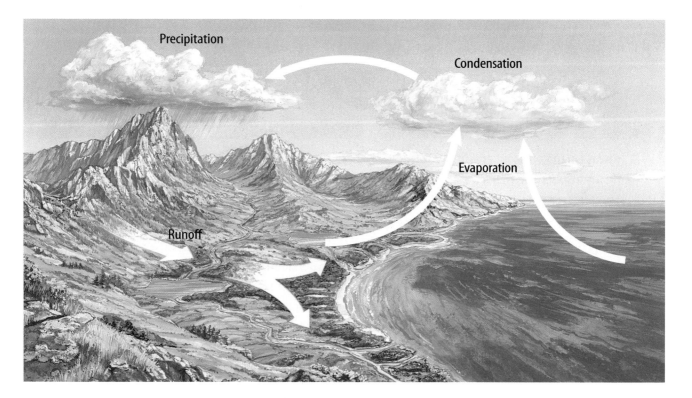

Precipitation

Condensation

Evaporation

Runoff

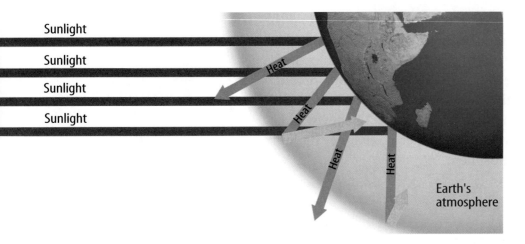

Sunlight

Sunlight

Sunlight

Sunlight

Heat

Heat

Heat

Heat

Earth's atmosphere

Figure 14
Earth's atmosphere creates a delicate balance between energy received and energy lost.

Earth's Atmosphere is Unique

On Earth, radiation from the Sun can be reflected into space, absorbed by the atmosphere, or absorbed by the surface and hydrosphere. Once it is absorbed, heat can be transferred by radiation, conduction, or convection. Earth's atmosphere, shown in **Figure 14,** helps control how much of the Sun's radiation is absorbed or lost.

✔ **Reading Check** *What helps control how much of the Sun's radiation is absorbed on Earth?*

Why doesn't life exist on Mars or Venus? Mars is a cold, life-less world because its atmosphere is too thin to support life or to hold much of the Sun's heat. Temperatuers on the surface of Mars range from 35° C to −170°C. On the other hand, Venus's atmosphere is so dense that almost no heat coming from the Sun can escape. The temperature on the surface of Venus is 470°C. Living things would burn instantly if they were placed on Venus's surface. Life on Earth exists because the atmosphere holds just the right amount of the Sun's energy.

Section ② Assessment

1. How does the Sun transfer energy to Earth?
2. How is Earth's atmosphere different from the atmosphere on Mars?
3. How is heat transferred from the stove to the water when you boil a pot of water?
4. Briefly describe the steps included in the water cycle.
5. **Think Critically** What would happen to the temperature of Earth's surface if the Sun's heat were not distributed throughout the atmosphere?

Skill Builder Activities

6. **Concept Mapping** Make a concept map that explains what happens to radiant energy that reaches Earth. **For more help, refer to the Science Skill Handbook.**

7. **Solving One-Step Equations** Earth is about 150 million km from the Sun. The radiation coming from the Sun travels at 300,000 km/s. How long does it take for radiation from the Sun to reach Earth? **For more help, refer to the Math Skill Handbook.**

SECTION 3

Air Movement

Forming Wind

Uneven heating of Earth's surface by the Sun causes some areas to be warmer than others. Recall from Section 2 that warmer air expands, becoming less dense than colder air. This causes air pressure to be generally lower where air is heated. Wind is the movement of air from an area of higher pressure to an area of lower pressure.

Heated Air Areas of Earth receive different amounts of radiation from the Sun because Earth is curved. **Figure 15** illustrates why the equator receives more radiation than areas to the north or south. The heated air at the equator is less dense, so it is displaced by denser, colder air, creating convection currents.

This cold, denser air comes from the poles, which receive less radiation from the Sun, making air at the poles much cooler. The resulting dense, high-pressure air sinks and moves along Earth's surface. However, dense air sinking as less-dense air rises does not explain everything about wind.

As You Read

What You'll Learn
- **Explain** why different latitudes on Earth receive different amounts of solar energy.
- **Describe** the Coriolis effect.
- **Locate** doldrums, trade winds, prevailing westerlies, polar easterlies, and jet streams.

Vocabulary
Coriolis effect   sea breeze
jet stream   land breeze

Why It's Important
Wind systems determine major weather patterns on Earth.

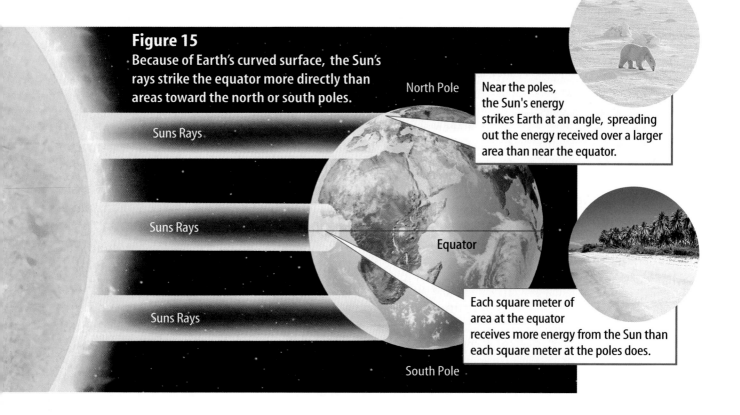

Figure 15
Because of Earth's curved surface, the Sun's rays strike the equator more directly than areas toward the north or south poles.

North Pole

Suns Rays

Suns Rays

Equator

Suns Rays

South Pole

Near the poles, the Sun's energy strikes Earth at an angle, spreading out the energy received over a larger area than near the equator.

Each square meter of area at the equator receives more energy from the Sun than each square meter at the poles does.

Figure 16
The Coriolis effect causes moving air to turn to the right in the northern hemisphere and to the left in the southern hemisphere.

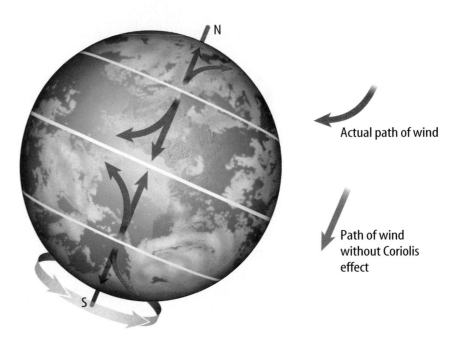

Actual path of wind

Path of wind without Coriolis effect

SCIENCE *Online*

Data Update Visit the Glencoe Science Web site at **science.glencoe.com** to collect data on global winds. Communicate to your class what you've learned.

The Coriolis Effect What would happen if you threw a ball to someone sitting directly across from you on a moving merry-go-round? Would the ball go to your friend? By the time the ball got to the opposite side, your friend would have moved and the ball would appear to have curved.

Like the merry-go-round, the rotation of Earth causes moving air and water to appear to turn to the right north of the equator and to the left south of the equator. This is called the **Coriolis** (kohr ee OH lus) **effect,** and is illustrated in **Figure 16.** The flow of air caused by differences in the amount of solar radiation received on Earth's surface and by the Coriolis effect creates distinct wind patterns on Earth's surface. These wind systems not only influence the weather, they also determine when and where ships and planes travel most efficiently.

Global Winds

How did Christopher Columbus get from Spain to the Americas? The *Nina,* the *Pinta,* and the *Santa Maria* had no source of power other than the wind in their sails. Early sailors discovered that the wind patterns on Earth helped them navigate the oceans. These wind systems are shown in **Figure 17.**

Sometimes sailors found little or no wind to move their sailing ships near the equator. It also rained nearly every afternoon. This windless, rainy zone near the equator is called the doldrums. Look again at **Figure 17.** Near the equator, the Sun heats the air and causes it to rise, creating low pressure and little wind. The rising air then cools, causing rain.

✔ **Reading Check** *What are the doldrums?*

Figure 17

The Sun's uneven heating of Earth's surface forms giant loops, or cells, of moving air. The Coriolis effect deflects the surface winds to the west or east, setting up belts of prevailing winds that distribute heat and moisture around the globe.

A WESTERLIES Near 30° north and south latitude, Earth's rotation deflects air from west to east as air moves toward the polar regions. In the United States, the westerlies move weather systems, such as this one along the Oklahoma-Texas border, from west to east.

B DOLDRUMS Along the equator, heating causes air to expand, creating a zone of low pressure. Cloudy, rainy weather, as shown here, develops almost every afternoon.

60° N — Polar easterlies

Westerlies

30° N — Trade winds

0° — Equatorial doldrums

Trade winds

30° S —

Westerlies

60°S— Polar easterlies

C TRADE WINDS Air warmed near the equator travels toward the Poles, but gradually cools and sinks. As the air flows back toward the low pressure of the doldrums, the Coriolis effect deflects the surface wind to the west. Early sailors, in ships like the one above, relied on these winds to navigate global trade routes.

D POLAR EASTERLIES In the polar regions, cold, dense air sinks and moves away from the Poles. Earth's rotation deflects this wind from east to west.

Surface Winds Between the equator and 30° latitude, air descending to Earth's surface creates steady winds. These are called trade winds because early sailors used their dependability to establish trade routes.

Between 30° and 60° latitude, winds called the prevailing westerlies blow in the opposite direction from the trade winds. Prevailing westerlies are responsible for much of the movement of weather across North America.

Polar easterlies are found near the poles. Near the north pole, easterlies blow from northeast to southwest. Near the south pole, polar easterlies blow from the southeast to the northwest.

Winds in the Upper Troposphere Narrow belts of strong winds, called **jet streams,** blow near the top of the troposphere. The polar jet stream forms at the boundary of cold, dry polar air to the north and warm, moist tropical air to the south, as shown in **Figure 18.** The jet stream moves faster in the winter because the difference between cold air and warm air is greater. The jet stream helps move storms across the country.

Jet pilots take advantage of the jet streams. When flying eastward, planes save time and fuel. Going west, planes fly at different altitudes to avoid the jet streams.

Local Wind Systems

Global wind systems determine the major weather patterns for the entire planet. Smaller wind systems affect local weather. If you live near a large body of water, you're familiar with two such wind systems—sea breezes and land breezes.

Figure 18
A strong current of air, called the jet stream, forms between cold, polar air and warm, tropical air.

A Flying from Boston to Seattle may take 1.5 h longer than flying from Seattle to Boston.

B The polar jet stream in North America usually is found between 10 km and 15 km above Earth's surface.

Cold air

Polar jet stream

Warm air

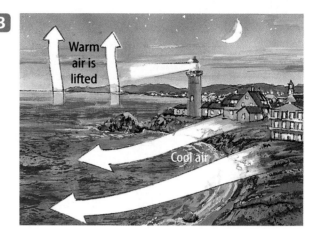

Sea Breezes Convection currents over areas where the land meets the sea can cause wind. A **sea breeze,** shown in **Figure 19,** is created during the day because solar radiation warms the land more than the water. Air over the land is heated by conduction. This heated air is less dense and has lower pressure. Cooler, denser air over the water has higher pressure and flows toward the warmer, less dense air. A convection current results, and wind blows from the sea toward the land.

✔ **Reading Check** *How does a sea breeze form?*

Land Breezes At night, land cools much more rapidly than ocean water. Air over the land becomes cooler than air over the ocean. Cooler, denser air above the land moves over the water, as the warm air over the water rises. Movement of air toward the water from the land is called a **land breeze.**

Figure 19
These daily winds occur because land heats up and cools off faster than water does. **A** During the day, cool air from the water moves over the land, creating a sea breeze. **B** At night, cool air over the land moves toward the warmer air over the water, creating a land breeze.

Section 3 Assessment

1. Why do some parts of Earth's surface, such as the equator, receive more of the Sun's heat than other regions?

2. How does the Coriolis effect influence wind circulation on Earth?

3. Why does little wind and lots of afternoon rain occur in the doldrums?

4. Which wind system helped early sailors navigate Earth's oceans?

5. **Think Critically** How does the jet stream help move storms across North America?

Skill Builder Activities

6. **Comparing and Contrasting** Compare and contrast sea breezes and land breezes. **For more help, refer to the** Science Skill Handbook.

7. **Using Graphics Software** Use graphics software and **Figure 17** to draw the wind systems on Earth. Make separate graphics of major wind circulation cells shown by black arrows. On another graphic, show major surface winds. Print your graphics and share them with your class. **For more help, refer to the** Technology Skill Handbook.

The Heat Is On

Sometimes, a plunge in a pool or lake on a hot summer day feels cool and refreshing. Why does the beach sand get so hot when the water remains cool? A few hours later, the water feels warmer than the land does. In this activity, you'll explore how water and land absorb heat.

Recognize the Problem

How do soil and water compare in their abilities to absorb and emit heat?

Form a Hypothesis

Form a hypothesis to explain how soil and water compare in their abilities to absorb and release heat. Write another hypothesis about how air temperatures above soil and above water differ during the day and night.

Safety Precautions

WARNING: *Be careful when handling the hot overhead light. Do not let the light or its cord make contact with water.*

Possible Materials

ring stand	clear plastic boxes (2)
soil	overhead light
metric ruler	with reflector
water	thermometers (4)
masking tape	*computer
colored pencils (4)	temperature probes

Alternate Materials

Goals

- **Design** an experiment to compare the rates of heat absorption and release for soil and water.
- **Observe** how these differing rates of heat absorption and release affect the air above soil and above water.

Test Your Hypothesis

Plan

1. As a group, agree upon and write your hypothesis.
2. **List** the steps that you need to take to test your hypothesis. Include in your plan how you will use your equipment to compare the rates of heat absorption and release for water and soil.
3. **Design** a data table in your Science Journal for both parts of your experiment—when the light is on and energy can be absorbed and when the light is off and energy is released to the environment.

Do

1. Make sure your teacher approves your plan and your data table before you start.
2. Carry out the experiment as planned.
3. During the experiment, record your observations and complete the data table in your Science Journal.
4. Include in your measurements the temperatures of the soil and the water. Also compare the rate of release of heat for water and soil. Include the temperatures of the air immediately above both of the substances. Allow 15 min for each test.

Analyze Your Data

1. Use your colored pencils and the information in your data tables to make line graphs. Show the rate of temperature increase for soil and water. Graph the rate of temperature decrease for soil and water after you turn the light off.

2. **Analyze** your graphs. When the light was on, which heated up faster—the soil or the water?

3. **Compare** how fast the air temperatures over the water changed with how fast the temperatures over the land changed after the light was turned off.

Draw Conclusions

1. Was your hypothesis supported or not? Explain.
2. **Infer** from your graphs which lost heat faster—the water or the soil.
3. **Compare** the temperatures of the air above the water and above the soil 15 minutes after the light was turned off. How do water and soil compare in their abilities to absorb and release heat?

*C*ommunicating
Your Data

Make a poster showing the steps you followed for your experiment. Include the graph of your data. **Display** your poster in the classroom. **For more help, refer to the Science Skill Handbook.**

Song of the Sky Loom[1]
Brian Swann, ed.

This Native American prayer comes from the Tewa people who are part of the Pueblo tribe. The poem is actually a chanted prayer used in ceremonial rituals.

Respond to the Reading

1. Why do the words *Mother Earth* and *Father Sky* appear on either side and above and below the rest of the words?

2. Why does the song use the image of a garment to describe Earth's atmosphere?

Mother Earth   Father Sky

we are your children

With tired backs we bring you gifts you love

Then weave for us a garment of brightness
its warp[2] the white light of morning,
weft[3] the red light of evening,
fringes the falling rain,
its border the standing rainbow.

Thus weave for us a garment of brightness
So we may walk fittingly where birds sing,
So we may walk fittingly where grass is green.

Mother Earth   Father Sky

[1] a machine or device from which cloth is produced

[2] threads that run lengthwise in a piece of cloth

[3] horizontal threads interlaced through the warp in a piece of cloth

Understanding Literature

Metaphor   A metaphor is a figure of speech that compares seemingly unlike things. Unlike a simile, a metaphor does not use the connecting words *like* or *as*. For instance, in the song you just read, Father Sky is a loom. A loom is a machine or device that weaves cloth. The song describes the relationship between Earth and sky as being a woven garment. Lines such as "weave for us a garment of brightness" serve as metaphors for how Mother Earth and Father Sky together create an atmosphere in which their "children," or humans, can thrive.

Science Connection   In this chapter, you learned about the composition of Earth's atmosphere. The atmosphere maintains the balance between the amount of heat absorbed from the Sun and the amount of heat that escapes back into space. You also learned about the water cycle and how water evaporates from Earth's surface back into the atmosphere. Using metaphor instead of scientific facts, the Tewa song conveys to the reader how the relationship between Earth and its atmosphere are important to all living things.

Linking Science and Writing

Creating a Metaphor   Write a four-line poem that uses a metaphor to describe rain. You can choose to write about a gentle spring rain or a thunderous rainstorm. Remember that a metaphor does not use the words *like* or *as*. Therefore, your poem should begin with something like "Rain is …" or "Heavy rain is …"

Career Connection

Meteorologist

Kim Perez is an on-air meteorologist for The Weather Channel, a national cable television network. She became interested in the weather when she was living in Cincinnati, Ohio. There, in 1974, she witnessed the largest tornado on record. Ms. Perez now broadcasts weather reports to millions of television viewers. Meteorologists study computer models of Earth's atmosphere. These models help them predict short-term and long-term weather conditions for the United States and the world.

SCIENCE *Online*   To learn more about careers in meteorology, visit the Glencoe Science Web site at **science.glencoe.com.**

Reviewing Main Ideas

Section 1 Earth's Atmosphere

1. Earth's atmosphere is made up mostly of gases, with some suspended solids and liquids. The unique atmosphere allows life on Earth to exist.

2. The atmosphere is divided into five layers with differant characteristics.

3. The ozone layer protects Earth from too much ultraviolet radiation, which can be harmful. *How do chlorofluoro-carbon molecules destroy ozone?*

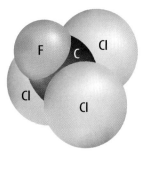

Section 2 Energy Transfer in the Atmosphere

1. Earth receives its energy from the Sun. Some of this energy is reflected back into space, and some is absorbed.

2. Heat is distributed in Earth's atmosphere by radiation, conduction, and convection.

3. Energy from the Sun powers the water cycle between the atmosphere and Earth's surface. *Clouds form during which part of the water cycle?*

4. Unlike the atmosphere on Mars or Venus, Earth's unique atmosphere maintains a balance between energy received and energy lost that keeps temperatures mild. This deli-cate balance allows life on Earth to exist.

Section 3 Air Movement

1. Because Earth's surface is curved, not all areas receive the same amount of solar radiation. This uneven heating causes temperature differences at Earth's surface.

2. Convection currents modified by the Coriolis effect produce Earth's global winds.

3. The polar jet stream is a strong current of wind found in the upper troposphere. It forms at the boundary between cold, polar air and warm, tropical air.

4. Land breezes and sea breezes occur near the ocean. *Why do winds change direction from day to night?*

FOLDABLES
Reading & Study Skills

After You Read

Draw pictures on the front of your Foldable of things that you might find in each layer of Earth's atmosphere.

Visualizing Main Ideas

Complete the following cycle map on the water cycle.

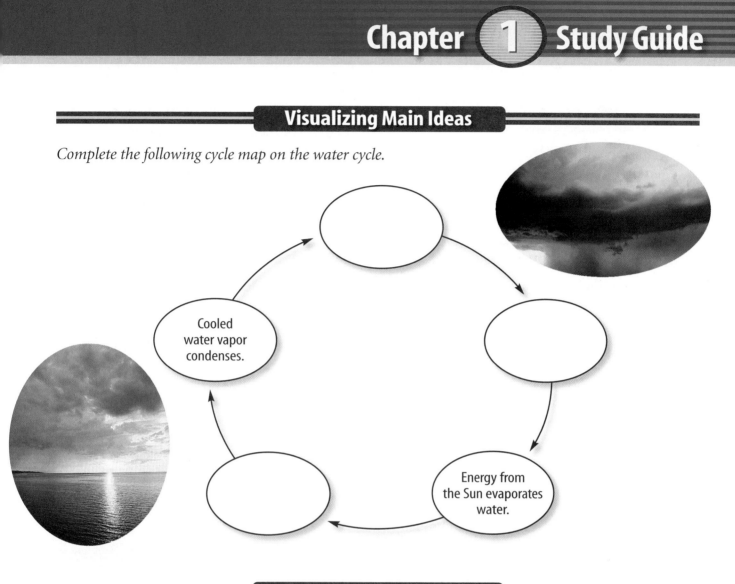

Cooled water vapor condenses.

Energy from the Sun evaporates water.

Vocabulary Review

Vocabulary Review

a. atmosphere
b. chlorofluorocarbon
c. condensation
d. conduction
e. convection
f. Coriolis effect
g. hydrosphere
h. ionosphere
i. jet stream
j. land breeze
k. ozone layer
l. radiation
m. sea breeze
n. troposphere
o. ultraviolet radiation

THE PRINCETON REVIEW Study Tip

Try to think of other ways that you might design an experiment to prove scientific principles.

Using Vocabulary

The sentences below include terms that have been used incorrectly. Change the incorrect terms so that the sentence reads correctly.

1. Chlorofluorocarbons are dangerous because they destroy the hydrosphere.

2. Narrow belts of strong winds called sea breezes blow near the top of the ionosphere.

3. The thin layer of air that surrounds Earth is called the troposphere.

4. Heat energy transferred in the form of waves is called condensation.

5. The ozone layer helps protect us from the Coriolis effect.

Chapter ① Assessment

Checking Concepts

Choose the word or phrase that best answers the question.

1. What is the most abundant gas in the atmosphere?
   A) oxygen
   B) water vapor
   C) argon
   D) nitrogen

2. What causes a brown haze near cities?
   A) conduction
   B) mud
   C) car exhaust
   D) wind

3. Which is the uppermost layer of the atmosphere?
   A) troposphere
   B) stratosphere
   C) exosphere
   D) thermosphere

4. What layer of the atmosphere has the most water?
   A) troposphere
   B) stratosphere
   C) mesosphere
   D) exosphere

5. What protects living things from too much ultraviolet radiation?
   A) the ozone layer
   B) oxygen
   C) nitrogen
   D) argon

6. Where is air pressure least?
   A) troposphere
   B) stratosphere
   C) exosphere
   D) thermosphere

7. How is energy transferred when objects are in contact?
   A) trade winds
   B) convection
   C) radiation
   D) conduction

8. Which surface winds are responsible for most of the weather movement across the United States?
   A) polar easterlies
   B) doldrums
   C) prevailing westerlies
   D) trade winds

9. What type of wind is a movement of air toward water?
   A) sea breeze
   B) doldrum
   C) land breeze
   D) barometer

10. What are narrow belts of strong winds near the top of the troposphere called?
    A) doldrums
    B) jet streams
    C) polar easterlies
    D) trade winds

Thinking Critically

11. Why are there few or no clouds in the stratosphere?

12. It is thought that life could not have existed on land until the ozone layer formed about 2 billion years ago. Why does life on land require an ozone layer?

13. Why do sea breezes occur during the day, but not at night?

14. Describe what happens when water vapor rises and cools.

15. Why does air pressure decrease with an increase in altitude?

Developing Skills

16. **Concept Mapping** Complete the cycle concept map below using the following phrases to explain how air moves to form a convection current: *Cool air moves toward warm air, cool air is warmed by conduction, warm air is lifted and cools*, and *cool air sinks.*

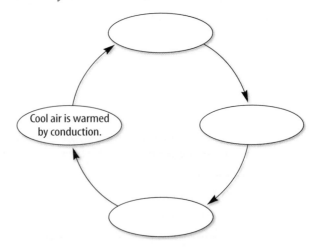

Cool air is warmed by conduction.

17. Drawing Conclusions In an experiment, a student measured the air temperature 1 m above the ground on a sunny afternoon and again in the same spot 1 h after sunset. The second reading was lower than the first. What can you infer from this?

18. Forming Hypotheses Carbon dioxide in the atmosphere prevents some radiation from Earth's surface from escaping to space. Hypothesize how the temperature on Earth might change if more carbon dioxide were released from burning fossil fuels.

19. Identifying and Manipulating Variables and Controls Design an experiment to find out how plants are affected by differing amounts of ultraviolet radiation. In the design, use filtering film made for car windows. What is the variable you are testing? What are your constants? Your controls?

20. Recognizing Cause and Effect Why is the inside of a car hotter than the outdoor temperature on a sunny summer day?

Performance Assessment

21. Poster Illustratate or find magazine photos of convection currents that occur in everyday life.

22. Experiment Design and conduct an experiment to find out how different surfaces such as asphalt, soil, sand, and grass absorb and reflect solar energy. Share the results with your class.

TECHNOLOGY

Go to the Glencoe Science Web site at **science.glencoe.com** or use the **Glencoe Science CD-ROM** for additional chapter assessment.

THE PRINCETON REVIEW Test Practice

Each layer of Earth's atmosphere has a unique composition and temperature. The four layers closest to Earth's surface are shown in the diagram below.

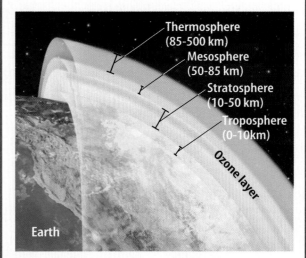

Study the diagram and answer the following questions.

1. In which part of the atmosphere is ozone located?
 A) Thermosphere   **C)** Stratosphere
 B) Troposphere   **D)** Mesosphere

2. According to the diagram, how far does the mesosphere extend above Earth's surface?
 F) 10 km   **H)** 50 km
 G) 85 km   **J)** 60 km

3. What is the correct order of atmospheric layers that the space shuttle goes through when landing on Earth?
 A) Mesosphere   **C)** Stratosphere
  Stratosphere   Troposphere
  Troposphere   Mesosphere
 B) Troposphere   **D)** Mesosphere
  Stratosphere   Troposphere
  Mesosphere   Stratosphere

Weather

It's summer and you've gone to your aunt's house in the country. You're playing baseball with your cousins, getting ready to bat, when suddenly you feel a strange sensation. The hot, humid air has suddenly turned cooler, and a strong breeze has kicked up. To the west, tall, black clouds are rapidly advancing. You see a flash of lightning and hear a loud clap of thunder. In this chapter, you'll learn how to measure weather conditions, how to interpret weather information, and make predictions.

What do you think?

Science Journal Look at the picture below with a classmate. Discuss what this might be or what is happening. Here's a hint: *It's calm in the center and rough around the edges.* Write your answer or best guess in your Science Journal.

How can it rain one day and be sunny the next? Powered by heat from the Sun, the air that surrounds you stirs and swirls. This constant mixing produces storms, calm weather, and everything in between. What causes rain and where does the water come from? Do the activity below to find out.

Demonstrate how rain forms

WARNING: *Boiling water and steam can cause burns.*

1. Bring a pan of water to a boil on a hot plate.

2. Carefully hold another pan containing ice cubes about 20 cm above the boiling water. Be sure to keep your hands and face away from the steam.

3. Keep the pan with the ice cubes in place until you see drops of water dripping from the bottom.

Observe

In your Science Journal, describe how the droplets formed. Infer where the water on the bottom of the pan came from.

Before You Read

FOLDABLES
Reading & Study
Skills

Making an Organizational Study Fold When information is grouped into clear categories, it is easier to make sense of what you are learning. Make the following Foldable to help you organize your thoughts about weather.

1. Stack two sheets of paper in front of you so the short side of both sheets is at the top.

2. Slide the top sheet up so that about 4 cm of the bottom sheet shows.

3. Fold both sheets top to bottom to form four tabs and staple along the top fold, as shown.

4. Label each flap *Weather, What is Weather, Weather Patterns,* and *Forecasting Weather,* as shown.

5. As you read the chapter, list what you learn under the appropriate flaps.

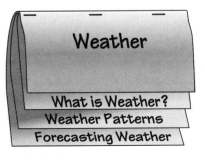

What is weather?

As You Read

What You'll Learn

- **Explain** how solar heating and water vapor in the atmosphere affect weather.
- **Discuss** how clouds form and how they are classified.
- **Describe** how rain, hail, sleet, and snow develop.

Vocabulary

weather
humidity
relative humidity
dew point
fog
precipitation

Why It's Important

Weather changes affect your daily activities.

Weather Factors

It might seem like small talk to you, but for farmers, truck drivers, pilots, and construction workers, the weather can have a huge impact on their livelihoods. Even professional athletes, especially golfers, follow weather patterns closely. You can describe what happens in different kinds of weather, but can you explain how it happens?

Weather refers to the state of the atmosphere at a specific time and place. Weather describes conditions such as air pressure, wind, temperature, and the amount of moisture in the air.

The Sun provides almost all of Earth's energy. Energy from the Sun evaporates water into the atmosphere where it forms clouds. Eventually, the water falls back to Earth as rain or snow. However, the Sun does more than evaporate water. It is also a source of heat energy. Heat from the Sun is absorbed by Earth's surface, which then heats the air above it. Weather, as shown in **Figure 1,** is the result of heat and Earth's air and water.

Figure 1
The Sun provides the energy that drives Earth's weather.
Can you find any storms in this photograph?

A When air is heated, it expands and becomes less dense. This creates lower pressure.

B Molecules in air are closer together in cooler temperatures, creating high pressure. Wind blows from higher pressure toward lower pressure.

Air Temperature During the summer when the Sun is hot and the air is still, a swim can be refreshing. But would a swim seem refreshing on a cold winter day? The temperature of air influences your daily activities.

Air is made up of molecules that are always moving randomly, even when there's no wind. Temperature is a measure of the average amount of motion of molecules. When the temperature is high, molecules in air move rapidly and it feels warm. When the temperature is low, molecules in air move less rapidly, and it feels cold.

Wind Why can you fly a kite on some days but not others? Kites fly because air is moving. Air moving in a specific direction is called wind. As the Sun warms the air, the air expands and becomes less dense. Warm, expanding air has low atmospheric pressure. Cooler air is denser and tends to sink, bringing about high atmospheric pressure. Wind results because air moves from regions of high pressure to regions of low pressure. You may have experienced this on a small scale if you've ever spent time along a beach, as in **Figure 2.**

Many instruments are used to measure wind direction and speed. Wind direction can be measured using a wind vane. A wind vane has an arrow that points in the direction from which the wind is blowing. A wind sock has one open end that catches the wind, causing the sock to point in the direction toward which the wind is blowing. Wind speed can be measured using an anemometer (a nuh MAH muh tur). Anemometers have rotating cups that spin faster when the wind is strong.

Figure 2
The temperature of air can affect air pressure. Wind is air moving from high pressure to low pressure.

Life Science
INTEGRATION

Birds and mammals maintain a fairly constant internal temperature, even when the temperature outside their bodies changes. On the other hand, the internal temperature of fish and reptiles changes when the temperature around them changes. Infer from this which group is more likely to survive a quick change in the weather.

Figure 3
Warmer air can have more water vapor than cooler air can because water vapor doesn't easily condense in warm air.

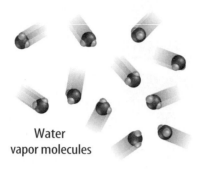

Water vapor molecules

Water droplets

A Water vapor molecules in warm air move rapidly. The molecules can't easily come together and condense.

B As air cools, water molecules in air move closer together. Some of them collide, allowing condensation to take place.

Determining Dew Point

Procedure

1. Partially fill a **metal can** with room-temperature **water.** Dry the outer surface of the can.
2. Place a **thermometer** in the water.
3. Slowly stir the water and add small amounts of **ice.**
4. On a data table in your **Science Journal,** note the exact water temperature at which a thin film of moisture first begins to form on the outside of the metal can.
5. Repeat steps 1 through 4 two more times.
6. The average of the three temperatures at which the moisture begins to appear is the dew point temperature of the air surrounding the metal container.

Analysis

1. What determines the dew point temperature?
2. Will the dew point change with increasing temperature if the amount of moisture in the air doesn't change? Explain.

Humidity Heat evaporates water into the atmosphere. Where does the water go? Water vapor molecules fit into spaces among the molecules that make up air. The amount of water vapor present in the air is called **humidity.**

Air doesn't always contain the same amount of water vapor. As you can see in **Figure 3,** more water vapor can be present when the air is warm than when it is cool. At warmer temperatures, the molecules of water vapor in air move quickly and don't easily come together. At cooler temperatures, molecules in air move more slowly. The slower movement allows water vapor molecules to collide with one another to form droplets of liquid water. Forming liquid water from water vapor is called condensation. When enough water vapor is present in air for condensation to take place, the air is saturated.

Reading Check *Why can more water vapor be present in warm air than in cold air?*

Relative Humidity On a hot, sticky afternoon, the weather forecaster reports that the humidity is 50 percent. How can the humidity be low when it feels so humid? Weather forecasters report the amount of moisture in the air as relative humidity. **Relative humidity** is a measure of the amount of water vapor present in the air compared to the amount needed for saturation at a specific temperature.

If you hear a weather forecaster say that the relative humidity is 50 percent, it means that the air contains 50 percent of the water needed for the air to be saturated.

As shown in **Figure 4,** air at 25°C is saturated when it contains 22 g of water vapor per cubic meter of air. The relative humidity is 100 percent. If air at 25°C contains 11 g of water vapor per cubic meter, the relative humidity is 50 percent.

Dew Point

When the temperature drops, less water vapor can be present in air. The water vapor in air will condense to a liquid or form ice crystals. The temperature at which air is saturated and condensation forms is the **dew point.** The dew point changes with the amount of water vapor in the air.

You've probably seen water droplets form on the outside of a glass of cold milk. The cold glass cooled the air next to it to its dew point. The water vapor in the surrounding air condensed and formed water droplets on the glass. In a similar way, when air near the ground cools to its dew point, water vapor condenses and forms dew. Frost may form when temperatures are near 0°C.

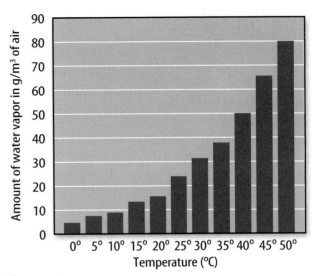

Figure 4
This graph shows that as the temperature of air increases, more water vapor can be present in the air.

Math Skills Activity

Calculating the Amount of Dew

Example Problem

One summer day, the relative humidity is 80 percent and the temperature is 35°C. Will the dew point be reached if the temperature falls to 25°C?

Solution

1 *This is what you know:*

From Figure 4

Air Temperature (°C)	Amount of Water Vapor Needed for Saturation (g)
35	37
25	24

2 *This is what you need to find:* x = amount of water vapor in 35°C air at 80 percent relative humidity. Is $x > 24$ g or is $x < 24$ g?

3 *This is how you solve the problem:* $x = .80 \, (37 \, g)$
$x = 29.6$ g of water vapor
29.6 g > 24 g, so the dew point is reached and dew will form

Practice Problem

If the relative humidity is 50 percent and the air temperature is 30°C, will the dew point be reached if the temperature falls to 20°C?

What clouds are in the sky today? To find out more about clouds, see the **Cloud Field Guide** at the back of this book.

Forming Clouds

Why are there clouds in the sky? Clouds form as warm air is forced upward, expands, and cools. **Figure 5** shows several ways that warm, moist air forms clouds. As the air cools, the amount of water vapor needed for saturation decreases and the relative humidity increases. When the relative humidity reaches 100 percent, the air is saturated. Water vapor soon begins to condense in tiny droplets around small particles such as dust and salt. These droplets of water are so small that they remain suspended in the air. Billions of these droplets form a cloud.

Classifying Clouds

Clouds are classified mainly by shape and height. Some clouds extend high into the sky, and others are low and flat. Some dense clouds bring rain or snow, while thin, wispy clouds appear on mostly sunny days. The shape and height of clouds vary with temperature, pressure, and the amount of water vapor in the atmosphere.

Figure 5
Clouds form when moist air is lifted and cools. This occurs where air is heated, at mountain ranges, and where cold air meets warm air.

A Rays from the Sun heat the ground and the air next to it. The warm air rises and cools. If the air is moist, some water vapor condenses and forms clouds.

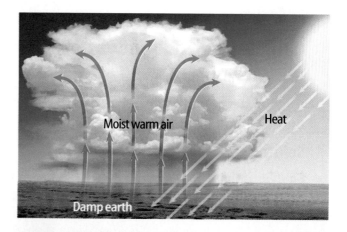

B As moist air moves over mountains, it is lifted and cools. Clouds formed in this way can cover mountains for long periods of time.

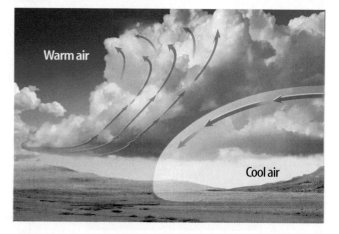

C When cool air meets warm, moist air, the warm air is lifted and cools. *What happens to the water vapor when the dew point is reached?*

Shape The three main cloud types are stratus, cumulus, and cirrus. Stratus clouds form layers, or smooth, even sheets in the sky. Stratus clouds usually form at low altitudes and may be associated with fair weather or rain or snow. When air is cooled to its dew point near the ground, it forms a stratus cloud called **fog,** as shown in **Figure 6.**

Cumulus (KYEW myuh lus) clouds are masses of puffy, white clouds, often with flat bases. They sometimes tower to great heights and can be associated with fair weather or thunderstorms.

Cirrus (SIHR us) clouds appear fibrous or curly. They are high, thin, white, feathery clouds made of ice crystals. Cirrus clouds are associated with fair weather, but they can indicate approaching storms.

Height Some prefixes of cloud names describe the height of the cloud base. The prefix *cirro-* describes high clouds, *alto-* describes middle-elevation clouds, and *strato-* refers to clouds at low elevations. Some clouds' names combine the altitude prefix with the term *stratus* or *cumulus*.

Cirrostratus clouds are high clouds, like those in **Figure 7.** Usually, cirrostratus clouds indicate fair weather, but they also can signal an approaching storm. Altostratus clouds form at middle levels. If the clouds are not too thick, sunlight can filter through them.

Figure 6
Fog surrounds the Golden Gate Bridge, San Francisco. Fog is a stratus cloud near the ground.

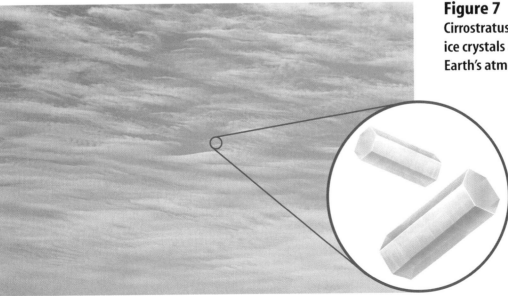
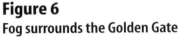

Figure 7
Cirrostratus clouds are made of ice crystals and form high in Earth's atmosphere.

Figure 8
Water vapor in air collects on particles to form water droplets or ice crystals. The type of precipitation that is received on the ground depends on the temperature of the air.

A When the air is warm, water vapor forms raindrops that fall as rain.

B When the air is cold, water vapor forms snowflakes.

Rain- or Snow-Producing Clouds Clouds associated with rain or snow often have the word nimbus attached to them. The term *nimbus* is Latin for "dark rain cloud" and this is a good description, because the water content of these clouds is so high that little sunlight can pass through them. When a cumulus cloud grows into a thunderstorm, it is called a cumulonimbus (kyew myuh loh NIHM bus) cloud. These clouds can tower to nearly 18,000 km. Nimbostratus clouds are layered clouds that can bring long, steady rain or snowfall.

Precipitation

Water falling from clouds is called **precipitation.** Precipitation occurs when cloud droplets combine and grow large enough to fall to Earth. The cloud droplets form around small particles, such as salt and dust. These particles are so small that a puff of smoke can contain millions of them.

You might have noticed that raindrops are not all the same size. The size of raindrops depends on several factors. One factor is the strength of updrafts in a cloud. Strong updrafts can keep drops suspended in the air where they can combine with other drops and grow larger. The rate of evaporation as a drop falls to Earth also can affect its size. If the air is dry, the size of raindrops can be reduced or they can completely evaporate before reaching the ground.

Air temperature determines whether water forms rain, snow, sleet, or hail. **Figure 8** shows these main types of precipitation. Drops of water falling in temperatures above freezing fall as rain. Snow forms when the air temperature is so cold that water vapor changes directly to a solid. Sleet forms when raindrops pass through a layer of freezing air near Earth's surface, forming ice pellets.

✔ **Reading Check** *What are the four main types of precipitation?*

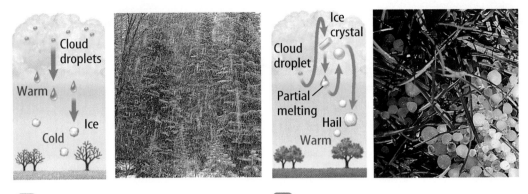

C When the air near the ground is cold, sleet, which is made up of many small ice pellets, falls.

D Hailstones are pellets of ice that form inside a cloud.

Hail Hail is precipitation in the form of lumps of ice. Hail forms in cumulonimbus clouds of a thunderstorm when water freezes in layers around a small nucleus of ice. Hailstones grow larger as they're tossed up and down by rising and falling air. Most hailstones are smaller than 2.5 cm but can grow larger than a softball. Of all forms of precipitation, hail produces the most damage immediately, especially if winds blow during a hailstorm. Falling hailstones can break windows and destroy crops.

If you understand the role of water vapor in the atmosphere, you can begin to understand weather. The relative humidity of the air helps determine whether a location will have a dry day or experience some form of precipitation. The temperature of the atmosphere determines the form of precipitation. Studying clouds can add to your ability to forecast weather.

Section 1 Assessment

1. When does water vapor in air condense?
2. What is the difference between humidity and relative humidity?
3. How do clouds form?
4. How does precipitation occur and what determines the type of precipitation that falls to Earth?
5. **Think Critically** Cumulonimbus clouds form when warm, moist air is suddenly lifted. How can the same cumulonimbus cloud produce rain and hail?

Skill Builder Activities

6. **Concept Mapping** Make a network-tree concept map that compares clouds and their descriptions. Use these terms: *cirrus, cumulus, stratus, feathery, fair weather, puffy, layered, precipitation, clouds, dark,* and *steady precipitation.* **For more help, refer to the** Science Skill Handbook.

7. **Making and Using Graphs** Use **Figure 4** to determine how much water vapor can be present in air when the temperature is 40℃. **For more help, refer to the** Science Skill Handbook.

Weather Patterns

As You Read

What You'll Learn

- **Describe** how weather is associated with fronts and high- and low-pressure areas.
- **Explain** how tornadoes develop from thunderstorms.
- **Discuss** the dangers of severe weather.

Vocabulary

air mass   hurricane
front   blizzard
tornado

Why It's Important

Air masses, pressure systems, and fronts cause weather to change.

Weather Changes

When you leave for school in the morning, the weather might be different from what it is when you head home in the afternoon. Because of the movement of air and moisture in the atmosphere, weather constantly changes.

Air Masses An **air mass** is a large body of air that has properties similar to the part of Earth's surface over which it develops. For example, an air mass that develops over land is dry compared with one that develops over water. An air mass that develops in the tropics is warmer than one that develops over northern regions. An air mass can cover thousands of square kilometers. When you observe a change in the weather from one day to the next, it is due to the movement of air masses. **Figure 9** shows air masses that affect the United States.

Figure 9
Six major air masses affect weather in the United States. Each air mass has the same characteristics of temperature and moisture content as the area over which it formed.

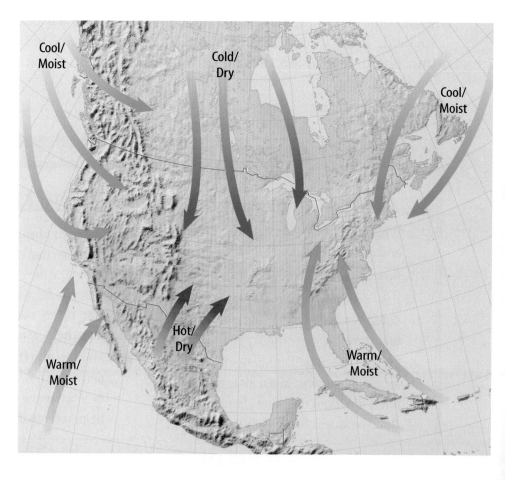

Highs and Lows

Atmospheric pressure varies over Earth's surface. Anyone who has watched a weather report on television has heard about high- and low-pressure systems. Recall that winds blow from areas of high pressure to areas of low pressure. As winds blow into a low-pressure area in the northern hemisphere, Earth's rotation causes these winds to swirl in a counterclockwise direction. Large, swirling areas of low pressure are called cyclones and are associated with stormy weather.

✔ Reading Check *How do winds move in a cyclone?*

Winds blow away from a center of high pressure. Earth's rotation causes these winds to spiral clockwise in the northern hemisphere. High-pressure areas are associated with fair weather and are called anticyclones. Air pressure is measured using a barometer, like the one shown in **Figure 10.**

Variation in atmospheric pressure affects the weather. Low pressure systems at Earth's surface are regions of rising air. In Section 1, you learned that clouds form when air is lifted and cools. Areas of low pressure usually have cloudy weather. Sinking motion in high-pressure air masses makes it difficult for air to rise and clouds to form. That's why high pressure usually means good weather.

Figure 10
A barometer measures atmospheric pressure. The red pointer points to the current pressure. *Watch how atmospheric pressure changes over time when you line up the white pointer to the one indicating the current pressure each day.*

Fronts

A boundary between two air masses of different density, moisture, or temperature is called a **front.** If you've seen a weather map in the newspaper or on the evening news, you've seen fronts represented by various types of curving lines.

Cloudiness, precipitation, and storms sometimes occur at frontal boundaries. Four types of fronts include cold, warm, occluded, and stationary.

Cold and Warm Fronts A cold front, shown on a map as a blue line with triangles, occurs when colder air advances toward warm air. The cold air wedges under the warm air like a plow. As the warm air is lifted, it cools and water vapor condenses, forming clouds. When the temperature difference between the cold and warm air is large, thunderstorms and even tornadoes may form.

Warm fronts form when lighter, warmer air advances over heavier, colder air. A warm front is drawn on weather maps as a red line with red semicircles.

Data Update Visit the Glencoe Science Web site at **science.glencoe.com** to find the current atmospheric pressure, temperature, and wind direction in your town or nearest city. Look up these weather conditons for a city west of your town. Forecast the weather for your town based on your research.

Occluded and Stationary Fronts An occluded front involves three air masses of different temperatures—colder air, cool air, and warm air. An occluded front may form when a cold air mass moves toward cooler air with warm air between the two. The colder air forces the warm air upward, closing off the warm air from the surface. Occluded fronts are shown on maps as purple lines with triangles and semicircles.

A stationary front occurs when a boundary between air masses stops advancing. Stationary fronts may remain in the same place for several days, producing light wind and precipitation. A stationary front is drawn on a weather map as an alternating red and blue line. Red semicircles point toward the cold air and blue triangles point toward the warm air. **Figure 11** summarizes the four types of fronts.

Figure 11
Cold, warm, occluded, and stationary fronts occur at the boundaries of air masses. Cloudiness and precipitation occur at front boundaries.

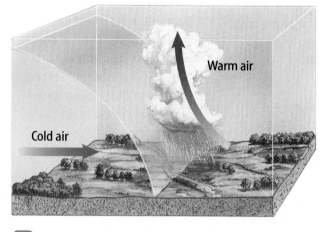

A A cold front can advance rapidly. Thunderstorms often form as warm air is suddenly lifted up over the cold air.

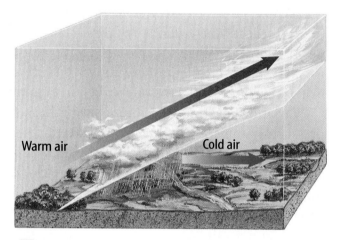

B Warm air slides over colder air along a warm front, forming a boundary with a gentle slope. This can lead to hours, if not days, of wet weather.

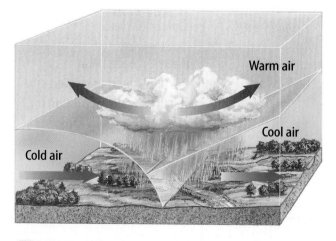

C The term *occlusion* means "closure." Colder air forces warm air upward, forming an occluded front that closes off the warm air from the surface.

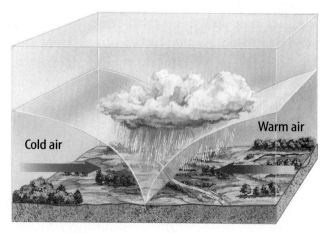

D A stationary front results when neither cold air nor warm air advances.

Severe Weather

Despite the weather, you usually can do your daily activities. If it's raining, you still go to school. You can still get there even if it snows a little. However, some weather conditions, such as those caused by thunderstorms, tornadoes, and blizzards, prevent you from going about your normal routine. Severe weather poses danger to people, structures, and animals.

Thunderstorms In a thunderstorm, heavy rain falls, lightning flashes, thunder roars, and hail might fall. What forces cause such extreme weather conditions? Thunderstorms occur in warm, moist air masses and along fronts. Warm, moist air can be rapidly forced upward where it cools and condenses, forming cumulonimbus clouds that can reach heights of 18 km, like the one in **Figure 12.** When rising air cools, water vapor condenses into water droplets or ice crystals. Smaller droplets collide to form larger ones, and the droplets fall through the cloud toward Earth's surface. The falling droplets collide with still more droplets and grow larger. Raindrops cool the air around them. This cool, dense air then sinks and spreads over Earth's surface. Sinking rain-cooled air and strong updrafts of warmer air cause the strong winds associated with thunderstorms. Hail also may form as ice crystals alternately fall to warmer layers and are lifted into colder layers by the strong updrafts inside cumulonimbus clouds.

Thunderstorm damage Sometimes thunderstorms can stall over a region, causing rain to fall heavily for a period of time. When streams cannot contain all the water running into them, flash flooding can occur. Flash floods can be dangerous because they occur with little warning.

Strong winds generated by thunderstorms also can cause damage. If a thunderstorm is accompanied by winds traveling faster than 89 km/h, it is classified as a severe thunderstorm. Hail from a thunderstorm can dent cars and the aluminum siding on houses. Although rain from thunderstorms helps crops grow, hail has been known to flatten and destroy entire crops in a matter of minutes.

Figure 12
Tall cumulonimbus clouds may form quickly as warm, moist air rapidly rises.

Figure 13
This time-elapsed photo shows a thunderstorm over Arizona.

Research Visit the Glencoe Science Web site at **science.glencoe.com** to research the number of lightning strikes in your state during the last year. Compare your findings with previous years. Communicate to your class what you learn.

Lightning and Thunder

What are lightning and thunder? Inside a storm cloud, warm air is lifted rapidly as cooler air sinks. This movement of air can cause different parts of a cloud to become oppositely charged. When current flows between regions of opposite electrical charge, lightning flashes. Lightning, as shown in **Figure 13,** can occur within a cloud, between clouds, or between a cloud and the ground.

Thunder results from the rapid heating of air around a bolt of lightning. Lightning can reach temperatures of about 30,000°C, which is more than five times the temperature of the surface of the Sun. This extreme heat causes air around the lightning to expand rapidly. Then it cools quickly and contracts. The rapid movement of the molecules forms sound waves heard as thunder.

Tornadoes Some of the most severe thunderstorms produce tornadoes. A **tornado** is a violent, whirling wind that moves in a narrow path over land. In severe thunderstorms, wind at different heights blows in different directions and at different speeds. This difference in wind speed and direction, called wind shear, creates a rotating column parallel to the ground. A thunderstorm's updraft can tilt the rotating column upward into the thunderstorm creating a funnel cloud. If the funnel comes into contact with Earth's surface, it is called a tornado.

✔ **Reading Check** *What causes a tornado to form?*

A tornado's destructive winds can rip apart buildings and uproot trees. High winds can blow through broken windows. When winds blow inside a house, they can lift off the roof and blow out the walls, making it look as though the building exploded. The updraft in the center of a powerful tornado can lift animals, cars, and even houses into the air. Although tornadoes rarely exceed 200 m in diameter and usually last only a few minutes, they often are extremely destructive. In May 1999, multiple thunderstorms produced more than 70 tornadoes in Kansas, Oklahoma, and Texas. This severe tornado outbreak caused 40 deaths, 100 injuries, and more than $1.2 billion in property damage.

Figure 14

Tornadoes are extremely rapid, rotating winds that form at the base of cumulonimbus clouds. Smaller tornadoes may even form inside larger ones. Luckily, most tornadoes remain on the ground for just a few minutes. During that time, however, they can cause considerable—and sometimes strange— damage, such as driving a fork into a tree.

Tornadoes often form from a type of cumulonimbus cloud called a wall cloud. Strong, spiraling updrafts of warm, moist air may form in these clouds. As air spins upward, a low-pressure area forms, and the cloud descends to the ground in a funnel. The tornado sucks up debris as it moves along the ground, forming a dust envelope.

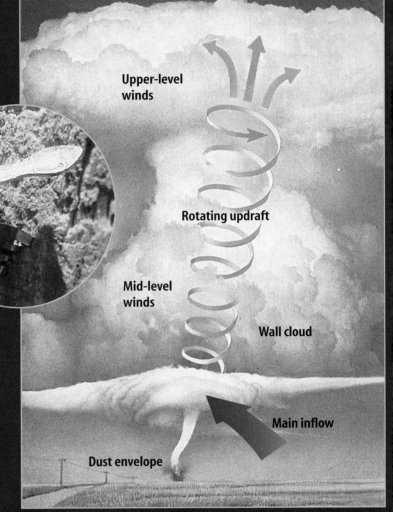

Upper-level winds

Rotating updraft

Mid-level winds

Wall cloud

Main inflow

Dust envelope

F0   F1   F2   F3   F4   F5

The Fujita Scale

	Wind speed (km/h)	Damage
F0	<116	Light: broken branches and chimneys
F1	116–180	Moderate: roofs damaged, mobile homes upturned
F2	181–253	Considerable: roofs torn off homes, large trees uprooted
F3	254–332	Severe: trains overturned, roofs and walls torn off
F4	333–419	Devastating: houses completely destroyed, cars picked up and carried elsewhere
F5	420–512	Incredible: total demolition

The Fujita scale, named after tornado expert Theodore Fujita, ranks tornadoes according to how much damage they cause. Fortunately, only one percent of tornadoes are classified as violent (F4 and F5).

Environmental Science

INTEGRATION

Some scientists hypothesize that Earth's ocean temperatures are increasing due to global warming. In your Science Journal, predict what might happen to the strength of hurricanes if Earth's oceans become warmer.

Figure 15
In this hurricane cross section, the small, red arrows indicate rising, warm, moist air. This air forms cumulus and cumulonimbus clouds in bands around the eye. The green arrows indicate cool, dry air sinking in the eye and between the cloud bands.

Hurricanes The most powerful storm is the hurricane. A **hurricane,** illustrated in **Figure 15,** is a large, swirling, low-pressure system that forms over the warm Atlantic ocean. It is like a machine that turns heat energy from the ocean into wind. A storm must have winds of at least 120 km/h to be called a hurricane. Similar storms are called typhoons in the Pacific Ocean and cyclones in the Indian Ocean.

Hurricanes are similar to low-pressure systems on land, but they are much stronger. In the Atlantic and Pacific Oceans, low pressure sometimes develops near the equator. In the northern hemisphere, winds around this low pressure begin rotating counterclockwise. The strongest hurricanes affecting North America usually begin as a low-pressure system east of Africa. Steered by surface winds, these storms can travel west, gaining strength from the heat and moisture of warm ocean water.

When a hurricane strikes land, high winds, tornadoes, heavy rains, and high waves can cause a lot of damage. Floods from the heavy rains can cause additional damage. Hurricane weather can destroy crops, demolish buildings, and kill people and other animals. As long as a hurricane is over water, the warm, moist air rises and provides energy for the storm. When a hurricane reaches land, however, its supply of energy disappears and the storm loses power.

Outflow

Descending air

Warm moist air

Eye

Spiral rain bands

Blizzards Severe storms also can occur in winter. If you live in the northern United States, you may have awakened from a winter night's sleep to a cold, howling wind and blowing snow, like the storm in **Figure 16.** The National Weather Service classifies a winter storm as a **blizzard** if the winds are 51 km/h, the temperature is −12°C or below, the visibility is less than 200 m in falling or blowing snow, and if these conditions persist for three hours or more.

Figure 16
Blizzards can be extremely dangerous because of their high winds, low temperatures, and poor visibility.

Severe Weather Safety When severe weather threatens, the National Weather Service issues a watch or warning. Watches are issued when conditions are favorable for severe thunderstorms, tornadoes, floods, blizzards, and hurricanes. During a watch, stay tuned to a radio or television station reporting the weather. When a warning is issued, severe weather conditions already exist. You should take immediate action. During a severe thunderstorm or tornado warning, take shelter in the basement or a room in the middle of the house away from windows. When a hurricane or flood watch is issued, be prepared to leave your home and move farther inland.

Blizzards can be blinding and have dangerously low temperatures with high winds. During a blizzard, stay indoors. Spending too much time outside can result in severe frostbite.

Section 2 Assessment

1. Why is fair weather common during periods of high pressure?

2. How does a cold front form? What effect does a cold front have on weather?

3. What causes lightning and thunder in a thunderstorm?

4. What is the difference between a watch and a warning? How can you keep safe during a hurricane warning?

5. **Think Critically** Explain why some fronts produce stronger storms than others.

Skill Builder Activities

6. **Recognizing Cause and Effect** Describe how an occluded front may form over your city and what effects it can have on the weather. **For more help, refer to the** Science Skill Handbook.

7. **Using an Electronic Spreadsheet** Make a spreadsheet comparing warm fronts, cold fronts, occluded fronts, and stationary fronts. Indicate what kind of clouds and weather systems form with each. **For more help, refer to the** Technology Skill Handbook.

Weather Forecasts

As You Read

What You'll Learn
- **Explain** how data are collected for weather maps and forecasts.
- **Identify** the symbols used in a weather station model.

Vocabulary
meteorologist   isotherm
station model   isobar

Why It's Important
Weather observations help you predict future weather events.

Weather Observations

You can determine current weather conditions by checking the thermometer and looking to see whether clouds are in the sky. You know when it's raining. You have a general idea of the weather because you are familiar with the typical weather where you live. If you live in Florida, you don't expect snow in the forecast. If you live in Maine, you assume it will snow every winter. What weather concerns do you have in your region?

A **meteorologist** (meet ee uh RAH luh jist) is a person who studies the weather. Meteorologists take measurements of temperature, air pressure, winds, humidity, and precipitation. Computers, weather satellites, Doppler radar shown in **Figure 17,** and instruments attached to balloons are used to gather data. Such instruments improve meteorologists' ability to predict the weather. Meteorologists use the information provided by weather instruments to make weather maps. These maps are used to make weather forecasts.

Forecasting Weather Meteorologists gather information about current weather and use computers to make predictions about future weather patterns. Because storms can be dangerous, you do not want to be unprepared for threatening weather. However, meteorologists cannot always predict the weather exactly because conditions can change rapidly.

The National Weather Service depends on two sources for its information—data collected from the upper atmosphere and data collected on Earth's surface. Meteorologists of the National Weather Service collect information recorded by satellites, instruments attached to weather balloons, and from radar. This information is used to describe weather conditions in the atmosphere above Earth's surface.

Figure 17
A meteorologist uses Doppler radar to track a tornado. Since the nineteenth century, technology has greatly improved weather forecasting.

Station Models When meteorologists gather data from Earth's surface, it is recorded on a map using a combination of symbols, forming a **station model.** A station model, like the one in **Figure 18,** shows the weather conditions at a specific location on Earth's surface. Information provided by station models and instruments in the upper atmosphere is entered into computers and used to forecast weather.

Temperature and Pressure In addition to station models, weather maps have lines that connect locations of equal temperature or pressure. A line that connects points of equal temperature is called an **isotherm** (I suh thurm). *Iso* means "same" and *therm* means "temperature." You probably have seen isotherms on weather maps on TV or in the newspaper.

An **isobar** is a line drawn to connect points of equal atmospheric pressure. You can tell how fast wind is blowing in an area by noting how closely isobars are spaced. Isobars that are close together indicate a large pressure difference over a small area. A large pressure difference causes strong winds. Isobars that are spread apart indicate a smaller difference in pressure. Winds in this area are gentler. Isobars also indicate the locations of high- and low-pressure areas.

Reading Check *How do isobars indicate wind speed?*

TRY AT HOME

Mini LAB

Measuring Rain

Procedure

1. You will need a **straight-sided container,** such as a soup or coffee can, **tape,** and a **ruler.**
2. Tape the ruler to the inner wall of your container.
3. Place the container on a level surface outdoors away from buildings or plants.
4. Measure the amount of water in your container after it rains. Continue to take measurements for a week.

Analysis

1. What was the average daily rainfall?
2. Why is it necessary to use containers with straight sides?

Figure 18
A station model shows the weather conditions at one specific location.

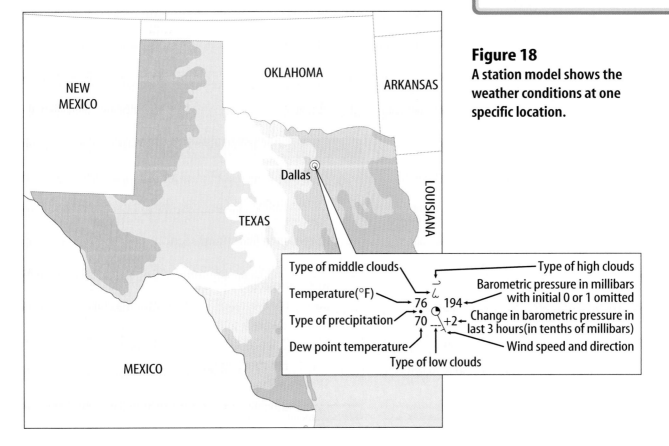

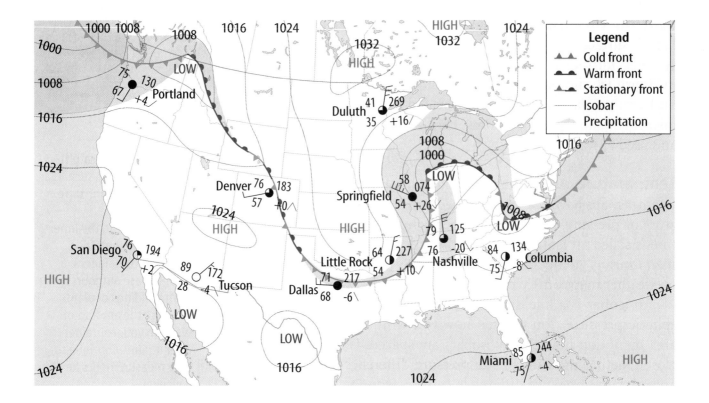

Figure 19
Highs, lows, isobars, and fronts on this weather map help meteorologists forecast the weather.

Weather Maps On a weather map like the one in **Figure 19,** pressure areas are drawn as circles with the word High or Low in the middle of the circle. Fronts are drawn as lines and symbols. When you watch weather forecasts on television, notice how weather fronts move from west to east. This is a pattern that meteorologists depend on to forecast weather.

Section ③ Assessment

1. What instruments do meteorologists use to collect weather data?

2. What is a station model?

3. Where does the National Weather Service get information to make weather maps?

4. What do closely spaced isobars on a weather map indicate?

5. **Think Critically** In the morning you hear a meteorologist forecast today's weather as sunny and warm. After school, it is raining. Why is the weather so hard to predict?

Skill Builder Activities

6. **Concept Mapping** Using a computer, make an events chain concept map for how a weather forecast is made. **For more help, refer to the** Science Skill Handbook.

7. **Communicating** Research what happened to American colonial troops at Valley Forge during the winter of 1777–1778. Imagine that you were a soldier during that winter. In your Science Journal, describe your experiences. **For more help, refer to the** Science Skill Handbook.

Activity

Reading a Weather Map

Meteorologists use a series of symbols to provide a picture of local and national weather conditions. With what you know, can you interpret weather information from weather map symbols?

What You'll Investigate
How do you read a weather map?

Materials
hand lens
Weather Map Symbols Appendix
Figure 19

Goals
■ **Learn** how to read a weather map.
■ **Use** information from a station model and maps to forecast weather.

Procedure
Use the information provided in the questions below and the Weather Map Symbols Appendix to learn how to read a weather map.

1. Find the station models on the map for Portland, Oregon, and Miami, Florida. Find the dew point, wind direction, barometric pressure, and temperature at each location.

2. Looking at the placement of the isobars, determine whether the wind would be stronger at Springfield, Illinois, or at San Diego, California. Record your answer. What is another way to determine the wind speed at these locations?

3. **Determine** the type of front near Dallas, Texas. Record your answer.

4. The triangles or half-circles are on the side of the line toward the direction the front is moving. What direction is the cold front located over Washington State moving?

Conclude and Apply

1. Locate the pressure system over southeast Kansas. Predict what will happen to the weather of Nashville, Tennessee, if this pressure system moves there.

2. Prevailing westerlies are winds responsible for the movement of much of the weather across the United States. Based on this, would you expect Columbia, South Carolina, to continue to have clear skies? Explain.

3. The direction line on the station model indicates the direction from which the wind blows. The wind is named for that direction. Infer from this the name of the wind blowing at Little Rock, Arkansas.

*C*ommunicating
Your Data

Pretend you are a meteorologist for a local TV news station. Make a poster of your weather data and present a weather forecast to your class. **For more help, refer to the** Science Skill Handbook.

Activity
Model and Invent

Measuring Wind Speed

When you watch a gust of wind blow leaves down the street, do you wonder how fast the wind is moving? For centuries, people could only guess at wind speeds, but in 1805, Admiral Beaufort of the British navy invented a method for estimating wind speeds based on their effect on sails. Later, Beaufort's system was modified for use on land. Meteorologists use a simple instrument called an anemometer to measure wind speeds, and they still use Beaufort's system to estimate the speed of the wind. What type of instrument or system can you invent to measure wind speed?

Recognize the Problem

How could you use simple materials to invent an instrument or system for measuring wind speeds?

Thinking Critically

What observations do you use to estimate the speed of the wind?

Goals
- **Invent** an instrument or devise a system for measuring wind speeds using common materials.
- **Devise** a method for using your invention or system to compare different wind speeds.

Possible Materials
paper
scissors
confetti
grass clippings
meterstick
*measuring tape
*Alternate materials

Data Source
Refer to Section 1 for more information about anemometers and other wind speed instruments. Consult the data table for information about Beaufort's wind speed scale.

Planning the Model

1. Scan the list of possible materials and choose the materials you will need to devise your system.

2. **Devise** a system to measure different wind speeds. Be certain the materials you use are light enough to be moved by slight breezes.

Check the Model Plans

1. **Describe** your plan to your teacher. Provide a sketch of your instrument or system and ask your teacher how you might improve its design.

2. Present your idea for measuring wind speed to the class in the form of a diagram or poster. Ask your classmates to suggest improvements in your design that will make your system more accurate or easy to use.

Beaufort's Wind Speed Scale	
Description	Wind Speed (km/h)
calm—smoke drifts up	less than 1
light air—smoke drifts with wind	1–5
light breeze—leaves rustle	6–11
gentle breeze—leaves move constantly	12–19
moderate breeze—branches move	20–29
fresh breeze—small trees sway	30–39
strong breeze—large branches move	40–50
moderate gale—whole trees move	51–61
fresh gale—twigs break	62–74
strong gale—slight damage to houses	75–87
whole gale—much damage to houses	88–101
storm—extensive damage	102–120
hurricane—extreme damage	more than 120

Making the Model

1. Confetti or grass clippings that are all the same size can be used to measure wind speed by dropping them from a specific height. Measuring the distances they travel in different strength winds will provide data for devising a wind speed scale.

2. Different sizes and shapes of paper also could be dropped into the wind, and the strength of the wind would be determined by measuring the distances traveled by these different types of paper.

Analyzing and Applying Results

1. **Explain** why it is important for meteorologists to measure wind speeds.

2. **Compare** your results with Beaufort's wind speed scale.

3. **Develop** a scale for your method.

4. **Evaluate** how well your system worked in gentle breezes and strong winds.

5. **Analyze** what problems may exist in the design of your system and suggest steps you could take to improve your design.

*C*ommunicating Your Data

Demonstrate your system for the class. Compare your results and measurements with the results of other classmates.

Rain

You listen to a meteorologist give the long-term weather forecast. Another week with no rain in sight. As a farmer, you are concerned that your crops are withering in the fields. Homeowners' lawns are turning brown. Wildfires are possible. Cattle are starving. And, if farmers' crops die, there could be a shortage of food and prices will go up for consumers.

Cloud seeding is an inexact science makers

Flares contain chemicals which will seed clouds.

Meanwhile, several states away, another farmer is listening to the weather report calling for another week of rain. Her crops are getting so water-soaked that they are beginning to rot.

Weather. Can't scientists find a way to better control it? The answer is...not exactly. Scientists have been experimenting with methods to control our weather since the 1940s. And nothing really works.

Cloud seeding is one such attempt. It uses technology to enhance the natural rainfall process. The idea has been used to create rain where it is needed or to reduce hail damage. Government officials also use cloud seeding or weather modification to try to reduce the force of a severe storm.

Some people seed a cloud by flying a plane above it and releasing highway-type flares with chemicals, such as silver iodide. Another method is to fly beneath the cloud and spray a chemical that can be carried into the cloud by air currents.

Flares are lodged under a plane. The pilot will drop them into potential rain clouds.

Cloud seeding doesn't work with clouds that have little water vapor or are not near the dew point. Seeding chemicals must be released into potential rain clouds. The chemicals provide nuclei for water molecules to cluster around. Water then falls to Earth as precipitation.

Cloud seeding does have its critics. If you seed clouds and cause rain for your area, aren't you preventing rain from falling in another area? Would that be considered "rain theft" by people who live in places where the cloudburst would naturally occur? What about those cloud-seeding agents? Could the cloud-seeding chemicals, such as silver iodide and acetone, affect the environment in a harmful way? Are humans meddling with nature which might create problems in ways that haven't been determined?

Currently, Montana, Pennsylvania, and New Mexico are states that don't allow cloud seeding within their state boundaries. But, officials in Texas and California, the two states with the largest number of cloud-seeding programs, feel strongly that cloud seeding is an important technology when it comes to dealing with weather.

CONNECTIONS **Debate** Learn more about cloud seeding and other methods of changing weather. Then debate whether or not cloud seeding can be considered "rain theft."

SCIENCE *Online* For more information, visit science.glencoe.com

Reviewing Main Ideas

Section 1 What is weather?

1. Important factors that determine weather include air pressure, wind, temperature, and the amount of moisture in the air.

2. More water vapor can be present in warm air than in cold air. Water vapor condenses when the dew point is reached. Clouds are formed when warm, moist air rises and cools to its dew point.

3. Rain, hail, sleet, and snow are types of precipitation. *What causes hail to form during severe thunderstorms?*

Section 2 Weather Patterns

1. Fronts form when air masses with different characteristics, such as temperature, moisture, or density, meet. Types of fronts include cold fronts, warm fronts, occluded fronts, and stationary fronts.

2. High atmospheric pressure at Earth's surface usually means good weather. Cloudy and stormy weather usually have low pressure.

3. Tornadoes are intense, whirling windstorms that can result from wind shears inside a thunderstorm.

4. Hurricanes and blizzards are large, severe storms with strong winds. *Why does a hurricane, shown below, lose strength as it moves over land?*

Section 3 Weather Forecasts

1. Meteorologists use information from radar, satellites, computers, and other weather instruments to make weather maps and forecasts.

2. Symbols on a station model indicate the weather at a particular location. *What is the dew point temperature on the station model shown here?*

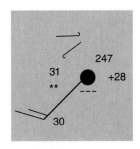

3. Weather maps include information about temperature and air pressure.

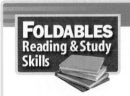

FOLDABLES
Reading & Study Skills

After You Read

To help you review facts about weather, use the Foldable you made at the beginning of the chapter.

Chapter 2 Study Guide

Visualizing Main Ideas

Complete the following concept map about air temperature, water vapor, and pressure.

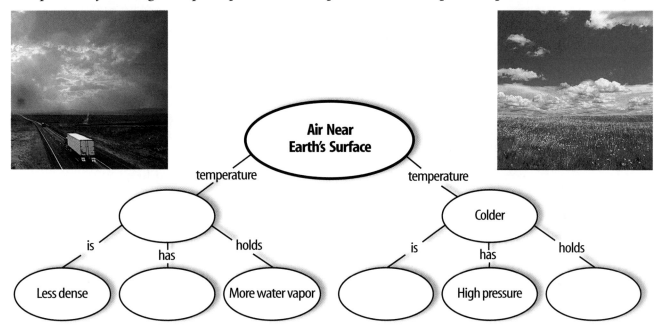

Vocabulary Review

Vocabulary Words

a. air mass
b. blizzard
c. dew point
d. fog
e. front
f. humidity
g. hurricane
h. isobar
i. isotherm
j. meteorologist
k. precipitation
l. relative humidity
m. station model
n. tornado
o. weather

Using Vocabulary

Explain the differences between the vocabulary words in each of the following sets.

1. air mass, front
2. humidity, relative humidity
3. relative humidity, dew point
4. dew point, precipitation
5. thunderstorm, tornado
6. blizzard, hurricane
7. meteorologist, station model
8. precipitation, fog
9. isobar, isotherm
10. isobar, front

Study Tip

After each day's lesson, make a practice quiz for yourself. Later, when you're studying for the test, take the practice quizzes that you created.

Checking Concepts

Choose the word or phrase that best answers the question.

1. Which type of air has a relative humidity of 100 percent?
A) humid   **C)** dry
B) temperate   **D)** saturated

2. What is a large body of air that has the same properties as the area over which it formed called?
A) air mass   **C)** front
B) station model **D)** isotherm

3. At what temperature does water vapor in air condense?
A) dew point   **C)** front
B) station model **D)** isobar

4. Which type of precipitation forms when water vapor changes directly into a solid?
A) rain   **C)** sleet
B) hail   **D)** snow

5. Which type of the following clouds are high feathery clouds made of ice crystals?
A) cirrus   **C)** cumulus
B) nimbus   **D)** stratus

6. Which type of front may form when cool air, cold air and warm air meet?
A) warm   **C)** stationary
B) cold   **D)** occluded

7. Which is issued when severe weather conditions exist and immediate action should be taken?
A) front   **C)** station model
B) watch   **D)** warning

8. Which term means the amount of water vapor in the air?
A) dew point   **C)** humidity
B) precipitation **D)** relative humidity

9. What does an anemometer measure?
A) air pressure   **C)** wind speed
B) relative humidity   **D)** precipitation

10. What is a large, swirling storm that forms over warm, tropical water called?
A) hurricane   **C)** blizzard
B) tornado   **D)** hailstorm

Thinking Critically

11. Explain the relationship between temperature and relative humidity.

12. Describe how air, water, and the Sun interact to cause weather.

13. Explain why northwest Washington often has rainy weather and southwest Texas is dry.

14. What does it mean if the relative humidity is 79 percent?

15. Why don't hurricanes form in Earth's polar regions?

Developing Skills

16. Comparing and Contrasting Compare and contrast the weather at a cold front to that at a warm front.

17. Observing and Inferring You take a hot shower. The mirror in the bathroom fogs up, like the one below. Infer from this information what has happened.

18. Recording Observations Use the cloud descriptions in Section 1 of this chapter to describe the weather at your location today. Then try to predict tomorrow's weather. Repeat for one week.

19. Concept Mapping Complete the sequence map below showing how precipitation forms.

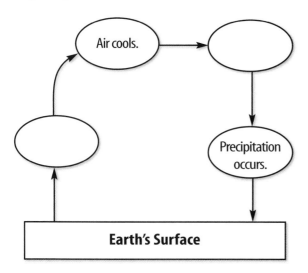

Air cools.

Precipitation occurs.

Earth's Surface

20. Comparing and Contrasting Compare and contrast tornadoes and thunderstorms.

Performance Assessment

21. Board Game Make a board game using weather terms. You could make cards to advance or retreat a token.

22. Design your own weather station. Record temperature, precipitation, and wind speed for one week.

TECHNOLOGY

Go to the Glencoe Science Web site at **science.glencoe.com** or use the **Glencoe Science CD-ROM** for additional chapter assessment.

THE PRINCETON REVIEW — Test Practice

Hurricanes are rated on a scale based on their wind speed and barometric pressure. The table below lists the hurricane category by the wind speed and pressure of the storm.

Hurricane Rating Scale		
Category	Wind Speed (km/h)	Barometric Pressure (millibars)
1	120–154	>980
2	155–177	965–980
3	178–209	945–964
4	210–250	920–944
5	>250	<920

Study the table and answer the following questions.

1. In 1992, Hurricane Andrew, with winds of 233 km/hr and a pressure of 922 mb struck southeast Florida. What category was Hurricane Andrew?

A) 1   **C)** 3
B) 2   **D)** 4

2. Which of the following best describes the pressure and wind when categorizing a hurricane?

F) Storm category increases as wind increases and pressure decreases.
G) Storm category increases as wind decreases and pressure increases.
H) Storm category increases as wind and pressure increase.
J) Storm category decreases as wind and pressure decrease.

Climate

As summer fades, trees take on the beautiful colors of autumn. As the temperature continues to drop throughout the season, those beautiful leaves will fall, and the bare branches will signify winter. What causes the change in seasons? Why do some places have four distinct seasons, while others have only a wet and dry season? In this chapter, you will learn what climate is, and how climates are classified. You also will learn what causes climate changes and how humans and animals adapt to different climates.

What do you think?

Science Journal Look at the picture below with a classmate. Discuss what you think this might be or what is happening. Here's a hint: *These are frozen, but they aren't trees.* Write your best guess in your Science Journal.

EXPLORE ACTIVITY

Y ou wouldn't go to Alaska to swim or to Jamaica to snow ski. You know the climates in these places aren't suited for these sports. In this activity, you'll explore the climates in different parts of the world.

Track the climates of the world

1. Obtain a world atlas, globe, or large classroom map. Select several cities from as many different parts of the world as possible.

2. Record the longitude and latitude of your cities. Note if they are near mountains or an ocean.

3. Research the average temperature of your cities. In what months are they hottest? Coldest? What is the average yearly rainfall? What kinds of plants and animals live in the region? Record your findings.

4. Compare your findings with those of the rest of your class. Can you see any relationship between latitude and climate? Do cities near an ocean or a mountain range have different climatic characteristics?

Observe

As you read the chapter, keep track of the daily weather conditions in your cities. Are these representative of the kind of climates your cities are supposed to have? Suggest reasons why day-to-day weather conditions may vary.

Before You Read

FOLDABLES
Reading & Study Skills

Making a Classify Study Fold Make the following Foldable to help you organize objects or events into groups based on their common features.

1. Place a sheet of paper in front of you so the short side is at the top. Fold the paper in half from top to bottom. Then fold it in half again top to bottom two more times. Unfold all the folds.

2. Using the fold lines as a guide, refold the paper into a fan. Unfold all the folds again.

3. Title your Foldable *Climate Classifications* and label the sections *Tropical, Mild, Dry, Continental, Polar,* and *High Elevation*.

4. As you read the chapter, define each and write notes on weather patterns on the back of each fold.

> *Climate Classification*
> *Tropical*
> *Mild*
> *Dry*
> *Continental*
> *Polar*
> *High Elevation*

What is climate?

As You Read

What You'll Learn

- **Describe** what determines climate.
- **Explain** how latitude and other factors affect the climate of a region.

Vocabulary

climate
tropics
polar zone
temperate zone

Why It's Important

Climate affects the way you live.

Climate

If you wandered through a tropical rain forest, you would see beautiful plants flowering in shades of pink and purple beneath a canopy of towering trees. A variety of exotic birds and other animals would dart among the tree branches and across the forest floor. The sounds of singing birds and croaking frogs would surround you. All of these organisms thrive in hot temperatures and abundant rainfall. Rain forests have a hot, wet climate. **Climate** is the pattern of weather that occurs in an area over many years. It determines the types of plants or animals that can survive, and it influences how people live.

Climate is determined by averaging the weather of a region over a long period of time, such as 30 years. Scientists average temperature, precipitation, air pressure, humidity, and number of days of sunshine to determine an area's climate. Some factors that affect the climate of a region include latitude, landforms, location of lakes and oceans, and ocean currents.

Latitude and Climate

As you can see in **Figure 1,** regions close to the equator receive the most solar radiation. Latitude, a measure of distance north or south of the equator, affects climate. **Figure 2** compares cities at different latitudes. The **tropics**—the region between latitudes 23°N and 23°S—receive the most solar radiation because the Sun shines almost directly over these areas. The tropics have temperatures that are always hot, except at high elevations. The **polar zones** extend from 66°N and 66°S latitude to the poles. Solar radiation hits these zones at a low angle, spreading energy over a large area. During winter, polar regions receive little or no solar radiation. Therefore, polar regions are never warm.

✔ **Reading Check** *How does latitude affect climate?*

Between the tropics and the polar zones are the **temperate zones.** Temperatures here are moderate. Most of the United States is in a temperate zone.

Figure 1
The tropics are warmer than the temperate zones and the polar zones because the tropics receive the most direct solar energy.

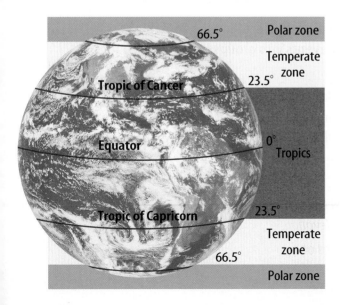

Polar zone
66.5°
Temperate zone
Tropic of Cancer
23.5°
Equator
0°
Tropics
Tropic of Capricorn
23.5°
Temperate zone
66.5°
Polar zone

Other Factors

In addition to the general climate divisions of polar, temperate, and tropical, natural features such as large bodies of water, ocean currents, and mountains affect climate within each zone. Large cities also change weather patterns and influence the local climate.

Large Bodies of Water If you live or have vacationed near an ocean, you may have noticed that water heats up and cools down more slowly than land does. This is because it takes a lot more heat to increase the temperature of water than it takes to increase the temperature of land. In addition, water must give up more heat than land does for it to cool. Large bodies of water can affect the climate of coastal areas by absorbing or giving off heat. This causes many coastal regions to be warmer in the winter and cooler in the summer than inland areas at similar latitude. Look at **Figure 2** again. You can see the effect of an ocean on climate by comparing the average temperatures in a coastal city and an inland city, both located at 37°N latitude.

Figure 2
This map shows average daily low temperatures in four cities during January and July. It also shows average yearly precipitation.

Mini LAB

Observing Solar Radiation

Procedure
1. Darken the room.
2. Hold a **flashlight** about 30 cm from a **globe.** Shine the light directly on the equator. With your finger, trace around the light.
3. Now, tilt the flashlight to shine on 30°N latitude. The size of the lighted area should increase. Repeat at 60°N latitude.

Analysis
1. How did the size and shape of the light beam change as you directed the light toward higher latitudes?
2. How does Earth's tilt affect the solar radiation received by different latitudes?

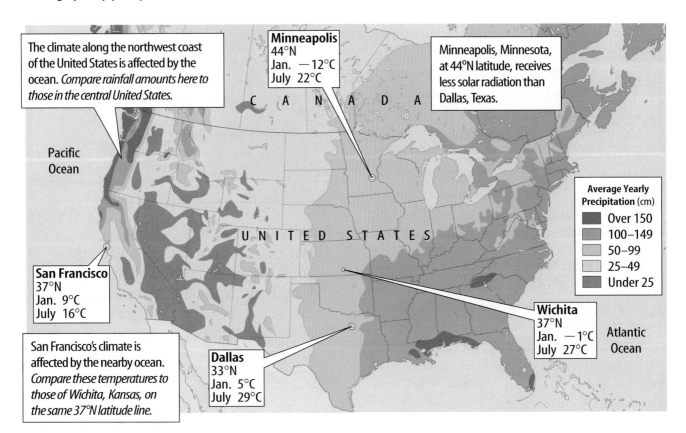

The climate along the northwest coast of the United States is affected by the ocean. *Compare rainfall amounts here to those in the central United States.*

Minneapolis
44°N
Jan. −12°C
July 22°C

Minneapolis, Minnesota, at 44°N latitude, receives less solar radiation than Dallas, Texas.

Pacific Ocean

C A N A D A

U N I T E D   S T A T E S

Average Yearly Precipitation (cm)
- Over 150
- 100–149
- 50–99
- 25–49
- Under 25

San Francisco
37°N
Jan. 9°C
July 16°C

San Francisco's climate is affected by the nearby ocean. *Compare these temperatures to those of Wichita, Kansas, on the same 37°N latitude line.*

Dallas
33°N
Jan. 5°C
July 29°C

Wichita
37°N
Jan. −1°C
July 27°C

Atlantic Ocean

When air rises over a mountain, the air expands and its temperature decreases, causing water vapor to condense and form rain. Temperature changes caused by air expanding or contracting also occur in some machines. Why does the air coming out of a bicycle pump feel cold?

Ocean Currents Ocean currents affect coastal climates. Warm currents begin near the equator and flow toward higher latitudes, warming the land regions they pass. When the currents cool off and flow back toward the equator, they cool the air and climates of nearby land.

✔ **Reading Check**   *How do ocean currents affect climate?*

Winds blowing from the sea are often moister than those blowing from land. Therefore, some coastal areas have wetter climates than places farther inland. Look at the northwest coast of the United States shown in **Figure 2.** The large amounts of precipitation in Washington, Oregon, and northern California can be explained by this moist ocean air.

Mountains At the same latitude, the climate is colder in the mountains than at sea level. When radiation from the Sun is absorbed by Earth's surface, it heats the land. Heat from Earth then warms the atmosphere. In the mountains, the air has fewer molecules to absorb this heat. This is because Earth's atmosphere gets thinner at higher altitudes.

Problem-Solving Activity

How do large cities influence temperature?

The temperature of rural areas surrounding a large city can differ from the temperature in the city's downtown by several degrees. This difference in temperature is called the heat-island effect. It is partly a result of the land in cities being covered with buildings, roads, and pavement, while rural areas have far more open space and vegetation. Do you think the heat-island effect can change as a city grows? Use your ability to interpret data to find out.

Identifying the Problem

The table lists the average summer high temperatures in and around a large metropolitan city in 1978 and 1993. By examining the data, can you tell if the heat-island effect has changed over time?

Average Summer Temperatures		
Distance from Downtown (km)	Temperatures (°C)	
	1978	1993
0	32.5	35
8	28.0	32.0
16	27.5	30.5
24	27.5	29.5

Solving the Problem

1. What distances from downtown experienced the greatest and smallest temperature change between 1978 and 1993? Can you account for the differences?
2. Suppose that in 1999 the average temperature in the downtown area was 36°C, but the temperature 24 km away was 33°C. Would you expect this? Explain.

A The windward side of a large mountain range—the side facing the wind—often receives heavy precipitation.

B Deserts are common on the leeward side—the side away from the wind—of mountain ranges.

Rainshadows Mountains also affect regional climates, as shown in **Figure 3.** On the windward side of a mountain range, air rises, cools, and drops its moisture. On the leeward side of a mountain range air descends, heats up, and dries the land. Deserts are common behind mountains.

Cities Large cities affect local climates. Streets, parking lots, and buildings heat up, in turn heating the air. Air pollution traps this heat, creating what is known as the heat-island effect. Temperatures in a city can be 5°C higher than in surrounding rural areas.

Figure 3
Large mountain ranges can affect climate by forcing air to rise over the windward side and to descend on the leeward side. *How can this cause the two sides of the Sierra Nevada Mountain Range to be so different?*

Section 1 Assessment

1. What factors determine the climate of a region?

2. Explain how two cities located at the same latitude can have different climates.

3. How do mountains affect climate?

4. What is the heat island effect?

5. **Think Critically** Explain why types of plants and animals found at different elevations on a mountain range might differ. Would latitude affect the elevation at which some organisms are found?

Skill Builder Activities

6. **Comparing and Contrasting** Compare and contrast tropical and polar climates. **For more help, refer to the** Science Skill Handbook.

7. **Solving One-Step Equations** The coolest average summer temperature in the United States is 2°C at Barrow, Alaska, and the warmest is 37°C at Death Valley, California. Calculate the range of average summer temperatures in the United States. **For more help, refer to the** Math Skill Handbook.

SECTION
2 Climate Types

As You Read

***What* You'll Learn**

- **Describe** a climate classification system.
- **Explain** how organisms adapt to particular climates.

Vocabulary
adaptation
hibernation

***Why* It's Important**
Many organisms can survive only in climates to which they are adapted.

Figure 4
The type of vegetation in a region depends on the climate.
What do these plants tell you about the climate shown here?

Classifying Climates

What is the climate like where you live? Would you call it generally warm? Usually wet and cold? Or different depending on the time of year? How would you classify the climate in your region? Life is full of familiar classification systems—from musical categories to food groups. Classifications help to organize your thoughts and to make your life more efficient. That's why Earth's climates also are classified and are organized into the various types that exist. Climatologists—people who study climates—usually use a system developed in 1918 by Wladimir Köppen to classify climates. Köppen observed that the types of plants found in a region depended on the climate of the area. **Figure 4** shows one region Köppen might have observed. He classified climates by using the temperature and precipitation of regions that had different plant types.

The climate classification system shown in **Figure 5** separates climates into six groups—tropical, mild, dry, continental, polar, and high elevation. These groups are further separated into types. For example, the dry climate classification is separated into semiarid and arid.

Adaptations

Climates vary around the world, and as Köppen observed, the type of climate that exists in an area determines the vegetation found there. Fir trees aren't found in deserts, nor are cacti found in rain forests. In fact, all organisms are best suited for certain climates. Organisms are adapted to their environment. An **adaptation** is any structure or behavior that helps an organism survive in its environment. Adaptations are inherited. They develop in a population over a long period of time. Once adapted to a particular climate, organisms may not be able to survive in other climates.

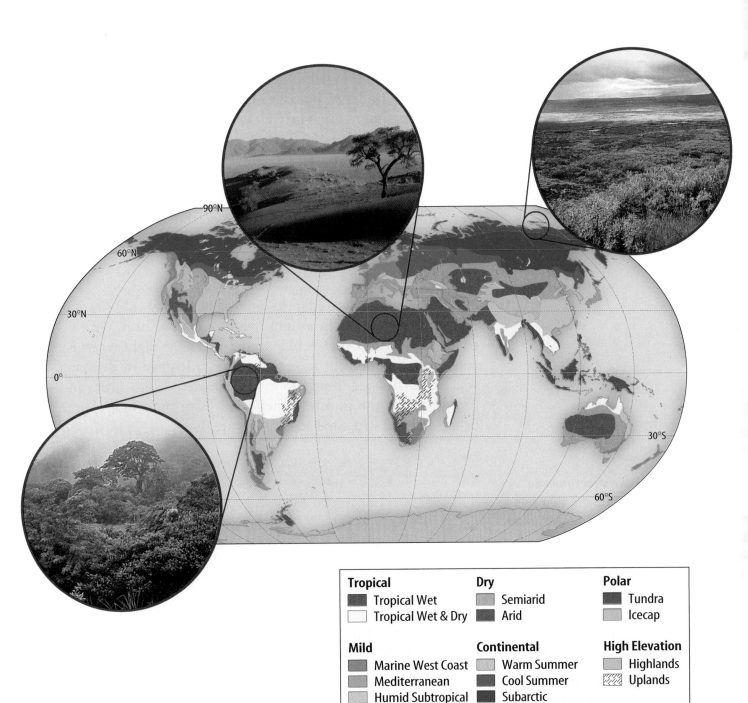

Tropical
- ■ Tropical Wet
- □ Tropical Wet & Dry

Dry
- ■ Semiarid
- ■ Arid

Polar
- ■ Tundra
- ■ Icecap

Mild
- ■ Marine West Coast
- ■ Mediterranean
- ■ Humid Subtropical

Continental
- ■ Warm Summer
- ■ Cool Summer
- ■ Subarctic

High Elevation
- ■ Highlands
- ▨ Uplands

Life Science
INTEGRATION

Structural Adaptations Some organisms have body structures that help them survive in certain climates. The fur of mammals is really hair that insulates them from cold temperatures. A cactus has a thick, fleshy stem. This structural adaptation helps a cactus hold water. The waxy stem covering prevents water inside the cactus from evaporating. Instead of broad leaves, these plants have spiny leaves that further reduce water loss.

✔ **Reading Check** *How do cacti conserve water?*

Figure 5
This map shows a climate classification system similar to the one developed by Köppen. *What patterns can you see in the locations of certain climate types?*

Behavioral Adaptations Some organisms display behavioral adaptations that help them survive in a particular climate. For example, rodents and certain other mammals undergo a period of greatly reduced activity in winter called **hibernation.** During hibernation, body temperature drops and body processes are reduced to a minimum. Some of the factors thought to trigger hibernation include cooler temperatures, shorter days, and lack of adequate food. The length of time that an animal hibernates varies depending on the particular species of animal and the environmental conditions.

✔ Reading Check *What is hibernation?*

Other animals have adapted differently. During cold weather, bees cluster together in a tight ball to conserve heat. On hot, sunny days, desert snakes hide under rocks. At night when it's cooler, they slither out in search of food. Instead of drinking water as turtles and lizards do in wet climates, desert turtles and lizards obtain the moisture they need from their food. Some behavioral and structural adaptations are shown in **Figure 6.**

Figure 6
Organisms have structural and behavioral adaptations that help them survive in particular climates.

A These hibernating bats have adapted their behavior to survive winter.

B The needles and the waxy skin of a cactus are structural adaptations to a desert climate. *How do these adaptations help cacti conserve water?*

C Polar bears have structural adaptations to keep them warm. The hairs of their fur trap air and heat.

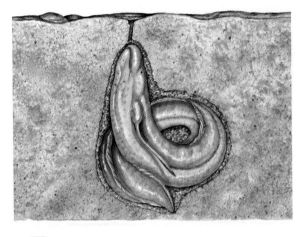

A

B

Figure 7
Lungfish survive periods of intense heat and drought by going into an inactive state called estivation. **A** During the dry season when water evaporates, lungfish dig into the mud and curl up in a small chamber they make at the lake's bottom. **B** During the wet season, lungfish reemerge to live in small lakes and pools.

Estivation Lungfish, shown in **Figure 7,** survive periods of intense heat by entering an inactive state called estivation (es tuh VAY shun). As the weather gets hot and water evaporates, the fish burrows into mud and covers itself in a leathery mixture of mud and mucus. It lives this way until the warm, dry months pass.

Like other organisms, you have adaptations that help you adjust to climate. In hot weather, your sweat glands release water onto your skin. The water evaporates, taking some heat with it. As a result, you become cooler. In cold weather, you may shiver to help your body stay warm. When you shiver, the rapid muscle movements produce some heat. What other adaptations to climate do people have?

Section 2 Assessment

1. How can climates be classified? What type of climate do you live in?

2. Use **Figure 5** and a world map to identify the climate type for each of the following locations: Cuba, North Korea, Egypt, and Uruguay.

3. What are some behavioral adaptations that allow animals to stay warm? What structural adaptations help keep animals warm?

4. How is hibernation different from estivation? How is it similar?

5. **Think Critically** What adaptations help dogs keep cool during hot weather?

Skill Builder Activities

6. **Forming Hypotheses** Some scientists have suggested that Earth's climate is getting warmer. What effects might this have on vegetation and animal life in various parts of the United States? **For more help, refer to the Science Skill Handbook.**

7. **Communicating** Research the types of vegetation found in the six climate regions shown in **Figure 5.** Write a paragraph in your Science Journal describing why vegetation can be used to help define climate boundaries. **For more help, refer to the Science Skill Handbook.**

Climatic Changes

As You Read

What **You'll Learn**

- **Explain** what causes seasons.
- **Describe** how El Niño affects climate.
- **Explore** possible causes of climatic change.

Vocabulary

season
El Niño
greenhouse effect
global warming
deforestation

Why **It's Important**

Changing climates could affect sea level and life on Earth.

Earth's Seasons

In temperate zones, you can play softball under the summer Sun and in the winter go sledding with friends. Weather changes with the season. **Seasons** are short periods of climatic change caused by changes in the amount of solar radiation an area receives. **Figure 8** shows Earth revolving around the Sun. Because Earth is tilted, different areas of Earth receive changing amounts of solar radiation throughout the year.

Seasonal Changes Because of fairly constant solar radiation near the equator, the tropics do not have much seasonal temperature change. However, they do experience dry and rainy seasons. The middle latitudes, or temperate zones, have warm summers and cool winters. Spring and fall are usually mild.

✔ **Reading Check** *What are seasons like in the tropics?*

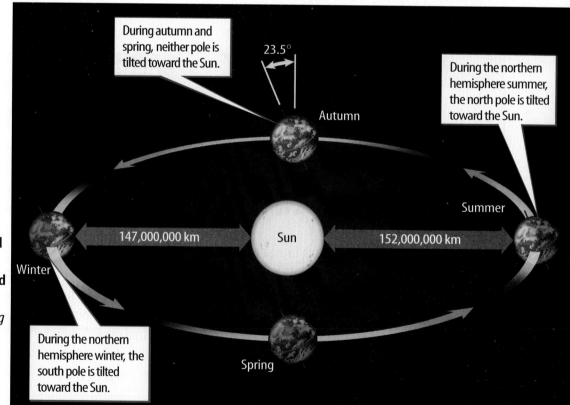

Figure 8
As Earth revolves around the Sun, different areas of Earth are tilted toward the Sun, which causes different seasons. *During which northern hemisphere season is Earth closer to the Sun?*

During autumn and spring, neither pole is tilted toward the Sun.

23.5°

During the northern hemisphere summer, the north pole is tilted toward the Sun.

Autumn

Summer

147,000,000 km   Sun   152,000,000 km

Winter

During the northern hemisphere winter, the south pole is tilted toward the Sun.

Spring

Figure 9
A strong El Niño, like the one that occurred in 1998, can affect weather patterns around the world.

A A severe drought struck Indonesia, contributing to forest fires.

B California was plagued by large storms that produced pounding surf and shoreline erosion.

High Latitudes During the year, the high latitudes near the poles have great differences in temperature and number of daylight hours. As shown in **Figure 8,** during summer in the northern hemisphere, the north pole is tilted toward the Sun. During summer at the north pole, the Sun doesn't set for nearly six months. During that same time, the Sun never rises at the south pole. At the equator days are about the same length all year long.

El Niño and La Niña

El Niño (el NEEN yoh) is a climatic event that involves the tropical Pacific Ocean and the atmosphere. During normal years, strong trade winds that blow east to west along the equator push warm surface water toward the western Pacific Ocean. Cold, deep water then is forced up from below along the coast of South America. During El Niño years, these winds weaken and sometimes reverse. The change in the winds allows warm, tropical water in the upper layers of the Pacific to flow back eastward to South America. Cold, deep water is no longer forced up from below. Ocean temperatures increase by 1°C to 7°C off the coast of Peru.

El Niño can affect weather patterns. It can alter the position and strength of one of the jet streams. This changes the atmospheric pressure off California and wind and precipitation patterns around the world. This can cause drought in Australia and Africa. This also affects monsoon rains in Indonesia and causes storms in California, as shown in **Figure 9.**

The opposite of El Niño is La Niña, shown in **Figure 10.** During La Niña, the winds blowing across the Pacific are stronger than normal, causing warm water to accumulate in the western Pacific. The water in the eastern Pacific near Peru is cooler than normal. La Niña may cause droughts in the southern United States and excess rainfall in the northwestern United States.

TRY AT HOME
Mini LAB

Modeling El Niño

Procedure
1. During El Niño, trade winds blowing across the Pacific Ocean from east to west slacken or even reverse. Surface waters move back toward the coast of Peru.
2. Add **warm water** to a **9 in by 13 in baking pan** until it is two-thirds full. Place the pan on a smooth countertop.
3. Blow as hard as you can across the surface of the water along the length of the pan. Next, blow with less force. Then, blow in the opposite direction.

Analysis
1. What happened to the water as you blew across its surface? What was different when you blew with less force and when you blew from the opposite direction?
2. Explain how this is similar to what happens during an El Niño event.

Figure 10

Weather in the United States can be affected by changes that occur thousands of kilometers away. Out in the middle of the Pacific Ocean, periodic warming and cooling of a huge mass of sea-water—phenomena known as El Niño and La Niña, respectively—can impact weather across North America. During normal years (right), when neither El Niño nor La Niña is in effect, strong winds tend to keep warm sur-face waters contained in the western Pacific while cooler water wells up to the surface in the eastern Pacific.

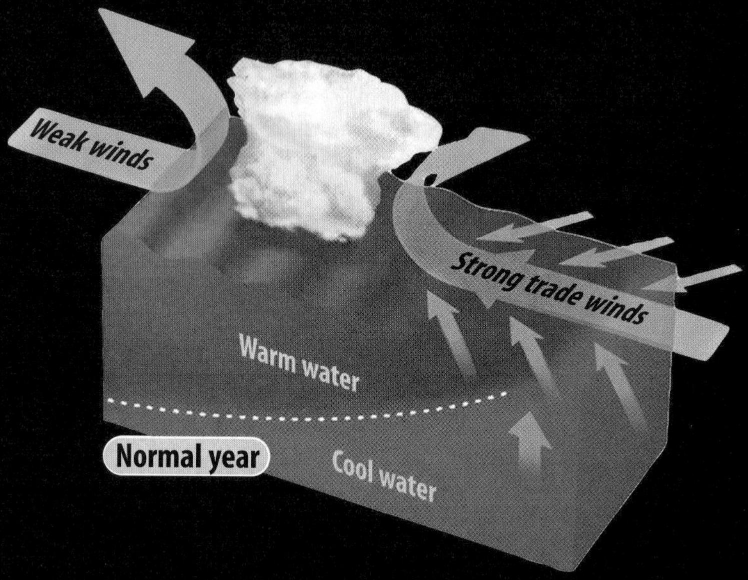

Weak winds

Strong trade winds

Warm water

Normal year   Cool water

EL NIÑO During El Niño years, winds blowing west weaken and may even reverse. When this hap-pens, warm waters in the western Pacific move eastward, preventing cold water from upwelling. These changes can alter global weather patterns and trigger heavier-than-normal precipitation across much of the United States.

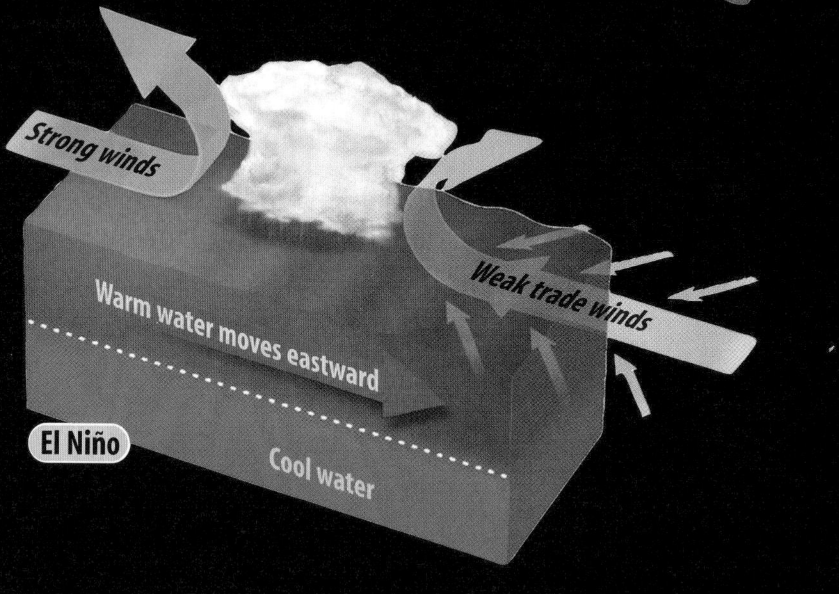

Strong winds

Weak trade winds

Warm water moves eastward

El Niño   Cool water

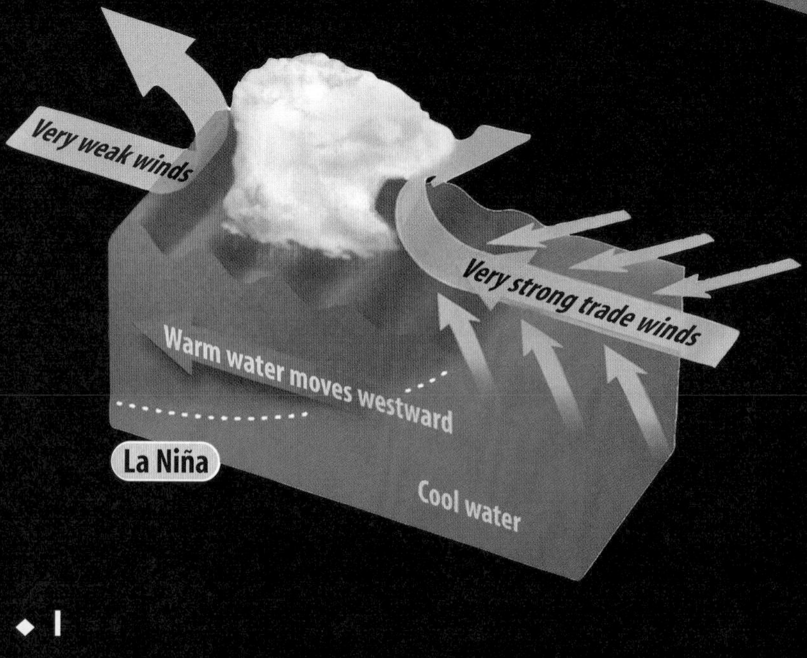

Very weak winds

Very strong trade winds

Warm water moves westward

La Niña   Cool water

LA NIÑA During La Niña years, stronger-than-normal winds push warm Pacific waters farther west, toward Asia. Cold, deep-sea waters then well up strongly in the east-ern Pacific, bringing cooler and often drier weather to many parts of the United States.

El Niño

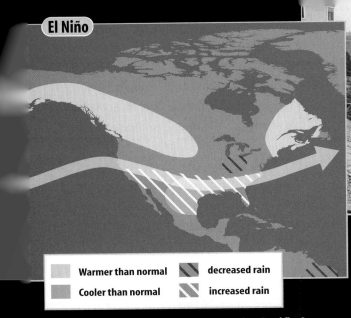

Warmer than normal | decreased rain
Cooler than normal | increased rain

Sun-warmed surface water spans the Pacific Ocean during El Niño years. Clouds form above the warm ocean, carrying moisture aloft. The jet stream, shown by the white arrow above, helps bring some of this warm, moist air to the United States.

▲ LANDSLIDE Heavy rains in California resulting from El Niño can lead to landslides. This upended house in Laguna Niguel, California, took a ride downhill during the El Niño storms of 1998.

La Niña

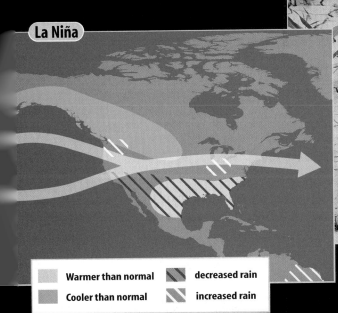

Warmer than normal | decreased rain
Cooler than normal | increased rain

During a typical La Niña year, warm ocean waters, clouds, and moisture are pushed away from North America. A weaker jet stream often brings cooler weather to the northern parts of the continent and hot, dry weather to southern areas.

▲ PARCHED LAND The Southeast may experience drought conditions, like those that struck the cornfields of Montgomery County, Maryland, during the La Niña summer of 1988.

Climatic Change

If you were exploring in Antarctica near Earth's south pole and found a 3-million-year-old fossil of a warm-weather plant or animal, what would it tell you? You might conclude that the climate of that region changed because Antarctica is much too cold for similar plants and animals to survive today. Some warm-weather fossils found in polar regions indicate that at times in Earth's past, worldwide climate was much warmer than at present. At other times Earth's climate has been much colder than it is today.

Sediments in many parts of the world show that at several different times in the past 2 million years, glaciers covered large parts of Earth's surface. These times are called ice ages. During the past 2 million years, ice ages have alternated with warm periods called interglacial intervals. Ice ages seem to last 60,000 to 100,000 years. Most interglacial periods are shorter, lasting 10,000 to 15,000 years. We are now in an interglacial interval that began about 11,500 years ago. Additional evidence suggests that climate can change even more quickly. Ice cores record climate in a way similar to tree rings. Cores drilled in Greenland show that during the last ice age, colder times lasting 1,000 to 2,000 years changed quickly to warmer spells that lasted about as long. **Figure 11** shows a scientist working with ice cores.

Figure 11
Each layer of ice in a core records detailed climate information for a single year. Some cores cover 300,000 years.

What causes climatic change?

Climatic change has many varied causes. These causes of climatic change can operate over short periods of time or very long periods of time. Catastrophic events, including meteorite collisions and large volcanic eruptions, can affect climate over short periods of time, such as a year or several years. These events add solid particles and liquid droplets to the upper atmosphere, which can change climate. Another factor that can alter Earth's climate is short- or long-term changes in solar output, which is the amount of energy given off by the Sun. Changes in Earth's movements in space affect climate over many thousands of years, and movement of Earth's crustal plates can change climate over millions of years. All of these things can work separately or together to alter Earth's climate.

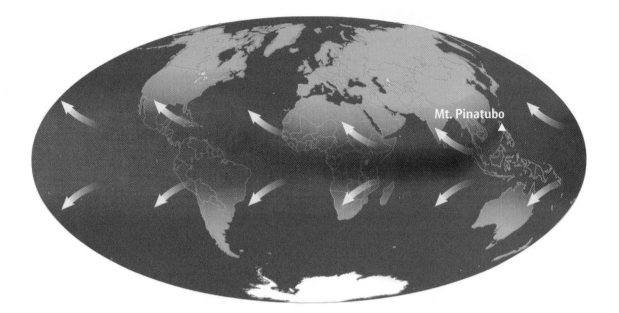

Mt. Pinatubo

Atmospheric Solids and Liquids Small solid and liquid particles always are present in Earth's atmosphere. These particles can enter the atmosphere naturally or be added to the atmosphere by humans as pollution. Some ways that particles enter the atmosphere naturally include volcanic eruptions, soot from fires, and wind erosion of soil particles. Humans add particles to the atmosphere through automobile exhaust and smokestack emissions. These small particles can affect climate.

Catastrophic events such as meteorite collisions and volcanic eruptions put enormous volumes of dust, ash, and other particles into the atmosphere. These particles block so much solar radiation that they can cool the planet. **Figure 12** shows how a major volcanic eruption affected Earth's atmosphere.

In cities, particles put into the atmosphere as pollution can change the local climate. These particles can increase the amount of cloud cover downwind from the city. Some studies have even suggested that rainfall amounts can be reduced in these areas. This may happen because many small cloud droplets form rather than larger droplets that could produce rain.

Energy from the Sun Solar radiation provides Earth's energy. If the output of radiation from the Sun varies, Earth's climate could change. Some changes in the amount of energy given off by the Sun seem to be related to the presence of sunspots. Sunspots are dark spots on the surface of the Sun. **WARNING:** *Never look directly at the Sun.* Evidence supporting the link between sunspots and climate includes an extremely cold period in Europe between 1645 and 1715. During this time, very few sunspots appeared on the Sun.

Figure 12
Mount Pinatubo in the Philippines erupted in 1991. During the eruption, particles were spread high into the atmosphere and circled the globe. Over time, particles spread around the world, blocking some of the Sun's energy from reaching Earth. The gray areas show how particles from the eruption moved around the world.

Health
INTEGRATION

Atmospheric particles produced as pollution can affect human health as well as climate. These small particles, often called particulates, can enter the lungs and cause tissue damage. People who have existing lung or heart problems are affected most seriously. Do research to find out what types of laws have been written to reduce particulate pollution.

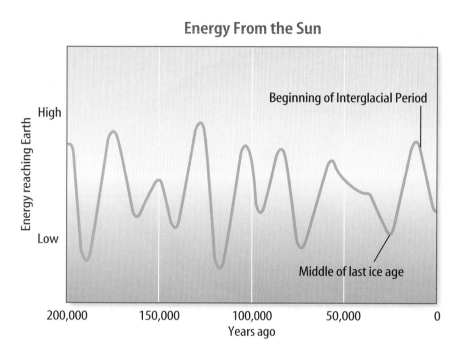

Energy From the Sun

High

Energy reaching Earth

Low

Beginning of Interglacial Period

Middle of last ice age

200,000   150,000   100,000   50,000   0

Years ago

Figure 13
The curving line shows how the amount of the Sun's energy that strikes the northern hemisphere changed over the last 200,000 years. *Describe the amount of energy that reached the northern hemisphere during the last ice age.*

Earth Movements Another explanation for some climatic changes involves Earth's movements in space. Earth's axis currently is tilted 23.5° from perpendicular to the plane of its orbit around the Sun. In the past, this tilt has increased to 24.5° and has decreased to 21.5°. When this tilt is at its maximum, the change between summer and winter is probably greater. Earth's tilt changes about every 41,000 years. Some scientists hypothesize that the change in tilt affects climate.

Two additional Earth movements also cause climatic change. Earth's axis wobbles in space just like the axis of a top wobbles when it begins to spin more slowly. This can affect the amount of solar energy received by different parts of Earth. Also, the shape of Earth's orbit changes. Sometimes it is more circular than at present and sometimes it is more flattened. The shape of Earth's orbit changes over a 100,000-year cycle.

Amount of Solar Energy These movements of Earth cause the amount of solar energy reaching different parts of Earth to vary over time, as shown in **Figure 13.** These changes might have caused glaciers to grow and shrink over the last few million years. However, they do not explain why glaciers have occurred so rarely over long spans of geologic time.

Crustal Plate Movement Another explanation for major climatic change over tens or hundreds of millions of years concerns the movement of Earth's crustal plates. The movement of continents and oceans affects the transfer of heat on Earth, which in turn affects wind and precipitation patterns. Through time, these altered patterns can change climate. One example of this is when movement of Earth's plates created the Himalaya about 40 million years ago. The growth of these mountains changed climate over much of Earth.

As you've learned, many theories attempt to answer questions about why Earth's climate has changed through the ages. Probably all of these things play some role in changing climates. More study needs to be done before all the factors that affect climate will be understood.

Climatic Changes Today

Beginning in 1994, representatives from many countries have met to discuss the greenhouse effect and global warming. These subjects also have appeared frequently in the headlines of newspapers and magazines. Some people are concerned that the greenhouse effect could be responsible for some present-day warming of Earth's atmosphere and oceans.

The **greenhouse effect** is a natural heating that occurs when certain gases in Earth's atmosphere trap heat. Radiation from the Sun strikes Earth's surface and causes it to warm. Some of this heat then is radiated back toward space. Greenhouse gases in the atmosphere absorb a portion of this heat. This keeps Earth warmer than it would be otherwise. The greenhouse effect is illustrated in **Figure 14.**

There are many natural greenhouse gases in Earth's atmosphere. Water vapor, carbon dioxide, and methane are some of the most important ones. Without these greenhouse gases, life would not be possible on Earth. Like Mars, Earth would be too cold. However, if the greenhouse effect is too strong, Earth could get too warm. High levels of carbon dioxide in its atmosphere indicate that this has happened on the planet Venus.

SCIENCE *Online*

Research Visit the Glencoe Science Web site at **science.glencoe.com** for more information about the greenhouse effect.

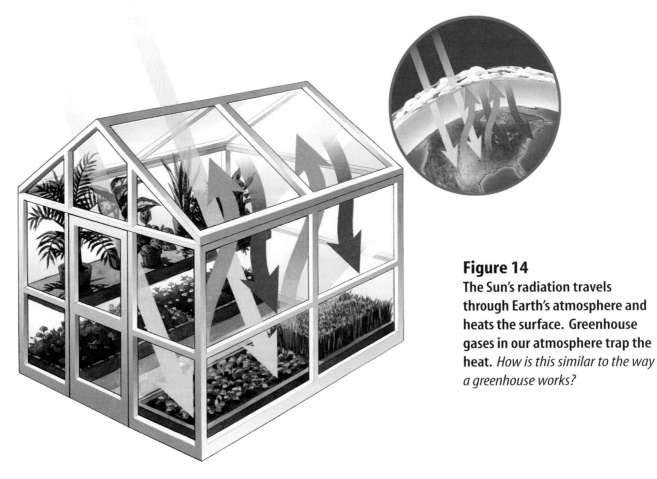

Figure 14
The Sun's radiation travels through Earth's atmosphere and heats the surface. Greenhouse gases in our atmosphere trap the heat. *How is this similar to the way a greenhouse works?*

Global Warming

Global warming means that the average global temperature of Earth is rising. One likely reason for global warming is the increase of greenhouse gases in our atmosphere. An increase in greenhouse gases increases the greenhouse effect. In the last 100 years, the surface temperature on Earth has increased 0.5°C. This might be a result of more greenhouse gases.

✔ **Reading Check** *How can greenhouse gases affect Earth's climate?*

If Earth's average temperature continues to rise, many glaciers could melt. When glaciers melt, the extra water causes sea levels to rise. Low-lying coastal areas would experience increased flooding. Already some ice caps and small glaciers are beginning to melt and recede, as shown in **Figure 15.** Sea level is rising in some places. Some scientific studies show that these events are related to Earth's increased temperature.

You learned in the previous section that organisms are adapted to their environments. When environments change, can organisms cope? In some tropical waters around the world, corals are dying. Many people think these deaths are caused by warmer water to which the corals are not adapted.

Some climate models show that in the future, Earth's temperatures will increase faster than they have in the last 100 years. Next, you will learn how human activity might contribute to global warming, and you will find out what you can do to help reduce the amount of greenhouse gases entering the atmosphere.

Figure 15
This glacier in Greenland might have receded from its previous position because of global warming. The pile of rock in front shows how far the glacier once reached.

Figure 16
When forests are cleared or burned, carbon dioxide levels increase in the atmosphere.
What can people do to help reduce CO_2 levels in the atmosphere?

Human Activities

Human activities affect the air in Earth's atmosphere. Burning fossil fuels and removing vegetation increase the amount of carbon dioxide (CO_2) in the atmosphere. Each year, the amount of carbon dioxide in the atmosphere continues to increase. Because carbon dioxide is a greenhouse gas, it might cause Earth's temperature to increase.

Burning Fossil Fuels When natural gas, oil, and coal are burned for energy, the carbon in these fossil fuels combines with atmospheric oxygen to form carbon dioxide. This increases the amount of carbon dioxide in Earth's atmosphere. Studies indicate that humans have increased carbon dioxide levels in the atmosphere by about 25 percent over the last 150 years.

Deforestation Destroying and cutting down forests, called **deforestation,** also affects the amount of carbon dioxide in the atmosphere. Forests, such as the one shown in **Figure 16,** are cleared for mining, roads, buildings, and grazing cattle. Large tracts of forest have been cleared in every country on Earth. Tropical forests have been decreasing at a rate of about one percent each year for the past two decades.

As trees grow, they take in carbon dioxide from the atmosphere. Trees use this carbon dioxide to produce wood and leaves. When trees are cut down, the carbon dioxide they could have removed from the atmosphere remains. Cut-down trees often are burned for fuel or to clear the land. Burning trees produces even more carbon dioxide.

SCIENCE *Online*

Research Visit the Glencoe Science Web site at **science.glencoe.com** for more information about deforestation. Communicate to your class what you learn.

Figure 17
Solar energy is beginning to fill some human energy needs.
A These solar panels in California generate electricity without adding CO_2 to the atmosphere.
B Solar-powered cars may be common in the future.

How to Reduce CO_2

What can you do to help reduce the amount of CO_2 in the atmosphere? Conserving electricity is one answer. When you conserve electricity, you reduce the amount of fossil fuel that is burned. One way to save fuel is to change daily activities that rely on energy from burning fossil fuels. Turn off the TV, for instance, when no one is watching it. Walk or ride a bike to the store, if possible, instead of using a car. People also can use different energy sources to meet their energy needs, as shown in **Figure 17.**

Another way to reduce CO_2 is to plant vegetation. As you've learned, plants remove carbon dioxide from the atmosphere. Correctly planted vegetation also can shelter homes from cold winds or the blazing Sun and reduce the use of electricity.

Section 3 Assessment

1. How is Earth's tilted axis responsible for seasons?

2. In what way does El Niño change the climate? What climate changes are caused by La Niña?

3. What factors can cause Earth's climate to change?

4. How are people adding carbon dioxide to the atmosphere?

5. **Think Critically** If Earth's climate continues to warm, how might your community be affected?

Skill Builder Activities

6. **Recognizing Cause and Effect** Using a globe, model the three movements of Earth in space that can cause climatic change. **For more help, refer to the** Science Skill Handbook.

7. **Using a Word Processor** Use word processing software to design a pamphlet to inform people why Earth's climate changes. What are your predictions for the future? On what evidence do you base these predictions? Include this evidence in your pamphlet. **For more help, refer to the** Technology Skill Handbook.

Activity

The Greenhouse Effect

Do you remember climbing into the car on a warm, sunny day? Why was it so hot inside the car when it wasn't that hot outside? It was hotter in the car because the car functioned like a greenhouse. You experienced the greenhouse effect.

What You'll Investigate

How can you demonstrate the greenhouse effect?

Materials

identical large, empty glass jars (2)
lid for one jar
nonmercury thermometers (3)

Goals

- ■ **Model** the greenhouse effect.
- ■ **Measure and graph** temperature changes.

Safety Precautions

Be careful when you handle glass thermometers. If a thermometer breaks, do not touch it. Have your teacher dispose of the glass safely.

Procedure

1. Lay a thermometer inside each jar.

2. Place the jars next to each other by a sunny window. Lay the third thermometer between the jars.

3. **Record** the temperatures of the three thermometers. They should be the same.

4. Place the lid on one jar.

5. **Record** the temperatures of all three thermometers at the end of 5, 10, and 15 min.

6. Make a line graph that shows the temperatures of the three thermometers for the 15 min of the experiment.

Conclude and Apply

1. **Explain** why you placed a thermometer between the two jars.

2. What were the constants in this experiment? What was the variable?

3. Which thermometer experienced the greatest temperature change during your experiment?

4. **Analyze** what occurred in this experiment. How was the lid in this experiment like the greenhouse gases in the atmosphere?

5. **Infer** from this experiment why you should never leave a pet inside a closed car in warm weather.

Communicating
Your Data

Give a brief speech describing your conclusions to your class. **For more help, refer to the** Science Skill Handbook.

Activity

Microclimates

A microclimate is a localized climate that differs from the main climate of a region. Buildings in a city, for instance, can affect the climate of the surrounding area. Large buildings can create microclimates by blocking the Sun or changing wind patterns.

What You'll Investigate

Does your school create microclimates?

Materials

thermometers
psychrometer
paper strip or wind sock
large cans (4 or 5)
beakers or rain gauges (4 or 5)
unlined paper

Alternate materials

Goals

- **Observe** temperature, wind speed, relative humidity, and precipitation in areas outside your school.
- **Identify** local microclimates.

Safety Precautions

WARNING: *If a thermometer breaks, do not touch it. Have your teacher dispose of the glass safely.*

Relative Humidity										
Dry Bulb Temperature (°C)	**Dry Bulb Temperature Minus Wet Bulb Temperature (°C)**									
	1	2	3	4	5	6	7	8	9	10
14	90	79	70	60	51	42	34	26	18	10
15	90	80	71	61	53	44	36	27	20	13
16	90	81	71	63	54	46	38	30	23	15
17	90	81	72	64	55	47	40	32	25	18
18	91	82	73	65	57	49	41	34	27	20
19	91	82	74	65	58	50	43	36	29	22
20	91	83	74	66	59	51	44	37	31	24
21	91	83	75	67	60	53	46	39	32	26
22	92	83	76	68	61	54	47	40	34	28
23	92	84	76	69	62	55	48	42	36	30
24	92	84	77	69	62	56	49	43	37	31
25	92	84	77	70	63	57	50	44	39	33

Procedure

1. Select four or five sites around your school building. Also, select a control site well away from the school.

2. Attach a thermometer to an object near each of the locations you selected. Set up a rain gauge, beaker, or can to collect precipitation.

3. Visit each site at two predetermined times, one in the morning and one in the afternoon, each day for a week. Record the temperature and measure any precipitation that might have fallen. Use a wind sock or paper strip to determine wind direction.

4. To find relative humidity, you'll need to use a psychrometer. A psychrometer is an instrument with two thermometers—one wet and one dry. As moisture from the wet thermometer evaporates, it takes heat energy from its environment, and the environment immediately around the wet thermometer cools. The thermometer records a lower temperature. Relative humidity can be found by finding the difference between the wet thermometer and the dry thermometer and by using the chart on the previous page. Record all of your weather data.

5. **Analyze** your data to find patterns. Make separate line graphs for temperature, relative humidity, and precipitation for your morning and afternoon data. Make a table showing wind direction data.

Conclude and Apply

1. Why did you take weather data at a control site away from the school building? How did the control help you analyze and interpret your data?

2. **Compare and contrast** weather data for each of your sites. What microclimates did you identify around your school building? How did these climates differ from the control site? How did they differ from each other?

3. **Infer** what conditions could have caused the microclimates that you identified. Are your microclimates similar to those that might exist in a large city? Explain.

Communicating Your Data

Use your graphs to make a large poster explaining your conclusions. Display your posters in the school building. **For more help, refer to the** Science Skill Handbook.

The Year There Was

Mount St. Helens in Washington state erupted in May 1980. Its ash cloud temporarily darkened the sky and was carried thousands of kilometers away by upper-air currents.

You've seen pictures of erupting volcanoes. One kind of volcano sends smoke, rock, and ash high into the air above the crater. Another kind of volcano erupts with fiery, red-hot rivers of lava snaking down its sides. Erupting volcanoes are nature's forces at their mightiest, causing destruction and death. But not everyone realizes how far-reaching the destruction can be.

Large volcanic eruptions can affect people thousands of kilometers away. In fact, major volcanic eruptions can have effects that reach around the globe.

An erupting volcano can temporarily change Earth's climate. The ash a volcano ejects into the atmosphere can create day after day without sunshine. Other particles move high into the atmosphere and are carried all the way around Earth, sometimes causing global temperatures to drop for several months.

The Summer That Never Came

An example of a volcanic eruption with wide-ranging effects occurred in 1783 in Iceland, an island nation in the North Atlantic Ocean. Winds carried a black cloud of ash from an erupting volcano in Iceland westward across northern Canada, Alaska, and across the Pacific Ocean to Japan. The summer turned bitterly cold in these places. Water froze, and heavy snowstorms pelted the land. Sulfurous gases from the erupting volcano combined with water to form particles of acid that reflected solar energy back into space. This "blanket" in the atmosphere kept the Sun's rays from heating up part of Earth.

The most tragic result of this eruption was the death of many Kauwerak people, who lived in western Alaska. Only a handful of Kauwerak survived the summer that never came. They had no opportunity to catch needed foods to keep them alive through the following winter.

No Summer

Erupting volcanoes can cause unusual changes in climate

A truck is dwarfed by clouds of volcanic ash during the eruption of Mt. Pinatubo in the Philippines. The volcano had been dormant for 611 years.

Another Year Without a Summer

In 1815, the eruption of Tambora, on the island of Sumbawa in Indonesia, is blamed for North America and Europe having "the year without a summer" in 1816. Once again, the blanket of acid particles, pushed by upper-level winds, caused areas far removed from the volcanic activity to face a drastic change in weather patterns. In New England in 1816, frosts occurred and snow fell well into June. Massive crop failures occurred in North America and Europe.

Only volcanoes that throw debris above the troposphere cause this kind of climatic change. Melissa Free, a researcher for the National Oceanographic and Atmospheric Administration, says, "If [debris] is in the troposphere, it is taken out and dissipated more rapidly by rainfall." But, Free says, to cause climatic change, "...the eruption has to be strong enough to push material above the troposphere and into the stratosphere." And that's what happened when Tambora erupted, leading to a very unusual summer.

CONNECTIONS Locate Using an atlas, locate Indonesia and Iceland. Using reference materials, find five facts about each place. Make a map of each nation and illustrate the map with your five facts.

SCIENCE

Online

For more information, visit
science.glencoe.com

Reviewing Main Ideas

Section 1 What is climate?

1. An area's climate is the average weather over a long period of time, such as 30 years.

2. The three main climate zones are tropical, polar, and temperate.

3. Features such as oceans, mountains, and even large cities affect climate. *What differences might you find in the climates on the opposite sides of this mountain range?*

Section 2 Climate Types

1. Climates can be classified by various characteristics, such as temperature, precipitation, and vegetation. World climates commonly are separated into six major groups.

2. Organisms have structural and behavioral adaptations that help them survive in particular climates. Many organisms can survive only in the climate they are adapted to.

3. Adaptations develop in a population over a long period of time.

Section 3 Climatic Changes

1. Seasons are caused by the tilt of Earth's axis as Earth revolves around the Sun.

2. El Niño disrupts normal temperature and precipitation patterns around the world. *How could El Niño help cause California mudflows like this one?*

3. Geological records show that over the past few million years, Earth's climate has alternated between ice ages and warmer periods called interglacials.

4. The greenhouse effect occurs when certain gases trap heat in Earth's atmosphere.

5. Humans might be contributing to global warming by producing greenhouse gases. Carbon dioxide enters the atmosphere when fossil fuels such as oil and coal are burned. *How can planting vegetation like the tree shown here help decrease greenhouse gases in the atmosphere?*

After You Read

FOLDABLES
Reading & Study Skills

To help you review the various aspects of the climate classification system, use the Classify Study Fold you made at the beginning of the chapter.

Visualizing Main Ideas

Complete the following concept map on climate.

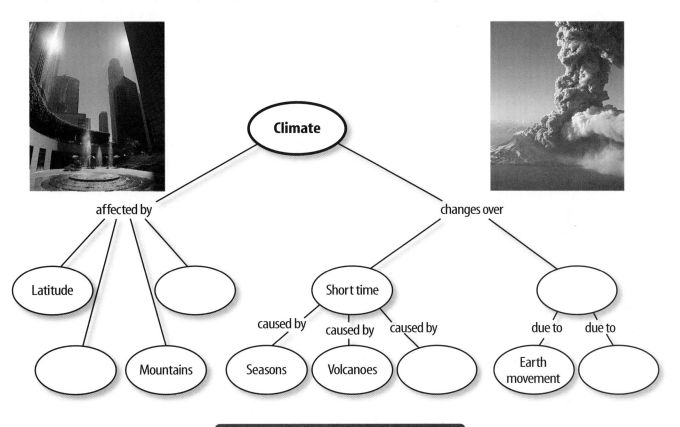

Climate

affected by
- Latitude
- (blank)
- (blank)
- Mountains

changes over

Short time
- caused by → Seasons
- caused by → Volcanoes
- caused by → (blank)

(blank)
- due to → Earth movement
- due to → (blank)

Vocabulary Review

Vocabulary Words

a. adaptation
b. climate
c. deforestation
d. El Niño
e. global warming
f. greenhouse effect
g. hibernation
h. polar zone
i. season
j. temperate zone
k. tropics

THE PRINCETON REVIEW **Study Tip**

Use tables and graphs to help you organize written material. For example, put the levels of biological organization in a table. Show what each level contains. Referring to the table may help you revise concepts quickly.

Using Vocabulary

The sentences below include vocabulary words that have been used incorrectly. Change the incorrect words so that the sentence reads correctly. Underline your change.

1. Earth's north pole is in the temperate zone.

2. Deforestation causes the Pacific Ocean to become warmer off the coast of Peru.

3. During adaptation, an animal's body temperature drops.

4. Season is the pattern of weather that occurs over many years.

5. Greenhouse effect means global temperatures are rising.

Checking Concepts

Choose the word or phrase that best answers the question.

1. What is commonly found in places where warm air crosses a mountain and descends?
   A) lakes   C) deserts
   B) rain forests   D) glaciers

2. During which of the following is the eastern Pacific warmer than normal?
   A) El Niño   C) summer
   B) La Niña   D) spring

3. Which of the following is a greenhouse gas in Earth's atmosphere?
   A) helium   C) hydrogen
   B) carbon dioxide D) oxygen

4. Which latitude receives the most direct rays of the Sun year-round?
   A) 60°N   C) 30°S
   B) 90°N   D) 0°

5. What happens as you climb a mountain?
   A) temperature decreases
   B) temperature increases
   C) air pressure increases
   D) air pressure remains constant

6. Which of the following is true of El Niño?
   A) It cools the Pacific Ocean near Peru.
   B) It causes flooding in Australia.
   C) It cools the waters off Alaska.
   D) It may occur when the trade winds slacken or reverse.

7. What do changes in Earth's orbit affect?
   A) Earth's shape   C) Earth's rotation
   B) Earth's climate D) Earth's tilt

8. The Köppen climate classification system includes categories based on precipitation and what other factor?
   A) temperature   C) winds
   B) air pressure   D) latitude

9. Which of the following is an example of structural adaptation?
   A) hibernation   C) fur
   B) migration   D) estivation

10. Which of these can people do in order to help reduce global warming?
    A) conserve energy C) produce methane
    B) burn coal   D) remove trees

Thinking Critically

11. Why might global warming lead to the extinction of some organisms?

12. What might you infer if you find fossils of tropical plants in a desert?

13. On a summer day, why would a Florida beach be cooler than an orange grove that is 2 km inland?

14. What would happen to global climates if the Sun emitted more energy?

15. Why will it be cooler if you climb to a higher elevation in a desert?

Developing Skills

16. **Making and Using Graphs** The following table gives average precipitation amounts for Phoenix, Arizona. Make a bar graph of these data. Which climate type do you think Phoenix represents?

Precipitation in Phoenix, Arizona	
Season	**Precipitation (cm)**
Winter	5.7
Spring	1.2
Summer	6.7
Autumn	5.9
Total	19.5

17. **Communicating** Explain how atmospheric pressure over the Pacific Ocean might affect the direction that the trade winds blow.

18. **Predicting** Make a chain-of-events chart to explain the effect of a major volcanic eruption on climate.

19. **Forming Hypotheses** A mountain glacier in South America has been getting smaller over several decades. What hypotheses should a scientist consider to explain why this is occurring?

20. **Concept Mapping** Complete the concept map using the following: *tropics, 0°–23° latitude, polar, temperature zones, temperate, 23°–66° latitude, 66° latitude to poles.*

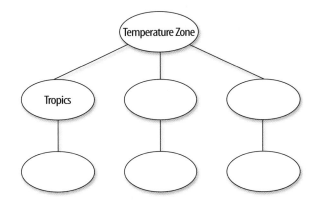

Performance Assessment

21. **Science Display** Make a display illustrating different factors that can affect climate. Be sure to include detailed diagrams and descriptions for each factor in your display. Present your display to the class.

TECHNOLOGY

Go to the Glencoe Science Web site at **science.glencoe.com** or use the **Glencoe Science CD-ROM** for additional chapter assessment.

THE PRINCETON REVIEW **Test Practice**

The graph below shows long-term variations in atmospheric carbon dioxide levels and global temperature.

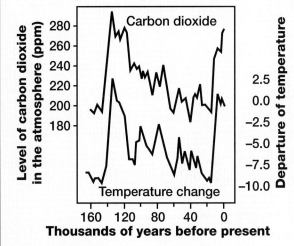

Study the graph and answer the following questions.

1. Which of these statements is TRUE according to the graph?
   A) Earth's mean temperature has never been hotter than it is today.
   B) The level of CO_2 has never been higher than today.
   C) The mean global temperature 60,000 years ago was less than today.
   D) The level of CO_2 in the atmosphere 80,000 years ago was 280 parts per million.

2. Which of the following statements BEST describes this graph?
   F) As CO_2 levels have increased, so has global temperature.
   G) As CO_2 levels have increased, global temperature has decreased.
   H) As global temperature has increased, CO_2 levels have decreased.
   J) No relationship exists between CO_2 and global temperatures.

4 Air Pollution

Looking out the window of the car, you notice the bright sunshine and clear sky. It's so bright and clear that you can see the buildings of the city miles away. Although the air looks clean, it still might be polluted. In this chapter, you will learn about substances in air that can affect your health and the health of other organisms. You will learn how laws in the United States help reduce the amount of harmful substances in the air. You also will learn what you can do to help reduce air pollution.

What do you think?

Science Journal Look at the picture below with a classmate. Discuss what this might be. Here's a hint: *It often is found in air, and it's microscopic.* Write your answer or best guess in your Science Journal.

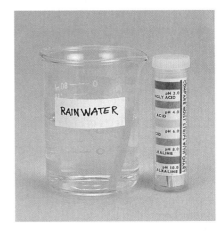

RAIN WATER

Some types of air pollutants from power plants and car exhaust can react with water in the atmosphere to produce acids. These acids then can return to Earth in precipitation. In this activity, you will determine if your region receives acidic precipitation.

Test precipitation

1. Collect some precipitation by placing a clean, glass jar on your schoolyard before a rain or snow.

2. Bring the jar indoors. If you collected snow, let it melt.

3. Pour some of the water into a clean 100-mL beaker. Use a piece of pH paper or a computer probe to test the pH of the water.

4. If the pH value you obtained was less than about 5.5, your region receives acid rain.

Observe

Write a paragraph in your Science Journal describing the pH of the precipitation you collected.

Before You Read

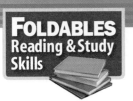

FOLDABLES
Reading & Study Skills

Making a Cause-and-Effect Study Fold **Make the following Foldable to help you understand the cause and effect relationship of air pollution.**

Causes of Air Pollution	Effects of Air Pollution

1. Place a sheet of paper in front of you so the long side is at the top. Fold the paper in half from the left side to the right side and unfold.

2. Label the left side of the paper *Causes of Air Pollution* and the right side *Effects of Air Pollution*. Refold the paper. Label the front *Air Pollution*.

3. Before you read the chapter, draw a picture of one cause of air pollution on the outside of your Foldable. As you read the chapter, list causes of air pollution on the inside of your Foldable.

1 Types and Causes of Air Pollution

As You Read

What You'll Learn

- **Identify** the sources of air pollution.
- **Describe** the effects of pollution on air quality.

Vocabulary

primary pollutant
secondary pollutant
photochemical smog
acid rain
particulate matter
toxic air pollutant
ozone layer

Why It's Important

Understanding the causes of air pollution will help you learn ways to prevent it.

What causes air pollution?

Nearly every organism depends on gases like oxygen in Earth's atmosphere to carry out life functions. In addition to essential gases, the air you breathe also contains pollutants, which are harmful substances that contaminate the environment.

Air pollution comes from human activities as well as natural events. Industry, construction, power generation, transportation, and agriculture are a few examples of human activities that can pollute the air. Natural events that contribute to air pollution include erupting volcanoes that spew out ash and toxic gases. Near Aso, a volcano in Japan, 71 people have been hospitalized since 1980 due to inhalation of volcanic gases. Smoke from forest fires and grass fires also can cause health problems.

Pollutants released directly into the air in a harmful form are called **primary pollutants,** some examples of which are shown in **Figure 1.** Pollutants that are not released directly into the air but form through chemical interactions in the atmosphere are called **secondary pollutants.** Secondary pollutants are responsible for most of the brown haze, or smog, that you see near cities.

Figure 1
Primary pollutants include ash and toxic gases from volcanoes, soot from trucks, and smoke from industry smokestacks.

C Nitrogen dioxide and ozone form smog.

B Ultraviolet rays from the Sun help form ozone.

A Nitrogen and organic compounds are released in car exhaust and form nitrogen dioxide.

Smog

The term *smog* originally was used to describe the combination of smoke and fog, but the smog you see near cities forms in a different way. Smog near cities is called **photochemical smog** because it forms with the help of sunlight. Photochemical smog forms when vehicles, some industries, and power plants release nitrogen compounds and organic compounds into the air. These substances react to form nitrogen dioxide. The nitrogen dioxide then can react in the presence of sunlight to eventually form ozone, a secondary pollutant, as shown in **Figure 2.** Ozone is a major component of smog, and nitrogen dioxide is a reddish-brown gas that contributes to the colored haze.

✔ Reading Check *How does photochemical smog form?*

Nature and Smog Nature can affect the formation of smog. In many cities, smog is not a problem because winds disperse the pollutants that cause smog to form. In some locations, however, landforms can add to smog development. Los Angeles, California, for example, is a city that lies in a basin surrounded by the Santa Monica Mountains to the northwest, the San Gabriel Mountains to the north and east, and the Santa Ana Mountains to the southeast. These surrounding mountains trap air in the Los Angeles region, preventing pollutants from being dispersed quickly. In addition, Los Angeles frequently has sunny, dry weather. When nitrogen compounds are added to the air and exposed to sunlight for long periods of time, thick blankets of smog can develop.

Figure 2
Pollutants from cars and other sources can cause urban smog.

Figure 3
A temperature inversion can worsen air pollution.

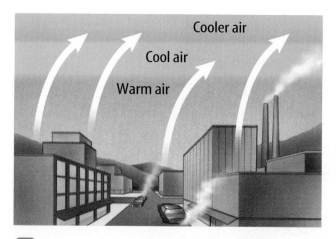

A Cool air usually overlies warm air near Earth's surface. Pollutants can be carried away from their source.

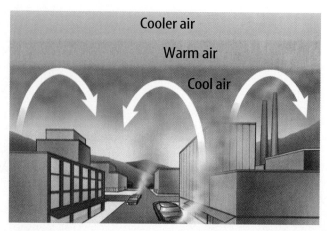

B During a temperature inversion, warm air overlies cool air, trapping air pollutants near the ground.

Temperature Inversions The atmosphere also can influence the formation of smog, as shown in **Figure 3.** Normally, temperatures in Earth's lower atmosphere are warmest near Earth's surface. However, a temperature inversion sometimes occurs. During an inversion, warm air overlies cool air, trapping the cool air near Earth's surface. A temperature inversion reduces the amount of mixing in the atmosphere and can cause pollutants to accumulate near Earth's surface.

✔ Reading Check *How does a temperature inversion contribute to smog formation?*

Acid Rain

Acids and bases are two terms that describe substances. A substance that is neither acidic nor basic is neutral. The pH scale, shown in **Figure 4,** indicates how acidic or how basic a substance is. A pH of 7 is neutral. Substances with a pH lower than 7 are acids. Substances with a pH above 7 are bases. Rainwater is naturally slightly acidic, but pollution sometimes can cause rainwater to be even more acidic.

Figure 4
Substances with a pH lower than 7 are acids. Those with a pH higher than 7 are bases. Rainwater naturally has a pH of about 5.6.

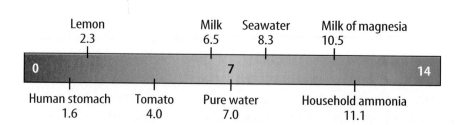

Acid Rain Sources Power plants burn fuels, like coal and oil, to produce the electricity that you need to light your home or power your stereo. Fuels also are burned for transportation and to heat your home. When fuels are burned, they release primary pollutants, such as sulfur dioxide and nitrogen oxides, into the air. These compounds rise into the atmosphere and combine with moisture in the air to form the secondary pollutants sulfuric and nitric acids.

Winds can carry acids long distances. The acids then can be returned to Earth's surface in precipitation. **Acid rain** is rain, snow, fog, and other forms of precipitation that have a pH less than 5.6. Acid rain can discolor painted surfaces, corrode metals, and damage concrete structures. It also can harm plant and animal life.

The Northeastern United States As shown in **Figure 5,** precipitation in the northeastern United States is more acidic than in other areas. Sulfur dioxides and nitrogen oxides released from midwestern power plants and other sources are carried by upper-level winds blowing from a generally westerly direction. The resulting acids that form in the atmosphere eventually return to Earth as acid rain. Many lakes in the northeastern United States have few fish due to acid rain.

Figure 5
The pH of precipitation varies across the United States.

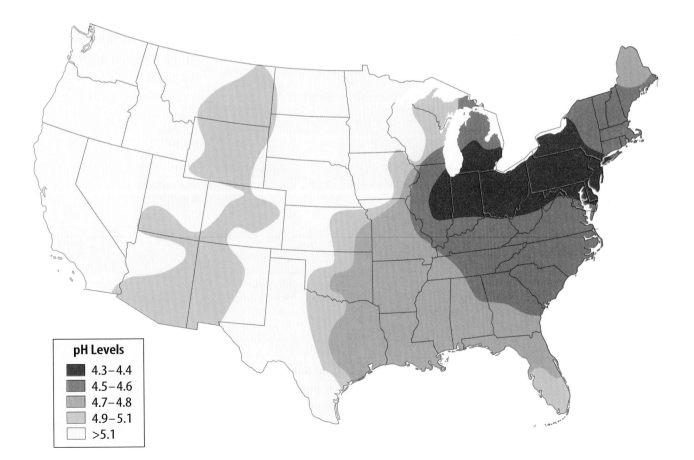

pH Levels
- 4.3–4.4
- 4.5–4.6
- 4.7–4.8
- 4.9–5.1
- >5.1

Observing Particulates

1. Spread **petroleum jelly** in a thin layer on a small **saucer**.
2. Place the saucer outside your home where it will not be disturbed.

Analysis

1. At the end of one day, examine the saucer.
2. Count the number of particulates you see in the petroleum jelly.
3. Infer where the particles might have come from.

Particulate Pollution

Air contains suspended solid particles and liquid droplets called **particulate matter.** Some particles enter the air directly and are therefore primary pollutants, such as smoke from a fire-place or soot in bus exhaust. Other particles, such as liquid droplets, can form from gases such as nitrogen or sulfur oxides as they combine with water in the air.

Coarse and Fine Particulates Larger particles make up coarse particulate matter and come from vehicles traveling on unpaved roads, construction activities, and dust picked up by wind. You can see coarse particulate matter easily when a lot of it is in the air, but the individual size of each particle is only about one-seventh the diameter of a human hair, as shown in **Figure 6.**

Fine particulate matter is much smaller than coarse particu-late matter—only about one-fourth the size of coarse particu-lates. Fine particulates are released into the air from fires, vehicle exhaust, factories, and power plants. Particulate matter can damage plants and buildings and harm your lungs.

Figure 6

Coarse particulate matter is about one-seventh the diameter of a human hair. Fine particulates are much smaller.

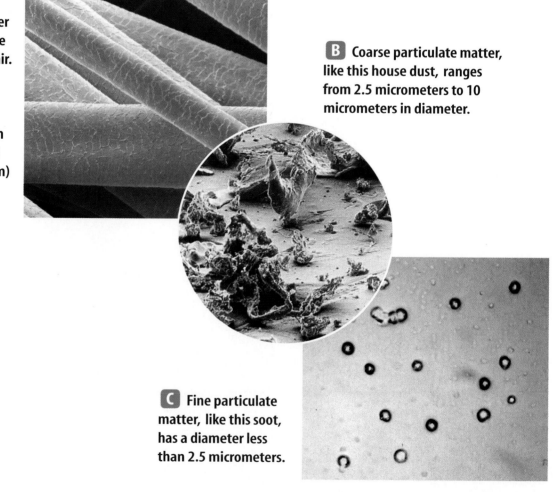

A The average human hair is approximately 70 micrometers (0.000 07 m) in diameter.

B Coarse particulate matter, like this house dust, ranges from 2.5 micrometers to 10 micrometers in diameter.

C Fine particulate matter, like this soot, has a diameter less than 2.5 micrometers.

Figure 7
Human-caused toxic air pollution comes from large factories, some small businesses, and transportation.

Mobile sources (41%) include cars, trucks, and planes.

Major sources (24%) include factories such as oil refineries, steel mills, and chemical manufacturers.

Area sources (35%) include small businesses such as gas stations and dry cleaners.

Toxic Pollutants and Carbon Monoxide

More than 180 different substances released into the air are called **toxic air pollutants** because they cause or might cause cancer or other serious human health problems. Toxic pollutants also can damage other organisms. Most of the toxic air pollution is released by human activities, like those in **Figure 7.** Some air toxics can be released from natural events such as fires and erupting volcanoes.

When fossil fuels are not completely burned, a gas called carbon monoxide forms. About 60 percent of this colorless, odorless gas comes from car exhaust. Concentrations of carbon monoxide increase when cars are stopped in traffic. Low levels of carbon monoxide can harm people with heart disease. Carbon monoxide is poisonous at high concentrations.

Chlorofluorocarbons

Since their discovery in 1928, people have been using chemicals called chlorofluorocarbons (KLOR oh flor oh kar buhns), or CFCs, in air conditioners, refrigerators, and aerosol sprays. For many years, CFCs were thought to be wonder compounds. They don't burn. They're easy to manufacture. They aren't toxic. Millions of tons of CFCs were manufactured and sold by the mid-1970s. In 1974, scientists F. Sherwood Rowland and Mario Molina of the University of California began to wonder where all these CFCs ended up. They theorized that these compounds could end up high in Earth's atmosphere and damage Earth's ozone layer.

SCIENCE *Online*

Research Visit the Glencoe Science Web site at **science.glencoe.com** to find out which chemicals are considered to be toxic air pollutants.

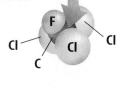

A Energetic rays from the Sun hit a CFC molecule.

Sun's rays

F
Cl   Cl   Cl
    C

B A chlorine atom breaks away.

Cl
F   Cl
Cl   Cl
    C

Cl
O   O

C The chlorine atom hits an ozone molecule.

O   O   Cl

F The oxygen atoms form an oxygen molecule. The chlorine atom is free to repeat the depletion process.

E An oxygen atom hits the chlorine monoxide molecule.

Cl
O
O

O   O
Cl
O

D The chlorine atom takes one oxygen atom to create chlorine monoxide, leaving behind one molecule of oxygen gas (O_2).

Figure 8
One chlorine atom can destroy nearly 100,000 molecules of ozone. If too many ozone molecules are destroyed, harmful radiation from the Sun could reach Earth.

Ozone Depletion About 20 km above Earth is the **ozone layer.** Ozone is a molecule made of three oxygen atoms, just like the ozone in smog. However, unlike smog, the ozone that exists at high altitudes helps Earth's organisms by absorbing some of the Sun's harmful rays.

In the mid-1980s, a severe depletion of ozone appeared over Antarctica. After researching, scientists discovered that CFCs are able to destroy ozone molecules, as shown in **Figure 8.**

In 1987, governments around the world agreed to restrict the use of CFCs gradually. By 1996, all industrialized nations halted production. Measurements taken in the upper atmosphere in 1996 show that the level of CFCs is beginning to decrease. However, scientists don't expect the ozone layer to recover until the middle of the twenty-first century.

Section 1 Assessment

1. What is the difference between primary and secondary air pollutants?

2. Which pollutants can react with water to form acid rain?

3. What causes photochemical smog?

4. What are three kinds of air pollution caused by burning fuels in vehicles?

5. **Think Critically** Why would Denver, Colorado, have smoggier air on some days than Portland, Oregon?

Skill Builder Activities

6. **Recognizing Cause and Effect** Explain how CFCs affect Earth's ozone layer. **For more help, refer to the** Science Skill Handbook.

7. **Solving One-Step Equations** If a person breathes air each day that contains 0.000 030 g of particulate matter, how many grams of particulate matter would a person breathe in one year? **For more help, refer to the** Math Skill Handbook.

Activity

Particulate Pollution

You know that strong winds can pick up and carry small particles such as silt from soil. However, particles also can be carried in air from a variety of sources on most any day. In this activity, you will examine particulates in the air.

What You'll Investigate

How much particulate matter is in the air? How do factors such as wind speed and location affect the amount of particulates?

Materials

vacuum cleaner	compass
paper filter (5)	anemometer
coffee filter	*local weather data source*
stereo microscope	paper confetti
hand lens	heavy-duty rubber band (5)
alternative materials	

Goals

- **Observe** particulates in the air.
- **Relate** particulate abundance to weather conditions and environment.

Safety Precautions

WARNING: *Do not use the vacuum cleaner during the rain or on a wet surface. Keep the cord away from moisture.*

Procedure

1. Find an outdoor location on your schoolyard where electrical power is available.
2. Each day for five days, determine the wind direction and speed at your location. Wind direction can be determined by dropping confetti and using a compass to determine the direction from which the wind is blowing. Wind speed can be determined using an anemometer. Alternately, the information

Particulate Data		
Day	Weather conditions	Particle types and number
1		
2		
3		
4		
5		

can be obtained from a frequently updated source of weather information. Also, record other weather conditions such as snow cover and whether it rained recently.

3. Wrap a large, paper filter around the intake hose of a vacuum cleaner. Fasten the filter to the hose by tightly wrapping it with a heavy-duty rubber band.
4. Turn the vacuum cleaner on and let it draw air at a height of about 1 m for 20 min. each day. You should use a different filter on each different day of your experiment.
5. Remove the filter and take it indoors. Draw a circle around the area where particles would have collected.
6. Examine the filter under a stereomicroscope. Count and describe any particles you observe.

Conclude and Apply

1. **Describe** the different types of particles collected on the filters.
2. **Examine** how wind conditions and other weather factors affected the number and type of particles collected each day.
3. **Infer** possible sources in your community for the particles.

2 Effects of Air Pollution

As You Read

What You'll Learn

- **Explain** how air pollution affects human health.
- **Describe** how air pollution affects Earth's organisms.
- **List** several ways that air pollution can damage buildings and structures.

Vocabulary

ultraviolet radiation
cataract
biomagnification

Why It's Important

Air pollution can harm organisms, human-built structures, and your health.

Air Pollution and Your Health

In the United States, about 62 million people breathe unhealthy air and approximately 250,000 people suffer from pollution-related breathing disorders. The United Nations estimates that at least 1.3 billion people around the world live in areas with dangerously polluted air.

The effects on your health from air pollution are listed in **Figure 9.** Health effects depend on how long you are exposed to the pollutant and how much of the pollutant is in the air. For example, you might notice watery eyes and shortness of breath on a smoggy day. When the air clears, you can breathe normally. If you breathe smoggy air for your entire life, you might have difficulty breathing when you get older.

Young children and elderly people suffer the most effects of pollution. With the same amount of exposure to pollutants, young children get much bigger doses for their size than adults do. When a child is young, all of his or her organs, including the brain, still are developing. Air pollution can affect the development of growing organs. Elderly people are at risk because they have been exposed to pollutants for a long time.

Figure 9
Health effects of air pollution depend on the concentration of pollutants and how long you are exposed to them.

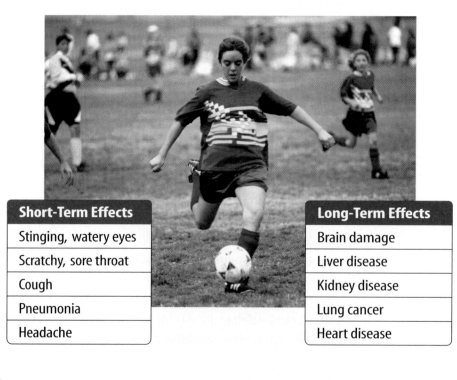

Short-Term Effects	Long-Term Effects
Stinging, watery eyes	Brain damage
Scratchy, sore throat	Liver disease
Cough	Kidney disease
Pneumonia	Lung cancer
Headache	Heart disease

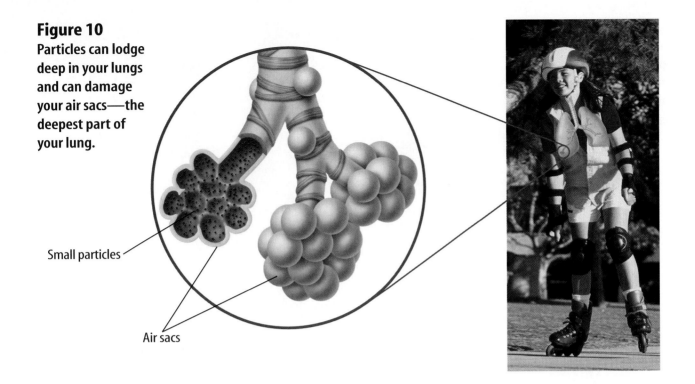

Figure 10
Particles can lodge deep in your lungs and can damage your air sacs—the deepest part of your lung.

Small particles

Air sacs

Smog and Carbon Monoxide Compounds found in smog can cause your eyes to water and sting. Long-term exposure to smog can increase your risk for lung infections, reduce your ability to breathe normally, and might make asthma worse. You also can develop chest pains and a cough.

Carbon monoxide affects your blood's ability to carry oxygen. High concentrations of this gas might affect your vision, your ability to concentrate, and your coordination. Very high levels can cause death.

Effects of Particulates and Toxic Pollutants Do you sneeze when you shake out a dusty rug? When you sneeze, you force the dust out of your respiratory system. Smaller particles, however, can penetrate deep into your lungs and cause part of the lungs to become inflamed, as shown in **Figure 10.** Over time, small particulate matter might damage your lungs permanently, making breathing difficult and forcing your heart to work harder than it should.

Toxic substances in air can damage many body systems. People exposed to toxic air pollutants can suffer from nerve damage, respiratory problems, and disorders of the reproductive system. They also can have an increased risk for cancer.

Exposure to a large amount of toxic air pollution over a short period of time can be deadly. On December 3, 1984, an accident at a pesticide factory in India released a cloud of toxic gas. Nearly 4,000 people died and 200,000 suffered permanent injuries such as blindness and heart disease.

Health
INTEGRATION

The tubes that carry air deep inside your lungs are lined with mucus-producing glands and small hair-like structures called cilia. The mucus traps particulate matter. The cilia move, constantly sweeping the mucus and the trapped particulate matter upward to your throat. Every time you swallow, you begin the process of clearing this mucus and particulate matter from your body. Cigarette smoking destroys the cilia over time. Infer what might happen to your lungs if you smoke cigarettes.

Figure 11
Malignant melanoma, a type of skin cancer that can be deadly, can be caused by exposure to the Sun's harmful rays.

Modeling Ozone Depletion

Procedure

1. Attach three **red polystyrene balls** together with **toothpicks** to form a triangle. This model represents the three oxygen atoms of an ozone molecule.
2. Attach three **green balls** and one **yellow ball** to a center **blue ball.** The green balls represent chlorine atoms; the yellow ball is a fluorine atom, and the blue ball represents a carbon atom. This is a model of a CFC molecule.
3. Detach one of the green balls from the CFC molecule and a red ball from the ozone molecule and connect these two balls.

Analysis

1. How is ozone different from oxygen gas?
2. What did you model during step 3 of the procedure?

Inhaling Acid When you inhale humid air from acid rain, acid can be deposited deep inside your lungs. Acid irritates the lung's sensitive tissues and reduces your ability to fight respiratory infections. Your lungs are responsible for moving oxygen into your blood. Damaged lungs cannot transfer oxygen to the blood easily, so the heart must work harder to pump oxygen to body cells. Over time, the heart can become stressed and weak.

Increased Ultraviolet Radiation Harmful rays from the Sun, called **ultraviolet radiation,** are blocked partially by the protective ozone layer. Each spring, an ozone hole forms over Antarctica, and ozone levels fall as much as 70 percent below normal. Even over the United States, the protective ozone layer is about five percent below normal in the summer and ten percent below normal in the winter.

In humans, increased ultraviolet radiation is linked to skin cancer. One type of skin cancer, malignant melanoma, shown in **Figure 11,** accounts for only four percent of skin cancer cases but causes about 79 percent of skin cancer deaths. About 47,700 people are diagnosed with malignant melanoma in the United States each year, and nearly 7,700 people die from it. The number of new melanomas diagnosed has more than doubled since 1973.

In addition to skin cancer, cataracts are more common in people who are exposed to high amounts of ultraviolet radiation. **Cataracts** are a form of eye damage that makes the lens of the eye cloudy. Ultraviolet radiation also can affect the immune system, which helps you fight illness.

✔ **Reading Check** *What are some health effects of increased ultraviolet radiation?*

You can protect yourself against excess ultraviolet radiation by avoiding outdoor activities during the middle of the day and by wearing long sleeves, a hat with a wide brim, sunglasses, and by using protective sunscreens.

Effects on Earth's Organisms

Animals are exposed to air pollutants when they inhale gases and small particles. Because air pollutants fall to Earth in rain or snow, animals also are exposed when they ingest pollutants in their food and water. Soft-bodied animals such as earthworms, or animals with thin, moist skin, such as amphibians, can absorb air pollutants directly through their skin.

Just like humans, young animals are not able to tolerate the same amount of pollution as adult animals can. Whether or not an animal will be affected by a pollutant depends on the kind of pollutant, the length of time the animal is exposed to the pollutant, and the amount of pollutant taken into the animal's body.

Concentrating Pollutants The concentration of a pollutant in the air might not be high enough to cause a problem. Some pollutants, however, stay in animal tissues when they eat or drink instead of passing through their bodies as waste. When these animals are eaten by other animals, many of the pollutants they were exposed to also are ingested by the predator. **Biomagnification** (BI oh mag nuh fuh KAY shun) is the process in which pollutant levels increase through the food chain, as shown in **Figure 12.** Some fish are not safe for humans to eat frequently because of biomagnification.

Figure 12
Pollutants from the air, such as the metal mercury, can end up in high concentrations in animals through biomagnification. Pollutants often are measured in parts per million, or ppm.

Mercury from air

Florida panther
110 ppm

Water
0.001 ppm

Racoon
24 ppm

Fish
0.9 ppm

Figure 13
Acids in rain or fog can make trees weak and strip the nutrients they need from the soil.

Acidic Lakes and Streams Recall that lower pH means higher acidity. The pH of some streams, lakes and rivers can decrease when acid rain falls. Many organisms require an environment with a narrow range of pH values.

In some streams and lakes in the United States and Canada, acid rain has eliminated certain fish species, such as brook trout. For example, hundreds of lakes in the Adirondack Mountains in New York are too acidic for fish to survive in. The Canadian government estimates that more than 14,000 lakes in eastern Canada are acidic. Acid rain is an even greater problem when snow melts. If a large amount of acidic snow falls in the winter and melts quickly in the spring, a sudden rush of acids flows into lakes and streams. Many fish and other organisms have been killed because of sudden pH changes.

Acid rain also can damage plants. At higher elevations, trees often are surrounded by fog. When the fog is acidic, trees suffer injury and are less able to resist pests and diseases. Some stands of evergreens in the Great Smoky Mountain National Park, as shown in **Figure 13,** have died from acidic exposure.

Acid Rain and Soils Acid rain can also affect soils. As acid rain moves through soil, it can strip away many of the nutrients that trees and other plants need to grow. Some regions of the United States, however, have naturally basic soils. In such regions, acid rain might not significantly affect vegetation. The higher pH of basic soils can help raise the pH of acid rain after it falls to the ground.

Smog The compounds in smog affect animals and plants. Smog affects the respiratory system of animals, causing irritation to the lining of the lungs. When plants are exposed to smog over a long period of time, the pollutants break down the waxy coating on their leaves. This results in water loss through the leaves and increases the effects of diseases, pests, drought, and frost. Scientists estimate that smog formed from vehicle exhaust damages $10 million worth of crops in California each year.

✔ **Reading Check** *What effects does smog have on plants and animals?*

The Ozone Layer As the ozone layer thins, Earth's organisms are exposed to more ultraviolet radiation. Small organisms called phytoplankton (FI toh PLANK tun) live in Earth's freshwater and oceans. They make food using carbon dioxide and water in the presence of sunlight. These organisms also are the basis of the food chain shown in **Figure 14.** Research shows that ultraviolet radiation can reduce the ability of phytoplankton to make food, decreasing their numbers. Ultraviolet radiation also might damage young crabs, shrimp, and some fish. In some animal species, growth is slowed and the ability to fight diseases is reduced.

Ultraviolet radiation might affect many agricultural crops such as rice by decreasing the plant's ability to fight diseases and pests. Even small increases in ultraviolet radiation might reduce the amount of rice grown per square kilometer. Rice is the main food source for more than half the world's population. The world population is growing, but the amount of land suitable for farming will not increase.

Reading Check *How might increasing ultraviolet radiation affect world rice production?*

Figure 14
Studies indicate that a 16 percent increase in ultraviolet radiation could decrease the amount of fish in antarctic waters by more than 6 million metric tons per year.

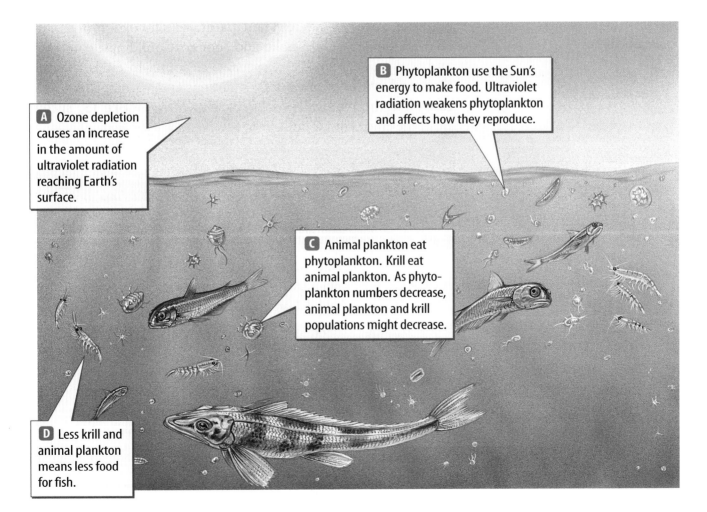

A Ozone depletion causes an increase in the amount of ultraviolet radiation reaching Earth's surface.

B Phytoplankton use the Sun's energy to make food. Ultraviolet radiation weakens phytoplankton and affects how they reproduce.

C Animal plankton eat phytoplankton. Krill eat animal plankton. As phytoplankton numbers decrease, animal plankton and krill populations might decrease.

D Less krill and animal plankton means less food for fish.

Figure 15
The pyramids in Egypt have withstood the Sun, wind, and sandstorms for more than 4,000 years. However, air pollution within the last 50 years has led to increased decay of these magnificent structures.

Damage to Materials and Structures

Air pollution not only affects your health and the health of other organisms, it also damages many materials. For example, acid rain is known to corrode metals, and deteriorate stone and paint. To reduce the damage on automobiles, some manufacturers use a special acid-resistant paint, which costs more than $61 million per year. Smoke and soot coat buildings, paintings and sculptures, requiring expensive cleaning. In cities all over the world, works of art, ornate buildings and statues, and structures like the pyramids of Egypt, shown in **Figure 15,** suffer from the effects of air pollution.

Section 2 Assessment

1. What are three ways that animals are exposed to air pollutants?
2. What are some effects of air pollution on human health?
3. Why are young children more affected by air pollutants than young adults are?
4. How does air pollution affect buildings and other structures?
5. **Think Critically** What might happen to carbon dioxide levels in Earth's atmosphere if ultraviolet radiation increases?

Skill Builder Activities

6. **Recognizing Cause and Effect** After a quick spring thaw of heavy snow, many fish are found dead in New York lakes. Explain why this happened. **For more help, refer to the** Science Skill Handbook.

7. **Using Graphics Software** Use a computer to create a pamphlet that describes the effects that acid rain might have on humans and other organisms. **For more help, refer to the** Technology Skill Handbook.

SECTION 3 Solutions to Air Pollution

History of Clean Air Laws

Between 1900 and 1970, motor vehicle use and industrial manufacturing expanded rapidly in the United States. Air in some parts of the country, especially in cities, became more polluted. The release of nitrogen oxides, which help form smog and acid rain, increased nearly 700 percent between 1900 and 1970.

Scientists and government officials recognized that air quality must be protected. Beginning in 1955, the U.S. Congress passed a series of laws to help protect the air you breathe. A summary of these laws is listed in **Table 1.** The U.S. Environmental Protection Agency has the responsibility of gathering and analyzing air pollution data from across the country and working to keep the country's air clean.

The Clean Air Act is a federal law that regulates air pollution over the entire country. Each state is responsible for making sure that the goals of the law are met. State agencies issue permits to power plants and industries, which limit what they can release into the air. Companies that exceed air pollution limits might have to pay a fine. Automobile exhaust is monitored in areas with poor air quality.

As You Read

***What* You'll Learn**

■ **Describe** air pollution laws in the United States.
■ **Identify** things you can do to reduce air pollution.

Vocabulary
ambient air
air quality standard
emission

***Why* It's Important**

Controlling the sources of air pollution will help keep your air clean.

Table 1 Summary of Clean Air Regulations in the United States

Name of Law	What It Does
Air Pollution Control Act of 1955	It granted $5 million annually for air pollution research. Although it did little to prevent air pollution, the law made the public aware of pollution problems.
Clean Air Act of 1963	This act granted $95 million per year to state and local governments for research and to create air pollution control programs. It also encouraged the use of technology to reduce air pollution from cars and electric power plants.
Clean Air Act of 1970	It set standards for specific pollutants in the air and placed strict limits on car exhaust and pollutants from new industries.
Clean Air Act of 1990	This act placed strict limits on car emissions and encouraged the use of cleaner-burning gasoline. It also forced companies to use the best technology available to reduce toxic emissions.

Ambient Air You know that air pollutants released in one part of the country can affect the air somewhere else. You also have learned that natural events, such as temperature inversions, can concentrate pollutants in an area. The air you breathe is called **ambient** (AM bee unt) **air.** Air pollution laws are written to help keep ambient air clean, no matter what the source of pollution is. Across the United States, scientists sample and test ambient air for particulate matter, carbon monoxide, sulfur dioxide, nitrogen dioxide, lead, and ozone. These pollutants cannot exceed a certain level, called an **air quality standard.** Areas that already have fairly clean air, such as national parks, have stricter air quality standards than cities do. As **Figure 16** illustrates, if an area has pollution levels above ambient air quality standards, controls can be placed on specific sources of air pollution.

Figure 16
The Clean Air Act of 1990 set standards for ambient air. These limits are met by controlling emissions from various sources.

Controlling the Source Pollutants released into the air from a particular source are called **emissions** (ee MIH shunz). Emissions are measured at industry smokestacks and automobile tailpipes. If ambient air quality standards are not met, emissions must be reduced.

Emissions can be controlled in two ways—by using devices that capture pollutants already created and by limiting the amount of pollutants produced in the first place. For example, auto exhaust used to contain many more pollutants than it does today. Since 1975, each new car sold in the United States has been equipped with a catalytic (ka tuh LIH tihk) converter, a device that changes harmful gases in car exhaust to less harmful ones. A catalytic converter and other emission control devices are shown in **Figure 17.**

✔ **Reading Check** *What two methods can be used to control emissions?*

Changing the way gasoline is produced has helped control the amount of pollutants in gasoline even before it is burned. Compounds such as alcohol can be added to gasoline to reduce tailpipe emissions. Since the 1990 Clean Air Act was enacted, only clean-burning gasoline can be sold in the smoggiest areas of the country.

SCIENCE *Online*

Research Visit the Glencoe Science Web site at **science.glencoe.com** to find an ambient air quality standard for a city near you.

Figure 17

In the past few decades new technologies have reduced air pollution by trapping pollutants at their sources. Devices such as smokestack scrubbers, electrostatic precipitators, and catalytic converters shown here use different methods to remove pollutants from exhaust gases.

▶ SMOKESTACK SCRUBBER Burning some types of coal to generate electricity produces large quantities of sulfur dioxide—a pollutant that can cause acid rain. The smokestacks of many coal-burning plants are equipped with anti-pollution devices called scrubbers.

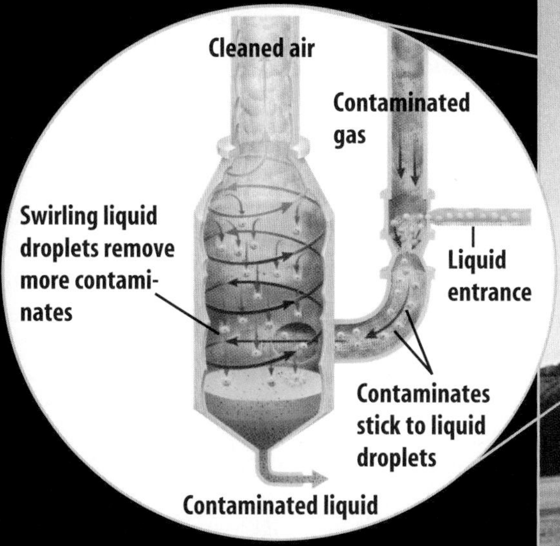

Cleaned air

Contaminated gas

Swirling liquid droplets remove more contaminates

Liquid entrance

Contaminates stick to liquid droplets

Contaminated liquid

▶ ELECTROSTATIC PRECIPITATOR As smoke enters an electrostatic precipitator, plates that line the interior of the device give polluting particles a positive charge. Negatively charged plates then attract the particles, "cleaning" the smoke. An electrostatic precipitator removes up to 99 percent of particulate matter from industrial emissions.

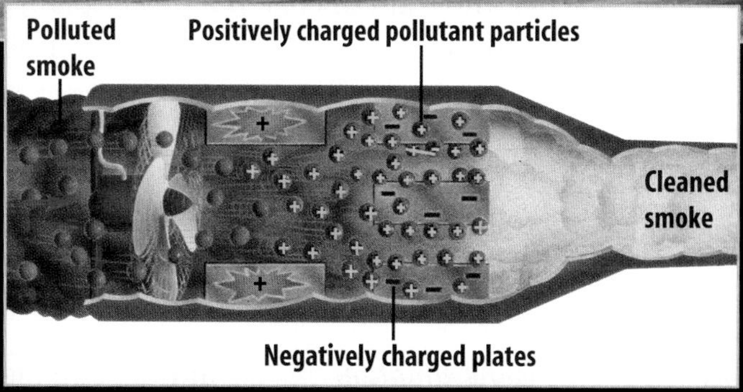

Polluted smoke

Positively charged pollutant particles

Cleaned smoke

Negatively charged plates

Exhaust from engine

◀ CATALYTIC CONVERTER Automobile exhaust gases pass over small beads coated with metals inside a catalytic converter. The metals cause chemical reactions that change most of the harmful gases into carbon dioxide and water.

Cleaned exhaust exits tailpipe

You Can Help

Laws and new technologies will help reduce air pollution, but you can be a part of the solution, too. When you reduce the amount of electricity you use, less fuel is burned at a power plant, and less pollution is released. Turn off lights and all appliances when you aren't using them. Turn down the thermostat in the winter and wear more layers of clothing. Open windows in the summer instead of using air conditioning. Using public transportation, riding a bike as shown in **Figure 18,** or car pooling will help keep the air clean.

Figure 18
Cars emit 0.6 g of nitrogen oxides per kilometer. Light trucks, minivans, and sport-utility vehicles can emit 1.1 g to 1.7 g per kilometer, depending on their size. *How many grams of nitrogen oxides would not be emitted if you rode your bike for 5 km instead of riding in a car?*

✔ **Reading Check** *How can you help reduce air pollution?*

Math Skills Activity

Calculating Pollution Caused by Burning Coal

Example Problem

Sulfur dioxide (SO_2) belongs to a family of gases that are formed when coal or oil is burned. It is considered to be a major air pollutant. Burning a certain type of coal produces about 0.01 kg of SO_2 per kilogram of coal. If a power plant burns 3 million kg of coal annually, how much SO_2 would be released?

Solution

1 *This is what you know:*   production rate = 0.01 kg of SO_2 /kg coal
annual use = 3,000,000 kg of coal

2 *This is what you need to find:*   annual emissions = kilograms of SO_2 produced each year

3 *This is the equation you need to use:*   annual emissions = (annual use) $\times$ (production rate)

4 *Substitute the known values:*   annual emissions = (3,000,000 kg coal) $\times$ (0.01 kg SO_2 /kg coal)
= 30,000 kg SO_2

Practice Problem

If a power plant burned 500,000 kg of coal annually, how much SO_2 would be produced?

For more help, refer to the Math Skill Handbook.

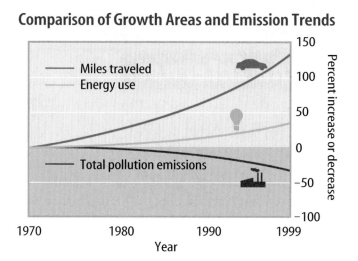

Comparison of Growth Areas and Emission Trends

Miles traveled
Energy use

Total pollution emissions

Percent increase or decrease

150
100
50
0
−50
−100

1970   1980   1990   1999

Year

Figure 19
The total amount of air pollutants released to the air above the United States has decreased since the passage of strict air pollution laws.

Are air pollution laws working?

As **Figure 19** shows, air quality in the United States has improved since 1990, even though energy use increased and people are driving more. Strict controls on sources of pollution have greatly increased the quality of the air you breathe. Even so, although the national trends for most air pollutants are decreasing, others, such as nitrogen dioxides, continue to rise. Smog levels are increasing in many rural areas, and the United States is home to more than 2,500 bodies of water whose fish are unsafe to eat because of biomagnification. As the United States population continues to increase, conservation and new technology can help reduce air pollution.

Section 3 Assessment

1. Why did air in some parts of the United States become more polluted from 1900 to 1970?

2. Ambient air is sampled and tested for which pollutants across the United States?

3. What did the 1970 Clean Air Act regulate?

4. How is air pollution reduced when energy is conserved?

5. **Think Critically** Why are air pollution standards written for ambient air instead of emissions?

Skill Builder Activities

6. **Drawing Conclusions** More people are moving to a city. Traffic congestion has increased and people are driving greater distances. Will ambient air quality remain the same if emissions per car don't change? **For more help, refer to the** Science Skill Handbook.

7. **Communicating** Write a letter to the editor of a newspaper explaining how everyone can help reduce air pollution. **For more help, refer to the** Science Skill Handbook.

Activity *Use the Internet*

Air Pollution Where You Live

The quality of the air you breathe can affect your health and the health of other organisms near your home. Clean air laws passed in 1970 and 1990 have helped increase air quality in many regions of the United States. By investigating your community's air quality, you can determine how changes in the laws have improved the air you breathe. You also can investigate methods people have used to help make air cleaner and healthier.

Recognize the Problem

How has the quality of the air in your community changed?

Form a Hypothesis

Air quality can be assessed many ways. For example, you can count the number of days per year when smog levels exceed healthful values. You also can collect statistics describing the number of people who develop respiratory problems. Form a hypothesis about whether air quality in your community has changed during the last 20 years.

Goals

- **Identify** sources of data that can be used to assess air quality.
- **Investigate** data to determine local air quality.
- **Evaluate** trends in data to identify patterns of change.
- **Identify** information that supports or refutes your hypothesis.

Data Source

SCIENCE*Online* Go to the Glencoe Science Web site at **science.glencoe.com** to get more information about air quality and for data collected by other students.

Test Your Hypothesis

Plan

1. Search for information about air quality indicators for your community or region. Data from federal, state, and local government sources can be helpful. Consider using information that has been collected by private groups.

2. Review carefully the data you find. What information illustrates the change in air quality during the last 20 years? Examine the data to determine trends.

3. Do the trends in the data show a continued increase in air quality? Has the air quality improved or worsened in an irregular pattern?

4. Look for other types of information that provide additional clues about your community's air quality over the years. For example, does gasoline sold in your area contain clean-burning additives?

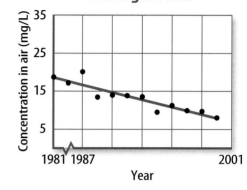

Trends in Carbon Monoxide Levels, Washington D.C.

Do

1. Make sure your teacher approves your plan before you start.

2. Create a table for your data.

Analyze Your Data

1. **Calculate** the five-year and ten-year averages for your data. Calculate the range of your data.

2. **Graph** the annual data and the five-year and ten-year averages.

3. **Describe** the air quality changes for your area in the last 20 years.

4. **List** additional information that describes changes in your community that might affect air quality.

Draw Conclusions

1. Overall, how would you assess the quality of your community's air? Has there been a change in the air quality? What indicators provide these data?

2. Does your data support or refute your hypothesis about air quality in your community? Why?

3. What strategies should you use to analyze and compare data from different sources?

Communicating Your Data

SCIENCE Online Find this *Use the Internet* activity on the Glencoe Science Web site at **science.glencoe.com**. Complete the table posted on the site. Compare your data to those of other students. Present your findings to your class.

Oops! Accidents in SCIENCE

SOMETIMES GREAT DISCOVERIES HAPPEN BY ACCIDENT!

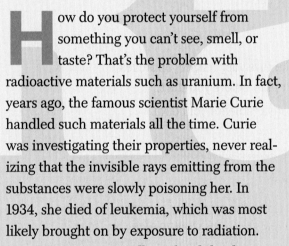

Geiger counters determine radioactivity.

Rad

How do you protect yourself from something you can't see, smell, or taste? That's the problem with radioactive materials such as uranium. In fact, years ago, the famous scientist Marie Curie handled such materials all the time. Curie was investigating their properties, never realizing that the invisible rays emitting from the substances were slowly poisoning her. In 1934, she died of leukemia, which was most likely brought on by exposure to radiation.

Scientists eventually realized the danger of radioactive materials. Many workers in uranium mines developed lung cancer as a result of being exposed to radioactive substances. Scientists also learned that as uranium begins to break down, it changes into different elements, such as thorium, protactinium (pro tak TIH nee um), and radium . . . all still radioactive.

In 1900, a German scientist, Friedrich Ernst Dorn, discovered that radium emitted a radioactive gas called radon. Still, most people didn't think radon gas was much to worry about.

Marie Curie was one of the first scientists to be exposed to radioactive materials.

Radon Levels

	LOW
	MODERATE
	HIGH

Map states labeled: Washington, Oregon, Idaho, Montana, North Dakota, Minnesota, Wisconsin, Michigan, Maine, New Hampshire, Vermont, Massachusetts, New York, Rhode Island, Connecticut, Pennsylvania, New Jersey, Delaware, Maryland, West Virginia, Virginia, Wyoming, South Dakota, Nebraska, Iowa, Illinois, Indiana, Ohio, Kentucky, North Carolina, South Carolina, Tennessee, Nevada, Utah, Colorado, Kansas, Missouri, California, Arizona, New Mexico, Oklahoma, Arkansas, Mississippi, Alabama, Georgia, Texas, Louisiana, Florida, Hawaii, Alaska

The Invisible Threat

Radon Worries

All that changed in 1984. An engineer at a nuclear power plant in Pennsylvania set off the radiation detectors at the plant one morning. Officials found no contamination that could have caused this to happen. So, where did the engineer get his radioactive contamination? The answer was completely unexpected—the engineer's home! The house had radiation levels 700 times higher than is considered to be safe for humans. Further study found that the house was built on rock that contained uranium and radon gas.

This caused people to wake up to the hazards of radon gas. Large deposits containing low amounts of uranium are found in many U.S. states. The radon gas can seep from the ground through small cracks and pores in the soil. Invisibly and without a smell, it can enter a home. Here's how it works. As warm air is lifted in your home, it creates an effect similar to the suction of a vacuum cleaner, helping the radon gas get pulled from the soil into your basement.

Fortunately, there are tests that people living in high-risk radon areas can conduct to detect levels of radon gas. And, if found, there are methods for removing radon gas from these buildings safely.

CONNECTIONS Use a map Locate the area where you live on the map above. Are high amounts of radon gas found in your state? According to the map, which states have low radon levels?

SCIENCE Online
For more information, visit

Chapter 4 Study Guide

Reviewing Main Ideas

Section 1 Types and Causes of Air Pollution

1. Human activities and nature can cause air pollution. *What types of pollutants are released from vehicles like this truck?*

2. Acid rain forms when sulfur dioxide and nitrogen oxides combine with moisture in the atmosphere.

3. Mountains, weather, and temperature inversions can add to smog development.

4. Toxic air pollutants come from vehicles, factories, and power plants. Natural sources, such as fires and volcanoes also produce toxins.

Section 2 Effects of Air Pollution

1. Animals are exposed to air pollutants when they inhale gases and particulates and ingest pollutants. Some soft-bodied organisms and amphibians also can absorb pollutants through their skin.

2. The ozone layer protects Earth from ultraviolet radiation. *What are some health effects caused by increased ultraviolet exposure?*

3. The greater the concentration of a pollutant is and the greater the length of time a person has been exposed to a pollutant is, the greater the health risk is. Depending on the exposure, smog, acid rain, and particulate pollution can cause minor discomfort or lead to long-term health problems.

4. Pollutants can increase in concentration as they biomagnify through food chains.

Section 3 Solutions to Air Pollution

1. The Environmental Protection Agency monitors ambient air for certain pollutants.

2. Air pollution control laws passed since 1955 have reduced air pollution levels significantly.

3. Technologies, such as catalytic converters on cars and scrubbers on smokestacks, help reduce air pollution levels. *How does adding substances to gasoline, like ethanol, help reduce air pollution?*

FOLDABLES
Reading & Study Skills

After You Read

On the inside of your Foldable, list the effects of air pollution. Draw a picture on the back of how the scene on the front would look without pollution.

Visualizing Main Ideas

Complete the following chart on the health effects of air pollution.

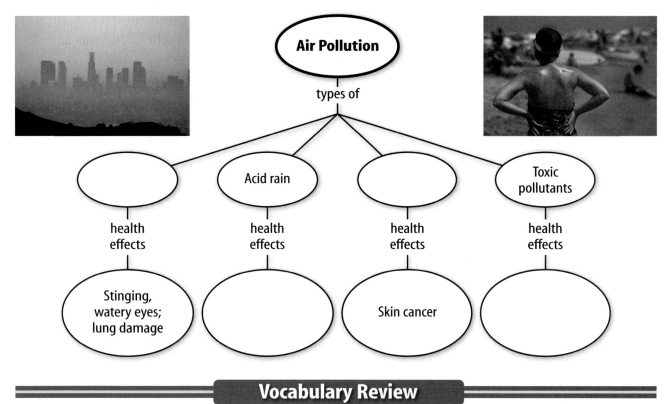

Air Pollution

types of

Acid rain

Toxic pollutants

health effects

health effects

health effects

health effects

Stinging, watery eyes; lung damage

Skin cancer

Vocabulary Review

Vocabulary Review

a. acid rain
b. air quality standard
c. ambient air
d. biomagnification
e. cataract
f. emission
g. ozone layer
h. particulate matter
i. photochemical smog
j. primary pollutant
k. secondary pollutant
l. toxic air pollutant
m. ultraviolet radiation

THE PRINCETON REVIEW **Study Tip**

Draw pictures of difficult concepts that are described in the chapter. Then label each picture with its concept. This will help you remember the concept more easily.

Using Vocabulary

Use what you know about the listed terms to answer the following questions.

1. How do pollutants form photochemical smog? Give an example of a secondary pollutant in smog.

2. Why are emissions controlled when ambient air doesn't meet an air quality standard?

3. Why didn't the ozone layer immediately recover despite the severe restriction of chlorofluorocarbon use in the mid-1990s?

4. Explain how sulfur dioxide emissions in the Midwest contribute to acid rain in the Northeast.

5. How can biomagnification of toxic air pollutants occur in the environment?

Chapter ④ Assessment

Checking Concepts

Choose the word or phrase that best answers the question.

1. What is the brown haze that forms over some cities called?
   A) CFCs   C) acid rain
   B) carbon monoxide   D) smog

2. Which of these forms when warm air acts as a barrier, preventing air from mixing?
   A) temperature inversion
   B) ozone depletion
   C) primary pollution
   D) secondary pollution

3. What is the pH of acid rain?
   A) greater than 7.6   C) lower than 5.6
   B) 5.6   D) 5.6 to 7.6

4. Which kind of atom in a chlorofluoro-carbon molecule destroys ozone molecules?
   A) hydrogen   C) carbon
   B) oxygen   D) chlorine

5. What does the ozone layer absorb?
   A) metals   C) acid rain
   B) UV radiation   D) particulates

6. What type of pollutant is about one-seventh the diameter of a human hair?
   A) coarse particulate matter
   B) fine particulate matter
   C) acid rain
   D) carbon monoxide

7. Which term is used to describe increasing pollutant levels through the food chain?
   A) ambient   C) biomagnification
   B) emission   D) acidity

8. About 60 percent of carbon monoxide comes from which source?
   A) power plants   C) car exhaust
   B) cleaning products   D) industry

9. What type of air pollution caused the death of nearly 4,000 people in India in 1984?
   A) carbon monoxide   C) particulates
   B) toxic pollutants   D) acid rain

10. Which emission control device was added to automobiles in the mid-1970s?
    A) catalytic converter
    B) smokestack scrubber
    C) alcohol
    D) electrostatic separator

Thinking Critically

11. How can traffic jams increase air pollution?

12. Why does air pollution affect the health of older people more than most young people?

13. Why are there air quality standards for ambient air?

14. What are three things you can do to help reduce air pollution?

15. Why is the concentration of some pollutants greater in birds and mammals than in the contaminated organisms they eat?

Developing Skills

16. **Recognizing Cause and Effect** It has been sunny and hot with little wind for more than a week in your city. The newspaper reports that smog levels are unhealthy. Explain the connection.

17. Converting Units Most air pollutants are measured in micrograms. There are 1,000 micrograms in 1 milligram and 1,000 milligrams in 1 gram. How many micrograms are in 1 gram?

18. Comparing and Contrasting Compare and contrast the effects of acid rain and ultraviolet radiation on organisms.

19. Researching Information Research to find out how antarctic organisms are affected by ozone depletion.

20. Communicating Illustrate how emissions from midwestern states can cause acid rain in the northeastern United States.

Performance Assessment

21. Make a Poster Research the pollutants found in cigarette smoke. Make a poster of how these chemicals harm your health.

22. Organize Activities To conserve energy in your school, place signs near light switches that remind people to turn off lights when they leave the room. Make signs encouraging students to carpool to school events.

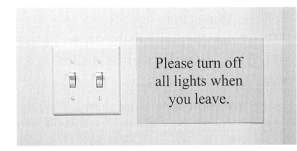

Please turn off all lights when you leave.

TECHNOLOGY

Go to the Glencoe Science Web site at **science.glencoe.com** or use the **Glencoe Science CD-ROM** for additional chapter assessment.

THE PRINCETON REVIEW **Test Practice**

Automobiles produced before the mid-1970s used leaded gasoline. Car engines have since been designed that don't require lead in gasoline. The graph below illustrates average lead emissions for the United States over a 20-year period.

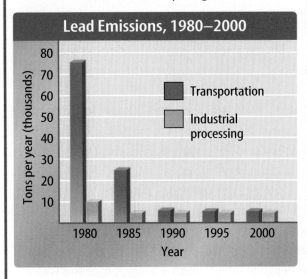

Lead Emissions, 1980–2000

Tons per year (thousands)

■ Transportation

□ Industrial processing

Year: 1980, 1985, 1990, 1995, 2000

Study the graph and answer the following questions.

1. Which of the following phrases describes lead emissions in 1980?
   A) Most came from industrial sources.
   B) Most came from transportation.
   C) Emissions were lower in 1980 than in 2000.
   D) Total emissions were 10,000 tons.

2. Which of the following likely is responsible for the reduction in emissions?
   F) Cars now use unleaded gasoline.
   G) People drive less.
   H) Industry has produced more products.
   J) More electricity is produced.

Reading Comprehension

Read the passage. Then read each question that follows the passage. Decide which is the best answer to each question.

Hurricanes: An Exchange Between Ocean and Atmosphere

Hurricanes are among the most feared of all weather storms in the Atlantic region. In the western Pacific they are known as typhoons, and in Australia and the Indian Ocean they are called cyclones. Hurricane season in the United States and Caribbean occurs each year between June and November.

Hurricanes over the Atlantic Ocean begin as low-pressure systems, usually in the tropical seas west of Africa. The trade winds blow these storms westward. Heat from the warm ocean water gives the system energy. Once the water temperature rises to 27°C, a hurricane can form.

To be classified as a hurricane, the wind speed of the storm must exceed 119 km/h. Hurricanes can last for several days and can reach heights up to 16 km above the water.

The Atlantic has about ten tropical storms each year. Of these, six of them might develop into full-blown hurricanes.

Hurricanes can cause severe damage to anything near them on the water. After a hurricane reaches land, it loses its source of energy—warm ocean water—and begins to weaken. Even though the strength of these storms fade as they reach shore, hurricanes frequently are responsible for bllions of dollars of damage and loss of lives.

Test-Taking Tip Take your time and read the passage carefully.

1. Which of the following was described first in the passage?
   A) Hurricanes can reach heights up to 16 km above the surface of the water.
   B) Hurricane season in the Atlantic region occurs between June and November.
   C) Hurricanes start to lose energy upon reaching land.
   D) Hurricanes can be suppressed by the high, strong winds of El Niño.

2. To classify as a hurricane, the wind speed of the storm must be more than _____.
   F) 27 km/h
   G) 16 km/h
   H) 119 km/h
   J) 140 km/h

3. What is the energy source of hurricanes?
   A) high winds
   B) warm ocean water
   C) trade winds
   D) cold air from land

Reasoning and Skills

Read each question and choose the best answer.

1. Jim and Todd noticed that some types of patio chairs were not as hot to sit in as others. Which of the following would be the BEST test of this hypothesis?

   A) Measure and record the height and weight of all the chairs.

   B) Sit in each one and feel which one was hotter.

   C) Find out where each chair was purchased from and compare prices.

   D) Record the surface temperature of each chair at the same time of day.

Test-Taking Tip Think of what type of scientific information would be needed to find out for certain the temperature of an object.

Things Found in Earth's Atmosphere	
Layer	**Found in Layer**
Troposphere	Most water vapor and gases
Stratosphere	Ozone
Mesosphere	Falling temperatures
Thermosphere	Very high temperatures

2. According to the table, ozone would be found in the _____.

   F) troposphere

   G) stratosphere

   H) mesosphere

   J) thermosphere

Test-Taking Tip Examine the table carefully. Find the word "ozone" in the table and follow the row back to the correct answer.

Type of Tornado	Damage
F0	Light: Broken branches and chimney
F1	Moderate: Roofs damage
F2	Considerable: Roofs torn off, trees uprooted
F3	Severe: Heavy roofs and walls torn off
F4	Devastating: Houses leveled
F5	Incredible: Houses picked up
F6	Total demolition

3. What type of tornado occurred near this home?

   A) light   **C)** considerable

   B) moderate   **D)** severe

Test-Taking Tip Study the graphic and circle all of the things damaged in the picture. Compare what you found to the information given in the table.

Student Resources

Student Resources

CONTENTS

Field GUIDE

C louds are like people—they come in many different sizes and shapes. Some tower thousands of meters in the sky. Others are like fragile wisps of cotton candy floating in the air. All clouds are formed by atmospheric conditions that in turn form Earth's weather. Using this field guide, you can learn to identify different types of clouds and try your hand at weather forecasting.

How Clouds Are Classified

Clouds are classified based on their shape and height. The height of a cloud is represented by the prefix used in its name. For example, a cirrocumulus (*cirro* + *cumulus*) cloud is a high cloud with a puffy shape.

Clouds

Key to Cloud Classification

The following symbols are used in this field guide to represent the height and shape of common clouds.

Key to Cloud Classification			
Height		**Shape**	
symbol	prefix	symbol	prefix
	Cirro Describes high clouds with bases starting above 6000 m.		**Cirrus** Latin meaning: hair Describes wispy, stringy clouds
	Alto Describes middle clouds with bases between 2000 m to 6000 m.		**Cumulus** Latin meaning: pile or heap. Describes puffy, lumpy-looking clouds
			Stratus Latin meaning: layer Describes featureless sheets of clouds
	Strato Refers to low clouds below 2000 m.		**Nimbus** Latin meaning: cloud Describes low, gray rain clouds

Field Activity

For a week, use this field guide to help you identify the clouds in your area. Observe the clouds two to three times each day. In your Science Journal, record the date, time, types of clouds observed, and the general weather conditions. What relationships can you infer between the weather and types of clouds that are present?

Cirrus

Feathery cirrus clouds are the highest clouds. They are formed of ice crystals. They usually signal fair weather, but they also can be a sign of changing weather.

Cirrostratus

These thin, sheetlike clouds often form ahead of advancing storms, particularly if they're followed by middle clouds.

Cirrocumulus

Cirrocumulus clouds are small, rounded, white puffs. They appear individually or in long rows. Their rippled pattern resembles the scales of fish. Hence, a sky full of cirrocumulus clouds is called a mackerel sky.

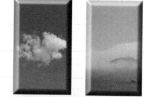

Altostratus

Gray or blue-gray altostratus clouds—they're never white—often cover the entire sky. They are a sign of widespread, steady rain ahead.

Altocumulus

These puffy, white or gray clouds look like rows of soft cotton balls. Randomly scattered altocumulus clouds can mean several days of fair weather. When the clouds resemble little castles, expect a thunderstorm by day's end.

Nimbostratus

Dark-gray nimbostratus clouds are associated with steady rain or snow. This precipitation is light to moderate—rarely heavy. Nimbostratus clouds often have streaks that extend to the ground.

Stratus

Low-lying stratus clouds cover the sky in a blanket of gray. Light rain or drizzle usually accompanies these clouds.

Stratocumulus

Low, lumpy stratocumulus clouds are often a sign of fair weather. To distinguish them from altocumulus clouds, extend your arm toward the cloud. An altocumulus cloud will be roughly the size of your thumbnail. A stratocumulus cloud will be about the size of your fist.

Cumulus

Small, scattered cumulus clouds with slight vertical growth signal fair weather. They have dome-shaped or tower-shaped tops, like cauliflower.

Cumulonimbus

These are thunderstorm clouds. They form near Earth's surface and grow to nearly 18,000 m. Lightning, thunder, and strong winds are associated with cumulonimbus clouds.

Lightning

When storm clouds form, the particles in clouds collide with one another, removing electrons from some and adding them to others. Positive charges accumulate at the top of the cloud, leaving the negative ones at the bottom. These negative charges repel electrons in the ground below. As a result, the ground beneath the cloud becomes positively charged. The negative charges in the cloud are attracted toward the positively charged ground. They move downward in a zigzag path called a stepped leader. As the leader approaches the ground, a streamer of positive charges rises to meet it. When they meet, a return stroke—an electric spark called lightning—blasts up to the cloud.

The cycle of leader and return strokes can repeat many times in less than a second to comprise a single flash of lightning that you see.

Common Types of Lightning

The most common type of lightning strikes from one part of a cloud to another part of the same cloud. This type of lightning can occur ten times more often than lightning from a cloud to the ground. Other forms include strikes from one cloud to a different cloud, and from a cloud to the surrounding air.

Cloud-to-Ground Lightning

This type of lightning is characterized by a single streak of light connecting the cloud and the ground or a streak with one or more forks in it. Occasionally, a tall object on Earth will initiate the leader strike, causing what is known as cloud-to-ground lightning.

Cloud-to-ground lightning

Field Activity

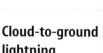

During a thunderstorm, observe lightning from a safe location in your home or school. Using this field guide, identify and record in your Science Journal the types of lightning you saw. Also, note the date and time of the thunderstorm in your Science Journal.

Cloud-to-Cloud Lightning

Cloud-to-cloud lightning is the most common type of lightning. It can occur between clouds (intercloud lightning) or within a cloud (intracloud lightning). The lightning is often hidden by the clouds, such that the clouds themselves seem to be glowing flashes of light.

Cloud-to-Air Lightning

When a lightning stroke ends in midair above a cloud or forks off the main stroke of cloud-to-ground lightning, it causes what is known as cloud-to-air lightning. This type of lightning is usually not as powerful or as bright as cloud-to-ground lightning.

Cloud-to-air lightning

Some forms of lightning differ in appearance from the forked flashes commonly considered to be lightning. However, the discharge in the cloud occurs for the same reason—to neutralize the accumulation of charge.

Sheet lightning

Sheet Lightning

Sheet lightning appears to fill a large section of the sky. Its appearance is caused by light reflecting off the water droplets in the clouds. The actual strokes of lightning are far away or hidden by the clouds. When the lightning is so far away that no thunder is heard, it is often called heat lightning and usually can be seen during summer nights.

Ribbon Lightning

Ribbon lightning is a thicker flash than ordinary cloud-to-ground lightning. In this case, wind blows the channel that is created by the return stroke sideways. Because each return stroke follows this channel, each is moved slightly to the side of the last stroke, making each return stroke of the flash visible, and thus a wider, ribbonlike band of light is produced.

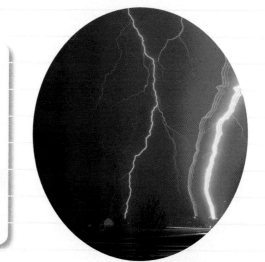

Ribbon lightning

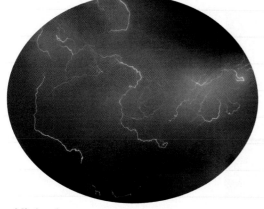

Bead lightning

Chain Lightning

Chain lightning, also called bead lightning, is distinguished by a dotted line of light as it fades. The cause is still uncertain, but it might be due to the observer's position relative to lightning or to parts of the flash being hidden by clouds or rain.

Some forms of lightning are rare or poorly understood and have different appearances than the previously described forms.

Sprites

Sprites are red or blue flashes of light that are sometimes cone shaped and occur high above a thundercloud, 60 to 100 km above Earth. The flashes are associated with thunderstorms that cover a vast area. Sprites are estimated to occur in about 1 percent of all lightning strokes.

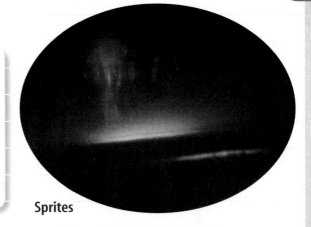

Sprites

Ball Lightning

There have been numerous eyewitness accounts of the existence of ball lightning, which appears as a sphere of red, yellow, orange or white light, usually between 1 cm to 1 m in size. Ball lightning seems to occur during thunderstorms, and appears within a few meters of the ground. The ball may move horizontally at a speed of a few meters per second, or may float in the air. Ball lightning usually lasts for several seconds and may vanish either quietly or explosively. Unlike other forms of lightning which can be seen by many observers at large distances, the small size of ball lightning and its random occurrence make it difficult to study. As a result, the causes of ball lightning still are not known, and even its existence is disputed.

St. Elmo's Fire

St. Elmo's Fire is a bluish-green glowing light that sometimes appears during thunderstorms around tall, pointed objects like the masts of ships and lightning rods. It also occurs around the wings and propellers of airplanes flying through thunderstorms. A sizzling or crackling noise often accompanies the glow. St. Elmo's Fire is caused by the strong electric field between the bottom of a thundercloud and the ground. This electric field is strongest around pointed objects. If this field is strong enough, it can pull electrons from atoms in the air. The glow is produced when these electrons collide with other atoms and molecules in the air.

Organizing Information

As you study science, you will make many observations and conduct investigations and experiments. You will also research information that is available from many sources. These activities will involve organizing and recording data. The quality of the data you collect and the way you organize it will determine how well others can understand and use it. In **Figure 1,** the student is obtaining and recording information using a thermometer.

Putting your observations in writing is an important way of communicating to others the information you have found and the results of your investigations and experiments.

Figure 1
Collecting data is one way to gather information directly.

Researching Information

Scientists work to build on and add to human knowledge of the world. Before moving in a new direction, it is important to gather the information that already is known about a subject. You will look for such information in various reference sources. Follow these steps to research information on a scientific subject:

Step 1 Determine exactly what you need to know about the subject. For instance, you might want to find out what happened when Mount St. Helens erupted in 1980.

Step 2 Make a list of questions, such as: When did the eruption begin? How long did it last? What kind of material was expelled and how much?

Step 3 Use multiple sources such as textbooks, encyclopedias, government documents, professional journals, science magazines, and the Internet.

Step 4 List where you found the sources. Make sure the sources you use are reliable and the most current available.

Evaluating Print and Nonprint Sources

Not all sources of information are reliable. Evaluate the sources you use for information, and use only those you know to be dependable. For example, suppose you live in an area where earthquakes are common and you want to know what to do to keep safe. You might find two Web sites on earthquake safety. One Web site contains "Earthquake Tips" written by a company that sells metal scrapings to help secure your hot-water tank to the wall. The other is a Web page on "Earthquake Safety" written by the U.S. Geological Survey. You would choose the second Web site as the more reliable source of information.

In science, information can change rapidly. Always consult the most current sources. A 1985 source about the Moon would not reflect the most recent research and findings.

Interpreting Scientific Illustrations

As you research a science topic, you will see drawings, diagrams, and photographs. Illustrations help you understand what you read. Some illustrations are included to help you understand an idea that you can't see easily by yourself. For instance, you can't see the layers of Earth, but you can look at a diagram of Earth's layers, as labeled in **Figure 2,** that helps you understand what the layers are and where they are located. Visualizing a drawing helps many people remember details more easily. Illustrations also provide examples that clarify difficult concepts or give additional information about the topic you are studying.

Most illustrations have a label or caption. A label or caption identifies the illustration or provides additional information to better explain it. Can you find the caption or labels in **Figure 2?**

Figure 2
This cross section shows a slice through Earth's interior and the positions of its layers.

Concept Mapping

If you were taking a car trip, you might take some sort of road map. By using a map, you begin to learn where you are in relation to other places on the map.

A concept map is similar to a road map, but a concept map shows relationships among ideas (or concepts) rather than places. It is a diagram that visually shows how concepts are related. Because a concept map shows relationships among ideas, it can make the meanings of ideas and terms clear and help you understand what you are studying.

Overall, concept maps are useful for breaking large concepts down into smaller parts, making learning easier.

Venn Diagram

Although it is not a concept map, a Venn diagram illustrates how two subjects compare and contrast. In other words, you can see the characteristics that the subjects have in common and those that they do not.

The Venn diagram in **Figure 3** shows the relationship between two types of rocks made from the same basic chemical. Both rocks share the chemical calcium carbonate. However, due to the way they are formed, one rock is the sedimentary rock limestone, and the other is the metamorphic rock marble.

Figure 3
A Venn diagram shows how objects or concepts are alike and how they are different.

Calcium
carbonate

Limestone
(sedimentary)

Marble
(metamorphic)

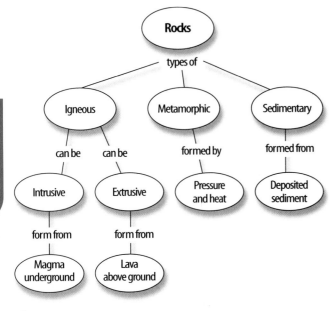

Figure 4
A network tree shows how concepts or objects are related.

Network Tree Look at the concept map in **Figure 4,** that shows the three main types of rock. This is called a network tree concept map. Notice how some words are in ovals while others are written across connecting lines. The words inside the ovals are science terms or concepts. The words written on the connecting lines describe the relationships between the concepts.

When constructing a network tree, write the topic on a note card or piece of paper. Write the major concepts related to that topic on separate note cards or pieces of paper. Then arrange them in order from general to specific. Branch the related concepts from the major concept and describe the relationships on the connecting lines. Continue branching to more specific concepts. Write the relation-ships between the concepts on the connecting lines until all concepts are mapped. Then examine the concept map for relationships that cross branches, and add them to the concept map.

Events Chain An events chain is another type of concept map. It models the order of items or their sequence. In science, an events chain can be used to describe a sequence of events, the steps in a procedure, or the stages of a process.

When making an events chain, first find the one event that starts the chain. This event is called the *initiating event.* Then, find the next event in the chain and continue until you reach an outcome. Suppose you are asked to describe why and how a sound might make an echo. You might draw an events chain such as the one in **Figure 5.** Notice that connecting words are not necessary in an events chain.

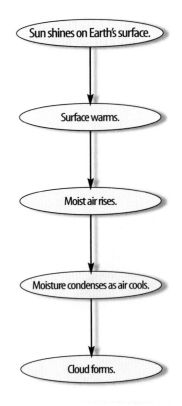

Figure 5
Events chains show the order of steps in a process or event.

Cycle Map A cycle concept map is a specific type of events chain map. In a cycle concept map, the series of events does not produce a final outcome. Instead, the last event in the chain relates back to the beginning event.

You first decide what event will be used as the beginning event. Once that is decided, you list events in order that occur after it. Words are written between events that describe what happens from one event to the next. The last event in a cycle concept map relates back to the beginning event. The number of events in a cycle concept varies, but is usually three or more. Look at the cycle map, as shown in **Figure 6.**

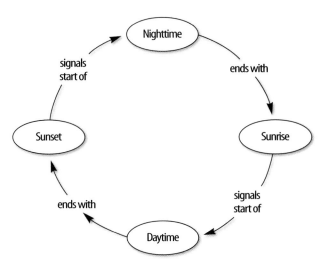

Figure 6
A cycle map shows events that occur in a cycle.

Spider Map A type of concept map that you can use for brainstorming is the spider map. When you have a central idea, you might find you have a jumble of ideas that relate to it but are not necessarily clearly related to each other. The spider map on sound in **Figure 7** shows that if you write these ideas outside the main concept, then you can begin to separate and group un-related terms so they become more useful.

Figure 7
A spider map allows you to list ideas that relate to a central topic but not necessarily to one another.

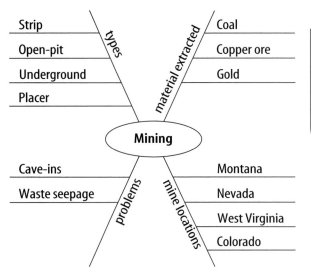

Writing a Paper

You will write papers often when researching science topics or reporting the results of investigations or experiments. Scientists frequently write papers to share their data and conclusions with other scientists and the public. When writing a paper, use these steps.

Step 1 Assemble your data by using graphs, tables, or a concept map. Create an outline.

Step 2 Start with an introduction that contains a clear statement of purpose and what you intend to discuss or prove.

Step 3 Organize the body into paragraphs. Each paragraph should start with a topic sentence, and the remaining sentences in that paragraph should support your point.

Step 4 Position data to help support your points.

Step 5 Summarize the main points and finish with a conclusion statement.

Step 6 Use tables, graphs, charts, and illustrations whenever possible.

You might say the work of a scientist is to solve problems. When you decide to find out why one corner of your yard is always soggy, you are problem solving, too. You might observe the corner is lower than the surrounding area and has less vegetation growing in it. You might decide to see whether planting some grass will keep the corner drier.

Scientists use orderly approaches to solve problems. The methods scientists use include identifying a question, making observations, forming a hypothesis, testing a hypothesis, analyzing results, and drawing conclusions.

Scientific investigations involve careful observation under controlled conditions. Such observation of an object or a process can suggest new and interesting questions about it. These questions sometimes lead to the formation of a hypothesis. Scientific investigations are designed to test a hypothesis.

Identifying a Question

The first step in a scientific investigation or experiment is to identify a question to be answered or a problem to be solved. You might be interested in knowing why a rock like the one in **Figure 8** looks the way it does.

Figure 8
When you find a rock, you might ask yourself, "How did this rock form?"

Forming Hypotheses

Hypotheses are based on observations that have been made. A hypothesis is a possible explanation based on previous knowledge and observations.

Perhaps a scientist has observed that thunderstorms happen more often on hot days than on cooler days. Based on these observations, the scientist can make a statement that he or she can test. The statement is a hypothesis. The hypothesis could be: *Warm temperatures cause thunderstorms*. A hypothesis has to be something you can test by using an investigation. A testable hypothesis is a valid hypothesis.

Predicting

When you apply a hypothesis, or general explanation, to a specific situation, you predict something about that situation. First, you must identify which hypothesis fits the situation you are considering. People use predictions to make everyday decisions. Based on previous observations and experiences, you might form a prediction that if warm temperatures cause thunderstorms, then more thunderstorms will occur in summer months than in spring months. Someone could use these predictions to plan when to take a camping trip or when to schedule an outdoor activity.

Testing a Hypothesis

To test a hypothesis, you need a procedure. A procedure is the plan you follow in your experiment. A procedure tells you what materials to use, as well as how and in what order to use them. When you follow a procedure, data are generated that support or do not support the original hypothesis statement.

For example, premium gasoline costs more than regular gasoline. Does premium gasoline increase the efficiency or fuel mileage of your family car? You decide to test the hypothesis: "If premium gasoline is more efficient, then it should increase the fuel mileage of my family's car." Then you write the procedure shown in **Figure 9** for your experiment and generate the data presented in the table below.

Figure 9
A procedure tells you what to do step by step.

> **Procedure**
> 1. Use regular gasoline for two weeks.
> 2. Record the number of kilometers between fill-ups and the amount of gasoline used.
> 3. Switch to premium gasoline for two weeks.
> 4. Record the number of kilometers between fill-ups and the amount of gasoline used.

Gasoline Data			
Type of Gasoline	Kilometers Traveled	Liters Used	Liters per Kilometer
Regular	762	45.34	0.059
Premium	661	42.30	0.064

These data show that premium gasoline is less efficient than regular gasoline in one particular car. It took more gasoline to travel 1 km (0.064) using premium gasoline than it did to travel 1 km using regular gasoline (0.059). This conclusion does not support the hypothesis.

Are all investigations alike? Keep in mind as you perform investigations in science that a hypothesis can be tested in many ways. Not every investigation makes use of all the ways that are described on these pages, and not all hypotheses are tested by investigations. Scientists encounter many variations in the methods that are used when they perform experiments. The skills in this handbook are here for you to use and practice.

Identifying and Manipulating Variables and Controls

In any experiment, it is important to keep everything the same except for the item you are testing. The one factor you change is called the independent variable. The factor that changes as a result of the independent variable is called the dependent variable. Always make sure you have only one independent variable. If you allow more than one, you will not know what causes the changes you observe in the dependent variable. Many experiments also have controls—individual instances or experimental subjects for which the independent variable is not changed. You can then compare the test results to the control results.

For example, in the fuel-mileage experiment, you made everything the same except the type of gasoline that was used. The driver, the type of automobile, and the type of driving were the same throughout. In this way, you could be sure that any mileage differences were caused by the type of fuel—the independent variable. The fuel mileage was the dependent variable.

If you could repeat the experiment using several automobiles of the same type on a standard driving track with the same driver, you could make one automobile a control by using regular gasoline over the four-week period.

Science Skill Handbook

Collecting Data

Whether you are carrying out an investigation or a short observational experiment, you will collect data, or information. Scientists collect data accurately as numbers and descriptions and organize it in specific ways.

Observing Scientists observe items and events, then record what they see. When they use only words to describe an observation, it is called qualitative data. For example, a scientist might describe the color, texture, or odor of a substance produced in a chemical reaction. Scientists' observations also can describe how much there is of something. These observations use numbers, as well as words, in the description and are called quantitative data. For example, if a sample of the element gold is described as being "shiny and very dense," the data are clearly qualitative. Quantitative data on this sample of gold might include "a mass of 30 g and a density of 19.3 g/cm^3." Quantitative data often are organized into tables. Then, from information in the table, a graph can be drawn. Graphs can reveal relationships that exist in experimental data.

When you make observations in science, you should examine the entire object or situation first, then look carefully for details. If you're looking at a rock sample, for instance, check the general color and pattern of the rock before using a hand lens to examine the small mineral grains that make up its underlying structure. Remember to record accurately everything you see.

Scientists try to make careful and accurate observations. When possible, they use instruments such as microscopes, metric rulers, graduated cylinders, thermometers, and balances. Measurements provide numerical data that can be repeated and checked.

Sampling When working with large numbers of objects or a large population, scientists usually cannot observe or study every one of them. Instead, they use a sample or a portion of the total number. To *sample* is to take a small, representative portion of the objects or organisms of a population for research. By making careful observations or manipulating variables within a portion of a group, information is discovered and conclusions are drawn that might apply to the whole population.

Estimating Scientific work also involves estimating. To *estimate* is to make a judgment about the amount or the number of something without measuring every part of an object or counting every member of a population. Scientists first measure or count the amount or number in a small sample. A chemist, for example, might remove a 10-g piece of a large rock that is rich in copper ore, such as the one shown in **Figure 10.** Then the chemist can determine the percentage of copper by mass and multiply that percentage by the mass of the rock to get an estimate of the total mass of copper in the rock.

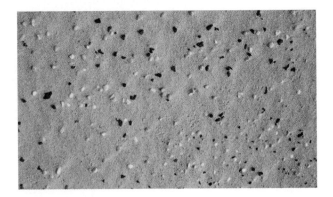

Figure 10
In a 1-meter frame positioned on a beach, count the pebbles that are longer than 2.5 cm. Multiply this number by the area of the beach. This will give you an estimate for the total number of pebbles on the beach.

Measuring in SI

The metric system of measurement was developed in 1795. A modern form of the metric system, called the International System, or SI, was adopted in 1960. SI provides standard measurements that all scientists around the world can understand.

The metric system is convenient because unit sizes vary by multiples of 10. When changing from smaller units to larger units, divide by a multiple of 10. When changing from larger units to smaller, multiply by a multiple of 10. To convert millimeters to centimeters, divide the millimeters by 10. To convert 30 mm to centimeters, divide 30 by 10 (30 mm equal 3 cm).

Prefixes are used to name units. Look at the table below for some common metric prefixes and their meanings. Do you see how the prefix *kilo-* attached to the unit *gram* is *kilogram*, or 1,000 g?

Metric Prefixes

Prefix	Symbol	Meaning	
kilo-	k	1,000	thousand
hecto-	h	100	hundred
deka-	da	10	ten
deci-	d	0.1	tenth
centi-	c	0.01	hundredth
milli-	m	0.001	thousandth

Now look at the metric ruler shown in **Figure 11.** The centimeter lines are the long, numbered lines, and the shorter lines are millimeter lines.

When using a metric ruler, line up the 0-cm mark with the end of the object being measured, and read the number of the unit where the object ends, in this instance it would be 4.5 cm.

Figure 11
This metric ruler shows centimeters and millimeter divisions.

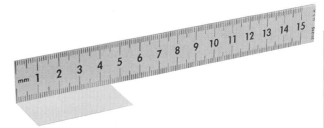

Liquid Volume In some science activities, you will measure liquids. The unit that is used to measure liquids is the liter. A liter has the volume of 1,000 cm³. The prefix *milli-* means "thousandth (0.001)." A milliliter is one thousandth of 1 L, and 1 L has the volume of 1,000 mL. One milliliter of liquid completely fills a cube measuring 1 cm on each side. Therefore, 1 mL equals 1 cm³.

You will use beakers and graduated cylinders to measure liquid volume. A graduated cylinder, as illustrated in **Figure 12,** is marked from bottom to top in milliliters. This one contains 79 mL of a liquid.

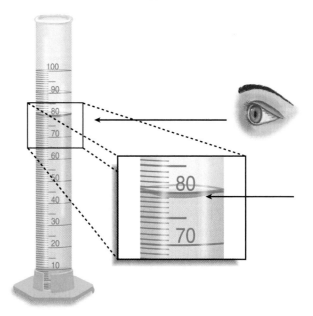

Figure 12
Graduated cylinders measure liquid volume.

Mass Scientists measure mass in grams. You might use a beam balance similar to the one shown in **Figure 13.** The balance has a pan on one side and a set of beams on the other side. Each beam has a rider that slides on the beam.

Before you find the mass of an object, slide all the riders back to the zero point. Check the pointer on the right to make sure it swings an equal distance above and below the zero point. If the swing is unequal, find and turn the adjusting screw until you have an equal swing.

Place an object on the pan. Slide the largest rider along its beam until the pointer drops below zero. Then move it back one notch. Repeat the process on each beam until the pointer swings an equal distance above and below the zero point. Sum the masses on each beam to find the mass of the object. Move all riders back to zero when finished.

Figure 13
A triple beam balance is used to determine the mass of an object.

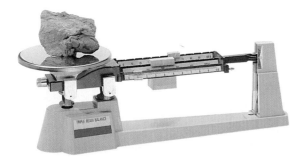

You should never place a hot object on the pan or pour chemicals directly onto the pan. Instead, find the mass of a clean container. Remove the container from the pan, then place the chemicals in the container. Find the mass of the container with the chemicals in it. To find the mass of the chemicals, subtract the mass of the empty container from the mass of the filled container.

Making and Using Tables

Browse through your textbook and you will see tables in the text and in the activities. In a table, data, or information, are arranged so that they are easier to understand. Activity tables help organize the data you collect during an activity so results can be interpreted.

Making Tables To make a table, list the items to be compared in the first column and the characteristics to be compared in the first row. The title should clearly indicate the content of the table, and the column or row heads should tell the reader what information is found in there. The table below lists materials collected for recycling on three weekly pick-up days. The inclusion of kilograms in parentheses also identifies for the reader that the figures are mass units.

Recyclable Materials Collected During Week			
Day of Week	Paper (kg)	Aluminum (kg)	Glass (kg)
Monday	5.0	4.0	12.0
Wednesday	4.0	1.0	10.0
Friday	2.5	2.0	10.0

Using Tables How much paper, in kilograms, is being recycled on Wednesday? Locate the column labeled "Paper (kg)" and the row "Wednesday." The information in the box where the column and row intersect is the answer. Did you answer "4.0"? How much aluminum, in kilograms, is being recycled on Friday? If you answered "2.0," you understand how to read the table. How much glass is collected for recycling each week? Locate the column labeled "Glass (kg)" and add the figures for all three rows. If you answered "32.0," then you know how to locate and use the data provided in the table.

Recording Data

To be useful, the data you collect must be recorded carefully. Accuracy is key. A well-thought-out experiment includes a way to record procedures, observations, and results accurately. Data tables are one way to organize and record results. Set up the tables you will need ahead of time so you can record the data right away.

Record information properly and neatly. Never put unidentified data on scraps of paper. Instead, data should be written in a notebook like the one in **Figure 14.** Write in pencil so information isn't lost if your data gets wet. At each point in the experiment, record your data and label it. That way, your information will be accurate and you will not have to determine what the figures mean when you look at your notes later.

Figure 14
Record data neatly and clearly so it is easy to understand.

Recording Observations

It is important to record observations accurately and completely. That is why you always should record observations in your notes immediately as you make them. It is easy to miss details or make mistakes when recording results from memory. Do not include your personal thoughts when you record your data. Record only what you observe to eliminate bias. For example, when you record the time required for five students to climb the same set of stairs, you would note which student took the longest time. However, you would not refer to that student's time as "the worst time of all the students in the group."

Making Models

You can organize the observations and other data you collect and record in many ways. Making models is one way to help you better understand the parts of a structure you have been observing or the way a process for which you have been taking various measurements works.

Models often show things that are too large or too small for normal viewing. For example, you normally won't see the inside of an atom. However, you can understand the structure of the atom better by making a three-dimensional model of an atom. The relative sizes, the positions, and the movements of protons, neutrons, and electrons can be explained in words. An atomic model made of a plastic-ball nucleus and pipe-cleaner electron shells can help you visualize how the parts of the atom relate to each other.

Other models can be devised on a computer. Some models, such as those that illustrate the chemical combinations of different elements, are mathematical and are represented by equations.

Making and Using Graphs

After scientists organize data in tables, they might display the data in a graph that shows the relationship of one variable to another. A graph makes interpretation and analysis of data easier. Three types of graphs are the line graph, the bar graph, and the circle graph.

Line Graphs A line graph like in **Figure 15** is used to show the relationship between two variables. The variables being compared go on two axes of the graph. For data from an experiment, the independent variable always goes on the horizontal axis, called the *x*-axis. The dependent variable always goes on the vertical axis, called the *y*-axis. After drawing your axes, label each with a scale. Next, plot the data points.

A data point is the intersection of the recorded value of the dependent variable for each tested value of the independent variable. After all the points are plotted, connect them.

Bar Graphs Bar graphs compare data that do not change continuously. Vertical bars show the relationships among data.

To make a bar graph, set up the *y*-axis as you did for the line graph. Draw vertical bars of equal size from the *x*-axis up to the point on the *y*-axis that represents value of *x*.

Figure 16
The amount of aluminum collected for recycling during one week can be shown as a bar graph or circle graph.

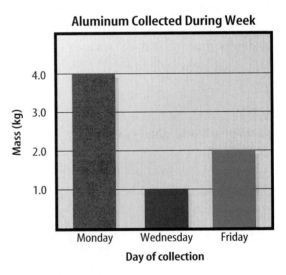

Circle Graphs A circle graph uses a circle divided into sections to display data as parts (fractions or percentages) of a whole. The size of each section corresponds to the fraction or percentage of the data that the section represents. So, the entire circle represents 100 percent, one-half represents 50 percent, one-fifth represents 20 percent, and so on.

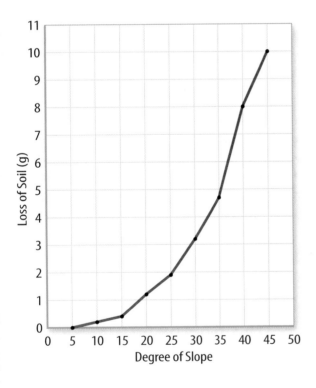

Figure 15
This line graph shows the relationship between degree of slope and the loss of soil in grams from a container during an experiment.

Analyzing Results

To determine the meaning of your observations and investigation results, you will need to look for patterns in the data. You can organize your information in several of the ways that are discussed in this handbook. Then you must think critically to determine what the data mean. Scientists use several approaches when they analyze the data they have collected and recorded. Each approach is useful for identifying specific patterns in the data.

Forming Operational Definitions

An operational definition defines an object by showing how it functions, works, or behaves. Such definitions are written in terms of how an object works or how it can be used; that is, they describe its job or purpose.

For example, a ruler can be defined as a tool that measures the length of an object (how it can be used). A ruler also can be defined as something that contains a series of marks that can be used as a standard when measuring (how it works).

Classifying

Classifying is the process of sorting objects or events into groups based on common features. When classifying, first observe the objects or events to be classified. Then select one feature that is shared by some members in the group but not by all. Place those members that share that feature into a subgroup. You can classify members into smaller and smaller subgroups based on characteristics.

How might you classify a group of rocks? You might first classify them by color, putting all of the black, white, and red rocks into separate groups. Within each group, you could then look for another common feature to classify further, such as size or whether the rocks have sharp or smooth edges.

Remember that when you classify, you are grouping objects or events for a purpose. For example, classifying rocks can be the first step in identifying them. You might know that obsidian is a black, shiny rock with sharp edges. To find it in a large group of rocks, you might start with the classification scheme mentioned. You'll locate obsidian within the group of black, sharp-edged rocks that you separate from the rest. Pumice could be located by its white color and by the fact that it contains many small holes called vesicles. Keep your purpose in mind as you select the features to form groups and subgroups.

Figure 17
Color is one of many characteristics that are used to classify rocks.

Comparing and Contrasting

Observations can be analyzed by noting the similarities and differences between two or more objects or events that you observe. When you look at objects or events to see how they are similar, you are comparing them. Contrasting is looking for differences in objects or events. The table below compares and contrasts the characteristics of two minerals.

Mineral Characteristics		
Mineral	Graphite	Gold
Color	black	bright yellow
Hardness	1–2	2.5–3
Luster	metallic	metallic
Uses	pencil "lead"	jewelry, electronics

Recognizing Cause and Effect

Have you ever heard a loud pop right before the power went out and then suggested that an electric transformer probably blew out? If so, you have observed an effect and inferred a cause. The event is the effect, and the reason for the event is the cause.

When scientists are unsure of the cause of a certain event, they design controlled experiments to determine what caused it.

Interpreting Data

The word *interpret* means "to explain the meaning of something." Look at the problem originally being explored in an experiment and figure out what the data show. Identify the control group and the test group so you can see whether or not changes in the independent variable have had an effect. Look for differences in the dependent variable between the control and test groups.

These differences you observe can be qualitative or quantitative. You would be able to describe a qualitative difference using only words, whereas you would measure a quantitative difference and describe it using numbers. If there are differences, the independent variable that is being tested could have had an effect. If no differences are found between the control and test groups, the variable that is being tested apparently had no effect.

For example, suppose that three beakers each contain 100 mL of water. The beakers are placed on hot plates, and two of the hot plates are turned on, but the third is left off for a period of 5 min. Suppose you are then asked to describe any differences in the water in the three beakers. A qualitative difference might be the appearance of bubbles rising to the top in the water that is being heated but no rising bubbles in the unheated water. A quantitative difference might be a difference in the amount of water that is present in the beakers.

Inferring Scientists often make inferences based on their observations. An inference is an attempt to explain, or interpret, observations or to indicate what caused what you observed. An inference is a type of conclusion.

When making an inference, be certain to use accurate data and accurately described observations. Analyze all of the data that you've collected. Then, based on everything you know, explain or interpret what you've observed.

Drawing Conclusions

When scientists have analyzed the data they collected, they proceed to draw conclusions about what the data mean. These conclusions are sometimes stated using words similar to those found in the hypothesis formed earlier in the process.

Conclusions To analyze your data, you must review all of the observations and measurements that you made and recorded. Recheck all data for accuracy. After your data are rechecked and organized, you are almost ready to draw a conclusion such as "salt water boils at a higher temperature than freshwater."

Before you can draw a conclusion, however, you must determine whether the data allow you to come to a conclusion that supports a hypothesis. Sometimes that will be the case, other times it will not.

If your data do not support a hypothesis, it does not mean that the hypothesis is wrong. It means only that the results of the investigation did not support the hypothesis. Maybe the experiment needs to be redesigned, but very likely, some of the initial observations on which the hypothesis was based were incomplete or biased. Perhaps more observation or research is needed to refine the hypothesis.

Avoiding Bias Sometimes drawing a conclusion involves making judgments. When you make a judgment, you form an opinion about what your data mean. It is important to be honest and to avoid reaching a conclusion if there were no supporting evidence for it or if it were based on a small sample. It also is important not to allow any expectations of results to bias your judgments. If possible, it is a good idea to collect additional data. Scientists do this all the time.

For example, the *Hubble Space Telescope* was sent into space in April, 1990, to provide scientists with clearer views of the universe. The *Hubble* is the size of a school bus and has a 2.4-m-diameter mirror. The *Hubble* helped scientists answer questions about the planet Pluto.

For many years, scientists had only been able to hypothesize about the surface of the planet Pluto. The *Hubble* has now provided pictures of Pluto's surface that show a rough texture with light and dark regions on it. This might be the best information about Pluto scientists will have until they are able to send a space probe to it.

Evaluating Others' Data and Conclusions

Sometimes scientists have to use data that they did not collect themselves, or they have to rely on observations and conclusions drawn by other researchers. In cases such as these, the data must be evaluated carefully.

How were the data obtained? How was the investigation done? Was it carried out properly? Has it been duplicated by other researchers? Were they able to follow the exact procedure? Did they come up with the same results? Look at the conclusion, as well. Would you reach the same conclusion from these results? Only when you have confidence in the data of others can you believe it is true and feel comfortable using it.

Communicating

The communication of ideas is an important part of the work of scientists. A discovery that is not reported will not advance the scientific community's understanding or knowledge. Communication among scientists also is important as a way of improving their investigations.

Scientists communicate in many ways, from writing articles in journals and magazines that explain their investigations and experiments, to announcing important discoveries on television and radio, to sharing ideas with colleagues on the Internet or presenting them as lectures.

Skill Handbooks

Computer Skills

People who study science rely on computers to record and store data and to analyze results from investigations. Whether you work in a laboratory or just need to write a lab report with tables, good computer skills are a necessity.

Using a Word Processor

Suppose your teacher has assigned a written report. After you've completed your research and decided how you want to write the information, you need to put all that information on paper. The easiest way to do this is with a word processing application on a computer.

A computer application that allows you to type your information, change it as many times as you need to, and then print it out so that it looks neat and clean is called a word processing application. You also can use this type of application to create tables and columns, add bullets or cartoon art to your page, include page numbers, and check your spelling.

Helpful Hints

■ If you aren't sure how to do something using your word processing program, look in the help menu. You will find a list of topics there to click on for help. After you locate the help topic you need, just follow the step-by-step instructions you see on your screen.

■ Just because you've spell checked your report doesn't mean that the spelling is perfect. The spell check feature can't catch misspelled words that look like other words. If you've accidentally typed *mind* instead of *mine*, the spell checker won't know the difference. Always reread your report to make sure you didn't miss any mistakes.

Figure 18
You can use computer programs to make graphs and tables.

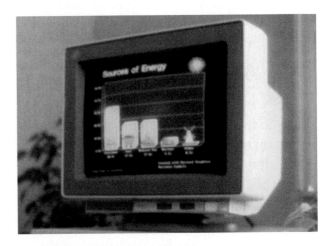

Using a Database

Imagine you're in the middle of a research project, busily gathering facts and information. You soon realize that it's becoming more difficult to organize and keep track of all the information. The tool to use to solve information overload is a database. Just as a file cabinet organizes paper records, a database organizes computer records. However, a database is more powerful than a simple file cabinet because at the click of a mouse, the contents can be reshuffled and reorganized. At computer-quick speeds, databases can sort information by any characteristics and filter data into multiple categories.

Helpful Hints

■ Before setting up a database, take some time to learn the features of your database software by practicing with established database software.

■ Periodically save your database as you enter data. That way, if something happens such as your computer malfunctions or the power goes off, you won't lose all of your work.

Doing a Database Search

When searching for information in a database, use the following search strategies to get the best results. These are the same search methods used for searching internet databases.

■ Place the word *and* between two words in your search if you want the database to look for any entries that have both the words. For example, "Earth *and* Mars" would give you information that mentions both Earth and Mars.

■ Place the word *or* between two words if you want the database to show entries that have at least one of the words. For example "Earth *or* Mars" would show you information that mentions either Earth or Mars.

■ Place the word *not* between two words if you want the database to look for entries that have the first word but do not have the second word. For example, "Moon *not* phases" would show you information that mentions the Moon but does not mention its phases.

In summary, databases can be used to store large amounts of information about a particular subject. Databases allow biologists, Earth scientists, and physical scientists to search for information quickly and accurately.

Using an Electronic Spreadsheet

Your science fair experiment has produced lots of numbers. How do you keep track of all the data, and how can you easily work out all the calculations needed? You can use a computer program called a spreadsheet to record data that involve numbers. A spreadsheet is an electronic mathematical worksheet.

Type your data in rows and columns, just as they would look in a data table on a sheet of paper. A spreadsheet uses simple math to do data calculations. For example, you could add, subtract, divide, or multiply any of the values in the spreadsheet by another number. You also could set up a series of math steps you want to apply to the data. If you want to add 12 to all the numbers and then multiply all the numbers by 10, the computer does all the calculations for you in the spreadsheet. Below is an example of a spreadsheet that records weather data.

Helpful Hints

■ Before you set up the spreadsheet, identify how you want to organize the data. Include any formulas you will need to use.

■ Make sure you have entered the correct data into the correct rows and columns.

■ You also can display your results in a graph. Pick the style of graph that best represents the data with which you are working.

Figure 19
A spreadsheet allows you to display large amounts of data and do calculations automatically.

	A	B	C	D	E
1	Readings	Temperature	Wind speed	Precipitation	
2	10:00 A.M.	21°C	24 km/h	–	
3	12:00 noon	23°C	26 km/h	–	
4	2:00 P.M.	25°C	24 km/h	light drizzle (.5cm)	

Using a Computerized Card Catalog

When you have a report or paper to research, you probably go to the library. To find the information you need in the library, you might have to use a computerized card catalog. This type of card catalog allows you to search for information by subject, by title, or by author. The computer then will display all the holdings the library has on the subject, title, or author requested.

A library's holdings can include books, magazines, databases, videos, and audio materials. When you have chosen something from this list, the computer will show whether an item is available and where in the library to find it.

Helpful Hints

- Remember that you can use the computer to search by subject, author, or title. If you know a book's author but not the title, you can search for all the books the library has by that author.
- When searching by subject, it's often most helpful to narrow your search by using specific search terms, such as *and, or,* and *not.* If you don't find enough sources, you can broaden your search.
- Pay attention to the type of materials found in your search. If you need a book, you can eliminate any videos or other resources that come up in your search.
- Knowing how your library is arranged can save you a lot of time. If you need help, the librarian will show you where certain types of materials are kept and how to find specific items.

Using Graphics Software

Are you having trouble finding that exact piece of art you're looking for? Do you have a picture in your mind of what you want but can't seem to find the right graphic to represent your ideas? To solve these problems, you can use graphics software. Graphics software allows you to create and change images and diagrams in almost unlimited ways. Typical uses for graphics software include arranging clip art, changing scanned images, and constructing pictures from scratch. Most graphics software applications work in similar ways. They use the same basic tools and functions. Once you master one graphics application, you can use other graphics applications.

Figure 20
Graphics software can use your data to draw bar graphs.

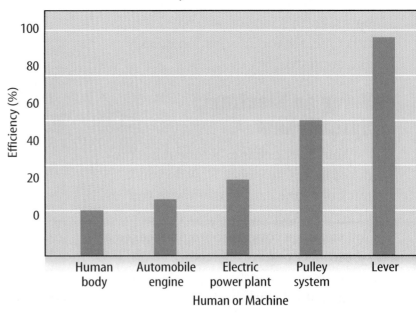

Efficiency of Humans and Machines

Figure 21

You can use this circle graph to find the names of the major gases that make up Earth's atmosphere.

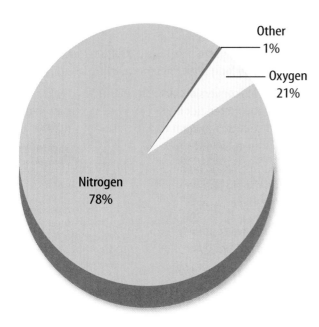

Other 1%

Oxygen 21%

Nitrogen 78%

Helpful Hints

- As with any method of drawing, the more you practice using the graphics software the better your results will be.
- Start by using the software to manipulate existing drawings. Once you master this, making your own illustrations will be easier.
- Clip art is available on CD-ROMs and the Internet. With these resources, finding a piece of clip art to suit your purposes is simple.
- As you work on a drawing, save it often.

Developing Multimedia Presentations

It's your turn—you have to present your science report to the entire class. How do you do it? You can use many different sources of information to get the class excited about your presentation. Posters, videos, photographs, sound, computers, and the Internet can help show your ideas.

First, determine what important points you want to make in your presentation. Then, write an outline of what materials and types of media would best illustrate those points. Maybe you could start with an outline on an overhead projector, then show a video, followed by something from the Internet or a slide show accompanied by music or recorded voices. You might choose to use a presentation builder computer application that can combine all these elements into one presentation. Make sure the presentation is well constructed to make the most impact on the audience.

Figure 21

Multimedia presentations use many types of print and electronic materials.

Helpful Hints

- Carefully consider what media will best communicate the point you are trying to make.
- Make sure you know how to use any equipment you will be using in your presentation.
- Practice the presentation several times.
- If possible, set up all of the equipment ahead of time. Make sure everything is working correctly.

Use this Math Skill Handbook to help solve problems you are given in this text. You might find it useful to review topics in this Math Skill Handbook first.

Converting Units

In science, quantities such as length, mass, and time sometimes are measured using different units. Suppose you want to know how many miles are in 12.7 km?

Conversion factors are used to change from one unit of measure to another. A conversion factor is a ratio that is equal to one. For example, there are 1,000 mL in 1 L, so 1,000 mL equals 1 L, or:

$$1,000 \text{ mL} = 1 \text{ L}$$

If both sides are divided by 1 L, this equation becomes:

$$\frac{1,000 \text{ mL}}{1 \text{ L}} = 1$$

The **ratio** on the left side of this equation is equal to one and is a conversion factor. You can make another conversion factor by dividing both sides of the top equation by 1,000 mL:

$$1 = \frac{1 \text{ L}}{1,000 \text{ mL}}$$

To **convert units,** you multiply by the appropriate conversion factor. For example, how many milliliters are in 1.255 L? To convert 1.255 L to milliliters, multiply 1.255 L by a conversion factor.

Use the **conversion factor** with new units (mL) in the numerator and the old units (L) in the denominator.

$$1.255 \text{ Ł} \times \frac{1,000 \text{ mL}}{1 \text{ Ł}} = 1,255 \text{ mL}$$

The unit L divides in this equation, just as if it were a number.

Example 1 There are 2.54 cm in 1 inch. If a meterstick has a length of 100 cm, how long is the meterstick in inches?

Step 1 Decide which conversion factor to use. You know the length of the meterstick in centimeters, so centimeters are the old units. You want to find the length in inches, so inch is the new unit.

Step 2 Form the conversion factor. Start with the relationship between the old and new units.

$$2.54 \text{ cm} = 1 \text{ inch}$$

Step 3 Form the conversion factor with the old unit (centimeter) on the bottom by dividing both sides by 2.54 cm.

$$1 = \frac{2.54 \text{ cm}}{2.54 \text{ cm}} = \frac{1 \text{ inch}}{2.54 \text{ cm}}$$

Step 4 Multiply the old measurement by the conversion factor.

$$100 \text{ cm} \times \frac{1 \text{ inch}}{2.54 \text{ cm}} = 39.37 \text{ inches}$$

The meter stick is 39.37 inches long.

Example 2 There are 365 days in one year. If a person is 14 years old, what is his or her age in days? (Ignore leap years)

Step 1 Decide which conversion factor to use. You want to convert years to days.

Step 2 Form the conversion factor. Start with the relation between the old and new units.

$$1 \text{ year} = 365 \text{ days}$$

Step 3 Form the conversion factor with the old unit (year) on the bottom by dividing both sides by 1 year.

$$1 = \frac{1 \text{ year}}{1 \text{ year}} = \frac{365 \text{ days}}{1 \text{ year}}$$

Step 4 Multiply the old measurement by the conversion factor:

$$14 \text{ years} \times \frac{365 \text{ days}}{1 \text{ year}} = 5,110 \text{ days}$$

The person's age is 5,110 days.

Practice Problem A book has a mass of 2.31 kg. If there are 1,000 g in 1 kg, what is the mass of the book in grams?

Skill Handbooks

A **fraction** is a number that compares a part to the whole. For example, in the fraction $\frac{2}{3}$, the 2 represents the part and the 3 represents the whole. In the fraction $\frac{2}{3}$, the top number, 2, is called the numerator. The bottom number, 3, is called the denominator.

Sometimes fractions are not written in their simplest form. To determine a fraction's **simplest form,** you must find the greatest common factor (GCF) of the numerator and denominator. The greatest common factor is the largest common factor of all the factors the two numbers have in common.

For example, because the number 3 divides into 12 and 30 evenly, it is a common factor of 12 and 30. However, because the number 6 is the largest number that evenly divides into 12 and 30, it is the **greatest common factor.**

After you find the greatest common factor, you can write a fraction in its simplest form. Divide both the numerator and the denominator by the greatest common factor. The number that results is the fraction in its **simplest form.**

Example Twelve of the 20 peaks in a mountain range have elevations over 10,000 m. What fraction of the peaks in the mountain range are over 10,000 m? Write the fraction in simplest form.

Step 1 Write the fraction.

$$\frac{part}{whole} = \frac{12}{20}$$

Step 2 To find the GCF of the numerator and denominator, list all of the factors of each number.

Factors of 12: 1, 2, 3, 4, 6, 12 (the numbers that divide evenly into 12)

Factors of 20: 1, 2, 4, 5, 10, 20 (the numbers that divide evenly into 20)

Step 3 List the common factors.

1, 2, 4.

Step 4 Choose the greatest factor in the list of common factors.

The GCF of 12 and 20 is 4.

Step 5 Divide the numerator and denominator by the GCF.

$$\frac{12 \div 4}{20 \div 4} = \frac{3}{5}$$

In the mountain range, $\frac{3}{5}$ of the peaks are over 10,000 m.

Practice Problem There are 90 rides at an amusement park. Of those rides, 66 have a height restriction. What fraction of the rides has a height restriction? Write the fraction in simplest form.

Math Skill Handbook

Calculating Ratios

A **ratio** is a comparison of two numbers by division.

Ratios can be written 3 to 5 or 3:5. Ratios also can be written as fractions, such as $\frac{3}{5}$. Ratios, like fractions, can be written in simplest form. Recall that a fraction is in **simplest form** when the greatest common factor (GCF) of the numerator and denominator is 1.

Example A particular geologic sample contains 40 kg of shale and 64 kg of granite. What is the ratio of shale to granite as a fraction in simplest form?

Step 1 Write the ratio as a fraction. $\frac{\text{shale}}{\text{granite}} = \frac{40}{64}$

Step 2 Express the fraction in simplest form. The GCF of 40 and 64 is 8.

$$\frac{40}{64} = \frac{40 \div 8}{64 \div 8} = \frac{5}{8}$$

The ratio of shale to granite in the sample is $\frac{5}{8}$.

Practice Problem Two metal rods measure 100 cm and 144 cm in length. What is the ratio of their lengths in simplest fraction form?

Using Decimals

A **decimal** is a fraction with a denominator of 10, 100, 1,000, or another power of 10. For example, 0.854 is the same as the fraction $\frac{854}{1,000}$.

In a decimal, the decimal point separates the ones place and the tenths place. For example, 0.27 means twenty-seven hundredths, or $\frac{27}{100}$, where 27 is the **number of units** out of 100 units. Any fraction can be written as a decimal using division.

Example Write $\frac{5}{8}$ as a decimal.

Step 1 Write a division problem with the numerator, 5, as the dividend and the denominator, 8, as the divisor. Write 5 as 5.000.

Step 2 Solve the problem.

```
      0.625
  8)5.000
      48
      20
      16
       40
       40
        0
```

Therefore, $\frac{5}{8} = 0.625$.

Practice Problem Write $\frac{19}{25}$ as a decimal.

Using Percentages

The word *percent* means "out of one hundred." A **percent** is a ratio that compares a number to 100. Suppose you read that 77 percent of Earth's surface is covered by water. That is the same as reading that the fraction of Earth's surface covered by water is $\frac{77}{100}$. To express a fraction as a percent, first find an equivalent decimal for the fraction. Then, multiply the decimal by 100 and add the percent symbol. For example, $\frac{1}{2} = 1 \div 2 = 0.5$. Then $0.5 = 0.50 = 50\%$.

Example Express $\frac{13}{20}$ as a percent.

Step 1 Find the equivalent decimal for the fraction.

$$\begin{array}{r} 0.65 \\ 20\overline{)13.00} \\ \underline{120} \\ 100 \\ \underline{100} \\ 0 \end{array}$$

Step 2 Rewrite the fraction $\frac{13}{20}$ as 0.65.

Step 3 Multiply 0.65 by 100 and add the % sign.

$0.65 \cdot 100 = 65 = 65\%$

So, $\frac{13}{20} = 65\%$.

Practice Problem In one year, 73 of 365 days were rainy in one city. What percent of the days in that city were rainy?

Using Precision and Significant Digits

When you make a **measurement,** the value you record depends on the precision of the measuring instrument. When adding or subtracting numbers with different precision, the answer is rounded to the smallest number of decimal places of any number in the sum or difference. When multiplying or dividing, the answer is rounded to the smallest number of significant figures of any number being multiplied or divided. When counting the number of **significant figures,** all digits are counted except zeros at the end of a number with no decimal such as 2,500, and zeros at the beginning of a decimal such as 0.03020.

Example The lengths 5.28 and 5.2 are measured in meters. Find the sum of these lengths and report the sum using the least precise measurement.

Step 1 Find the sum.

$$\begin{array}{ll} 5.28 \text{ m} & 2 \text{ digits after the decimal} \\ + \ 5.2 \ \text{ m} & 1 \text{ digit after the decimal} \\ \hline 10.48 \text{ m} & \end{array}$$

Step 2 Round to one digit after the decimal because the least number of digits after the decimal of the numbers being added is 1.

The sum is 10.5 m.

Practice Problem Multiply the numbers in the example using the rule for multiplying and dividing. Report the answer with the correct number of significant figures.

Solving One-Step Equations

An **equation** is a statement that two things are equal. For example, $A = B$ is an equation that states that A is equal to B.

Sometimes one side of the equation will contain a **variable** whose value is not known. In the equation $3x = 12$, the variable is x.

The equation is solved when the variable is replaced with a value that makes both sides of the equation equal to each other. For example, the solution of the equation $3x = 12$ is $x = 4$. If the x is replaced with 4, then the equation becomes $3 \cdot 4 = 12$, or $12 = 12$.

To solve an equation such as $8x = 40$, divide both sides of the equation by the number that multiplies the variable.

$$8x = 40$$
$$\frac{8x}{8} = \frac{40}{8}$$
$$x = 5$$

You can check your answer by replacing the variable with your solution and seeing if both sides of the equation are the same.

$$8x = 8 \cdot 5 = 40$$

The left and right sides of the equation are the same, so $x = 5$ is the solution.

Sometimes an equation is written in this way: $a = bc$. This also is called a **formula.** The letters can be replaced by numbers, but the numbers must still make both sides of the equation the same.

Example 1 Solve the equation $10x = 35$.

Step 1 Find the solution by dividing each side of the equation by 10.

$$10x = 35 \qquad \frac{10x}{10} = \frac{35}{10} \qquad x = 3.5$$

Step 2 Check the solution.

$$10x = 35 \qquad 10 \times 3.5 = 35 \qquad 35 = 35$$

Both sides of the equation are equal, so $x = 3.5$ is the solution to the equation.

Example 2 In the formula $a = bc$, find the value of c if $a = 20$ and $b = 2$.

Step 1 Rearrange the formula so the unknown value is by itself on one side of the equation by dividing both sides by b.

$$a = bc$$
$$\frac{a}{b} = \frac{bc}{b}$$
$$\frac{a}{b} = c$$

Step 2 Replace the variables a and b with the values that are given.

$$\frac{a}{b} = c$$
$$\frac{20}{2} = c$$
$$10 = c$$

Step 3 Check the solution.

$$a = bc$$
$$20 = 2 \times 10$$
$$20 = 20$$

Both sides of the equation are equal, so $c = 10$ is the solution when $a = 20$ and $b = 2$.

Practice Problem In the formula $h = gd$, find the value of d if $g = 12.3$ and $h = 17.4$.

Using Proportions

A **proportion** is an equation that shows that two ratios are equivalent. The ratios $\frac{2}{4}$ and $\frac{5}{10}$ are equivalent, so they can be written as $\frac{2}{4} = \frac{5}{10}$. This equation is an example of a proportion.

When two ratios form a proportion, the **cross products** are equal. To find the cross products in the proportion $\frac{2}{4} = \frac{5}{10}$, multiply the 2 and the 10, and the 4 and the 5. Therefore $2 \cdot 10 = 4 \cdot 5$, **or** $20 = 20$.

Because you know that both proportions are equal, you can use cross products to find a missing term in a proportion. This is known as **solving the proportion.** Solving a proportion is similar to solving an equation.

Example The heights of a tree and a pole are proportional to the lengths of their shadows. The tree casts a shadow of 24 m at the same time that a 6-m pole casts a shadow of 4 m. What is the height of the tree?

Step 1 Write a proportion.

$$\frac{\text{height of tree}}{\text{height of pole}} = \frac{\text{length of tree's shadow}}{\text{length of pole's shadow}}$$

Step 2 Substitute the known values into the proportion. Let h represent the unknown value, the height of the tree.

$$\frac{h}{6} = \frac{24}{4}$$

Step 3 Find the cross products.

$$h \cdot 4 = 6 \cdot 24$$

Step 4 Simplify the equation.

$$4h = 144$$

Step 5 Divide each side by 4.

$$\frac{4h}{4} = \frac{144}{4}$$

$$h = 36$$

The height of the tree is 36 m.

Practice Problem The ratios of the weights of two objects on the Moon and on Earth are in proportion. A rock weighing 3 N on the Moon weighs 18 N on Earth. How much would a rock that weighs 5 N on the Moon weigh on Earth?

Using Statistics

Statistics is the branch of mathematics that deals with collecting, analyzing, and presenting data. In statistics, there are three common ways to summarize the data with a single number—the mean, the median, and the mode.

The **mean** of a set of data is the arithmetic average. It is found by adding the numbers in the data set and dividing by the number of items in the set.

The **median** is the middle number in a set of data when the data are arranged in numerical order. If there were an even number of data points, the median would be the mean of the two middle numbers.

The **mode** of a set of data is the number or item that appears most often.

Another number that often is used to describe a set of data is the range. The **range** is the difference between the largest number and the smallest number in a set of data.

A **frequency table** shows how many times each piece of data occurs, usually in a survey. The frequency table below shows the results of a student survey on favorite color.

Color	Tally	Frequency
red	IIII	4
blue	IIII	5
black	II	2
green	III	3
purple	IIII II	7
yellow	IIII I	6

Based on the frequency table data, which color is the favorite?

Example The high temperatures (in °C) on five consecutive days at a desert observation station are 39°, 37°, 44°, 36°, and 44°. Find the mean, median, mode, and range of this set.

To find the mean:
Step 1 Find the sum of the numbers.

$$39 + 37 + 44 + 36 + 44 = 200$$

Step 2 Divide the sum by the number of items, which is 5.

$$200 \div 5 = 40$$

The mean high temperature is 40°C.

To find the median:
Step 1 Arrange the temperatures from least to greatest.

$$36, \ 37, \ \underline{39}, \ 44, \ 44$$

Step 2 Determine the middle temperature.

The median high temperature is 39°C.

To find the mode:
Step 1 Group the numbers that are the same together.

$$44, 44, 36, 37, 39$$

Step 2 Determine the number that occurs most in the set.

$$\underline{44, 44}, 36, 37, 39$$

The mode measure is 44°C.

To find the range:
Step 1 Arrange the temperatures from largest to smallest.

$$44, 44, 39, 37, 36$$

Step 2 Determine the largest and smallest temperature in the set.

$$\underline{44}, 44, 39, 37, \underline{36}$$

Step 3 Find the difference between the largest and smallest temperatures.

$$44 - 36 = 8$$

The range is 8°C.

Practice Problem Find the mean, median, mode, and range for the data set 8, 4, 12, 8, 11, 14, 16.

Safety in the Science Classroom

1. Always obtain your teacher's permission to begin an investigation.

2. Study the procedure. If you have questions, ask your teacher. Be sure you understand any safety symbols shown on the page.

3. Use the safety equipment provided for you. Goggles and a safety apron should be worn during most investigations.

4. Always slant test tubes away from yourself and others when heating them or adding substances to them.

5. Never eat or drink in the lab, and never use lab glassware as food or drink containers. Never inhale chemicals. Do not taste any substances or draw any material into a tube with your mouth.

6. Report any spill, accident, or injury, no matter how small, immediately to your teacher, then follow his or her instructions.

7. Know the location and proper use of the fire extinguisher, safety shower, fire blanket, first aid kit, and fire alarm.

8. Keep all materials away from open flames. Tie back long hair and tie down loose clothing.

9. If your clothing should catch fire, smother it with the fire blanket, or get under a safety shower. NEVER RUN.

10. If a fire should occur, turn off the gas then leave the room according to established procedures.

Follow these procedures as you clean up your work area

1. Turn off the water and gas. Disconnect electrical devices.

2. Clean all pieces of equipment and return all materials to their proper places.

3. Dispose of chemicals and other materials as directed by your teacher. Place broken glass and solid substances in the proper containers. Make sure never to discard materials in the sink.

4. Clean your work area. Wash your hands thoroughly after working in the laboratory.

First Aid	
Injury	**Safe Response ALWAYS NOTIFY YOUR TEACHER IMMEDIATELY**
Burns	Apply cold water.
Cuts and Bruises	Stop any bleeding by applying direct pressure. Cover cuts with a clean dressing. Apply ice packs or cold compresses to bruises.
Fainting	Leave the person lying down. Loosen any tight clothing and keep crowds away.
Foreign Matter in Eye	Flush with plenty of water. Use eyewash bottle or fountain.
Poisoning	Note the suspected poisoning agent.
Any Spills on Skin	Flush with large amounts of water or use safety shower.

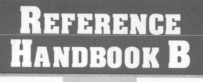

Reference Handbook

SI—Metric/English, English/Metric Conversions

	When you want to convert:	To:	Multiply by:
Length	inches	centimeters	2.54
	centimeters	inches	0.39
	yards	meters	0.91
	meters	yards	1.09
	miles	kilometers	1.61
	kilometers	miles	0.62
Mass and Weight*	ounces	grams	28.35
	grams	ounces	0.04
	pounds	kilograms	0.45
	kilograms	pounds	2.2
	tons (short)	tonnes (metric tons)	0.91
	tonnes (metric tons)	tons (short)	1.10
	pounds	newtons	4.45
	newtons	pounds	0.22
Volume	cubic inches	cubic centimeters	16.39
	cubic centimeters	cubic inches	0.06
	liters	quarts	1.06
	quarts	liters	0.95
	gallons	liters	3.78
Area	square inches	square centimeters	6.45
	square centimeters	square inches	0.16
	square yards	square meters	0.83
	square meters	square yards	1.19
	square miles	square kilometers	2.59
	square kilometers	square miles	0.39
	hectares	acres	2.47
	acres	hectares	0.40
Temperature	To convert °Celsius to °Fahrenheit		$°C \times 9/5 + 32$
	To convert °Fahrenheit to °Celsius		$5/9 \, (°F - 32)$

*Weight is measured in standard Earth gravity.

Weather Map Symbols

Sample Station Model

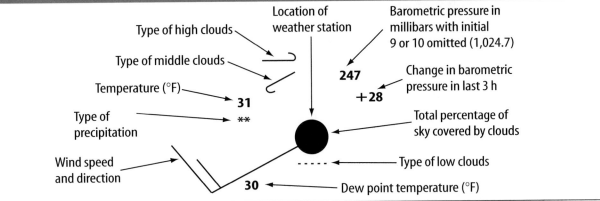

Type of high clouds

Type of middle clouds

Temperature (°F) — **31**

Type of precipitation — ******

Wind speed and direction

Location of weather station

Barometric pressure in millibars with initial 9 or 10 omitted (1,024.7) — **247**

Change in barometric pressure in last 3 h — **+28**

Total percentage of sky covered by clouds

Type of low clouds — **- - - - -**

Dew point temperature (°F) — **30**

Sample Plotted Report at Each Station

Precipitation		Wind Speed and Direction		Sky Coverage		Some Types of High Clouds	
≡	Fog	○	0 calm	○	No cover	⌐⌐	Scattered cirrus
★	Snow	/	1–2 knots	◐	1/10 or less	⌐⌐	Dense cirrus in patches
●	Rain	⌐/	3–7 knots	◕	2/10 to 3/10	∼⌐	Veil of cirrus covering entire sky
⊺	Thunderstorm	⌐/	8–12 knots	◑	4/10	⌐	Cirrus not covering entire sky
,	Drizzle	⋁/	13–17 knots	◑	–		
▽	Showers	⋁/	18–22 knots	◕	6/10		
		⋁⋁/	23–27 knots	◕	7/10		
		⋁/	48–52 knots	◐	Overcast with openings		
		1 knot = 1.852 km/h		●	Completely overcast		

Some Types of Middle Clouds		Some Types of Low Clouds		Fronts and Pressure Systems	
∠	Thin altostratus layer	◠	Cumulus of fair weather	(H) or High (L) or Low	Center of high- or low-pressure system
⫽	Thick altostratus layer	◡	Stratocumulus	▲▲▲▲	Cold front
∽	Thin altostratus in patches	- - - - -	Fractocumulus of bad weather	●●●●	Warm front
∽	Thin altostratus in bands	—	Stratus of fair weather	▲●▲▲	Occluded front
				●▲●▲	Stationary front

REFERENCE HANDBOOK D

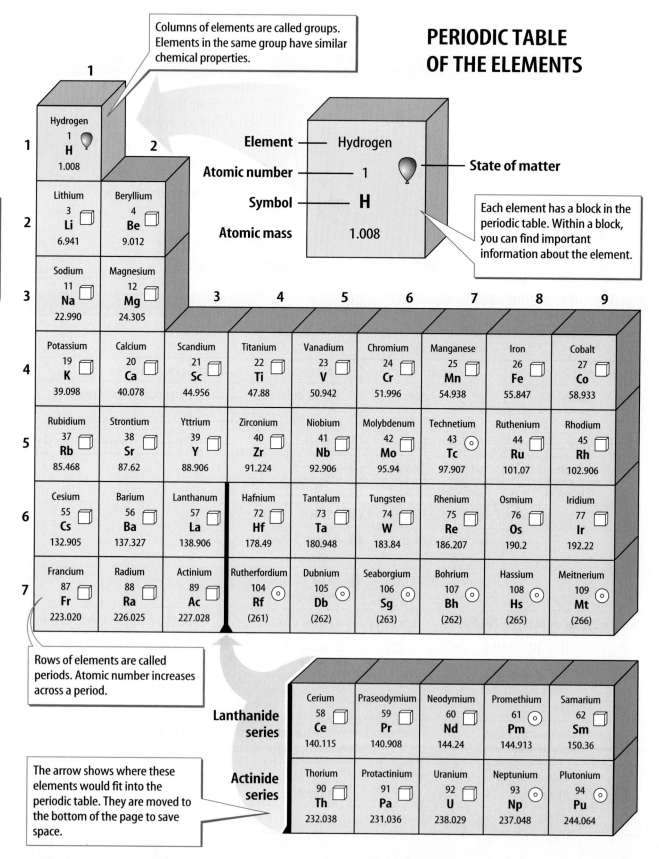

PERIODIC TABLE OF THE ELEMENTS

Reference Handbook

Gas

Liquid

Solid

⊙ Synthetic elements

The first three symbols tell you the state of matter of the element at room temperature. The fourth symbol identifies human-made, or synthetic, elements.

Metal

Metalloid

Nonmetal

Recently discovered

The color of an element's block tells you if the element is a metal, nonmetal, metalloid, or has been discovered so recently that more study is needed.

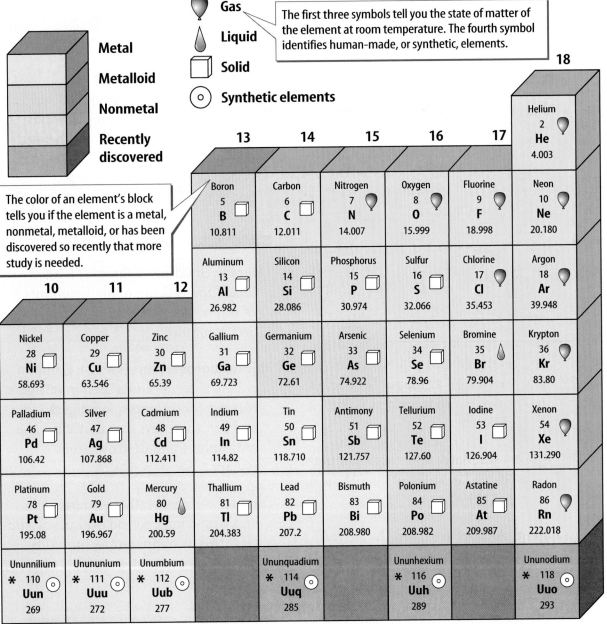

18

Helium
2
He
4.003

13

Boron
5
B
10.811

Carbon
6
C
12.011

Nitrogen
7
N
14.007

Oxygen
8
O
15.999

Fluorine
9
F
18.998

Neon
10
Ne
20.180

14

Aluminum
13
Al
26.982

Silicon
14
Si
28.086

Phosphorus
15
P
30.974

Sulfur
16
S
32.066

Chlorine
17
Cl
35.453

Argon
18
Ar
39.948

15

10 **11** **12**

Nickel
28
Ni
58.693

Copper
29
Cu
63.546

Zinc
30
Zn
65.39

Gallium
31
Ga
69.723

Germanium
32
Ge
72.61

Arsenic
33
As
74.922

Selenium
34
Se
78.96

Bromine
35
Br
79.904

Krypton
36
Kr
83.80

Palladium
46
Pd
106.42

Silver
47
Ag
107.868

Cadmium
48
Cd
112.411

Indium
49
In
114.82

Tin
50
Sn
118.710

Antimony
51
Sb
121.757

Tellurium
52
Te
127.60

Iodine
53
I
126.904

Xenon
54
Xe
131.290

Platinum
78
Pt
195.08

Gold
79
Au
196.967

Mercury
80
Hg
200.59

Thallium
81
Tl
204.383

Lead
82
Pb
207.2

Bismuth
83
Bi
208.980

Polonium
84
Po
208.982

Astatine
85
At
209.987

Radon
86
Rn
222.018

Ununnilium
✱ 110 ⊙
Uun
269

Unununium
✱ 111 ⊙
Uuu
272

Ununbium
✱ 112 ⊙
Uub
277

Ununquadium
✱ 114 ⊙
Uuq
285

Ununhexium
✱ 116 ⊙
Uuh
289

Ununodium
✱ 118 ⊙
Uuo
293

✱ Names not officially assigned.

Europium
63
Eu
151.965

Gadolinium
64
Gd
157.25

Terbium
65
Tb
158.925

Dysprosium
66
Dy
162.50

Holmium
67
Ho
164.930

Erbium
68
Er
167.26

Thulium
69
Tm
168.934

Ytterbium
70
Yb
173.04

Lutetium
71
Lu
174.967

Americium
95 ⊙
Am
243.061

Curium
96 ⊙
Cm
247.070

Berkelium
97 ⊙
Bk
247.070

Californium
98 ⊙
Cf
251.080

Einsteinium
99 ⊙
Es
252.083

Fermium
100 ⊙
Fm
257.095

Mendelevium
101 ⊙
Md
258.099

Nobelium
102 ⊙
No
259.101

Lawrencium
103 ⊙
Lr
260.105

16 **17**

Reference Handbook

English Glossary

This glossary defines each key term that appears in bold type in the text. It also shows the chapter, section, and page number where you can find the word used.

A

acid rain: rain, snow, fog, and other forms of precipitation with a pH below 5.6 that can harm plant and animal life and is formed when sulfur dioxide and nitrogen oxides combine with moisture in the atmosphere. (Chap. 4, Sec. 1, p. 99)

adaptation: any structural or behavioral change that helps an organism survive in its particular environment. (Chap. 3, Sec. 2, p. 70)

air mass: large body of air that has the same characteristics of temperature and moisture content as the part of Earth's surface over which it formed. (Chap. 2, Sec. 2, p. 44)

air quality standard: level that a pollutant cannot exceed in ambient air. (Chap. 4, Sec. 3, p. 112)

ambient (AM bee yent) **air:** the air you breathe. (Chap. 4, Sec. 3, p. 112)

atmosphere: Earth's air, which is made up of a thin layer of gases, solids, and liquids; forms a protective layer around the planet and is divided into five distinct layers. (Chap. 1, Sec. 1, p. 8)

B

biomagnification (BI oh mag nih fih cay shun): process in which pollutant levels increase through the food chain. (Chap. 4, Sec. 2, p. 107)

blizzard: winter storm that lasts at least three hours with temperatures of −12°C or below, poor visibility, and winds of at least 51 km/h; body temperature drops, and body processes slow down. (Chap. 2, Sec. 2, p. 51) (Chap. 3, Sec. 2, p. 72)

C

cataract: clouding of the eye's lens, linked to exposure to high amounts of ultraviolet radiation. (Chap. 4, Sec. 2, p. 106)

chlorofluorocarbons (CFCs): group of chemical compounds used in refrigerators, air conditioners, foam packaging, and aerosol sprays that may enter the atmosphere and destroy ozone. (Chap. 1, Sec. 1, p. 14)

climate: average weather pattern in an area over a long period of time; can be classified by temperature, humidity, precipitation, and vegetation. (Chap. 3, Sec. 1, p. 66)

condensation: process in which water vapor changes to a liquid. (Chap. 1, Sec. 2, p. 19)

conduction: transfer of energy that occurs when molecules bump into each other. (Chap. 1, Sec. 2, p. 18)

convection: transfer of heat by the flow of material. (Chap. 1, Sec. 2, p. 18)

English Glossary

Coriolis (kor ee OH lus) **effect:** causes moving air and water to turn left in the southern hemisphere and turn right in the northern hemisphere due to Earth's rotation. (Chap. 1, Sec. 3, p. 22)

D

deforestation: destruction and cutting down of forests—often to clear land for mining, roads, and grazing of cattle—resulting in increased atmospheric CO_2 levels. (Chap. 3, Sec. 3, p. 83)

dew point: temperature at which air is saturated and condensation forms. (Chap. 2, Sec. 1, p. 39)

E

El Niño (el NEEN yoh): climatic event that begins in the tropical Pacific Ocean; may occur when trade winds weaken or reverse, and can disrupt normal temperature and precipitation patterns around the world. (Chap. 3, Sec. 3, p. 75)

emission (ih MIH shen): pollutant released into the air from a given source, such as an automobile tailpipe. (Chap. 4, Sec. 3, p. 112)

F

fog: a stratus cloud that forms when air is cooled to its dew point near the ground. (Chap. 2, Sec. 1, p. 41)

front: boundary between two air masses with different temperatures, density, or moisture; can be cold, warm, occluded, and stationary. (Chap. 2, Sec. 2, p. 45)

G

global warming: increase in the average global temperature of Earth. (Chap. 3, Sec. 3, p. 82)

greenhouse effect: natural heating that occurs when certain gases in Earth's atmosphere, such as methane, CO_2, and water vapor, trap heat. (Chap. 3, Sec. 3, p. 81)

H

hibernation: behavioral adaptation for winter survival in which an animal's activity is greatly reduced and its body temperature drops. (Chap. 3, Sec. 2, p. 72)

humidity: amount of water vapor held in the air. (Chap. 2, Sec. 1, p. 38)

hurricane: large, severe storm that forms over tropical oceans, has winds of at least 120 km/h, and loses power when it reaches land. (Chap. 2, Sec. 2, p. 50)

hydrosphere: all the water on Earth's surface. (Chap. 1, Sec. 2, p. 19)

I

ionosphere: layer of electrically charged particles in the thermosphere that absorbs AM radio waves during the day and reflects them back at night. (Chap. 1, Sec. 1, p. 11)

isobars: lines drawn on a weather map that connect points having equal atmospheric pressure; also indicate the location of high- and low-pressure areas and can show wind speed. (Chap. 2, Sec. 3, p. 53)

English Glossary

English Glossary

isotherm (I suh thurm): line drawn on a weather map that connects points having equal temperature. (Chap. 2, Sec. 3, p. 53)

J

jet stream: narrow belt of strong winds that blows near the top of the troposphere. (Chap. 1, Sec. 3, p. 24)

L

land breeze: movement of air from land to sea at night, created when cooler, denser air from the land forces up warmer air over the sea. (Chap. 1, Sec. 3, p. 25)

M

meteorologist (meet ee uh RAHL uh just): studies weather and uses information from Doppler radar, weather satellites, computers and other instruments to make weather maps and provide forecasts. (Chap. 2, Sec. 3, p. 52)

O

ozone layer: layer of the stratosphere with a high concentration of ozone; absorbs most of the Sun's harmful ultraviolet radiation. (Chap. 1, Sec. 1, p. 14) (Chap. 4, Sec. 1, p. 102)

P

particulate matter: solid particles and liquid droplets suspended in the air. (Chap. 4, Sec. 1, p. 100)

photochemical smog: brown haze formed when secondary pollutants interact with sunlight. (Chap. 4, Sec. 1, p. 97)

polar zones: climate zones that receive solar radiation at a low angle, extend from 66°N and S latitude to the poles, and are never warm. (Chap. 3, Sec. 1, p. 66)

precipitation: water falling from clouds—including rain, snow, sleet, and hail—whose form is determined by air temperature. (Chap. 2, Sec. 1, p. 42)

primary pollutant: substance released directly into the air in a harmful form, including volcanic gases, soot from trucks, and smoke from forest fires. (Chap. 4, Sec. 1, p. 96)

R

radiation: energy transferred by waves or rays. (Chap. 1, Sec. 2, p. 18)

relative humidity: measure of the amount of moisture held in the air compared with the amount it can hold at a given temperature; can range from 0 percent to 100 percent. (Chap. 2, Sec. 1, p. 38)

S

sea breeze: movement of air from sea to land during the day when cooler air from above the water moves over the land, forcing the heated, less dense air above the land to rise. (Chap. 1, Sec. 3, p. 25)

season: short period of climate change in an area caused by the tilt of Earth's axis as Earth revolves around the Sun. (Chap. 3, Sec. 3, p. 74)

secondary pollutant: substance that pollutes the air after reacting with other substances in Earth's atmosphere. (Chap. 4, Sec. 1, p. 96)

station model: indicates weather conditions at a specific location, using a combination of symbols on a map. (Chap. 2, Sec. 3, p. 53)

T

temperate zones: climate zones with moderate temperatures that are located between the tropics and the polar zones. (Chap. 3, Sec. 1, p. 66) the location of high- and low-pressure areas and can show wind speed. (Chap. 2, Sec. 3, p. 53)

tornado: violent, whirling windstorm that crosses land in a narrow path and can result from wind shears inside a thunderhead. (Chap. 2, Sec. 2, p. 48)

toxic air pollutant: substance released into the air that can cause health problems, including cancer. (Chap. 4, Sec. 1, p. 101)

tropics: climate zone that receives the most solar radiation, is located between latitudes 23°N and 23°S, and is always hot, except at high elevations. (Chap. 3, Sec. 1, p. 66)

troposphere: layer of Earth's atmosphere that is closest to the ground; contains 99 percent of the water vapor and 75 percent of the atmospheric gases, and is where clouds and weather occur. (Chap. 1, Sec. 1, p. 10)

U

ultraviolet radiation: a type of energy that comes to Earth from the Sun, can damage skin and cause cancer, and is mostly absorbed by the ozone layer. (Chap. 1, Sec. 1, p. 14) (Chap. 4, Sec. 2, p. 106)

W

weather: state of the atmosphere at a specific time and place, determined by factors including air pressure, amount of moisture in the air, temperature, and wind. (Chap. 2, Sec. 1, p. 36)

Spanish Glossary

Este glossario define cada término clave que aparece en negrillas en el texto. También muestra el capítulo, la sección y el número de página en donde se usa dicho término.

acid rain / lluvia ácida: lluvia, nieve, neblina y otras formas de precipitación con un pH menor de 5.5 que pueden causar daños a la vida vegetal y animal y la cual se forma de la combinación del dióxido de azufre y óxidos de nitrógeno con la humedad en la atmósfera. (Cap. 4, Sec. 1, pág. 99)

adaptation / adaptación: todo cambio estructural o de comportamiento que le ayuda a un organismo a sobrevivir en un ambiente en particular. (Cap. 3, Sec. 2, pág. 70)

air mass / masa de aire: flujo enorme de aire que tiene las mismas características de temperatura y contenido de humedad que la superficie terrestre sobre la cual se formó. (Cap. 2, Sec. 2, pág. 44)

air quality standard / estándar de calidad el aire: nivel que no puede exceder un contaminante en el aire ambiental. (Cap. 4, Sec. 3, pág. 112)

ambient air / aire ambiental: el aire que respiras. (Cap. 4, Sec. 3, pág. 112)

atmosphere / atmósfera: el aire de la Tierra, el cual está compuesto por una capa tenue de gases, sólidos y líquidos; forma una capa protectora alrededor del planeta y está dividida en cinco capas distintivas. (Cap. 1, Sec. 1, pág. 8)

biomagnification / bioaumento: proceso en que los niveles de contaminantes aumentan a través de la cadena alimenticia. (Cap. 4, Sec. 2, pág. 107)

blizzard / ventisca: tormenta invernal que dura por lo menos tres horas, con temperaturas de −12°C o más bajas, poca visibilidad y vientos de por lo menos 51 km/h. (Cap. 2, Sec. 2, pág. 51; Cap. 3, Sec. 2, pág. 72)

C

cataract / catarata: oscurecimiento del cristalino del ojo; vinculado a la exposición de altas cantidades de radiación ultravioleta. (Cap. 4, Sec. 2, pág. 106)

chlorofluorocarbons / clorofluorocarburos: grupo de compuestos químicos que se utilizan en los artefactos de refrigeración, los acondicionadores de aire, los empaques de espuma y los rociadores de aerosol; estos compuestos químicos pueden penetrar en la atmósfera y destruir el ozono. (Cap. 1, Sec. 1, pág. 14)

climate / clima: patrón de tiempo promedio en una área a lo largo de un período largo de tiempo; puede clasificarse según la temperatura, la humedad, la precipitación y la vegetación. (Cap. 3, Sec. 1, pág. 66)

condensation / condensación: proceso en el cual el vapor de agua se transforma en un líquido. (Cap. 1, Sec. 2, pág. 19)

conduction / conducción: transferencia de energía que ocurre cuando las moléculas chocan entre sí. (Cap. 1, Sec. 2, pág. 18)

convection / convección: transferencia de calor a través del flujo de un material. (Cap. 1, Sec. 2, pág. 18)

Spanish Glossary

Coriolis effect / efecto de Coriolis: es la causa de que el aire y el agua en movimiento giren a la izquierda en el hemisferio sur y a la derecha en el hemisferio norte, debido a la rotación de la Tierra. (Cap. 1, Sec. 3, pág. 22)

deforestation / deforestación: destrucción y tala de bosques en que a menudo se despeja la tierra para la minería, la construcción de caminos y el pastoreo del ganado y la cual resulta en aumentos en los niveles atmosféricos de CO_2. (Cap. 3, Sec. 3, pág. 83)

dew point / punto de condensación: temperatura a la cual el aire se satura y se forma la condensación. (Cap. 2, Sec. 1, pág. 39)

El Niño / El Niño: fenómeno climático que comienza en el océano Pacífico tropical; puede ocurrir debido al debilitamiento o inversión de los vientos alisios, y puede interrumpir los patrones normales de temperatura y precipitación por todo el mundo. (Cap. 3, Sec. 3, pág. 75)

emission / emisión: contaminante liberado en el aire proveniente de una fuente dada, como el tubo de escape de un automóvil. (Cap. 4, Sec. 3, pág. 112)

fog / neblina: una nube estrato que se forma cuando el aire se enfría hasta su punto de rocío, cerca de la superficie terrestre. (Cap. 2, Sec. 1, pág. 41)

front / frente: límite entre dos masas de aire que poseen diferentes temperaturas, densidad o humedad; puede ser frío, cálido, ocluido y estacionario. (Cap. 2, Sec. 2, pág. 45)

global warming / calentamiento global: aumento en el promedio de la temperatura global de la Tierra. (Cap. 3, Sec. 3, pág. 82)

greenhouse effect / efecto de invernadero: calentamiento natural que ocurre cuando ciertos gases en la atmósfera de la Tierra, por ejemplo, el metano, el CO_2 y el vapor de agua, atrapan el calor. (Cap. 3, Sec. 3, pág. 81)

hibernation / hibernación: adaptación del comportamiento para sobrevivir el invierno en que un animal disminuye considerablemente sus actividades corporales, la temperatura de su cuerpo baja y los procesos corporales se vuelven más lentos. (Cap. 3, Sec. 2, pág. 72

humidity / humedad: cantidad de vapor de agua que sostiene el aire. (Cap. 2, Sec. 1, pág. 38)

hurricane / huracán: tormenta extensa y severa que se forma sobre los océanos tropicales, con vientos de por lo menos 120 km/h y que pierde fuerza al llegar a tierra firme. (Cap. 2, Sec. 2, pág. 50)

hydrosphere / hidrosfera: toda el agua de la superficie terrestre. (Cap. 1, Sec. 2, pág. 19)

Spanish Glossary

I

ionosphere / ionosfera: capa de partículas cargadas eléctricamente en la termosfera que absorbe las ondas radiales AM durante el día y las vuelve a reflejar durante la noche. (Cap. 1, Sec. 1, pág. 11)

isobars / isobaras: líneas que se trazan en un mapa meteorológico conectando puntos que tienen la misma presión atmosférica; también indican la ubicación de las áreas de alta y de baja presión y pueden mostrar la velocidad del viento. (Cap. 2, Sec. 3, pág. 53)

isotherm / isoterma: línea que se traza en un mapa meteorológico conectando puntos que tienen la misma temperatura. (Cap. 2, Sec. 3, pág. 53)

J

jet stream / corriente de chorro: franja estrecha de vientos fuertes que sopla cerca de la troposfera. (Cap. 1, Sec. 3, pág. 24)

L

land breeze / brisa terrestre: movimiento de aire nocturno desde la tierra hacia el mar y que se forma cuando el aire más frío y denso proveniente de la tierra fuerza el aire más cálido a ascender sobre el mar. (Cap. 1, Sec. 3, pág. 25)

M

meteorologist / meteorólogo: persona que estudia el tiempo y usa información del radar Doppler, de los satélites meteorológicos, computadoras y otros instrumentos para hacer mapas meteorológicos y pronósticos del tiempo. (Cap. 2, Sec. 3, pág. 52)

O

ozone layer / capa de ozono: capa de la estratosfera con una alta concentración de ozono; absorbe la mayor parte de la radiación ultravioleta dañina proveniente del Sol. (Cap. 1, Sec. 1, pág. 14; Cap. 4, Sec. 1, pág. 102)

P

particulate matter / macropartículas: partículas sólidas y gotitas líquidas suspendidas en el aire. (Cap. 4, Sec. 1, pág. 100)

photochemical smog / smog fotoquímico: neblina pardusca que se forma de la interacción de los contaminantes secundarios con la luz solar. (Cap. 4, Sec. 1, pág. 97)

polar zones / zonas polares: zona climática que recibe la radiación solar a un ángulo bajo; se extiende desde la latitud 66°N y S hasta los polos y en donde nunca hace calor. (Cap. 3, Sec. 1, pág. 66)

precipitation / precipitación: agua que cae de las nubes, incluye la lluvia, la nieve, la cellisca y el granizo, y cuya forma la determina la temperatura del aire. (Cap. 2, Sec. 1, pág. 42)

primary pollutant / contaminante primario: sustancia liberada directamente en el aire de manera dañina; incluye gases volcánicos, hollín proveniente de camiones y humo de incendios forestales. (Cap. 4, Sec. 1, pág. 96)

R

radiation / radiación: energía que transmiten las ondas o los rayos. (Cap. 1, Sec. 2, pág. 18)

relative humidity / humedad relativa: medida de la cantidad de humedad que sostiene el aire, comparada con la cantidad de humedad que el aire puede sostener a una temperatura dada; puede variar de 0 por ciento a 100 por ciento. (Cap. 2, Sec. 1, pág. 38)

sea breeze / brisa marina: movimiento de aire diurno desde el mar hacia la tierra; se forma cuando el aire más frío sobre el agua se mueve hacia el interior forzando el ascenso del aire calentado y menos denso sobre la tierra. (Cap. 1, Sec. 3, pág. 25)

season / estación: período corto de cambio climático en un área causado por la inclinación de eje terrestre a medida que la Tierra gira alrededor del Sol. (Cap. 3, Sec. 3, pág. 74)

secondary pollutant / contaminante secundario: sustancia que contamina el aire después de reaccionar con otras sustancias en la atmósfera terrestre. (Cap. 4, Sec. 1, pág. 96)

station model / código meteorológico: indica las condiciones del tiempo en un lugar específico, mediante el uso de símbolos en un mapa. (Cap. 2, Sec. 3, pág. 53)

temperate zones / zona templada: zonas climáticas con temperaturas moderadas, las cuales se encuentran entre los trópicos y las zonas polares. (Cap. 3, Sec. 1, pág. 66) la ubicación de áreas de alta y baja presión y que pueden mostrar la velocidad del viento. (Cap. 2, Sec. 3, pág. 53)

tornado / tornado: tormenta de viento violento y arremolinado que se mueve sobre una estrecha trayectoria sobre la tierra y que puede ser resultado de los vientos laterales dentro de una tormenta eléctrica. (Cap. 2, Sec. 2, pág. 48)

toxic air pollutant / contaminante del aire tóxico: sustancia liberada en el aire que puede causar problemas de salud, incluyendo el cáncer. (Cap. 4, Sec. 1, pág. 101)

tropics / trópicos: zona climática que recibe la mayor cantidad de radiación solar; está ubicada entre los 23°N y los 23°S y en donde siempre hace calor, con excepción de las altas elevaciones. (Cap. 3, Sec. 1, pág. 66)

troposphere / troposfera: capa de la atmósfera terrestre más próxima a la tierra, contiene un 99 por ciento de vapor de agua y un 75 por ciento de los gases atmosféricos; es la región donde se forman las nubes y ocurre el estado del tiempo. (Cap. 1, Sec. 1, pág. 10)

ultraviolet radiation / radiación ultravioleta: tipo de energía que llega a la Tierra proveniente del Sol; puede causar daños a la piel y ocasionar cáncer; gran parte de esta radiación es absorbida por la capa de ozono. (Cap. 1, Sec. 1, pág. 14; Cap. 4, Sec. 2, pág. 106)

weather / tiempo: estado de la atmósfera en un momento y lugar específicos, determinado por factores que incluyen la presión atmosférica, la cantidad de humedad en el aire, la temperatura y el viento. (Cap. 2, Sec. 1, pág. 36)

Index

The index for *The Air Around You* will help you locate major topics in the book quickly and easily. Each entry in the index is followed by the number of the pages on which the entry is discussed. A page number given in boldfaced type indicates the page on which that entry is defined. A page number given in italic type indicates a page on which the entry is used in an illustration or photograph. The abbreviation *act.* indicates a page on which the entry is used in an activity.

Index

Art Credits

Glencoe would like to acknowledge the artists and agencies who participated in illustrating this program: Absolute Science Illustration; Andrew Evansen; Argosy; Articulate Graphics; Craig Attebery represented by Frank & Jeff Lavaty; CHK America; Gagliano Graphics; Pedro Julio Gonzalez represented by Melissa Turk & The Artist Network; Robert Hynes represented by Mendola Ltd.; Morgan Cain & Associates; JTH Illustration; Laurie O'Keefe; Matthew Pippin represented by Beranbaum Artist's Representative; Precision Graphics; Publisher's Art; Rolin Graphics, Inc.; Wendy Smith represented by Melissa Turk & The Artist Network; Kevin Torline represented by Berendsen and Associates, Inc.; WILDlife ART; Phil Wilson represented by Cliff Knecht Artist Representative; Zoo Botanica.

Photo Credits

Abbreviation Key: AA=Animals Animals; AH=Aaron Haupt; AMP=Amanita Pictures; BC=Bruce Coleman, Inc.; CB=CORBIS; DM=Doug Martin; DRK=DRK Photo; ES=Earth Scenes; FP=Fundamental Photographs; GH=Grant Heilman Photography; IC=Icon Images; KS=KS Studios; LA=Liaison Agency; MB=Mark Burnett; MM=Matt Meadows; PE=PhotoEdit; PD=PhotoDisc; PQ=PictureQuest; PR=Photo Researchers; SB=Stock Boston; TSA=Tom Stack & Associates; TSM=The Stock Market; VU=Visuals Unlimited.

Cover NASA/Science Photo Library/PR; **iv v** CB; **vi** Jeffrey Howe/VU; **1** Fritz Pölking/Peter Arnold, Inc.; **2** (t)Galen Rowell/CB, (b)Jeffrey Howe/VU; **3** (t)Yoav Levy/Photo-Take NYC/PQ, (b)Dave Martin/AP/Wide World Photos; **4** Lawrence Migdale/SB/PQ; **5** Luis M. Alvarez/AP/Wide World Photos; **6** Lester V. Bergman/CB; **6-7** David Keaton/TSM; **7** First Image; **8** NASA; **9** (t)David S. Addison/VU; (bl)Frank Rossotto/TSM; (br)Larry Lee/CB; **12** Laurence Fordyce/CB; **14** DM; **15** NASA/GSFC; **16** Michael Newman/PE; **18** Larry Fisher/Masterfile; **21** (t)Dan Guravich/PR, (b)Bill Brooks/Masterfile; **23** (t)Gene Moore/Photo-Take NYC/PQ, (cl)Phil Schermeister/CB, (cr)Stephen R. Wagner, (bl)Joel W. Rogers, (br)Kevin Schafer/CB; **24** Bill Brooks/Masterfile; **26 27** David Young-Wolff/PE; **27** Courtesy The Weather Channel; **28** Bob Rowan/CB; **30** (l)J.A. Kraulis/Masterfile, (r)CB; **31** (l)Tom Bean/DRK, (r)Keith Kent/Science Photo Library/PR; **34** NASA; **34-35** Michael S. Yamashita/CB; **35** KS; **36** Kevin Horgan/Stone; **37** Fabio Colombini/ES; **41** (t)Charles O'Rear/CB, (b)Joyce Photographics/PR; **42** (l)Roy Morsch/TSM, (r)Mark McDermott/Stone; **43** (l)Mark E. Gibson/VU, (r)EPI Nancy Adams/TSA; **45** Van Bucher/Science Source/PR; **47** Jeffrey Howe/VU; **48** Roy Johnson/

TSA; **49** (t)Warren Faidley/Weatherstock, (b)Robert Hynes; **50** NASA/Science Photo Library/PR; **51** Fritz Pölking/Peter Arnold, Inc.; **52** Howard Bluestein/Science Source/PR; **55** MB; **56** (t)Marc Epstein/DRK, (b)Timothy Fuller; **58** Erik Rank/Photonica; **59** Courtesy Weather Modification, Inc.; **60** (l)Peter Miller/Science Source/PR, Inc., (r)Gary Williams/LA; **61** (l)George D. Lepp/PR, (r)Janet Foster/Masterfile; **62** Bob Daemmrich; **64** Pekka Parviainen/PR; **64-65** Rod Planck/PR; **65** AH; **66** CB; **69** (l)William Leonard/DRK, (r)Bob Rowan, Progressive Image/CB; **70** John Shaw/TSA; **71** (tl)David Hosking/CB, (tr)Yva Momatiuk & John Eastcott/PR, (b)Michael Melford/The Image Bank; **72** (t)S.R. Maglione/PR, (bl)Fritz Pölking/VU, (br)Jack Grove/TSA; **73** Zig Zeszczynski/AA; **75** (l)Jonathan Head/AP/Wide World Photos, (r)Jim Corwin/Index Stock; **77** (t)A. Ramey/PE, (b)Peter Beck/Pictor; **78** Galen Rowell/Mountain Light; **82** John Bolzan; **83** Chip & Jill Isenhart/TSA; **84** (l)Jim Sugar Photography/CB, (r)AFP/CB; **85** MM; **87** DM; **88** Gary Rosenquist; **88-89** Alberto Garcia/Saba; **90** (t)Paul Sakuma/AP/Wide World Photos, (c)Galen Rowell/Mountain Light, (b)Michael Melford/The Image Bank; **91** (l)Spencer Grant/PE, (r)Steve Kaufman/DRK; **100** Bruce Iverson; **100-101** C. Moore/CB; **101** Dominic Oldershaw; **102** (l)Krafft-Explorer/PR, (r)Holger Weitzel/CB; **106** (t)Andrew Syred/Science Photo Library/PR, (bl)Bruce Iverson, (br)David Scharf/Peter Arnold, Inc.; **107** (tl)Powerstock-ZEFA/Index Stock, (tr)Rob Garbarini/Index Stock, (b)Tony Freeman/PE; **109** Timothy Fuller; **110 111** David Young-Wolff/PE; **112** (l)Dr. P. Marazzi/PR, (r)Rafael Macia/PR; **114** William Johnson/SB; **116** Roger Ressmeyer/CB; **118** Dan Habib/Impact Visuals/PQ; **119** (tl)Stephen R. Wagner, (tr)John Sohlden/VU, (bl)Charles D. Winter/PR, (br)Stephen R. Wagner; **120** (t)David Weintraub/SB, (b)Karl Lugmaier;Viennaslide Photoagency/CB; **122** (t)David Weintraub/SB, (b)Oliver Benn/Stone; **124** (t)Hank Morgan/ PR, (b)CB-Bettmann; **126** (t)SuperStock, (c)Timothy Fuller, (b)Wendell Metzen/Index Stock; **126-127** PD; **127** (l)Nik Wheeler/CB, (r)Owen Franken/SB/PQ; **128** Winifried Wisniewski/CB; **129** MB; **129** (t)Ruth Dixon, (c)Bryan Pickering/Eye Ubiquitous/CB, (b)Rod Currie/Stone; **130** (t)Warren Faidley/Weatherstock, (c)James N. Westwater, (b)Steve Austin/Papilio/CB; **131** (tl)Chinch Gryniewicz/Ecoscene/CB, (tr)MB, (bl)Annie Griffiths Belt/CB, (br)James N. Westwater; **132** CB; **133** (l)Bill Vaine/CB, (r)John Dudak/PhotoTake NYC/PQ; **134** (t)Richard Hamilton Smith/CB, (c)NOAA Photo Library/Central Library, OAR/ERL/National Severe Storms Laboratory (NSSL), (b)Jeffry W. Myers/CB; **135** Geophysical Institute, University of Alaska Fairbanks via RE/MAX/AP/Wide World Photo; **136** Michell D. Bridwell/PE; **140** David Young-Wolff/PE; **142** Kaz Chiba/PD; **143** Dominic Oldershaw; **144** StudiOhio; **145** MM; **147** (tl tr c)Mark Steinmetz, (bl)Elaine Shay, (br)Brent Turner/BLT Productions; **150** Paul Barton/TSM; **153** AH.

PERIODIC TABLE OF THE ELEMENTS

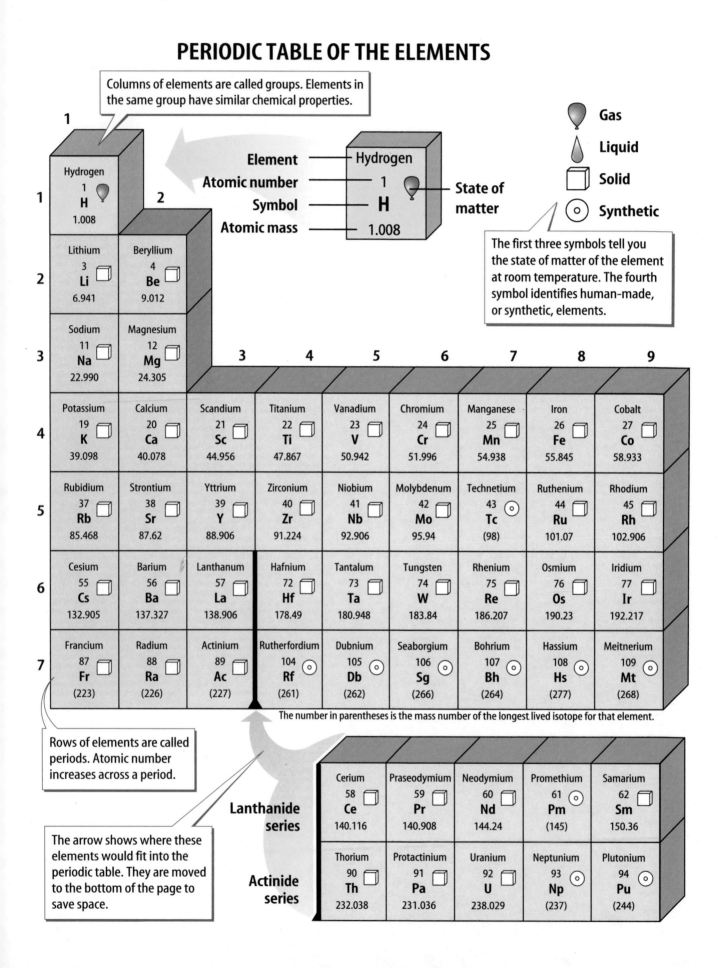

Columns of elements are called groups. Elements in the same group have similar chemical properties.

Element — Hydrogen
Atomic number — 1
Symbol — H
Atomic mass — 1.008

State of matter

Gas
Liquid
Solid
Synthetic

The first three symbols tell you the state of matter of the element at room temperature. The fourth symbol identifies human-made, or synthetic, elements.

The number in parentheses is the mass number of the longest lived isotope for that element.

Rows of elements are called periods. Atomic number increases across a period.

The arrow shows where these elements would fit into the periodic table. They are moved to the bottom of the page to save space.

Lanthanide series

Cerium	Praseodymium	Neodymium	Promethium	Samarium
58	59	60	61	62
Ce	**Pr**	**Nd**	**Pm**	**Sm**
140.116	140.908	144.24	(145)	150.36

Actinide series

Thorium	Protactinium	Uranium	Neptunium	Plutonium
90	91	92	93	94
Th	**Pa**	**U**	**Np**	**Pu**
232.038	231.036	238.029	(237)	(244)